JOHN D
ON EDUC

JOHN DEWEY
ON EDUCATION

Selected Writings

Edited and with an Introduction by

REGINALD D. ARCHAMBAULT

The University of Chicago Press

CHICAGO AND LONDON

The University of Chicago Press, Chicago 60637
The University of Chicago Press, Ltd., London

© Copyright 1964, by Random House, Inc.
All rights reserved. Published 1964
Phoenix Edition 1974
Printed in the United States of America

International Standard Book Number: 0–226–14390–2
Library of Congress Catalog Card Number: 64–18939

Reginald D. Archambault is a professor of philosophy of education at Brown University. He has a
long-standing interest in John Dewey's philosophy of
education and has published several articles and books
on Dewey and his works, including an edition of his
Lectures in the Philosophy of Education, 1899. His
main scholarly interest is in the philosophical analysis of educational concepts.

ACKNOWLEDGMENTS

My special thanks go to Morris Philipson of Random House whose patience is apparently inexhaustible.

I am deeply indebted to the following publishers for permission to reprint from Dewey's works:

The Macmillan Company, for passages from *Democracy and Education,* Copyright 1916 by The Macmillan Company, renewed 1944 by John Dewey.

Kappa Delta Pi Fraternity, for passages from *Experience and Education,* 1938.

The University of Chicago Press, for passages from *Theory of Valuation* (International Encyclopedia of Unified Science, Vol. II, Foundations of the Unity of Science, No. 4), 1939.

The John Dewey Society, for "Progressive Education and the Science of Education," originally published in *Progressive Education,* 1928, V, 197-204.

Harvard University Press, for passages from *The Way Out of Educational Confusion,* 1931.

D. C. Heath and Co., for passages from *How We Think,* 1933.

The American Association for the Advancement of Science, for "Science as Subject Matter and as Method," *Science,* XXXI, No. 787, pp. 121-127, 28 January 1910.

School and Society, for "The Relation of Science and Philosophy as a Basis of Education," *School and Society,* XLVII, pp. 470-473, 9 April 1938.

The Barnes Foundation Press for the following chapters by John Dewey, from *Art and Education,* by John Dewey, Albert C. Barnes, Laurence Buermeyer, Thomas Munro, Paul Guillaume, Mary Mullen, Violette de Mazia: "Experience, Nature and Art," pp. 3-12, "Affective Thought in Logic and Painting," pp. 63-73, and "Individuality and Experience," pp. 175-183, 1929.

Holt, Rinehart and Winston, for passages from *Human Nature and Conduct,* Copyright 1922 by Henry Holt and Company, Copyright renewed 1950 in the name of John Dewey; and *Characters and Events,* Vol. II, 1929, edited by Joseph Ratner, Copyright 1922, renewed 1950.

The New Era for "The Need for a Philosophy of Education," from *The New Era in Home and School,* London, November, 1934, XV, pp. 211-214.

I am also indebted to Mrs. John Dewey for consent to publish the above passages from *Art and Education.*

I wish to note that the comprehensive bibliography of Dewey's writing, *John Dewey, A Centennial Bibliography,* compiled by Milton Halsey Thomas (Chicago: The University of Chicago Press, 1962), has been invaluable in the preparation of this book.

The idea that lay back of my educational undertaking was a rather abstract one of the relation of knowledge and action. My school work translated this into a much more vital form. I reached fairly early in the growth of my ideas a belief in the intimate and indissoluble connection of means used and ends reached. The fruits of responsiveness in these matters leave confirmed ideas first aroused on more technical grounds of philosophical study. My belief in the office of intelligence as a continuously reconstructive agency is at least a faithful report of my own life and experience.

—JOHN DEWEY

PREFACE

This book represents an attempt to collect, in systematic form, Dewey's major writings on education, together with certain basic statements of his philosophic position that are relevant to understanding his educational views. Since his writings are so numerous, and since a collection of all of those which have relevance to education is impossible, there will be many who will disagree with the choice of writings included here. I can only plead that they seem to me most basic, not only for understanding Dewey's pedagogical principles, but for illustrating the relation between his educational theory and the principles of his general philosophy.

The aim of the book is to prompt a fresh look at Dewey's educational theory. It is a commonplace that everyone talks about Dewey and no one reads him. It is my hope that a comprehensive collection of this kind will facilitate a careful, critical reading of Dewey's views, on the part of scholars and students of education.

CONTENTS

Preface   ix

Introduction   xiii

I. PHILOSOPHY AND EDUCATION

Need for a Philosophy of Education   3
The Relation of Science and Philosophy as a Basis for
    Education   15

II. ETHICS AND EDUCATION

Logical Conditions of a Scientific Treatment of Morality   23
Human Nature and Conduct   61
The Nature of Aims   70
What is Freedom?   81
Ends and Values   89
The Continuum of Ends-Means   97
Ethical Principles Underlying Education   108

III. AESTHETICS AND EDUCATION

Affective Thought in Logic and Painting   141
Individuality and Experience   149
Experience, Nature and Art   157

IV. SCIENCE AND EDUCATION

Progressive Education and the Science of Education   169
Science as Subject-Matter and as Method   182

V. PSYCHOLOGY AND EDUCATION

What Psychology Can Do for the Teacher 195
Why Reflective Thinking Must Be an Educational Aim 212
School Conditions and the Training of Thought 229
The Process and Product of Reflective Activity: Psychological Process and Logical Form 242
Interest in Relation to Training of the Will 260

VI. SOCIETY AND EDUCATION

American Education and Culture 289
The School and Society 295

VII. PRINCIPLES OF PEDAGOGY

The Relation of Theory to Practice in Education 313
The Child and the Curriculum 339
The Nature of Subject Matter 359
Progressive Organization of Subject-Matter 373
The Nature of Method 387
The Educational Situation: As Concerns Secondary Education 404
The Way Out of Educational Confusion 422
My Pedagogic Creed 427

INTRODUCTION

These remarks are intended to be descriptive, rather than critical, and analytic rather than historical. A great deal has been written regarding the social and philosophical milieu in which Dewey matured, and to which he reacted so violently.[1] His early training in Scotch commonsense philosophy at Vermont, and his introduction to the dynamism and continuity of Hegelianism as a graduate student at Johns Hopkins were early influences that nourished his thought. Influence of dialectical reasoning never left him, and the "empty religiosity" of Scotch philosophy was something to which he soon reacted. From William James he learned the principles of the new functional psychology; from Charles Sanders Peirce the Darwinian framework of challenge, response, irritation and doubt that would serve as the basis for his theory of inquiry; from George Herbert Mead the importance of the new social psychology.

These were positive influences, but perhaps more important were the "negative conditions" that he found all around him. The chief of these was formal philosophy's "nauseous idealism" characterized by the thought of Josiah Royce. In the influence of Social Darwinism and the Gospel of Wealth he

---

[1] See, for example, Morton G. White, *The Origin of Dewey's Instrumentalism* (New York: The Viking Press, 1949), as well as Philip P. Wiener, *Evolution and the Founders of Pragmatism* (Cambridge: Harvard University Press, 1949). Dewey himself describes the influences on his thought in early and subsequent years in the autobiographical essay "From Absolutism to Experimentalism," in G. P. Adams and W. P. Montague, eds., *Contemporary American Philosophy: Personal Statements* (New York: The Macmillan Co., 1930, II, pp. 13-27).

saw ample evidence, in the field of politics, of a tendency to neglect, distort, and cover problems rather than to solve them. In psychology he saw the perpetuation of the doctrine of faculty psychology and the mind-body dualism. But the most dramatic deficiencies he found in the schools themselves. For there he saw, in actual practice, a violation of all common sense for the sake of perpetuating a totally inadequate and outmoded theory. The actual conditions are well described by Lawrence Cremin, in his history of the progressive education movement.[2] A new and complex modern society was arising, born of immigration, exploding population, and drastic social change. Yet the schools were totally unprepared to meet the challenge of this new society. It is this situation that he confronted, appraised and criticized almost at the outset of his career. And it was this problem that prompted an early development of his pedagogical principles, which he stated in *My Pedagogic Creed* in 1897 (reprinted in this volume). The essential features of this solution were to remain unchanged, although they would be softened as the intensity of battle subsided later in his career.

I. Philosophy, Science and Education

The selections in this volume are classified under several headings—Education and Aesthetics, Education and Science, etc. If these headings suggest a separation between the several facets of Dewey's thought, then they have not served a proper function. They are intended to serve as convenient and familiar artificial categories that illustrate the relations between the aspects of Dewey's thought, the complementarity of them, the consistency among them, and the contribution of each to a systematic and complete philosophy of education. For just as Dewey strove, in his basic philosophy, to eradicate dualisms and "either-ors," and to merge concepts traditionally kept distinct, similarly in education he attempted to bring to-

---

[2] *The Transformation of the School* (New York: Alfred A. Knopf, 1961).

gether all aspects of intellectual activity, and to illustrate, often in great detail, how all phases of activity merge in the philosophical activity which is education.

Hence, the notion of truth as warranted assertability mirrors his belief in the experimental method in general as the principal means toward knowledge; and this, in turn, is reflected in his belief in the "project method" as a principal means of organizing the curriculum of the schools on a "scientific," or experimental basis. Yet although the various aspects of Dewey's philosophy are intricately interrelated, so that distinctions are blurred between ethics and psychology, psychology and logic, logic and science, and science and aesthetics, certain notions are central to all others. His central views are found in his philosophy of science, and his belief in its central role in all philosophical thought, as well as its applicability to a wide range of practical affairs.

To understand anything of his philosophy of education, then, it is essential to understand Dewey's conception of science. It is not an extremely complicated idea, although he often referred to it as being highly theoretical. Its basis is biological. The human organism seeks a state of rest or equilibrium. It seeks an adjustment to its environment. This tendency in the human organism is fundamental, tied as it is to the most basic physiological needs which must be fulfilled if life, a primary value, is to be sustained. Earlier Peirce, in his famous essay on "The Fixation of Belief," (1877), had pointed out that this state of satisfaction can be achieved in several ways—by using the method of tenacity, through which an individual could cling to beliefs merely because they were comfortable; the method of authority, based on an appeal to authority or tradition; the *a priori* method, based on taste and intuition; and finally the method of science, consisting of control, public test, and the possibility of reasonable proof and consensus.

Dewey was greatly influenced by this point of view. He took this simple idea, with its essential aspects, and developed it consistently so that it served as the basis of his theories in all phases of philosophy, and particularly in his philosophy of education. The key notions in Dewey's idea of the scientific method of thinking are control, experiment, and objective test. His aim, reiterated constantly, is to bring the scientific method of reflective thought to all phases of human activity, including politics, art, and morals. In the basic model of scientific method is contained the key points of his instrumentalist or experimentalist version of the philosophy of pragmatism that he adopted from Peirce and William James.

The individual is faced with a problem that is real and meaningful to him. Between the recognition of the problem and its solution are five aspects of reflective thought: (1) suggestions—leaping forward to a solution; (2) the clarification of the problem which is to be solved; (3) the use of hypotheses; (4) reasoning about the possible results of acting on one or another hypothesis and choosing one; (5) testing the hypothesis by overt or imaginative action.[3]

Several aspects of this schema are important. To begin with, it initiates the process of inquiry or deliberation with a "felt need," or a "real doubt," as Peirce would call it. Philosophic inquiry should take its clue from inquiry into matters of common sense and personal import where finding a workable solution is important. Here we see the substitution of genuine psychological doubt—real irritation—for the "feigned doubt" of traditional philosophy, best characterized in the work of Descartes, who claimed that he would decide "to doubt everything."

In the second phase, that of the isolation and clarification of the problem which is to be solved, we see an early plea for the elimination of pseudo problems and for the postulation of problems that are susceptible to solution, at least in principle. This is the conversion of mere emotional befuddlement into an *intellectual* problem. It is the movement from mere irritation to an examination of actual conditions.

In the third phase we find the first use of the key scientific term "hypothesis," a tentative, projected solution to the problem that is to be balanced and weighed in relation to rival solutions. Here we find the first suggestion of highly

---

[3] Paraphrased from John Dewey, *How We Think* (Boston: D. C. Heath and Co., 1933), p. 107 ff.

controlled and systematic activity, of waiting, and of the projection of consequences. James had said that earlier philosophies had looked to the past, but that pragmatism looked to the future, to the consequences.

In the fourth phase is the full projection of consequences, the "dramatic rehearsal" in the imagination, the creative consideration of ideas in new configurations, that is characterized by strict intellectual control.

In the final phase is the testing of the hypothesis, the use of the idea as instrument, the verification of the idea, the proof of the extent of its "practical bearing."

In this brief description of scientific method can be found, then, most of the key ideas in Dewey's philosophy. It is based in experience. It deals with genuine pressing problems that stem from felt needs. It is characterized by control. Its solutions are tentative but useful. Its method is the method of science. And, like modern science, it not only consists in carefully controlled thought, but also aims at control of the environment and improvement of the environment by creative and reflective thought. Just as Greek science was characterized by categorization of concrete phenomena, and by a discovery of concrete qualities, ancient philosophy described a world of static dualisms. Modern philosophy, using the method of science, can create a new world by establishing new configurations and abstract relations.

So it was not only the actual content and method of science that interested, and indeed preoccupied Dewey, but the connotations that were associated with science: objectivity, honesty, freedom, openendedness. Philosophy was to follow the spirit of science, not only in its approach to problems of metaphysics and epistemology, but also in the fields of ethics and aesthetics. There was to be one major mode of knowing which could be applied consistently in all areas of thought. If this were to be done it would obviously require a political structure that would in itself be an implementation of the scientific mode of thought. Dewey saw democracy as the political manifestation of scientific method, with its combination of purposiveness and objectivity, freedom and discipline, individual speculation and public verification. Democracy and science came closest to being the only absolutes in Dewey's experimentalist philosophy.

The aim of education is the development of reflective, creative, responsible thought. Hence, Dewey's whole conception of science, and its methods and its aims is directly relevant to education. It is relevant in both the broad and the narrow sense. Scientific method serves as a direct model for educational methodology at every stage of instruction. In its purest form, it is reflected in "the project method" that starts with the felt needs of students, which are later refined into problem projects, the setting up of plans or hypotheses, and the testing of the hypotheses in searching for satisfactory completion of the project.[4] But Dewey's broader *conception* of science as a total and unique mode of thought bears on all of his educational ideas. It serves as the model for reflective thought. It defines the subject matter of instruction as a mode of thinking and doing. It serves as a model for active, practical projects where hypotheses can be acted out and acted upon. It defines the relation between freedom and discipline, emotion and control, interest and effort. And above all, it offers a method for determining the aims of education, and the relation between means and ends in the educative process.

II. Science, Value and Education

Dewey's conception of the relation between science and value is the most revolutionary aspect of his thought. He established his notion of this relation very early in his career, and the first comprehensive statement of it, which remained basically unchanged throughout his career, was in the early *Logical Conditions for a Scientific Treatment of Morality* in 1903 (reprinted in this volume). Again, the premise is simple. Morals should not belong to a separate sphere, distinct from and opposed to the world of fact. The act of valuing is properly susceptible to scientific treatment, for just as de-

---

[4] See, for example, the selections in this volume from *How We Think, School and Society, The Child and the Curriculum,* among many others.

cisions in any area of endeavor require criteria and justification which can be provided by specific inquiry, similarly then, judgments in the "moral sphere" are not distinct from those in science or practical affairs. They are, to use Dewey's word, "continuous." This principle of continuity runs throughout his writing. The basis of the principle is again the belief in the centrality of science as a way of doing.

Just as scientific inquiry is initiated by *doubt*—a psychological factor—similarly ethical activity is initiated by desire and confusion. Ethics is cast in a naturalistic framework. Moral activity starts with desire, proceeds by an examination of projected consequences and ends in satisfaction. This naturalistic framework is not new to Dewey. It is as old as philosophy itself, and found its most popular expression in the utilitarianism of Bentham and Mill, who called for a hedonistic calculus to measure the probable consequences of a moral act, and who concentrated on naturalistic pleasure as a basis for value. For Dewey, however, the formula is not simple, and in its complexity rests its novelty. For Dewey's ethical theory, while using a naturalistic framework, goes beyond mere naturalism in invoking the scientific method itself as a criterion for value.

Dewey's first concern is to break down the dichotomy between means and ends which has haunted philosophy since ancient times. Not only is the ethical sphere continuous with the practical, but ends are continuous with means. In his attempt to dramatize the relation, he refers to it as the continuum of "ends-means," simultaneously reversing the traditional order and merging the notions. Ends are projected consequences of action in real experience, not separate states belonging to a future and different experience. Again he uses the hyphen in order to give immediacy to moral aims, by calling them "ends-in-view." Just as the scientist seeks a solution to a problem in order to eliminate doubt, the individual in an ethical situation seeks an end-in-view which will insure a temporary state of rest, a settled situation, a sense of completeness or closure.

The psychologist understands the importance of habit in conduct. It provides stability. Yet it also leads to rigidity.

Since no habits or beliefs can satisfy all situations, particularly new ones brought on by ever-changing conditions, rigid habitual forms of behavior can lead only to stagnation. The situation is similar in ethics. There must be criteria for action, and these criteria must be supra-personal and justifiable, but they cannot rest on mere tradition, intuition, or authority. Nor can they be justified by invoking another sphere. At the same time they must be flexible, adaptible, susceptible to change. The simple naturalism of Bentham and Mill failed to satisfy these conditions for several reasons. It concentrated on the one factor of pleasure to the exclusion of all others, and in so doing neglected a multiplicity of subtle and paradoxical forms of satisfaction. It committed the naturalistic fallacy of equating the "desired" with the "desirable," of confusing wishes with goods. It failed, then, to distinguish the satisfying from the satisfactory, and it thus failed to provide an adequate criterion for value.

Dewey saw the scientific method of investigation, combined with naturalistic desire, as providing a realistic, flexible, and stable approach to ethics. Desires, when examined in the light of their causes and consequences, he claimed, do not remain merely "de facto." They are transformed, because they are subjected to the discipline of inquiry. They are seen in a total context. They are not acted upon in order to bring about immediate pleasure or satisfaction. They are examined in an attempt to test their "satisfactoriness." This is done by projecting the probable results or consequences of choosing one solution to a moral problem which is causing irritation and forcing choice. One must examine alternate ends-in-view, hypothesize, deliberate, perform a "dramatic rehearsal in the imagination," consider the long-range consequences. When this activity is performed, when intelligence is applied to a situation where desire is central, then the "merely desired" is judged to be desirable. The merely "de facto" is transformed into "de jure."

The criterion, then, far from being a static yardstick, is the intelligent method of science itself, in all of its complexity. Yet just as science employs public test in order to insure objectivity and public verification, the method of science in ethics insures objectivity in moral judgments and public justification. Science provides a body of belief, tested and accepted and susceptible to change. A scientific ethic provides a similar set of belief habits to guide conduct. Science provides only probable knowledge. The method of science in ethics provides for stability and reasonable security, but no certainty.

The relations to education are clear. Ethics is central to the educational enterprise since it is concerned with establishing a basis for determining the ends of education, the relation of means and methods to those ends, and a general classification of educational values. Dewey's total approach to these problems is controlled by the ethical principles outlined above. The ends of education are not fixed. They are changeable and must be modified in relation to shifting environmental conditions, the most important of which are changes in society. The chief aims of education must be stated in terms of *processes* rather than static states—the promotion of reflective behavior, the promotion of growth and health. Education, then, must be its own end.

These principles were stated by Dewey very early in his career, in *Ethical Principles Underlying Education,* in 1903 (reprinted in this volume). They remained substantially unchanged throughout his career. In that article he states that ethical theory is "two faced," dealing with the psychological and the social. He then relates this basic distinction to educational theory. Education must provide for the development of the individual and for his participation in society. It cannot do this by neglecting his individuality by forcing rigid patterns of socially-approved behavior upon him, for if it does it will prevent him from being creative, and hence block the only avenue for his eventual contribution to the society. Just as freedom and discipline are interrelated, individual expression and social necessity must be considered together. Education does not consist in promoting the "full-flowering" of the individual, considered without regard to his participation in the group. Nor does it consist in the rigid imposition of values. All genuine education is liberating, and certainly needs freedom and discipline. A major aim of education is to make the child morally responsible so that as an adult he can help to create new rules and become reasonably self-sufficient. This can only be done by avoiding indoctrination and establishing a framework in the school where the balance between individual desires and social needs can be constantly maintained. If this is to be a genuine aim of education, then directives must be stated in terms of processes, since there are no inviolate moral rules that can be taught to the child. If the aim of promoting freedom and responsibility is to be genuine, then the desire of the child, which is the impetus for moral activity, must not be squelched but nurtured, modified, and directed.

Hence the ethical theory and the educational theory become one. There is no "intellectual education" oppcsed to "moral education," for moral education, properly conceived, is intellectual, in that it is centered in reflective thought. Intellectual education is moral, in that it deals with problems of genuine personal and social import. There is no formula or axiology that can apply to either.

III. Central Concepts in Dewey's Educational Theory

Education is a conscious, purposive, informed activity. The central notions involved in education, then, are (1) the aim of the activity; (2) the agent responsible for the activity (the teacher); (3) the subject of the activity (the pupil); and (4) the means by which the aim is achieved (curriculum and method). With the relation between science, value, and education established, we can turn briefly to a description of these aspects of education.

Ends and Means in Education. "End" is an ambiguous term in education, for it refers to the outcomes of instruction, and it is often unclear whether the outcome that one has in mind is an immediate objective or effect, or the *result of* achieving certain specific objectives. Traditionally, the ends of education are stated broadly and vaguely in terms of "freedom" or "wisdom" or "the full development of the individual." Dewey fought a long battle against the vagueness in postulation of educational ends, and in doing so, deliberately introduced vaguely stated aims of his own. However, there is a major difference in the two kinds of ambiguity, the one that he fought, and the one that he fostered. The ambiguity in traditional conceptions of educational aims rested, he felt, on a failure to recognize the essential relation between ends and means. In his classic statement of the relation between the two in his *Theory of Valuation,* 1939 (reprinted in this volume), he emphasized the continuity and reciprocity between means and ends, stating that ends, if they are to be at all meaningful, must be defined in terms of the means which would be used in their attainment. Without such a description ends are empty. It is for this reason that he invokes an equally vague notion of the end of education as growth, for in doing so he emphasizes the need for flexibility, continuity, and dynamism, and some considerable lack of predictability regarding the ends of education, that is, in the precise results (attitudes, beliefs, tendencies, skills) that are to be achieved through the educative process.

Educational Aims. On the other hand aims, considered as specific objectives of instruction, must be postulated on the basis of pupil purposes, local conditions, social demands, and that skill and knowledge which is needed in order to complete worthy projects. The exact aims of instruction cannot be legislated, for they depend on a cluster of variables that are unique to a particular place and time. For a given situation, short-range aims must be relatively specific. Yet any school situation, since it is experimental in nature, has a quality of unpredictability. To try to specify, in exact detail, the precise knowledge that a student is to achieve, is to consider ends as remote, distinct, and separate from practical contingencies and the dynamic purposes of pupils.

Means in Education. Just as aims must be flexible and related to the needs of the pupils and the community at any given time, there must also be room for a much wider variety of means in education. Dewey's early school work was devoted largely to an attempt to destroy the static form of instruction which he called the "assign-study-recite" technique, with all of its accoutrements of pupils at attention.

fixed desks and chairs, a stern disciplinary attitude on the part of the teacher. Dewey here saw a converse difficulty stemming from a failure to recognize the continuity of means and ends: a type of static knowledge resulting from a rigid form of instruction which ostensibly aimed at ultimate intellectual freedom. The method of solution, he claimed, is determined by the problem to be solved. As problems change, modes of solution must also change. The complex series of problems that should make up the curriculum of the modern school could not be solved by using methods of instruction based on formal discipline and faculty psychology. The fundamental difficulty with traditional means of instruction was their psychological base, which considered the child a passive receptor of external data, his will a force to be controlled and checked, his desires to be mischievous and immature. For Dewey this misconception created the need for a totally new manner of education, which in turn necessitated a redefinition of the role of the teacher and the pupil, subject matter, and, as we have seen, aims.

The pupil should be looked upon as willful, purposive, curious, active. The teacher should be considered a guide who should help the pupil to achieve his own purposes. The subject matter of instruction should be completely redefined in terms of those facts, ideas, and objects that are helpful in fulfilling pupil purposes. The classroom should be looked upon as a total environment where physical and social conditions, as well as abstract intellectual material are essential features that effect the learning process. With this totally new manner of education must come a broader concept of method of instruction. For teaching, properly conceived, could not be said to consist of "instruction" at all. The teacher should be a catalytic agent who, by providing materials, clues, information, suggestions, clarifications—could create a setting that would be conducive to learning. And since there should be no separation between education and life, teaching method should properly encompass the kinds of experience traditionally held to be foreign to the proper province of the school: the recreation of cultural epochs through artifacts, the imitation of industrial processes, the substitution of actual experience and observation for mere vicarious experience. Above all, the total means of instruction should be centered on the live, meaningful, and important problem to be grappled with and solved.

The relation of means and ends, then, can be seen to come properly full circle.

Subject Matter and Curriculum. One of the chief components of the educational process is, of course, subject matter, a concept that has been the cause of more confusion than any other in educational theory. For traditional educational theory the content of instruction consisted of "subjects" or disciplines, derived from the past, and consisting of a logically organized series of facts, ideas, propositions and theories, usually arranged in an order of increasing degrees of complexity. Each discipline was looked upon as distinct, and there was a tendency to consider the subject, as traditionally organized, as inviolate. Rather than use the subject to aid in getting people to learn by reorganizing it, traditional education sought to "instill" the subject in its pure form, either through strong methods of discipline, or by means of sugar-coating that would make the bitter pill more palatable. For Dewey nothing could be more illogical, and hence more ineffective. Just as in all instances of the failure to recognize the relation between ends and means, this particular case demonstrated the failure to consider the actual effects of education by attributing an automatic ultimate end that would be derived from the direct imposition of a subject. The very manner of education, Dewey argued, prevented the acquisition of its stated aim. Instead of leading to richer and wider experience for the child, it prompted his hatred for the subject. Dewey's solution to the problem of the definition and prescription of the context of instruction was not merely the destruction of subjects as such, but a completely new conception of what the concept of "subject matter" should be. For him it was a dynamic concept, best described in the past tense, as "those things actually acted upon in a situation having a purpose." Organized knowledge, important as it might be, needs to be subservient to the purpose of instruction. There is nothing sacred about traditional subjects. Ideas, propositions, and theories are brought in as needed in the solution of problems. As problems become more complex, then more systematized knowledge is necessary. Yet even here the organization of knowledge should not be merely according to the dictates of tradition, but on the basis of its relevance to live intellectual issues.

What emerges from the Dewey analysis is a dynamic conception of subject matter, or the content of instruction, as consisting not only in the sentences, ideas and propositions presented, but the *way* in which they are presented by the teacher, and the *way* in which they are treated by the pupil. The total subject matter encountered in the formal education interval represents the actual content of instruction.

The Pupil. At this point the central role of the pupil becomes clear. He is the purpose for which the educational enterprise exists. Since democracy receives its impetus from creative individuals, the contribution of education to the society consists in the development of free, imaginative and creative individuals. Analogously, the educative process is fired and sustained by the impulse that comes from the desires, interests, and purposes of pupils. Just as the social order progresses most steadily and dynamically by maximum opportunity for individual expression, that school runs best which operates on the principle of individual development for its pupils. It is in this sense that the school can be properly considered "child-centered." In his psychology, Dewey maintained that "the *meaning* of native impulse is not native—the meaning results from intelligent manipulation." Similarly the meaning, and hence the direction of true education, does not rest in the native impulses, desires, and interests of the pupils. These are to be transformed into a reasonable pattern imposed by more experienced members of the adult society. Yet they provide the energy for learning and instruction. They provide the desires that will be transformed into the desirable. They provide the central *focus* for instruction.

The School and Society. The school is not to become a microcosm of society, but should provide a purified, simplified, and artificially balanced environment that will insure a healthy atmosphere for growth. It should be more "realistic," then, than "naturalistic." Dewey shared some of Rousseau's distrust of contemporary institutions, and felt that the function of the school was not merely to provide a means for pupils to fit into society, but also a means for them to change it for the better. This did not imply a system of indoctrination in order to provide the means for building a specific "new social order." Nor, however, did it imply shielding students from the evils and complexities of the contemporary society in order to insure a loyalty to the *status quo*. For Dewey one of the broad functions of education was to provide for cultural transmission *and* cultural renewal. In his educational theory, he sometimes invoked an organismic view of society as a body to be nourished so that it might progress and grow. Yet the characteristic means by which he would promote this growth would be by focusing on the development of free and creative individuals.

Education, then, must promote creativity and stability, individuality and social consciousness. The chief means for this were to be found in the environment of the school in general, and in the method of instruction in particular. The pupil is constantly made to share in activities, and indeed, to co-operate in planning the curriculum, and hence the total *environment* of the school. His purposes then become associated with the purposes of others, and he recognizes and participates in a general purpose, which is not totally unlike Rousseau's notion of the "general will." Yet he is not expected merely to "adjust," either to his own interests, the needs of the group, or the superficial needs of the present adult society. He is to be irritated. He is to change the group. He is to be denied easy adjustment.

In the activities of the classroom he engages in scientific method and democratic procedure. He is not preparing for future preparation in a society "outside." He is actively engaged in creating and sustaining a society "inside" that is essentially life-like.

The Role of the Teacher.   The teacher is the agent who is chiefly responsible for this highly complex process of education. It is his task to provide a setting conducive to learning, *i.e.*, to prompt the development of ideas in the pupil. In doing this he himself must become a learner. Dewey looks upon the relation between teacher and pupil as reciprocal. They should plan together and learn from each other. The teacher is not an authority in dispensing ideas to be absorbed by his pupils, but a guide, stimulus, and catalyst in getting the child to make his own relations and connections, his own ideas. In doing this the modern teacher must take into consideration a great variety of factors that the traditional teacher considered extraneous: the total physical setting, since this, rather than merely the "subject" alone makes up the environment for learning; the psychology of the individual pupils, so that differences in motivation, intelligence, and orientation can be taken into account; the social psychology of the group, since general interests, needs and purposes will serve as the basis for developing the curriculum; the psychological principles of learning, memory, transfer, and motivation, so that learning can be efficient and economical.

In order to accomplish all of this the teacher must be a well-educated professional. He must have a broad range of general knowledge on which to draw in developing units of instruction for his pupils. He must have a sound grounding in educational theory so that he understands the philosophical, psychological and sociological foundations of education. He must be able to see the reciprocal relation between theory and practice so that teaching is not reduced to a mere practical activity without grounding in theoretical science, or an abstract science that has little relation to practice. Teaching is a professional activity to the extent that it rests on principles of procedure. As the science of psychology matures this body of theory will become broader and deeper and the expertism of the teacher in promoting effective learning will become greater. Yet he will never become an "authority" in matters of morals, or merely a model of conduct. His role is to be the chief agent for the liberation of the student.

IV. Conclusion

We began these remarks by pointing out the interrelatedness of the various aspects of Dewey's thought. We have seen how the principle of continuity runs throughout all of his writings, based on the fundamental relation between means and ends, and evident in his conception of the relation between mind and body, theory and practice, aim and method, science and value. The principle extends to the relation between philosophy and education. He sums up his view on this matter in his famous statement from *Democracy and Education:* "If we are willing to conceive of education as the process of forming fundamental dispositions, intellectual and emotional, toward nature and fellow men, philosophy may even be defined *as the general theory of education.*" [5] Because of this dynamic relationship between his educational theory and the basic principles of his philosophic thought we have in his educational philosophy an unprecedented instance of basic theoretical principles exemplified in practice at every turn, and conversely, a set of broad prescriptions for educational practice that are clearly and directly justified at several levels. For example, in his theory of method we find a justification in psychological principles, based in turn on a theory of mind, which is based ultimately on a fundamental philosophical doctrine of evolutionary adjustment. Hence we have a theory of education that is consistently related to basic principles, which is, then, vertically continuous. Yet, as we have seen, it is also horizontally continuous in that the psychological, logical, ethical and aesthetic are merged, in any given policy, based as they are in a fundamental philosophy of science.

This quality of his work should offer an obvious and important caveat to students of Dewey's educational theory: that his educational principles can only be understood in the context of his total philosophy. It is unfortunate that so many of his critics, and indeed, his followers, have failed to recognize

---

[5] John Dewey, *Democracy and Education* (New York: The Macmillan Co., 1916), p. 328.

this fact. For this failure has led to superficial acceptance or oversimplified statements of his views ("the child-centered school," "I teach children, not subject matter," "learn by doing") on the one hand, and misdirected criticism on the other ("the easy philosophy of life adjustment," "country-club existentialism," "directionless activity").

There are many areas of Dewey's work that are susceptible to criticism, and recently there has been a growing body of work that is at once sophisticated, appreciative, and deeply critical of Dewey's views. It is not the function of this essay to examine these areas. One of the aims of publishing this volume is to bring together, in a comprehensive fashion, a significant number of Dewey's writings in education and the philosophy on which they are based, in order to invite a fresh look at his views. Implicit in the principle of selection, and in this introductory essay, is the notion that criticism of Dewey's educational theory must, in order to be valid, deal with his basic philosophical principles. These principles, and the educational prescriptions and controversies that spring from them, are as vital today as they were when they exploded on the educational horizon at the turn of the century. We should be able, with distance and fresh perspective, to "reconstruct" them, to use a favorite term of Dewey's, so that their value for us can be revitalized.

REGINALD D. ARCHAMBAULT

Grinnell College
Grinnell, Iowa
December, 1963

I

Philosophy
and
Education

THE NEED FOR A PHILOSOPHY
OF EDUCATION *

The phrase "progressive education" is one, if not of protest, at least of contrast, of contrast with an education which was predominantly static in subject-matter, authoritarian in methods, and mainly passive and receptive from the side of the young. But the philosophy of education must go beyond any idea of education that is formed by way of contrast, reaction and protest. For it is an attempt to discover what education *is* and how it takes place. Only when we identify education with schooling does it seem to be a simple thing to tell what education actually is, and yet a clear idea of what it *is* gives us our only criterion for judging and directing what goes on in schools.

It is sometimes supposed that it is the business of the philosophy of education to tell what education *should* be. But the only way of deciding what education should be, at least, the only way which does not lead us into the clouds, is discovery of what actually takes place when education really occurs. And before we can formulate a philosophy of education we must know how human nature is constituted in the

---

* This selection appeared originally in *The New Era in Home and School,* 1934.

concrete; we must know about the working of actual social forces; we must know about the operations through which basic raw materials are modified into something of greater value. The need for a philosophy of education is thus fundamentally the need for finding out what education really *is*. We have to take those cases in which we find there is a real development of desirable powers, and then find out how this development took place. Then we can project what has taken place in these instances as a guide for directing our other efforts. The need for this discovery and this projection is the need for a philosophy of education.

What then is education when we find actual satisfactory specimens of it in existence? In the first place, it is a process of development, of growth. And it is the *process* and not merely the result that is important. A truly healthy person is not something fixed and completed. He is a person whose processes and activities go on in such a way that he will continue to be healthy. Similarly, an educated person is the person who has the power to go on and get more education. Just what do we mean by growth, by development? Some of the early educational philosophers, like Rousseau and his followers, made much use of the analogy of the development of a seed into the full-grown plant. They used this analogy to draw the conclusion that in human beings there are latent capacities which, if they are only left to themselves, will ultimately flower and bear fruit. So they framed the notion of *natural* development as opposed to a directed growth which they regarded as artificial.

But in the first place the growth of a seed is limited as compared with that of a human being; its future is largely prescribed by its antecedent nature. It has not got the capacities for growth in different directions toward different outcomes that are characteristic of the more flexible and richly endowed human young. The latter is also, if you please, a seed, a collection of germinal powers, but he may become a sturdy oak, a willow that bends with every wind, a thorny cactus or a poisonous weed.

This fact suggests a second fallacy. Even the seed of a plant does not grow simply of itself. It must have light, air and moisture in order to grow. Its development is after all controlled by conditions and forces that are outside of it. Native inherent forces must interact with those of its surroundings if there is to be life and development. In fact, development, even with a plant, is a matter of the *kind of interaction* that goes on between itself and the conditions and forces that form its environment. A stunned oak, a stalk of maize that bears few ears with only a few scattered grains, exhibit so-called natural development as truly as does the noble tree with expanding branches or the ear of maize that wins the prize at an exhibition. The difference in result may in part be due to native stock, but it is also due in part to what the environment has provided. And even the finest native stock would come to an untimely end or result in a miserable product if its own energies could not interact with favorable conditions of light, moisture, air, etc.

Since there are two factors involved in the existence of any interaction, the idea and ideal of education must take account of both. Traditional school methods and subject-matter failed to take into account the *diversity* of capacities and needs that exists in different human beings. It virtually assumed that, for purposes of education at least, all human beings are as much alike as peas in a pod, and it therefore provided a uniform curriculum for all.

In the second place, it failed to recognize that the *initiative* in growth comes from the needs and powers of the pupil. The *first* step in the interaction that results in growth comes from the reaching out of the tentacles of the individual, from an effort, at first blind, to procure the materials that his potentialities demand in order that they may come into action and find satisfaction. As with the body, hunger and power of taking and assimilating nourishment are the first necessities. Without them, the food that is theoretically most nutritious is offered in vain. Nothing would be more extraordinary if we had a proper system of education than the assumption, now so commonly made, that the mind of the individual is naturally averse to learning, and has to be either browbeaten or coaxed into action. Every mind, even of the youngest, is naturally or inherently seeking for those modes of active operation that are within the limits of its capacities—precisely as the body of the baby is constantly active as long as the infant is awake. The problem, a difficult and delicate one, is to discover what tendencies are especially seeking expression at a particular time and just what materials and methods will serve to evoke and direct a truly educative development.

The practical counterpart of the failure of traditional education to see that the initiative in learning and growth is with the individual learner lay in the method of imposition from the side of the teacher and reception, absorption, from the side of the pupil. Unwillingness to learn naturally follows when there is failure to take into account tendencies that are urgent in the existing make-up of an individual. All sorts of external devices then have to be resorted to in order to achieve absorption and retention of imposed subject-matter and skills. This method of teaching may be compared to inscribing records upon a passive phonographic disc to result in giving back what has been inscribed when the proper button is pressed in recitation or examination.

It is impossible, of course, for any teacher not to observe that there *are* real differences among pupils. But because these differences are not carried back to concrete differences in individuality, to differences in needs, in desires, in direction of native interest, they are too often generalized by being summed up under two main heads. Some pupils are just naturally bright while others are dull and stupid! Some are docile and obedient and others are unruly and troublesome! Conformity then becomes the criterion by which the pupil is judged in spite of the fact that initiative, originality and independence are precious qualities in life.

While the raw material and the starting-point of growth are found in native capacities, the environing conditions which it is the duty of the educator to furnish are the indispensable means by which intrinsic possibilities are developed. Native capacities are the beginning, the starting-point. They are not the end and they do not of themselves decide the end. A gardener, a worker of metals, will not get far in his work if he does not observe and pay attention to the properties of the material he deals with. But if he permits these properties to dictate what he does, he will not get *anywhere*. Development will be arrested, not promoted. He must bring to his consideration of what he finds an ideal of possibilities not realized. This idea and ideal must be in line with the constitution of the raw material; it must not do violence to them; it must express *their* possibilities. But, nevertheless, it cannot be extracted from any study of them as they now exist. It must come from seeing them imaginatively, reflectively; and hence it must come from a source other than what is already at hand.

In the case of the educator the demand for imaginative insight into possibilities is greater. The gardener and worker in metals may take as their measure of the end to be accomplished the things that have already been done with plants and ores, although if they are original or inventive they will introduce some variation. But human individuals vary in their structure and possibilities as plants and metals do not. While the educator must use results that have already been accomplished he cannot, if he is truly an educator, make them his final and complete standard. Like the artist he has the problem of creating something that is not the exact duplicate of anything that has been wrought and achieved previously.

In any case, development, growth, involve change, modification, and modification in definite directions. It is quite possible for a teacher, under the supposed sanction of the idea of cultivating individuality, to fixate a pupil more or less at his existing level. Respect for individuality is primarily *intellectual*. It signifies studying the individual to see what is there to work with. Having this sympathetic understanding, the *practical* work then begins, for the practical work is one of modification, of changing, of reconstruction continued without end. The change must at least be towards more effective techniques, towards greater self-reliance, towards a more thoughtful and inquiring disposition, one more capable of persistent effort in meeting obstacles.

The weakness of some schools and teachers that would like to claim the name of progressive is that in reaction from the traditional method of external and authoritative imposition, they stop short with the recognition of the importance of giving free scope to native capacities and interests. They do not, in the first place, examine closely enough and long enough to find out what these actually may be. In the second place, they are inclined to take the individual traits that are showing themselves as finalities, instead of possibilities which by suitable direction can be transformed into something of greater significance, value and effectiveness. There is still current in many quarters the idea that evolution and development are simply matters of unfolding from within and that the unfolding will take place almost automatically if hands are kept off.

This point of view is natural as a reaction from the manifest evils of external imposition. But there is an alternative; and this alternative is not just a middle course or compromise between the two procedures. It is something radically different from either. Existing likes and powers are to be treated as possibilities, as starting-points, that are absolutely necessary for any healthy development. But development involves a point *towards* which as well as one *from* which; it involves constant movement in a given direction. Then when the point that is for the time being the goal and end is reached, it is in its turn but the starting-point of further reconstruction. The great problems of the adult who has to deal with the young is to see, and to feel deeply as well as merely to see intellectually, the forces that are moving in the young; but it is to see them as possibilities, as signs and promises; to interpret them, in short, in the light of what they may come to be. Nor does the task end there. It is bound up with the further problem of judging and devising the conditions, the materials, both physical, such as tools of work, and moral and social, which will, once more, so *interact* with existing powers and preferences as to bring about transformation in the desired direction.

The essential weakness of the old and traditional education was not just that it emphasized the necessity for provision of definite subject-matter and activities. These things *are* necessities for anything that can rightly be called education. The weakness and evil was that the imagination of educators did not go beyond provision of a fixed and rigid environment of subject-matter, one drawn moreover from sources altogether too remote from the experiences of the pupil. What is needed in the new education is more attention, not less, to subject-matter and to progress in technique. But when I say more, I do not mean more in quantity of the same old kind. I mean an imaginative vision which sees that no prescribed and ready-made scheme can possibly determine the exact subject-matter that will best promote the educative growth of every individual young person; that every new individual sets a new problem; that he calls for at least a somewhat different emphasis in subject-matter presented. There is nothing more blindly obtuse than the convention which supposes that the matter actually contained in textbooks of arithmetic, history, geography, etc., is just what will further the educational development of all children.

But withdrawal from the hard and fast and narrow contents of the old curriculum is only the negative side of the matter. If we do not go on and go far in the positive direction of providing a body of subject-matter much richer, more varied and flexible, and also in truth more definite, judged in terms of the experience of those being educated, than traditional education supplied, we shall tend to leave an educational vacuum in which anything may happen. Complete isolation is impossible in nature. The young live in some environment whether we intend it or not, and this environment is constantly interacting with what children and youth bring to it, and the result is the shaping of their interests, minds and character—either educatively or mis-educatively. If the professed educator abdicates his responsibility for judging and selecting the kind of environment that his best understanding leads him to think will be conducive to growth, then the young are left at the mercy of all the unorganized and casual forces of the modern social environment that inevitably play upon them as long as they live. In the educative environment the knowledge, judgment and experience of the teacher is a greater, not a smaller factor, than it is in the traditional school. The difference is that the teacher operates not as a magistrate set on high and marked by arbitrary authority but as a friendly co-partner and guide in a common enterprise.

Development, however, is a *continuous* process, and continuity signifies consecutiveness of action. Here was the strong point of the traditional education at its best. The subject-matter of the classics and mathematics involved of necessity, for those who mastered it, a consecutive and orderly development along definite lines. Here lies perhaps the greatest problem of the newer efforts in education. It is comparatively easy to improvise, to try a little of this today and this week and then something else tomorrow and next week. Things are done on the basis of some immediate interest and stimulation but without sufficient regard to what it leads to, as to whether or not something more difficult, setting new demands for information, need for acquisition of greater adequacy in technique and for new modes of skill, is led up to and grows naturally out of what is started. The need for taking account of spontaneous and uncoerced interest and activity is a genuine need; but without care and thought it results, all too readily, in a detached multiplicity of isolated short-time activities or projects, and the continuity necessary for growth is lost. Indeed, the new education processes require much more planning ahead on the part of teachers than did the old—for there the planning was all done in advance by the fixed curriculum.

I have spoken of the importance of environment, but a sound philosophy of education requires that the general term environment be specified. It must be seen to be dominantly human and its values as social. Through the influence of the social environment each person becomes saturated with the customs, the beliefs, the purposes, skills, hopes and fears of the cultural group to which he belongs. The features of even his physical surroundings come to him through the eyes and ears of the community. Hills and plains, plants and animals, climate and change of seasons, are clothed with the memories and traditions, and characteristic occupations and interests, of the society of which he is part. In the earlier years of education, it is particularly important that subject-matter be presented in its human context and setting. Here is one of the commonest failures of the school. We are told that instruction must proceed from the concrete to the abstract, but it is forgotten that in the experience of the child only that which has a human value and function is concrete. In his nature study and geography, physical things are presented to him as if they were independent and complete in themselves. But in the actual experience of a child, these things have a meaning for him only as they enter into human life. Even those distinctively human products, reading and writing, which have developed for the purposes of furthering human association, of making human contacts closer and richer, are treated as if they were subjects in themselves. They are not used as friendly speech is used in ordinary life, and so for the child they become abstract, a kind of mystery that belongs to the school but not to life outside the school.

As the material of genuine development is that of human contacts and associations, so the end, the value that is the criterion and directing guide of educational work, is social. The acquisition of skills is not an end in itself. They are things to be put to use, and that use is their contribution to a common and shared life. They are intended, indeed, to make an individual more capable of self-support and of self-respecting independence. But unless this end is placed in the context of services rendered to others, skills gained will be put to an egoistic and selfish use, and may be employed as means of a trained shrewdness in which one person gets the better of others. Too often, indeed, the schools, through reliance upon the spur of competition and the bestowing of special honors and prizes, only build up and strengthen the disposition that makes an individual when he leaves school employ his special talents and superior skill to outwit his fellows without respect for the welfare of others.

What is true of the skills acquired in school, is true also of the knowledge gained there. The educational end and the ultimate test of the value of what is learned is its use and application in carrying on and improving the common life of all. It should never be forgotten that the background of the traditional educational system is a class society and that opportunity for instruction in certain subjects, especially literary ones and in mathematics beyond the rudiments of simple arithmetical subjects, was reserved for the wellborn and the well-to-do. Because of this fact, knowledge of these subjects became a badge of cultural superiority and social status. For many persons the possession of knowledge was a means of display, almost of showing off. Useful knowledge, on the other hand, was necessary only for those who were compelled by their class status to work for a living. A class stigma attached to it, and the uselessness of knowledge for all purposes save purely personal culture was proof of its higher quality.

Even after education in many countries was made universal, these standards of value persisted. There is no greater egoism than that of learning when it is treated simply as a mark of personal distinction to be held and cherished for its own sake. Yet the only way of eliminating this quality of exclusiveness is that all conditions of the school environment should tend in actual practice to develop in individuals the realization that knowledge is a possession held in trust for the furthering of the well-being of all.

Perhaps the greatest need of and for a philosophy of education at the present time is the urgent need that exists for making clear in idea and effective in practice that its end is social, and that the criterion to be applied in estimating the value of the practices that exist in schools is also social. It is true that the aim of education is development of individuals to the utmost of their potentialities. But this statement in isolation leaves unanswered the question as to what is the measure of the development. A society of free individuals in which all, through their own work, contribute to the liberation and enrichment of the lives of others, is the only environment in which any individual can really grow normally to his full stature. An environment in which some are practically enslaved, degraded, limited, will always react to create conditions that prevent the full development even of those who fancy they enjoy complete freedom for unhindered growth.

There are two outstanding reasons why in the conditions of

the world at present a philosophy of education must make the social aim of education the central article in its creed. The world is rapidly industrialized. Individual groups, tribes and races, once living completely untouched by the economic regime of modern capitalistic industry, now find almost every phase of their lives affected for better or worse—and often for worse—by the expansion of that system. What the Geneva Commission reported after a study of natives in the mining districts of South Africa, holds of peoples all over the world, with proper change of some of the terms used: "The investment of Western capital in African industries has made the Native dependent upon the demand of the world markets for the products of his labor and the resources of his continent." In a world that has so largely engaged in a mad and often brutally harsh race for material gain by means of ruthless competition, it behooves the school to make ceaseless and intelligently organized effort to develop above all else the will for co-operation and the spirit which sees in every other individual one who has an equal right to share in the cultural and material fruits of collective human invention, industry, skill and knowledge. The supremacy of this aim in mind and character is necessary for other reasons than as an offset to the spirit of inhumanity bred by economic competition and exploitation. It is necessary to prepare the coming generation for a new and more just and humane society which is sure to come, and which, unless hearts and minds are prepared by education, is likely to come attended with all the evils that result from social changes effected by violence.

The other need especially urgent at the present time is connected with the unprecedented wave of nationalistic sentiment, of racial and national prejudice, of readiness to resort to the ordeal of arms to settle questions, that animates the world at the present time. The schools of the world must have somehow failed grievously or the rise of this evil spirit on so vast a scale would not have been possible. The best excuse, probably, that can be made is that schools and educators were caught unawares. Who could have dreamed that the demon of fear, suspicion, prejudice and hatred, would take possession of men's minds in the way it has done? But that excuse is no longer available. We now know the enemy; it is out in the open. Unless the schools of the world can engage in a common effort to rebuild the spirit of common understanding, of mutual sympathy and goodwill among all peoples and races, to exercise the demon of prejudice, isolation and hatred, the schools themselves are likely to be submerged by the general return to barbarism, which is the sure outcome of present tendencies if they go on unchecked by the forces which education alone can evoke and fortify.

THE RELATION OF
SCIENCE AND PHILOSOPHY AS
THE BASIS OF EDUCATION *

Empirical and experimental philosophy has no quarrel with science, either in itself or in its application to education. On the contrary, scientific conclusions and methods are the chief ally of an empirical philosophy of education. For according to empirical philosophy, science provides the only means we have for learning about man and the world in which he lives. Some have thought that this fact makes philosophy unnecessary. They have supposed that the admission that science is supreme in the field of knowledge covers the whole ground of human experience. The elimination does rule out *one* kind of philosophy, namely, that which held that philosophy is a higher form of knowledge than the scientific kind, one which furnishes knowledge of ultimate higher reality. But it does not follow from the elimination of this particular type of philosophy that philosophy itself must go.

It would follow if man were simply and only a knowing being. But he is not. He is also an acting being, a creature with desires, hopes, fears, purposes and habits. To the aver-

---

* This selection appeared originally in *School and Society*, 1938.

age person knowledge itself is of importance because of its bearing upon what he needs to do and to make. It helps him in clarifying his wants, in constructing his ends and in finding means for realizing them. There exist, in other words, values as well as known facts and principles, and philosophy is concerned primarily with values—with the ends for the sake of which man acts. Given the most extensive and accurate system of knowledge, and man is still faced with the question of what he is going to do about it and what he is going to do with the knowledge in his possession.

In this matter of the connection of what is known with values, science is an ally of an empirical philosophy against absolute philosophies which pretend that fixed and eternal truths are known by means of organs and methods that are independent of science. The objection to this position is not merely theoretical. The practical objections to it are that it strengthens appeal to authority and promotes controversies which cannot be settled by the use of the methods of inquiry and proof that have been worked out in the sciences. The only remaining alternative is the use of coercion and force, either openly or covertly through falling back on customs and institutions as they happen to exist. There is no great danger that the present-day revival in some quarters of Greek and medieval philosophies of eternal first principles will make much headway as a theoretical philosophy. There is always danger that such philosophies will have practical influence in reinforcing established social authority that is exercised in behalf of maintenance of the *status quo*. Against this danger, an experimental philosophy stands in firm alliance with the methods by which the natural sciences arrive at warranted truths.

The philosophy of education is not a poor relation of general philosophy even though it is often so treated even by philosophers. It is ultimately the most significant phase of philosophy. For it is through the processes of education that knowledge is obtained, while these educational processes do not terminate in mere acquisition of knowledge and related forms of skill. They attempt to integrate the knowledge gained into enduring dispositions and attitudes. It is not too much to say that education is *the* outstanding means by which union of knowledge and the values that actually work in actual conduct is brought about. The difference between educational practices that are influenced by a well-thought-out philosophy, and practices that are not so influenced is that between education conducted with some clear idea of the ends in the way of ruling attitudes of desire and purpose that are to be created, and an education that is conducted blindly, under the control of customs and traditions that have not been examined or in response to immediate social pressures. This difference does not come about because of any inherent sacredness in what is called philosophy, but because any effort to clarify the ends to be attained is, as far as it goes, philosophical.

The need for such systematic clarification is especially urgent at the present time. Applications of natural science have made an enormous difference in human relations. They have revolutionized the means of production and distribution of commodities and services. They have effected an equally great change in communication and all the means for influencing the public opinion upon which political action depends. These applications decide, more than any other force or set of forces, the conditions under which human beings live together and under which they act, enjoy and suffer. Moreover, they have produced communities that are in a state of rapid change. Wherever the effect of the applications of science has been felt, human relations have ceased to be static. Old forms have been invaded and often undermined, in the family, in politics and even in moral and religious habits as well as in the narrower field of economic arrangements. Almost all current social problems have their source here. Finally, ends and values that were formed in the pre-scientific period and the institutions of great power that were formed in the same period retain their influence. Human life, both individually and collectively, is disturbed, confused and conflicting.

Either the instrumentalities of education will ignore this state of affairs and the schools will go their own way, confining themselves for the most part to providing standardized knowledge and forms of skill as ends in themselves, modified only by concessions to temporary social pressures, or they will face the question of the relation of school-education to the needs and possibilities of the social situation. If the latter problem is faced, then there arise problems of the re-adaptation of materials of the curriculum, methods of instruction and the social organization of the school. A philosophy of education can not settle once for all how these problems shall be resolved. But it can enforce perception of the nature of these problems, and can give suggestions of value as to the only ways in which they can satisfactorily be dealt with. Administrators and teachers who are imbued with the ideas can test and develop them in their actual work so that, through union of theory and practice, the philosophy of education will be a living, growing thing.

I come back, then, to the question of the alliance of empirical pragmatic philosophy with science against both a philosophy of truths and principles that are alleged to be superior to any that can be ascertained by empirical methods of science, and also against dogmatic authority, custom, routine and the pressure of immediate circumstances. Science used in the educational field can ascertain the actual facts, and can generalize them on the basis of relations of cause and effect. It can not itself settle the value of the consequences that result from even the best use of more economical and effective methods as causes of effects produced. The consequences have to be evaluated in the light of what is known about social problems, evils and needs. But without the knowledge of actual conditions and of relations of cause and effect, any values that are set up as ends are bare ideals in the sense in which "ideal" means utopian, without means for its realization.

I shall mention two or three matters in which the need for cooperation between philosophy and science is especially intimate. Since scientific method depends upon first-hand experimentally controlled experiences, any philosophic application of the scientific point of view will emphasize the need of such experiences in the school, as over against mere acquisition of ready-made information that is supplied in isolation from the students' own experience. So far, it will be in line with what is called the "progressive" movement in education. But it will be an influence in counteracting any tendencies that may exist in progressive education to slur the importance of continuity in the experiences that are had and the importance of organization. Unless the science of education on its own ground and behalf emphasizes *subject-matters* which contain within themselves the promise and power of continuous growth in the direction of organization, it is false to its own position as scientific. In cooperation with a philosophy of education, it can lend invaluable aid in seeing to it that the chosen subject-matters are also such that they progressively develop toward formation of attitudes of understanding the world in which students and teachers live and towards forming the attitudes of purpose, desire and action which will make pupils effective in dealing with social conditions.

Another point of common interest concerns the place in the schools of the sciences, especially the place of the habits which form scientific attitude and method. The sciences had to battle against entrenched foes to obtain recognition in the curriculum. In a formal sense, the battle has been won, but not yet in a substantial sense. For scientific subject-matter is still more or less segregated as a special body of facts and truths. The full victory will not be won until every subject and lesson is taught in connection with its bearing upon creation and growth of the kind of power of observation, inquiry, reflection and testing that are the heart of scientific intelligence. Experimental philosophy is at one with the genuine spirit of a scientific attitude in the endeavor to obtain for scientific method this central place in education.

Finally, the science and philosophy of education can and should work together in overcoming the split between knowledge and action, between theory and practice, which now affects both education and society so seriously and harmfully. Indeed, it is not too much to say that institution of a happy marriage between theory and practice is in the end the chief meaning of a science and a philosophy of education that work together for common ends.

II

Ethics
and
Education

II

Ethics

and

Education

LOGICAL CONDITIONS
OF A SCIENTIFIC TREATMENT
OF MORALITY *

SEC. I · *The Use of the Term "Scientific"*

The familiar notion that science is a body of systematized knowledge will serve to introduce consideration of the term "scientific" as it is employed here. The phrase "body of systematized knowledge" may be taken in different senses. It may designate a property which resides inherently in arranged facts, apart from the ways in which the facts have been settled upon to be facts, and apart from the way in which their arrangement has been secured. Or, it may mean the intellectual activities of observing, describing, comparing, inferring, experimenting, and testing, which are necessary in obtaining facts and in putting them into coherent form. The term should include both of these meanings. But since the static property of arrangement is dependent upon antecedent dynamic processes, it is necessary to make explicit such dependence. We need to throw the emphasis in using the term "scientific" first upon methods, and then upon results through reference to methods. As used in this article,

---

* This selection was published originally as a pamphlet by the University of Chicago Press, 1903.

"scientific" means regular methods of controlling the formation of judgments regarding some subject-matter.

The transition from an ordinary to a scientific attitude of mind coincides with ceasing to take certain things for granted and assuming a critical or inquiring and testing attitude. This transformation means that some belief and its accompanying statement are no longer taken as self-sufficing and complete in themselves, but are regarded as *conclusions*. To regard a statement as a conclusion means(1) that its basis and ground lie outside of itself. This reference beyond itself sets us upon the search for prior assertions which are needed in order to make this one, *i.e.*, upon inquiry. (2) Such prior statements are considered with reference to their bearings or import in the determination of some further statement, *i.e.*, a consequent. The meaning or significance of a given statement lies, logically, in other statements to which we are committed in making the one in question. Thus we are set upon reasoning, the development of the assertions to which a particular assertion or view commits and entitles us. Our attitude becomes scientific in the degree in which we look in both directions with respect to every judgment passed; first, checking or testing its validity by reference to possibility of making other and more certain judgments with which this one is bound up; secondly, fixing its meaning (or significance) by reference to its use in making other statements. The determination of *validity* by reference to possibility of making other judgments upon which the one in question depends, and the determination of *meaning* by reference to the necessity of making other statements to which the one in question entitles us, are the two marks of scientific procedure.

So far as we engage in this procedure, we look at our respective acts of judging not as independent and detached, but as an interrelated system, within which every assertion entitles us to other assertions (which must be carefully deduced since they constitute its meaning) and to which we are entitled only through other assertions (so that they must be carefully searched for). "Scientific" as used in this article thus means the possibility of establishing an order of judgments such that each one when made is of use in determining other judgments, thereby securing control of their formation.

Such a conception of "scientific," throwing the emphasis upon the inherent logic of an inquiry rather than upon the particular form which the results of the inquiry assume, may serve to obviate some of the objections which at once suggest themselves when there is mention of a science of conduct. Unless this conception is emphasized, the term "science" is likely to suggest those bodies of knowledge which are most familiar to us in physical matters; and thus to give the impression that what is sought is reduction of matters of conduct to similarly physical or even quasi-mathematical form. It is, however, analogy with the method of inquiry, not with the final product, which is intended. Yet, while this explanation may preclude certain objections, it is far, in the present state of discussion, from removing all objections and thus securing a free and open field. The point of view expressly disclaims any effort to reduce the statement of matters of conduct to forms comparable with those of physical science. But it also expressly proclaims an identity of logical procedure in the two cases. This assertion will meet with sharp and flat denial. Hence, before developing the logic of moral science, it is necessary to discuss the objections which affirm such an inherent disparity between moral judgments and physical judgments that there is no ground in the control of the judging activity in one case for inferring the possibility of like control in the other.

SEC. 2 · *The Possibility of Logical Control of Moral Judgments*

In considering this possibility, we are met, as just indicated, by an assertion that there is something in the very nature of conduct which prevents the use of logical methods in the way they are employed in other recognized spheres of scientific inquiry. The objection implies that *moral* judgments are of such character that nothing can be systematically extracted from one of them which is of use in facilitating and guaranteeing the formation of others. It denies, from the logical side, the continuity of moral experience. If there were such continuity, any one judgment could be dealt with in such a way as to make of it a conscious tool for forming other judgments. The ground of denial of continuity in moral experience rests upon the belief that the basis and justifying principle of the ethical judgment is found in transcendental conceptions, viz., considerations which do not flow from the course of experience as that is judged in terms of itself, but which have a signficance independent of the course of experience as such.

The assertion of such logical disparity assumes a variety of forms, all coming back to pretty much the same presupposition. One way of putting the matter is that ethical judgments are immediate and intuitive. If this be true, an ethical judgment cannot be considered a conclusion; and hence there can be no question of putting it into orderly intellectual (or logical) relations with other like judgments. A merely immediate judgment is, by the nature of the case, incapable of either intellectual rectification or of intellectual application. This view finds expression in popular consciousness in the notion that scientific judgments depend upon reason, while moral valuations proceed from a separate faculty, conscience, having its own criteria and methods not amenable to intellectual supervision.

Another way of affirming radical disparity is that scientific judgments depend upon the principle of causation, which of necessity carries with it the dependence of one phenomenon upon another, and thus the possibility of stating every fact in connection with the statement of some other fact; while moral judgments involve the principle of final cause, of end and ideal. Hence to endeavor to control the construction and affirmation of any content of moral judgment by reference to antecedent propositions is to destroy its peculiar moral quality. Or, as it is popularly expressed, ethical judgment is ethical just because it is not scientific; because it deals with norms, values, ideals, not with given facts; with what *ought* to be, estimated through pure spiritual aspiration, not with what *is*, decided after investigation.

Pretty much the same point of view is expressed when it is said that scientific judgments, as such, state facts in terms of sequences in time and of co-existences in space. Wherever we are dealing with relations of this sort, it is apparent that a knowledge of one term or member serves as a guide and check in the assertion of the existence and character of the other term or member. But moral judgments, it is said, deal with actions which are still to be performed. Consequently in this case characteristic meaning is found only in the qualities which exist *after* and by means of the judgment. For this reason, moral judgment is often supposed to transcend anything found in past experience, and so, once more, to try to control a moral judgment through the medium of other judgments is to eliminate its distinctive ethical quality. This notion finds its popular equivalent in the conviction that moral judgments relate to realities where freedom is implicated in such a way that no intellectual control is possible. The judgment is considered to be based, not upon objective facts, but upon arbitrary choice or volition expressed in a certain sort of approval or disapproval.

I have no intention of discussing these points in their full bearing. I shall reduce them to a single logical formulation, and then discuss the latter in its most general significance. The justification of the single statement, as a formulation of the objections just set forth (and of other like ones), will not be attempted, for further discussion does not turn upon that point. When generalized, the various statements of the logical gulf between the moral judgment and the scientific reduces itself to an assertion of two antinomies: one, the separation between the universal and the individual; the other, between the intellectual and the practical. And these two antinomies finally reduce themselves to one: Scientific statements refer to *generic conditions* and relations, which are therefore capable of complete and objective statement; ethical judgments refer to an *individual act* which by its very nature transcends objective statement. The ground of separation is that scientific judgment is universal, hence only hypothetical, and hence incapable of relating to acts, while moral judgment is categorical, and thus individualized, and hence refers to acts. The scientific judgment states that where some condition or set of conditions is found, there also is found a specified other condition or set of conditions. The moral judgment states that a certain end has categorical value, and is thus to be realized without any reference whatsoever to antecedent conditions or facts. The scientific judgment states a connection of conditions; the moral judgment states the unconditioned claim of an idea to be made real.

This formulation of the logic of the problem under consideration fixes attention upon the two points which are in need of discussion. First: Is it true that scientific judgment deals with contents which have, in and of themselves, a universal nature—that its whole significance is exhausted in setting forth a certain connection of conditions? Secondly: Is it true that the attempt to regulate, by means of an intellectual technique, moral judgments—which, of course, are thoroughly individualized—destroys or in any way lessens distinctively ethical value?

In discussing the two questions just propounded, I shall endeavor to show: First, that scientific judgments have all the logical characteristics of ethical judgments; since they refer (1) to individual cases, and (2) to acts. I shall endeavor to show that the scientific judgment, the formulation of a connection of condition, has its origin, and is developed and employed for the specific and sole purpose of freeing and reinforcing acts of judgment that apply to unique and individual cases. In other words, I shall try to show that there is no question of eliminating the distinctive quality of ethical judgments by assimilating them to a different logical type, found in so-called scientific judgments; precisely because the logical type, found in so-called scientific judgments is one which already takes due account of individualization and activity. I shall, then, secondly, endeavor to show that individualized ethical judgments require for their control generic propositions, which state a connection of relevant conditions in general (or objective) form; and that it is possible to direct inquiry so as to arrive at such universals. And finally, I shall briefly set forth the three typical lines along which the construction of such generic scientific propositions must proceed, if there is to a scientific treatment of ethics.

SEC. 3 · *Nature of Scientific Judgments*

The proposition that scientific judgments are hypothetic because they are universal is almost commonplace in recent logical theory. There is no doubt that there is a sense in which this proposition states an unquestioned truth. The aim of science is law. A law is adequate in the degree in which it takes the form, if not of an equation, at least of formulation of constancy, of relationship, or order. It is clear that any law, whether stated as formulation of order or as an equation, conveys, in and of itself, not an individualized reality, but a certain connection of conditions. Up to this point there is no dispute. When, however, it is argued that this direct and obvious concern of science with generic statements exhausts the logical significance of scientific method, certain fundamental presuppositions and certain fundamental bearings are ignored; and the logical question at issue is begged. The real question is not whether science aims at statements which take the form of universals, or formulae of connection of conditions, but *how* it comes to do so, and *what it does with* the universal statements after they have been secured.

In other words, we have, first, to ask for the logical import of generic judgments. Accordingly, not questioning the importance of general formulae as the objective content of the sciences, this section will endeavor to show that such importance lies in the development of "sciences" or bodies of generic formulae as instrumentalities and methods of controlling individualized judgments.

1. The boast and pride of modern science is its distinctly empirical and experimental character. The term "empirical" refers to origin and development of scientific statements out of concrete experiences; the term "experimental" refers to the testing and checking of the so-called laws and universals by reference to their application in further concrete experience. If this notion of science be correct, it shows, without further argument, that generic propositions occupy a purely intermediate position. They are neither initial nor final. They are the bridges by which we pass over from one particular experi-

ence to another; they are individual experiences put into such shape as to be available in regulating other experiences. Otherwise scientific laws would be only intellectual abstractions tested on the basis of their own reciprocal consistencies; and the trait which is supposed to demarcate science from medieval speculation would at once fade away.

Moreover if the generic character of propositions of physical and biological sciences were ultimate, such propositions would be entirely useless from a practical point of view; they would be quite incapable of practical application because they would be isolated from intellectual continuity with the particular cases to which application is sought. No amount of purely deductive manipulation of abstractions brings a resulting conclusion any nearer a concrete fact than were the original premises. Deduction introduces in regular sequence new ideas, and thus complicates the general content. But to suppose that by complicating the content of a proposition we get nearer the individual of experience is the fallacy at once of mediaeval realism and of the ontological argument for the existence of God. No range of synthesis of universal propositions in chemistry, physics, and biology would (if such propositions were logically self-sufficing) assist us in building a bridge or in locating the source of an epidemic of typhoid fever. If, however, such propositions and their deductive synthesis are to be interpreted in the sense of the manufacturing and employing of intellectual tools for the express purpose of facilitating our individual experiences, the outcome is quite other.

The empirical origin, the experimental test, and the practical use of the statements of science are enough of themselves to indicate the impossibility of holding to any fixed logical division of judgments into universal as scientific, and individual as practical. It suggests that what we term science is just the forging and arranging of instrumentalities for dealing with individual cases of experience—cases which, if individual, are just as unique and irreplaceable as are those of moral life. We might even say that the very fact which leads us upon a superficial view into believing in the logical separation of the generic judgment from the individual, viz, the existence of a large and self-contained body of universal propositions, is proof that as to some individual experiences we have already worked out methods of regulating our reflective transactions with them, while for another phase of experience this work remains to be done; *i.e.*, is the problem of current ethical science.

The consideration of the technique by which the desired end of control is accomplished does not belong here. It suffices to note that the hypothetic judgment is a most potent instrumentality. If we inhibit the tendency to say, "This, *A*, is *B*," and can (1) find ground for saying, "Wherever there is *mn* there is *B*," and can (2) show that wherever there is *op* there is *mn*, and (3) have a technique for discovering the presence of *op* in *A*, we shall have warrant for identifying This, *A*, as *B*, even if all the outward and customary traits are lacking, and even if this *A*, presents certain traits which without the mediation of a generic proposition, would have inevitably led us to identify it as *C*. Identification, in other words, is secure only when it can be made through (1) breaking up the unanalyzed This of naïve judgment into determinate traits, (2) breaking up the predicate into a similar combination of elements, and (3) establishing uniform connection between some of the elements in the subject and some in the predicate. All judgments of everyday life, and indeed all judgments in such sciences as geology, geography, history, zoölogy, and botany (all sciences that have to do with historic narration or with description of space coexistences), come back ultimately to questions of identification. Even judgments in physics and chemistry, in their ultimate and concrete form, are concerned with individual cases. Of all the sciences, mathematics alone[1] is concerned with pure general propositions—hence the indispensable significance of mathematics as a *tool* for all judgments of tech-

---

[1] If it were necessary for the purpose of this argument, it could of course be shown that reference to individual cases is involved in all mathematics. Within mathematical science, symbols (and diagrams are symbols) are individual objects of just the same logical nature as are metals and acids in chemistry and as are rocks and fossils in geology.

nology and of the other sciences. It also is true in all the arts, whether commercial, professional, or artistic, that judgments reduce themselves to matters of correct identification. Observation, diagnosis, interpretation, and expert skill all display themselves in transactions with individual cases as such.

2. Thus far we have seen that the importance of generic statements in science is no ground for assuming a disparity in their logic from that of a scientific treatment of conduct. Indeed, since we have found that generic propositions originate, develop, and find their test in control of individual cases, the presumption is of similarity rather than of dissimilarity. Can we extend the parallelism farther? Does it apply equally well to the other characteristic trait of ethical judgment, viz., its reference to an act?

Just as modern logic has seized upon the hypothetic and universal character of scientific statements, relegating their bearing upon individual judgments into the background (but in truth so relegating them only because that bearing is always taken for granted), so modern logic has emphasized the aspect of content in judgment at the expense of the act of judging. I shall now try to show, however, that this emphasis also occurs because reference to act is so thoroughly taken for granted that it is possible to ignore it—that is, fail to give it explicit statement. I shall try to show that every judgment must be regarded as an act; that, indeed, the individual character of judgment proper, which has just been brought out, means, in final analysis, that the judgment is a unique act for which there is no substitute.

Our fundamental point is the control of the content or meaning which is asserted in any given judgment. How can such control be obtained? So far we have spoken as if the content of one judgment might be elaborated simply by reference to the content of another—particularly as if the content of an individual judgment, a judgment of identification, might be secured by reference to the content of a universal or hypothetic proposition. In truth, there is no such thing as control of one content by mere reference to another content as such. To recognize this impossibility is to recognize that the control of the formation of the judgment is always through the medium of an act by which the respective contents of both the individual judgment and of the universal proposition are selected and brought into relationship to each other. There is no road open from any generic formula to an individual judgment. The road leads through the habits and mental attitudes of the one engaged in judging. The universal gets logical force, as well as existence, only in the acts by which it is invented and constructed as a tool and then is employed for the purpose for which it was intended.

I shall accordingly try to show that activity shows itself at every critical point in the formation of judgment: (*a*) that it shows itself in the genesis of the generic or universal employed; (*b*) that it shows itself in the selection of the particular subject-matter which is judged; and (*c*) that it shows itself in the way in which the validity of the hypothesis is tested and verified, and the significance of the particular subject-matter determined.

a) So far we have assumed the possibility of building up and selecting for use some generic principle which controls the identification reached in an individual case. We cannot, that is to say, regulate judgments of the type, "This is typhoid," or, "That is Bela's comet," unless we have certain generic concepts, which are defined as connection of particular conditions, and unless we know when and how to select from the stock of such concepts at our disposal the particular one required. The entire science considered as a body of formulae having coherent relations to one another is just a system of possible predicates—that is, of possible standpoints or methods to be employed in qualifying some particular experience whose nature or meaning is not clear to us. It furnishes us with a set of tools from which choice has to be made. The choice, of course, depends upon the needs of the particular facts which have to be discriminated and identified in the given case—just as the carpenter decides, on the basis of what he is going to do, whether he will take a hammer, a saw, or a plane from his tool-chest. One might as well suppose that the existence of possible candidates for office, plus the mathematically possible combinations and permutations of them, constitutes an election of one of them to office, as to suppose that a specific judgment follows from even an ideally exhaustive system of general principles. The logical process includes, as an organic part of itself, the selection and reference of that particular one of the system which is relevant to the particular case. This individualized selection and adaptation is an integral portion of the logic of the situation. And such selection and adjustment is clearly in the nature of an action.

Nor must we fail to make clear that we are concerned, not with selecting and adapting a ready-made universal, but with the *origin* of the universal wholly for the sake of just such adaptation. If individual cases in experiences never gave us any difficulty in identification, if they never set any problem, universals would simply not exist, to say nothing of being used. The universal is precisely such a statement of experience as will facilitate and guarantee the valuation of individualized experiences. It has no existence, as it has no check of validity, outside of such a function. In some cases where science has already made considerable headway, we may, without error, speak as if universals were already at hand, as if the only question were which one of them to pick out and employ. But such a way of speaking must not blind us to the fact that it was only because of the need of some more objective way of determining given cases that a universal ever originated and took on form and character. Did not the universal develop as medium of conciliation in just the same sort of situation of conflict as that in which it finds its use, such use would be absolutely arbitrary and consequently without logical limit. The activity which selects and employs is logical, not extra-logical, just because the tool selected and employed has been invented and developed precisely for the sake of just such future selection and use.[2]

---

[2] The point of view which is here presented is, of course, distinctly pragmatic. I am not quite sure, however, of the implications of certain forms of pragmatism. They sometimes seem to imply that a rational or logical statement is all right up to a certain point, but has fixed external limits, so that at critical points recourse must be had to considerations which are distinctly of an irrational or extra-logical order, and this recourse is identified with choice and

b) The individualized act (or choice) in judgments of identification shows itself not only in selection from a body of alternatives of the specific predicate required, but in the determination of the "This," or subject, as well. Students of logic are familiar with the distinction between the fact of particularity and the qualifications or distinguishing traits of a particular—a distinction which has been variously termed one between the "That" and the "What," or between "This" and "Thisness." [3] Thisness refers to a quality which, however sensuous it be (such as hot, red, loud), may yet in its own meaning belong equally well to a large number of particulars. It is something a presentation *has,* rather than what it just *is.* Such a variety of applications is involved in the very notion of quality. It makes all qualities capable of consideration as degrees. It is responsible for the ease with which names of qualities transform themselves into abstract terms, blue into blueness, loud into loudness, hot into heat, etc.

The particularity, or better, singularity, of the judgment is constituted by the immediate demonstrative reference of the "This." [4] This demonstrative character means a preferential selection; it is a matter of action. Or, from the psychological side, the sensory quality becomes specific only in motor re-

---

"activity." The practical and the logical are thus opposed to each other. It is just the opposite which I am endeavoring to sustain, viz., that the logical is an inherent or organic expression of the practical, and hence is fulfilling its own logical basis and aim when it functions practically. I have no desire to show that what we term "science" is arbitrarily limited by *outside* ethical considerations; and that consequently science cannot intrude itself into the ethical sphere; but precisely the contrary, viz., that just because science is a mode of controlling our active relations with the world of experienced things, ethical experience is supremely in need of such regulation. And by "practical" I mean only regulated change in experienced values.

[3] This distinction in recent logic has been brought out with great force and clearness by Bradley, *Principles of Logic* (London, 1883), pp. 63-7.

[4] It is hardly necessary to point out that the article "the" is a weakened demonstrative, and that the pronouns, including "it," all have demonstrative reference.

sponse. Red, blue, hot, etc., as immediate experiences, always involve motor adjustments which determine them. Change the kind of motor adjustment and the quality of the experience changes; diminish it and the quality relapses more and more into indefinite vagueness. The selection of any particular "This" as the immediate subject of judgment is not arbitrary, however, but is dependent upon the end involved in the interest which is uppermost. Theoretically, any object within the range of perception, or any quality or any element of any one object, may function as the "This," or the subject-matter to be determined in judgment. Purely objectively, there is no reason for choosing any one of the infinite possibilities rather than another. But the aim in view (which, of course, finds its expression in the predicate of the judgment) gives a basis for deciding what object or what element of any object is logically fit. The implication of selective activity is thus an organic part of the logical operation, and not an arbitrary practical addition clapped on after the logical activity as such is complete. The very same interest which leads to the building up and selection of the universal leads to the constructive selection of the immediate data or material with reference to which the universal is to be employed.[5]

c) The experimental character of all scientific identification is a commonplace. It is so commonplace that we are apt to overlook its tremendous import—the unconditional necessity of overt activity to the integrity of the logical process as such. As we have just seen, an act is involved in the determination of both the predicate, or the interpreting meaning,

---

[5] Hence in accepting Bradley's distinction between "This" and "Thisness" we cannot accept the peculiar interpretation which he gives it. According to his way of looking at it, no strictly *logical* connection is possible between "This" and "Thisness." "Thisness" alone has logical significance; the "This" is determined by considerations entirely beyond intellectual control; indeed, it marks the fact that a reality lying outside of the act of judging has broken in upon, or forced itself into, a region of logical ideas or meanings, this peculiar and coercive irruption being an essential attendant of the *finite* extremely limited character of our experience.

and of the "This," or fact to be identified. Were not both of these acts correlatives in a larger scheme of change of value in experience, they would both be arbitrary; and their ultimate appropriateness or adaptation to each other would be a sheer miracle. If one arbitrary act of choice reached forth to lay hold of some predicate from out of the whole system of possible qualifications, while another act of choice, entirely independent in origin, reached out to seize a given area from the whole possible region of sense-perceptions, it would be the sheerest accident if the two selections thus made should fit into each other, should play into each other's hands.

But if one and the same end or interest operates in regulating both selections, the case stands quite otherwise. In such case, the experimental activity of verification is the carrying on of precisely the same purpose which found expression in the choice of subject and predicate respectively. It is in no sense a third process, but is the entire activity which we have already considered in two partial but typical aspects. The choice of meaning or predicate is always made with reference to the individual case to be interpreted; and the constitution of the particular objective case is always colored throughout by the point of view or idea with reference to which it is to be utilized. This reciprocal reference is the check or test continuously employed; and any particular more obvious experimental activity of verification means simply that conditions are such that the checking process is rendered overt.

I have now endeavored to show that if we take scientific judgment in its only ultimate form, viz, that which identifies or discriminates an individualized portion of experience, judgment appears as an act of judging the act showing itself both in the selection and determination of the subject and the predicate, and in the determination of their values with reference or in respect to each other, hence in deciding as to truth and validity.

Since in the discussion I have used a terminology which is hardly self-explanatory, and have introduced a variety of statements which to many will appear, in the present state or condition of logical discussion, to need rather than to afford support, I may point out that the force of the argument resides in matters capable of complete empirical confirmation. The truth or falsity of the conclusion reached depends upon these two notions:

First, every judgment is in its concrete reality an act of attention, and, like all attention, involves the functioning of an interest or end and the deploying of habits and impulsive tendencies (which ultimately involve motor adjustments) in the service of that interest. Hence it involves selection as regards both the object of attention and the standpoint and mode of "apperceiving" or interpreting. Change the interest or end, and the selected material (the subject of the judgment) changes, and the point of view from which it is regarded (and consequently the kind of predication) changes also.

Second, the abstract generalizing propositions of science have developed out of the needs of such individualized judgments or acts of attention; they have assumed their present form—that is, developed their characteristic structure or contents—as instrumentalities for enabling an individual judgment to do its work most effectively; that is to say, to accomplish most surely and economically the end for which it is undertaken. Consequently the value or validity of such concepts is constantly checked through a use which, by its success and failure, passes upon the competency of general principles, etc., to serve the regulative function for which they are instituted.[6]

So far as the scientific judgment is identified as an act, all *a priori* reason disappears for drawing a line between the

---

[6] It might check the prevalent tendency to draw sharp lines between philosophy as merely normative and the sciences as merely descriptive to realize that all generic scientific propositions, all statements of laws, all equations and formulae, are strictly normative in character, having as their sole excuse for being, and their sole test of worth, their capacity to regulate descriptions of individual cases. And the view that they are shorthand registers, or abstract descriptions, confirms instead of refuting this view. Why make a shorthand and abstract statement if it does not operate instrumentally in first-hand dealings with reality?

logic of the material of the recognized sciences and that of conduct. We are thus free to proceed, if we can find any positive basis. The recognition that the activity of judging does not exist in general, but is of such a nature as to require reference to an initial point of departure and to a terminal fulfilment, supplies exactly this positive ground. The act of judging is not merely an active experience at large, but one which requires specific motivation. There must be some stimulus which moves to performing this particular sort of act rather than some other. Why engage in that particular kind of activity that we call judging? Conceivably some other activity might be going on—the sawing of wood, the painting of a picture, the cornering of the wheat market, the administering of reproof. There must be something outside the most complete and correct collection of intellectual propositions which induces to engage in the occupation of judging rather than in some other active pursuit. Science furnishes conditions which are to be used in the most effective execution of the judging activity, *if* one means to judge at all. But it presupposes the If. No theoretical system can settle that the individual shall at a given moment judge rather than do something else. Only the whole scheme of conduct as focusing in the interests of an individual can afford that determining stimulus.

Not only must a practical motive be found for the use of the organized scientific system, but a similar motive must be found for its correct and adequate use. The logical value of any intellectual proposition, its distinctively logical significance as distinct from existence as mere *ens rationis,* depends upon practical, and ultimately upon moral, considerations. The interest must be of a kind not only to move the individual to judge, but to induce him to judge critically, bringing into use all necessary precautions and all available resources which may insure the maximum probability of truth in the conclusion. The system of science (employing the term "science" to mean an organized intellectual content) is absolutely dependent for logical worth upon a moral interest: the sincere aim to judge truly. Remove such an interest, and the scientific system becomes a purely aesthetic object, which may awaken emotional response in virtue of its internal harmony and symmetry, but which has no logical import. If we suppose, once more, that it is a case of identification of typhoid fever, it is the professional, social, and scientific interests of the physician which lead him to take the trouble and pains to get all the data that bear upon the forming of judgment, and to consider with sufficient deliberateness as to bring to bear the necessary instrumentalities of interpretation. The intellectual contents get a logical function only through a specific motive which is outside of them barely as contents, but which is absolutely bound up with them in logical function.

If the use made of scientific resources, of technique of observation and experiment, of systems of classification, etc., in directing the act of judging (and thereby fixing the content of the judgment) depends upon the interest and disposition of the situation, we have only to make such dependence explicit, and the so-called scientific judgment appears definitely as a moral judgment. If the physician is careless and arbitrary because of overanxiety to get his work done, or if he lets his pecuniary needs influence his manner of judgment, we may say that he has failed both logically and morally. Scientifically he has not employed the methods at command for directing his act of judging so as to give it maximum correctness. But the ground for such logical failure lies in his own habit or disposition. The generic propositions or universals of science can take effect, in a word, only through the medium of the habits and impulsive tendencies of the one who judges. They have no *modus operandi* of their own.[7]

---

[7] So far as I know, Mr. Charles S. Peirce was the first to call attention to this principle, and to insist upon its fundamental logical import (see *Monist*, Vol. II, pp. 534-6, 549-56). Mr. Peirce states it as the principle of continuity: A past idea can operate only so far as it is physically continuous with that upon which it operates. A general idea is simply a living and expanding feeling, and habit is a statement of the specific mode of operation of a given mental continuum. I have reached the above conclusion along such diverse lines that, without in any way minimizing the priority of Mr. Peirce's statement, or its more generalized logical

The possibility of a distinctively moral quality attaching to an intellectual activity is due to the fact that there is no particular point at which one habit begins and others leave off. If a given habit could become entirely isolated and detached, we might have an act of judging dependent upon a purely intellectual technique, upon a habit of using specialized skill in dealing with certain matters, irrespective of any ethical qualifications. But the principle of the continuum is absolute. Not only through habit does a given mental attitude expand into a particular case, but every habit in its own operation may directly or indirectly call up any other habit. The term "character" denotes this complex continuum of interactions in its office of influencing final judgment.

SEC. 4 · *The Logical Character of Ethical Judgment*

We now recur to our original proposition: Scientific treatment of any subject means command of an apparatus which may be used to control the formation of judgments in all matters appertaining to that subject. We have done away with the *a priori* objection that the subject matter to which recognized scientific judgments apply is so unlike that with which moral judgments are concerned that there is no common denominator. We are now free to revert to the original question: What are the differentiating logical conditions of a scientific treatment of conduct? Every sort of judgment has its own end to reach; and the instrumentalities (the categories and methods used) must vary as the end varies. If in general we conceive the logical nature of scientific technique, of formulae, universals, etc., to reside in their adaptation to guaranteeing the act of judging in accomplishing a purpose, we are thereby committed to the further proposition that the logical apparatus needed varies as the ends to be reached are diverse. If, then, there is anything typically distinctive in the end which the act of ethical judging has to subserve, there must be

character, I feel that my own statement has something of the value of an independent confirmation.

equally distinctive features in the logic of its scientific treatment.

The question thus recurs to the characteristic differential features of the ethical judgment as such. These features readily present themselves if we return to those cases of scientific identification in which ethical considerations become explicit. There are cases, we saw, in which the nature of the identification—and its consequent truth or falsity—is *consciously* dependent upon the attitude or disposition of the judger. The term "consciously" differentiates a peculiar type of judgment. In all cases of individual judgment there is an act; and in all cases the act is an expression of interest and thus of habit, and finally of the whole body of habit or character. But in many cases this implication of character remains a presupposition. It is not necessary to take notice of it. It is part of the practical conditions of making a judgment; but is no part of the logical conditions, and hence is not called upon to enter into a content—a conscious objectification in the judgment. To regard it as a practical instead of a logical condition means that while it is necessary to *any* judgment, the one act of judgment in question requires it no more than any other. It affects all *alike;* and this very impartiality of reference is equivalent to no reference at all as regards the truth or falsity of the particular judgment. Judging in such cases is controlled by reference to conditions of another quality than those of character; its presented data are judged in terms of objects of the same order or quality as themselves. Not only is there no conscious inclusion of interest and disposition within the content judged, but there is express holding off, inhibition, of all elements proceeding from the judger. From the standpoint of judgments of this type, such elements are regarded as logically merely subjective, and hence as disturbing factors with respect to the attainment of truth. It is no paradox to say that the activity of the agent in the act of judging expresses itself in effort to prevent its activity from having any influence upon the material judged. Accordingly through such judgments "external" objects are determined, the activity of the judges being kept absolutely neutral or indifferent as to its reference. The same idea is expressed by saying that the operation of motive and character may be presupposed, and thence left out of account, when they are so uniform in their exercise that they make no difference with respect to the *particular* object or content judged.

But whenever the implication of character, the operation of habit and interest, is recognized as a factor affecting the quality of the specific object judged, the logical aim makes it necessary to take notice of this fact by making the relationship an explicit element of content in the subject-matter undergoing judgment. When character is not an indifferent or neutral factor, when it qualitatively colors the meaning of the situation which the judger presents to himself, a characteristic feature is introduced into the very object judged; one which is not a mere refinement, homogeneous in kind with facts already given, but one which transforms their significance, because introducing into the very content judged the standard of valuation. In other words, character as a practical condition becomes *logical* when its influence is preferential in effect— when instead of being a uniform and impartial condition of any judgment it is, if left to itself (or unstated), a determinant of *this* content-value of judgment rather than that. Put from the other side, in the "intellectual" judgment, it makes no *difference* to character *what* object is judged, so be it the one judged is judged accurately, while in the moral judgment the nub of the matter is the difference which the determination of the content as this or that effects in character as a necessary condition of judging *qua* judging.

The express reference to disposition makes the object an active object, viz., a process defined by certain limits—given facts on one side and the same facts as transformed by agency of a given type on the other. The object judged is active, not "external," because it requires an act of judging, not merely as antecedent, but as a necessary element in its own structure. In judgments of the distinctively intellectual type, the assumption is that such activity as is necessary to effect certain combinations and distinctions will keep itself outside the material judged, retiring as soon as it has done its work in bringing together the elements that belong together and removing those that have no business. But in the ethical judgment the assumption is in the contrary sense, viz., that the situation is made what it is through the attitude which finds expression in the very act of judging. From the strictly logical standpoint (without reference, that is, to overtly moral considerations) the ethical judgment thus has a distinctive aim of its own; it is engaged in judging a subject-matter, in whose determination the attitude or disposition which leads to the act of judging is a factor.

It follows immediately that the aim of the ethical judgment may be stated as follows: Its purpose is to construct the *act* of judgment as itself a complex objective content. It goes back of the judging act as that is employed in distinctively intellectual processes, and makes its quality and nature (as distinct from its form—a question for psychology) an object of consideration. Just because character or disposition is involved in the material passed in review and organized in judgment, character is determined by the judgment. This is a fact of tremendous ethical significance; but here its import is not ethical, but logical. It shows that we are dealing, from the strictly logical point of view, with a characteristic type of judgment—that in which the conditions of judging activity are themselves to be objectively determined. The judger is engaged in judging himself; and thereby in so far is fixing the conditions of all further judgments of any type whatsoever. Put in more psychological terms, we may say the judgment realizes, through conscious deliberation and choice, a certain motive hitherto more or less vague and impulsive; or it expresses a habit in such a way as not merely to strengthen it practically, but as to bring to consciousness both its emotional worth and its significance in terms of certain kinds of consequences. But from the logical standpoint we say that the judger is consciously engaged in constructing as an object (and thereby giving objective form and structure to) the controlling condition of every exercise of judgment.

SEC. 5 · *The Categories of a Science of Ethics*

The ethical judgment is one which effects an absolutely reciprocal determination of the situation judged, and of the character or disposition which is expressed in the act of judging. Any particular moral judgment must necessarily reflect within itself all the characteristics which are essential to moral judgment *ueberhaupt*. No matter how striking or how unique the material of any particular ethical experience, it is at least an ethical experience; and as such its consideration or interpretation must conform to the conditions involved in the very act of judging. A judgment which institutes the reciprocal determination just described has its own characteristic structure or organization. The work that it has to do gives it certain limiting or defining elements and properties. These constitute the ultimate Terms or Categories of all ethical science. Moreover, since these terms are reflected in every moral experience that is in course of judgment, they do not remain formal or barren, but are instruments of analysis of any concrete situation that is subjected to scientific scrutiny.

The distinctively intellectual judgment, that of construing one object in terms of other similar objects, has necessarily its own inherent structure which supplies the ultimate categories of all physical science. Units of space, time, mass, energy, etc., define to us the limiting conditions under which judgments of this type do their work. Now, a type of judgment which determines a situation in terms of character, which is concerned with constructing what may be termed indifferently an active situation or a consciously active agency, has a like logical title to the standpoints and methods as the tools, which are necessary to its task. Ethical discussion is full of such terms: the natural and the spiritual, the sensuous and the ideal, the standard and the right, obligation and duty, freedom and responsibility, are samples. The discussion and use of these terms suffer, however, from a fundamental difficulty. The terms are generally taken as somehow given ready-made and hence as independent and isolated things. Then theory concerns itself, first, with debating as to whether the categories have validity or not; and, secondly, as to what their specific significance is. The discussion is arbitrary precisely because the categories are not taken as limiting terms; as constituent elements in a logical operation which, having its own task to perform, must have the means or tools necessary for its successful accomplishing. Consequently the primary condition of a scientific treatment of ethics is that the fundamental terms, the intellectual standpoints and instrumentalities used be discussed with reference to the position they occupy and the part they play in a judgment of a peculiar type, viz., one which brings about the reciprocal objective determination of an active situation and a psychical disposition.

When the categories receive the fate which is meted out to them in current discussion, when they are taken up in accidental because isolated ways, there is no method of controlling formation of judgment regarding them. Consequently other judgments which depend upon their use are in an increasing measure uncontrolled. The very tools which are necessary in order that more specific judgments may work economically and effectively are only vaguely known as to their own structure and modes of operation. Naturally they are bungled in employ. Because categories are discussed as if they had some ready-made independent meaning, each of its own, there is no check upon the meaning which is assigned to any one of them, and no recognized standard for judging the validity of any. Only reference to a situation within which the categories emerge and function can furnish the basis for estimation of their value and import. Otherwise the definition of basic ethical terms is left to argumentation based upon opinion, an opinion which snatches at some of the more obvious features of the situation (and thereby may always possess some measure of truth), and which, failing to grasp the situation as a whole, fails to grasp the exact significance of its characteristic terms. Discussion, for instance, about what constitutes the ethical standard—whether conduciveness to happiness, or approximation to perfection of being—must be relatively futile, until there is some method of determining by reference to the logical necessity of the case what *anything* must be and mean in order to be a standard at all. We lack a definition of standard in terms of the essential conditions of the ethical judgment and situation. Such a definition of standard would not indeed give us an off-hand view of the make-up of moral value such as might be utilized for forming moral precepts, but it will set before us certain conditions which any candidate for the office of moral standard must be capable of fulfilling; and will thereby serve as an instrument in criticizing the various claimants for the position of standard, whether these offer themselves in generic theory or in the affairs of concrete conduct. Similarly, theorists have been attempting to tell what the ideal of man is, what is *summum bonum,* what is man's duty, what are his responsibilities, to prove that he is possessed or not possessed of freedom, without any regulated way of defining the content of the terms "ideal," "good," "duty," etc. If these terms have any verifiable proper meaning of their own, it is as limiting traits of that type of judgment which institutes the reciprocal identification of mental attitude in judging and subject-matter judged. An analysis of the make-up of judgment of this type must reveal all the distinctions which have claim to the title of fundamental ethical categories. Whatever element of meaning reveals itself as a constituent part of such a judgment has all the claim to validity which moral experience itself possesses; a term which is not exhibited within such an analysis has no title to validity. The differential meaning of any one of the terms is dependent upon the particular part it plays in the development and termination of judgments of this sort.

SEC. 6 · *Psychological Analysis as a Condition of Controlling Ethical Judgments*

If it be true that a moral judgment is one in which the content finally affirmed is affected at every point by the disposition of the judger (since he interprets the situation that confronts him in terms of his own attitude), it follows at once that one portion of the generic theory necessary for adequate control of individual moral judgments will consist in an objective analysis of disposition as it affects action through the medium of judgment. Everyone knows, as simple matter of fact, that a large part of existing treatises on morals are filled with discussions concerning desirable and undesirable traits of character—virtues and vices; with conscience as a function of character; with discussions of intention, motive, choice, as expressions of, and as ways of forming, character. Moreover, a concrete discussion of freedom, responsibility, etc., is carried on as a problem of the relationship of character to the media of action. The reciprocal determination, already set forth, of character and the content judged shows that such discussions are not mere practical desiderata, not yet a mere clearing up of incidental points, but integral portions of any adequate ethical theory.

If character or disposition reflects itself at every point in the constitution of the content finally set forth in judgment, it is clear that control of such judgment depends upon ability to state, in universalized form, the related elements constituting character an objective fact.[8] Our particular judgments regarding physical things are controlled only in so far as we have, independent of and prior to any particular emergency in experience, a knowledge of certain conditions to be observed in judging every physical object as physical. It is through reference to such laws, or statements of connected conditions, that we get the impartiality or objectivity which enables us to judge in a particular crisis unswerved by purely immediate considerations. We get away from the coercive immediacy of the experience, and into a position to look at it clearly and thoroughly. Since character is a fact entering into any moral judgment passed, ability of control depends upon our power to state character in terms of generic

---

[8] Of course, the terms "object" and "objective" are used in a logical sense, not as equivalent to "physical," which denotes simply one form which the logical object may take. Dr. Stuart's article on "Valuation as a Logical Process" in *Studies in Logical Theory* (The University of Chicago Press, 1903) may be referred to for a discussion of the study of the logical significance of the term "object" and its bearing upon the objectivity of economic and ethical judgments.

relation of conditions, which conditions are detachable from the pressure of circumstance in the particular case. Psychological analysis is the instrument by which character is transformed from its absorption in the values of immediate experience into an objective, scientific fact. It is indeed, a statement of experience in terms of its modes of control of its own evolving.

Even popular consciousness is aware of many ways in which active dispositions modify judgment in a moral sense; and is accustomed to take advantage of its knowledge to regulate moral judgments. A score of proverbs could be collected expressing ways in which psychological attitudes affect moral valuation. The ideas in such statements as the following are commonplaces to the plain man: Habit, wont, and use dull the power of observation; passion blinds and confuses the power of reflection; self-interest makes the judger alert to certain aspects of the situation judged; impulse hurries the mind on uncritically to a conclusion; ends, ideals, arouse, when contemplated, emotions that tend to fill consciousness, and which, as they swell, first restrict and then eliminate power of judgment. Such statements, which might be indefinitely increased, are not only popularly known, but are commonly used in formation of a kind of hygiene of moral action.

Psychology proper differs from the aggregate of such statements through setting forth *how* various dispositions operate in bringing about the effects attributed to them. Just what are the various distinguishable mental attitudes and tendencies? How do they hang together? How does one call forth or preclude another? We need an inventory of the different characteristic dispositions; and an account of how each is connected, both in the way of stimulation and inhibition, with every other. Psychological analysis answers this need. While it can answer this need only through development of scientific constructs which present themselves in experience only as results of the psychological examination, yet it is true that the typical attitudes and dispositions are familiar as functions of every-day experience. It is equally true that even the most atomic psychology employs generalized statements about the ways in which certain "states of consciousness" or elements (the constructs referred to) regularly introduce certain other "states." The theory of association is, indeed, just a generalization concerning an objective sequence of elements which reflects to the psychologist the sequence of attitudes or dispositions which are found in the immediate course of experience. In particular the sensationalists not only admit but claim that the association of other states of consciousness with states of pleasure and pain have uniform tendencies which may be reduced to universal propositions; and which may be employed to formulate principles exhibited in all conduct. If such is the case with psychological atomism, every step toward recognition of a more organized, or inherently complex, mental structure multiplies the number and range of possible propositions relating to connection of conditions among psychic states—statements which, if true at all, have exactly the same logical validity that is possessed by any "physical law." And in so far as these "states" are symbols of the attitudes and habits which operate in our immediate experience, every such proposition is at once translatable into one regarding the way in which character is constituted —just the type of generic statement required by a scientific ethics.

Psychology of course does not aim at reinstating the immediate experience of the individual; nor does it aim at describing that experience in its immediate values, whether aesthetic, social, or ethical It reduces the immediate experience to a series of dispositions, attitudes, or states which are taken as either conditions or signatures of life-experience. It is not the full experience-of-seeing-a-tree it is concerned with, but the experience reduced by abstraction to an attitude or state of perception; it is not the concrete getting angry, with all its personal and social implications, but anger as one species of a generic mental disposition known as emotion. It is not concerned with a concrete judgment as such—to say nothing of moral judgment. But psychological analysis finds in experience the typical attitudes it deals with, and only abstracts them so that they may be objectively stated.

Every statement of moral theory which purports to relate

to our moral consciousness sets forth relations whose truth must ultimately be tested through psychological analysis—just as every judgment regarding a special physical phenomenon must finally satisfy certain generic conditions of physical reality set forth in physical analysis.

Psychological analysis does not, for example, set before us an end or ideal actually experienced, whether moral or otherwise. It does not purport to tell us *what* the end or ideal is. But psychological analysis shows us just what forming and entertaining an end means. Psychological analysis abstracts from the concrete make-up of an end, as that is found as matter of direct experience, and because of (not in spite of) that abstraction sets before us having-an-end in terms of its conditions and its effects, that is, in terms of taking other characteristic attitudes which are present in other experiences.

Hence purely psychologic propositions are indispensable to any concrete moral theory. The logical analysis of the process of moral judgment, setting forth its inherent organization or structure with reference to the peculiar logical function it has to accomplish, furnishes the categories or limiting terms of ethical science, and supplies their formal meaning, their definition. But the logical category, say, of end or ideal becomes concrete only as some individual has actually experience of and with ends—and this involves the act or attitude of forming and entertaining them. So the category of standard becomes more than a possible intellectual tool only as some individual actually engages in an experience concerned with right and wrong, and which, when viewed objectively, is regarded as a judgment. The entertaining of ends, the adjudging of values—such acts are character-phenomena. Considered in abstraction from their immediate matter in experience, viz., just as acts, states, or dispositions, they are character-phenomena as these present themselves to psychological analyis. Even to consider any experience, or any phase of an experience, as an ideal is to reflect upon that experience; it is to abstract and to classify. It involves passing judgment *upon* an experience; something beyond the concrete experiencing. It is, as far as it goes, psychological analysis—that is, it is a process of exactly the same order and implying just the same distinctions and terms as are found in psychological science. But the latter, in making abstraction and classification conscious processes, enables us to control them, instead of merely indulging in them.

Hence it is futile to insist that psychology cannot "give" the moral ideal, and that consequently there must be recourse to transcendental considerations—to metaphysics. Metaphysics, in the sense of a logical analysis of that type of judgment which determines the agent and the content of judgment in complete reciprocity to each other, may "give" the ideal —that is, it may show how the form or category of ideal is a constitutive element in this type of judgment, and hence has whatever of validity attaches to this mode of judging. But such a logical analysis is far from transcendental metaphysics; and in any case we thus obtain only the category of ideal as a standpoint or terminus of a *possible* moral judgment. There is no question here of ideal as immediately experienced. Only living, not metaphysics any more than psychology, can "give" an ideal in this sense. But when ethical theory makes statements regarding the importance of ideals for character and conduct, when it lays stress upon the significance of this, rather than that, kind of ideal, it is engaged in setting forth general relations of conditions; and there is absolutely no way of testing the validity of such statements with respect to their claim of generality or objectivity save by an analysis of mental dispositions which shows what is meant by having-an-ideal in terms of its antecedents and consequences. If any general statement whatsoever can be made about ideals, it is because the mental attitude corresponding to conceiving an ideal can be abstracted, and placed in a certain connection with attitudes which represent abstracts of other experiences. To have an ideal, to form and entertain one, must be a fact, or else ideals are absolute non-existence and non-sense. To discuss what it is to have an ideal is to engage in psychological analysis. If the having-an-ideal can be stated in terms of sequence with other similar attitudes, then we have a psychological generic statement (or "law") which can be employed as a tool of analysis in reflecting upon concrete moral experiences, just as the "law" of falling bodies is of use in controlling our judgment of pile-drivers, the trajectory of shells, etc. The possibility of *generalized propositions* regarding any character-phenomenon stands and falls with the possibility of psychological analysis revealing regular association or coordination of certain tendencies, habits, or dispositions with one another. Hence the continued reiteration that psychology as a natural science deals only with facts, while ethics is concerned with values, norms, ideals which *ought* to be whether they exist or no, is either aside from the point, or else proves the impossibility of making any general statements, metaphysical as well as practical and scientific, about such matters.

SEC. 7 · *Sociological Analysis as a Condition of Controlling Ethical Judgments*

We revert once more to our fundamental consideration: the reciprocal determination in moral judgment of the act of judging and the content judged. As we have just seen, adequate control of an act as determining a content involves the possibility of making character an object of scientific analysis—of stating it as a system of related conditions or an object complete in itself—a universal. We have now to recognize the converse, viz., that we can control the judgment of the act, hence of character as expressed in act, only as we have a method of analyzing the *content* in itself—that is, in abstraction from its bearings upon action.

The ethical problem needs to be approached from the point of view of the act as modifying the content, and of the content as modifying the act; so that, on one hand, we require, prior to a particular moral crisis, a statement in universal terms of the mechanism of the attitudes and dispositions which determine judgment about action; while on the other hand, we need a similar prior analysis and classification of the situations which call forth such judgment. Which portion of the scientific apparatus we bring most prominently into play in any given case depends upon the circumstances of that case as influencing the probable source of error. If the situation or scene of action (by which we mean the conditions which provoke or stimulate the act of moral judging) is fairly familiar, we may assume that the source of error in judgment lies in the disposition which is back of the experience—that if we can only secure the right motive on the part of the judger, the judgment itself will be correct. In other cases circumstances are reversed. We can fairly presuppose or take for granted a right attitude on the part of the judger; the problematic factor has to do with the interpretation of the situation. In this case what is needed for right judgment is a satisfactory knowledge of the "facts of the case." Given that, the existing motive will take care of the rest. It is this latter aspect of the matter that we now have to discuss.

The only way in which the agent can judge himself as an agent, and thereby control his act—that is, conceive of himself as the one who is to do a certain thing—is by finding out the situation which puts upon him the necessity of judging it in order that he may decide upon a certain course of action. As soon as a conclusion is reached as to the nature of the scene of action, a conclusion is also reached as to what the agent is to do, and this decides in turn what sort of an agent he is to be. The merely intellectual judgment may be marked off as one in which a content or object is fixed in terms of some other object or content, homogeneous in worth, and where accordingly it is a necessary part of the procedure to suppress participation in judging of traits which proceed from, or refer to, the disposition of the judger. But judgments which are ethical (not merely intellectual) make no such abstraction. They expressly and positively include the participation of the judger in the content judged, and of the object judged in the determination of the judger. In other words, the object judged or situation constructed in moral judgment is not an external object cold, remote, and indifferent, but is most uniquely, intimately, and completely the agent's own object, or is the agent *as object*.

Such being the case, what is required in order to form such a judgment of the scene or conditions of action as will facilitate the most adequate possible construing of the agent? I reply: A social science which will analyze a content as a combination of elements in the same way that psychological analysis determines an act as a set of attitudes. It is assumed that the situation which calls forth distinctively moral judgment is a social situation, which accordingly can be adequately described only through methods of sociological analysis. I am aware that (even admitting the necessity of some sort of scientific interpretation of the scene of action) it is something of a jump to say that such science must be sociological in character. The logical gap could be covered only by carrying the discussion of the categories of moral judgment to the point where their social value would explicitly show itself. Such analysis is apart from my present purpose. Here I need only recur to the proposition of the reciprocal determination, in the ethical judgment, of the judger and the content judged, and suggest that this idea requires in its logical development the conclusion that, since the judger is personal, the content judged must ultimately be personal too— so that the moral judgment really institutes a relationship between persons, relationship between persons being what we mean by "social."

But in any case some way of getting an objective statement of the situation, a statement in terms of connection of conditions, is necessary. Certain descriptive sciences are necessary and in many cases no one would deny that elements of associated life enter into the facts to be described. But even if it be admitted that the scene is social, this characterization does not exhaust the description. Any scene of action which is social is *also* cosmic or physical. It is also biological. Hence the absolute impossibility of ruling out the physical and biological sciences from bearing upon ethical science. If ethical theory require, as one of its necessary conditions, ability to describe in terms of itself the situation which demands moral judgment, any proposition, whether of mechanics, chemistry, geography, physiology, or history, which facilitates and guarantees the adequacy and truth of the description, becomes in virtue of that fact an important auxiliary of ethical science.

In other words, the postulate of moral science is the continuity of scientific judgment. This proposition is denied by both the materialistic and transcendental schools of philosophy. The transcendental school draws such a fixed line between the region of moral and of cosmic values that by no possibility can propositions which refer to the latter become auxiliary or instrumental with respect to the former. The fact that advance of physical and biological science so profoundly modifies moral problems, and hence moral judgments, and hence once more moral values, may serve as an argument against transcendental ethics—since, according to the latter, such obvious facts would be impossibilities. Materialism denies equally the principle of continuity of judgment. It confuses continuity of method, the possibility of using a general statement regarding one object as a tool in the determination of some other, with immediate identity of subject-matter. Instead of recognizing the *continuity* of ethical with other forms of experience, it wipes out ethical experience by assimilating it not simply with reference to logical method, but in its own ontological structure, to another form of objects defined in judgment—that is, the physical form. If it is once recognized that *all* scientific judgments, physical as well as ethical, are ultimately concerned with getting experience stated in objective (that is general) terms for the sake of the direction of further experience, there will, on the one hand, be no hesitation in using any sort of statement that can be of use in the formation of other judgments, whatever be their topic or reference; and, on the other hand, there will be no thought of trying to explain away the *distinctive* traits of any type of experience. Since human life is continuous, the possibility of using any one mode of experience to assist in the formation of any other is the ultimate postulate of *all* science—non-ethical and ethical alike. And this possibility of use, of application, of instrumental service, makes it possible and necessary to employ "materialistic" science in the construction of ethical theory, and also protects in this application ethical values from deterioration and dissolution.

In conclusion, it may avoid misapprehension if I say that the considerations set forth in this paper do not involve any pedantic assumption regarding the necessity of using science, or logical control, in any particular instance of moral experience. The larger part, infinitely the larger part, of our concrete contact with physical nature takes place without conscious reference to the methods, or even the results, of physical science. Yet no one questions the fundamental importance of physical science. This importance discovers itself in two ways:

First, when we come to peculiarly difficult problems (whether of interpretation or of inventive construction), physical science puts us in possession of tools of conscious analysis and of synthesis. It enables us to economize our time and effort, and to proceed with the maximum probability of success to solution of the problem which confronts us. This use is conscious and deliberate. It involves the critical application of the technique and already established conclusions of science to cases of such complexity and perplexity that they would remain unsolved and undealt with, were it not for scientific resources.

In the second place, physical science has a wide sphere of application which involves no *conscious* reference whatsoever. Previous scientific methods and investigations have taken effect in our own mental habits and in the material dealt with. Our unconscious ways of apprehending, of interpreting, of deliberating, are saturated with products of prior conscious critical science. We thus get the benefit, in our intellectual commerce with particular situations, of scientific operations which we have forgotten, and even of those which we individually have never performed. Science has become incarnate in our immediate attitude toward the world about us, and is embodied in that world itself. Every time that we solve a difficulty by sending a telegram, crossing a bridge, lighting the gas, boarding a railroad train, consulting a thermometer, we are controlling the formation of a judgment by use of so much precipitated and condensed science. Science has pre-formed, in many of its features, the situation with reference to which we have to judge; and it is this objective delimitation and structural reinforcement which, answering at every point to the conformation of habit, most assists intelligence in the details of its behavior.

There is every reason to suppose that the analogy holds with reference to a science of conduct. Such a science can be built up only through reference to cases which at the outset need explicit critical direction in judgment. We need to know what the social situation is in which we find ourselves required to act, so that we may know what it is right to do. We need to know what is the effect of some mental disposition upon our way of looking at life and thereby upon our conduct. Through clearing up the social situation, through making objective to ourselves our own motives and their consequences, we build up generic propositions: statements of experience as a connection of conditions, that is, in the form of objects. Such statements are used and applied in dealing with further problems. Gradually their use becomes more and more habitual. The "theory" becomes a part of our total apparatus. The social situation takes on a certain form or organization. It is pre-classified as of a certain sort, as of a certain genus and even species of this sort; the only question which remains is discrimination of the particular variety. Again, we get into the habit of taking into account certain sources of error in our own disposition as these affect our judgments of behavior, and thereby bring them sufficiently under control so that the need of conscious reference to their intellectual formulation diminishes. As physical science has brought about an organization of the physical world along with an organization of practical habits of dealing with that world, so ethical science will effect an organization of the social world and a corresponding organization of the mental habits through which the individual relates himself to it. With this clearing up of the field and organs of moral action, conscious recourse to theory will, as in physical cases, limit itself to problems of unusual perplexity and to constructions of a large degree of novelty.

Summary

1. By "scientific" is meant methods of control of formation of judgments.

2. Such control is obtained only by ability to abstract certain elements in the experience judged, and to state them as connections of conditions, *i.e.,* as "objects," or universals.

3. Such statements constitute the bulk of the recognized sciences. They are generic propositions, or laws, put, as a rule, in the hypothetic form if *M,* then *N.* But such generic propositions are the instruments of science, not science itself. Science has its life in judgments of identification, and it is for their sake that generic propositions (or universals, or laws) are constructed and tested or verified.

4. Such judgments of concrete identification are individualized, and are also acts. The presence of action as a logical element appears indirectly in (*a*) the selection of the subject, (*b*) the determination of the predicate, and (*c*) most directly in the copula—the entire process of the reciprocal forming and testing of tentative subjects and predicates.

5. Judgments are "intellectual" in logical type so far as this reference to behavior may be presupposed, and thereby not required to be consciously set forth or exposed. This happens whenever the action involved is impartial in its influence upon the quality of the content judged. Judgments are "moral" in logical type so far as the presence of activity in affecting the content of judgment is seen consciously to affect itself—or whenever the reciprocal determination of activity and content becomes itself an object of judgment whose determination is a prerequisite for further successful judgments.

6. Control of moral judgment requires ability to constitute the reciprocal determination of activity and content into an "object." This has three phases: First, a statement of the limiting forms of that type of judgment which is concerned with construing an activity and a content in terms of each other. The limiting terms of such a type of judgment constitute the characteristic features, or categories, of the object of ethical science, just as the limiting terms of the judgment which construes one object in terms of another object constitute the categories of physical science. A discussion of moral judgment from this point of view may be termed "The Logic of Conduct." Second, an abstraction of the activity, which views it as a system of attitudes or dispositions involved in having experience, and states it (since a system) as an object constituted by definite connections of diverse attitudes with the attitude of judging—viz., the science of psychology. Third, a

similar abstraction of the "content," which views it as a system of social elements which form the scene or situation in which action is to occur, and with reference to which, therefore, the actor is to be formed—viz., sociological science.

7. The whole discussion implies that the determination of objects as objects, even when involving no conscious reference whatever to conduct, is, after all, for the sake of the development of further experience. This further development is change, transformation of existing experience, and thus is *active*. So far as this development is intentionally directed through the construction of objects as objects, there is not only active experience, but *regulated activity, i.e.,* conduct, behavior, practice. Therefore, all determination of objects as objects (including the sciences which construct physical objects) has reference to change of experience, of experience as activity; and, when this reference passes from abstraction to application (from negative to positive), has reference to conscious control of the nature of the change (*i.e.,* deliberate change), and thereby gets ethical significance. This principle may be termed *the postulate of continuity of experience.* This principle, on the one hand, protects the integrity of the moral judgment, revealing its supremacy and the corresponding instrumental or auxiliary character of the intellectual judgment (whether physical, psychological, or social); and, upon the other, protects the moral judgment from isolation (*i.e.,* from transcendentalism), bringing it into working relations of reciprocal assistance with all judgments about the subject-matter of experience, even those of the most markedly mechanical and physiological sort.

HUMAN NATURE AND CONDUCT

Introduction*

"Give a dog a bad name and hang him." Human nature has been the dog of professional moralists, and consequences accord with the proverb. Man's nature has been regarded with suspicion, with fear, with sour looks, sometimes with enthusiasm for its possibilities but only when these were placed in contrast with its actualities. It has appeared to be so evilly disposed that the business of morality was to prune and curb it; it would be thought better of if it could be replaced by something else. It has been supposed that morality would be quite superfluous were it not for the inherent weakness, bordering on depravity, of human nature. Some writers with a more genial conception have attributed the current blackening to theologians who have thought to honor the divine by disparaging the human. Theologians have doubtless taken a gloomier view of man than have pagans and secularists. But this explanation doesn't take us far. For after all these theologians are themselves human, and they would have been without influence if the human audience had not somehow responded to them.

Morality is largely concerned with controlling human nature. When we are attempting to control anything we are

---

* This Introduction was written for *Human Nature and Conduct*, published by Henry Holt, 1922.

acutely aware of what resists us. So moralists were led, perhaps, to think of human nature as evil because of its reluctance to yield to control, its rebelliousness under the yoke. But this explanation only raises another question. Why did morality set up rules so foreign to human nature? The ends it insisted upon, the regulations it imposed, were after all outgrowths of human nature. Why then was human nature so averse to them? Moreover rules can be obeyed and ideals realized only as they appeal to something in human nature and awaken in it an active response. Moral principles that exalt themselves by degrading human nature are in effect committing suicide. Or else they involve human nature in unending civil war, and treat it as a hopeless mess of contradictory forces.

We are forced therefore to consider the nature and origin of that control of human nature with which morals has been occupied. And the fact which is forced upon us when we raise this question is the existence of classes. Control has been vested in an oligarchy. Indifference to regulation has grown in the gap which separates the ruled from the rulers. Parents, priests, chiefs, social censors have supplied aims, aims which were foreign to those upon whom they were imposed, to the young, laymen, ordinary folk; a few have given and administered rule, and the mass have in a passable fashion and with reluctance obeyed. Everybody knows that good children are those who make as little trouble as possible for their elders, and since most of them cause a good deal of annoyance they must be naughty by nature. Generally speaking, good people have been those who did what they were told to do, and lack of eager compliance is a sign of something wrong in their nature.

But no matter how much men in authority have turned moral rules into an agency of class supremacy, any theory which attributes the origin of rule to deliberate design is false. To take advantage of conditions after they have come into existence is one thing; to create them for the sake of an advantage to accrue is quite another thing. We must go back of the bare fact of social division into superior and inferior. To say that accident produced social conditions is to perceive they were not produced by intelligence. Lack of understanding of human nature is the primary cause of disregard for it. Lack of insight always ends in despising or else unreasoned admiration. When men had no scientific knowledge of physical nature they either passively submitted to it or sought to control it magically. What cannot be understood cannot be managed intelligently. It has to be forced into subjection from without. The opaqueness of human nature to reason is equivalent to a belief in its intrinsic irregularity. Hence a decline in the authority of social oligarchy was accompanied by a rise of scientific interest in human nature. This means that the make-up and working of human forces afford a basis for moral ideas and ideals. Our science of human nature in comparison with physical sciences is rudimentary, and morals which are concerned with the health, efficiency and happiness of a development of human nature are correspondingly elementary. These pages are a discussion of some phases of the ethical change involved in positive respect for human nature when the latter is associated with scientific knowledge. We may anticipate the general nature of this change through considering the evils which have resulted from severing morals from the actualities of human physiology and psychology. There is a pathology of goodness as well as of evil; that is, of that sort of goodness which is nurtured by this separation. The badness of good people, for the most part recorded only in fiction, is the revenge taken by human nature for the injuries heaped upon it in the name of morality. In the first place, morals cut off from positive roots in man's nature is bound to be mainly negative. Practical emphasis falls upon avoidance, escape of evil, upon not doing things, observing prohibitions. Negative morals assume as many forms as there are types of temperament subject to it. Its commonest form is the protective coloration of a neutral respectability, an insipidity of character. For one man who thanks God that he is not as other men there are a thousand to offer thanks that they are as other men, sufficiently as others are to escape attention. Absence of social blame is the usual mark of goodness for it shows that evil has been avoided. Blame is most readily averted by being so much like everybody else that one passes unnoticed. Conventional morality is a drab morality, in which the only fatal thing is to be conspicuous. If there be flavor left in it, then some natural traits have somehow escaped being subdued. To be so good as to attract notice is to be priggish, too good for this world. The same psychology that brands the convicted criminal as forever a social outcast makes it the part of a gentleman not to obtrude virtues noticeably upon others.

The Puritan is never popular, not even in a society of Puritans. In case of a pinch, the mass prefer to be good fellows rather than to be good men. Polite vice is preferable to eccentricity and ceases to be vice. Morals that professedly neglect human nature end by emphasizing those qualities of human nature that are most commonplace and average; they exaggerate the herd instinct to conformity. Professional guardians of morality who have been exacting with respect to themselves have accepted avoidance of conspicuous evil as enough for the masses. One of the most instructive things in all human history is the system of concessions, tolerances, mitigations and reprieves which the Catholic Church with its official supernatural morality has devised for the multitude. Elevation of the spirit above everything natural is tempered by organized leniency for the frailties of flesh. To uphold an aloof realm of strictly ideal realities is admitted to be possible only for a few. Protestantism, except in its most zealous forms, has accomplished the same result by a sharp separation between religion and morality in which a higher justification by faith disposes at one stroke of daily lapses into the gregarious morals of average conduct.

There are always ruder forceful natures who cannot tame themselves to the required level of colorless conformity. To them conventional morality appears as an organized futility; though they are usually unconscious of their own attitude since they are heartily in favor of morality for the mass as making it easier to manage them. Their only standard is success, putting things over, getting things done. Being good is to them practically synonymous with ineffectuality; and accomplishment, achievement is its own justification. They know by experience that much is forgiven to those who succeed, and they leave goodness to the stupid, to those whom they qualify as boobs. Their gregarious nature finds sufficient outlet in the conspicuous tribute they pay to all established institutions as guardians of ideal interests, and in their denunciations of all who openly defy conventionalized ideals. Or they discover that they are the chosen agents of a higher morality and walk subject to specially ordained laws. Hypocrisy in the sense of a deliberate covering up of a will to evil by loud-voiced protestations of virtue is one of the rarest of occurrences. But the combination in the same person of an intensely executive nature with a love of popular approval is bound, in the face of conventional morality, to produce what the critical term hypocrisy.

Another reaction to the separation of morals from human nature is a romantic glorification of natural impulse as something superior to all moral claims. There are those who lack the persistent force of the executive will to break through conventions and to use them for their own purposes, but who unite sensitiveness with intensity of desire. Fastening upon the conventional element in morality, they hold that all morality is a conventionality hampering to the development of individuality. Although appetites are the commonest things in human nature, the least distinctive or individualized, they identify unrestraint in satisfaction of appetite with free realization of individuality. They treat subjection to passion as a manifestation of freedom in the degree in which it shocks the bourgeois. The urgent need for a transvaluation of morals is caricatured by the notion that an avoidance of the avoidances of conventional morals constitutes positive achievement. While the executive type keeps its eyes on actual conditions so as to manipulate them, this school abrogates objective intelligence in behalf of sentiment, and withdraws into little coteries of emancipated souls.

There are others who take seriously the idea of morals separated from the ordinary actualities of humanity and who attempt to live up to it. Some become engrossed in spiritual egotism. They are preoccupied with the state of their character, concerned for the purity of their motives and the goodness of their souls. The exaltation of conceit which sometimes accompanies this absorption can produce a corrosive inhumanity which exceeds the possibilities of any other known form of selfishness. In other cases, persistent preoccupation with the thought of an ideal realm breeds morbid discontent with surroundings, or induces a futile withdrawal into an inner world where all facts are fair to the eye. The needs of actual conditions are neglected, or dealt with in a half-hearted way, because in the light of the ideal they are so mean and sordid. To speak of evils, to strive seriously for change, shows a low mind. Or, again, the ideal becomes a refuge, an asylum, a way of escape from tiresome responsibilities. In varied ways men come to live in two worlds, one the actual, the other the ideal. Some are tortured by the sense of their irreconcilability. Others alternate between the two, compensating for the strains of renunciation involved in membership in the ideal realm by pleasurable excursions into the delights of the actual.

If we turn from concrete effects upon character to theoretical issues, we single out the discussion regarding freedom of will as typical of the consequences that come from separating morals from human nature. Men are wearied with bootless discussion, and anxious to dismiss it as a metaphysical subtlety. But nevertheless it contains within itself the most practical of all moral questions, the nature of freedom and the means of its achieving. The separation of morals from human nature leads to a separation of human nature in its moral aspects from the rest of nature, and from ordinary social habits and endeavors which are found in business, civic life, the run of companionships and recreations. These things are thought of at most as places where moral notions need to be applied, not as places where moral ideas are to be studied and moral energies generated. In short, the severance of morals from human nature ends by driving morals inwards from the public open out-of-doors air and light of day into the obscurities and privacies of an inner life. The significance of the traditional discussion of free will is that it reflects precisely a separation of moral activity from nature and the public life of men.

One has to turn from moral theories to the general human struggle for political, economic and religious liberty, for freedom of thought, speech, assemblage and creed, to find significant reality in the conception of freedom of will. Then one finds himself out of the stiflingly close atmosphere of an inner consciousness and in the open-air world. The cost of confining moral freedom to an inner region is the almost complete severance of ethics from politics and economics. The former is regarded as summed up in edifying exhortations, and the latter as connected with arts of expediency separated from larger issues of good.

In short, there are two schools of social reform. One bases itself upon the notion of a morality which springs from an inner freedom, something mysteriously cooped up within personality. It asserts that the only way to change institutions is for men to purify their own hearts, and that when this has been accomplished, change of institutions will follow of itself. The other school denies the existence of any such inner power, and in so doing conceives that it has denied all moral freedom. It says that men are made what they are by the forces of the environment, that human nature is purely malleable, and that till institutions are changed, nothing can be done. Clearly this leaves the outcome as hopeless as does an appeal to an inner rectitude and benevolence. For it provides no leverage for change of environment. It throws us back upon accident, usually disguised as a necessary law of history or evolution, and trusts to some violent change, symbolized by civil war, to usher in an abrupt millennium. There is an alternative to being penned in between these two theories. We can recognize that all conduct is *interaction* between elements of human nature and the environment, natural and social. Then we shall see that progress proceeds in two ways, and that freedom is found in that kind of interaction which maintains an environment in which human desire and choice count for something. There are in truth forces in man as well as without him. While they are infinitely frail in comparison with exterior forces, yet they may have the support of a foreseeing and contriving intelligence. When we look at the problem as one of an adjustment to be intelligently attained, the issue shifts from within personality to an engineering issue, the establishment of arts of education and social guidance.

The idea persists that there is something materialistic about natural science and that morals are degraded by having anything seriously to do with material things. If a sect should arise proclaiming that men ought to purify their lungs completely before they ever drew a breath it ought to win many adherents from professed moralists. For the neglect of sciences that deal specifically with facts of the natural and social environment leads to a side-tracking of moral forces into an unreal privacy of an unreal self. It is impossible to say how much of the remediable suffering of the world is due to the fact that physical science is looked upon as merely physical. It is impossible to say how much of the unnecessary slavery of the world is due to the conception that moral issues can be settled within conscience or human sentiment apart from consistent study of facts and application of specific knowledge in industry, law and politics. Outside of manufacturing and transportation, science gets its chance in war. These facts perpetuate war and the hardest, most brutal side of modern industry. Each sign of disregard for the moral potentialities of physical science drafts the conscience of mankind away from concern with the interactions of man and nature which must be mastered if freedom is to be a reality. It diverts intelligence to anxious preoccupation with the unrealities of a purely inner life, or strengthens reliance upon outbursts of sentimental affection. The masses swarm to the occult for assistance. The cultivated smile contemptuously. They might smile, as the saying goes, out of the other side of their mouths if they realized how recourse to the occult exhibits the practical logic of their own beliefs. For both rest upon a separation of moral ideas and feelings from knowable facts of life, man and the world.

It is not pretended that a moral theory based upon realities of human nature and a study of the specific connections of these realities with those of physical science would do away with moral struggle and defeat. It would not make the moral life as simple a matter as wending one's way along a well-lighted boulevard. All action is an invasion of the future, of the unknown. Conflict and uncertainty are ultimate traits. But morals based upon concern with facts and deriving guidance from knowledge of them would at least locate the points of effective endeavor and would focus available resources upon them. It would put an end to the impossible attempt to live in two unrelated worlds. It would destroy fixed distinction between the human and the physical, as well as that between the moral and the industrial and political. A morals based on study of human nature instead of upon disregard for it would find the facts of man continuous with those of the rest of nature and would thereby ally ethics with physics and biology. It would find the nature and activities of one person coterminous with those of other human beings, and therefore link ethics with the study of history, sociology, law and economics.

Such a morals would not automatically solve moral problems, nor resolve perplexities. But it would enable us to state problems in such forms that action could be courageously and intelligently directed to their solution. It would not assure us against failure, but it would render failure a source of instruction. It would not protect us against the future emergence of equally serious moral difficulties, but it would enable us to approach the always recurring troubles with a fund of growing knowledge which would add significant values to our conduct even when we overtly failed—as we should continue to do. Until the integrity of morals with human nature and of both with the environment is recognized, we shall be deprived of the aid of past experience to cope with the most acute and deep problems of life. Accurate and extensive knowledge will continue to operate only in dealing with purely technical problems. The intelligent acknowledgment of the continuity of nature, man and society will alone secure a growth of morals which will be serious without being fanatical, aspiring without sentimentality, adapted to reality without conventionality, sensible without taking the form of calculation of profits, idealistic without being romantic.

THE NATURE OF AIMS *

Our problem now concerns the nature of ends, that is ends-in-view or aims. The essential elements in the problem have already been stated. It has been pointed out that the ends, objectives, of conduct are those foreseen consequences which influence present deliberation and which finally bring it to rest by furnishing an adequate stimulus to overt action. Consequently ends arise and function within action. They are not, as current theories too often imply, things lying beyong activity at which the latter is directed. They are not strictly speaking ends or termini of action at all. They are terminals of deliberation, and so turning points *in* activity. Many opposed moral theories agree however in placing ends beyond action, although they differ in their notions of what the ends are. The utilitarian sets up pleasure as such an outside-and-beyond, as something necessary to induce action and in which it terminates. Many harsh critics of utilitarianism have however agreed that there is some end in which action terminates, a final goal. They have denied that pleasure is such an outside aim, and put perfection or self-realization in its place. The entire popular notion of "ideals" is infected with this conception of some fixed end beyond activity at which we

---

* This selection appeared originally in *Human Nature and Conduct*, 1922.

should aim. According to this view ends-in-themselves come before aims. We have a moral aim only as our purpose coincides with some end-in-itself. We *ought* to aim at the latter whether we actually do or not.

When men believed that fixed ends existed for all normal changes in nature, the conception of similar ends for men was but a special case of a general belief. If the changes in a tree from acorn to full-grown oak were regulated by an end which was somehow immanent or potential in all the less perfect forms, and if change was simply the effort to realize a perfect or complete form, then the acceptance of a like view for human conduct was consonant with the rest of what passed for science. Such a view, consistent and systematic, was foisted by Aristotle upon western culture and endured for two thousand years. When the notion was expelled from natural science by the intellectual revolution of the seventeenth century, logically it should also have disappeared from the theory of human action. But man is not logical and his intellectual history is a record of mental reserves and compromises. He hangs on to what he can in his old beliefs even when he is compelled to surrender their logical basis. So the doctrine of fixed ends-in-themselves at which human acts are —or should be—directed and by which they are regulated if they are regulated at all persisted in morals, and was made the cornerstone of orthodox moral theory. The immediate effect was to dislocate moral from natural science, to divide man's world as it never had been divided in prior culture. One point of view, one method and spirit animated inquiry into natural occurrences; a radically opposite set of ideas prevailed about man's affairs. Completion of the scientific change begun in the seventeenth century thus depends upon a revision of the current notion of ends of action as fixed limits and conclusions.

In fact, ends are ends-in-view or aims. They arise out of natural effects or consequences which in the beginning are hit upon, stumbled upon so far as any purpose is concerned. Men *like* some of the consequences and *dislike* others. Henceforth (or till attraction and repulsion alter) attaining or averting similar consequences are aims or ends. These consequences constitute the meaning and value of an activity as it comes under deliberation. Meantime of course imagination is busy. Old consequences are enhanced, recombined, modified in imagination. Invention operates. Actual consequences, that is effects which have happened in the past, become possible future consequences of acts still to be performed. This operation of imaginative thought complicates the relation of ends to activity, but it does not alter the substantial fact: Ends are foreseen consequences which arise in the course of activity and which are employed to give activity added meaning and to direct its further course. They are in no sense ends *of* action. In being ends of *deliberation* they are redirecting pivots *in* action.

Men shoot and throw. At first this is done as an "instinctive" or natural reaction to some situation. The result when it is observed gives a new meaning to the activity. Henceforth men in throwing and shooting think of it in terms of its outcome; they act intelligently or have an end. Liking the activity in its acquired meaning, they not only "take aim" when they throw instead of throwing at random, but they find or make targets of which to aim. This is the origin and nature of "goals" of action. They are ways of defining and deepening the meaning of activity. Having an end or aim is thus a characteristic of *present* activity. It is the means by which an activity becomes adapted when otherwise it would be blind and disorderly, or by which it gets meaning when otherwise it would be mechanical. In a strict sense an end-in-view is a *means* in present action; present action is not a means to a remote end. Men do not shoot because targets exist, but they set up targets in order that throwing and shooting may be more effective and significant.

A mariner does not sail towards the stars, but by noting the stars he is aided in conducting his present activity of sailing. A port or harbor is his objective, but only in the sense of *reaching* it not of taking possession of it. The harbor stands in his thought as a significant point at which his activity will need re-direction. Activity will not cease when the port is attained, but merely the *present direction* of activity. The port is as truly the beginning of another mode of activity as it is the termination of the present one. The only reason we ignore this fact is because it is empirically taken for granted. We know without thinking that our "ends" are perforce beginnings. But theories of ends and ideals have converted a theoretical ignoring which is equivalent to practical acknowledgment into an intellectual denial, and have thereby confused and perverted the nature of ends.

Even the most important among all the consequences of an act is not necessarily its aim. Results which are objectively most important may not even be thought of at all; ordinarily a man does not think in connection with exercise of his profession that it will sustain him and his family in existence. The end-thought-of is uniquely important, but it is indispensable to state the respect in which it is important. It gives the decisive clew to the act to be performed under the existing circumstances. It is that particular foreseen object that will stimulate the act which relieves existing troubles, straightens out existing entanglements. In a temporary annoyance, even if only that caused by the singing of a mosquito, the thought of that which gives relief may engross the mind in spite of consequences much more important, objectively speaking. Moralists have deplored such facts as evidence of levity. But the remedy, if a remedy be needed, is not found in insisting upon the importance of ends in general. It is found in a change of the dispositions which make things either immediately troublesome or tolerable or agreeable.

When ends are regarded as literally ends to action rather than as directive stimuli to present choice they are frozen and isolated. It makes no difference whether the "end" is "natural" good like health or a "moral" good like honesty. Set up as complete and exclusive, as demanding and justifying action as a means to itself, it leads to narrowness; in extreme cases fanaticism, in considerateness, arrogance and hypocrisy. Joshua's reputed success in getting the sun to stand still to serve his desire is recognized to have involved a miracle. But moral theorists constantly assume that the continuous course of events can be arrested at the point of a particular object; that men can plunge with their own desires into the unceasing flow of changes, and seize upon some object as their end irrespective of everything else. The use of intelligence to discover the object that will best operate as a releasing and unifying stimulus in the existing situation is discounted. One reminds one's self that one's end is justice or charity or professional achievement or putting over a deal for a needed public improvement, and further questionings and qualms are stilled.

It is customary to suppose that such methods merely ignore the question of the morality of the means which are used to secure the end desired. Common sense revolts against the maxim, conveniently laid off upon Jesuits or other faraway people, that the end justifies the means. There is no incorrectness in saying that the question of means employed is overlooked in such cases. But analysis would go further if it were also pointed out that overlooking means is only a device for failing to note those ends, or consequences, which, if they were noted would be seen to be so evil that action would be estopped. Certainly nothing can justify or condemn means except ends, results. But we have to include consequences impartially. Even admitting that lying will save a man's soul, whatever that may mean, it would still be true that lying will have other consequences, namely, the usual consequences that follow from tampering with good faith and that lead lying to be condemned. It is wilful folly to fasten upon some single end or consequence which is liked, and permit the view of that to blot from perception all other undesired and undesirable consequences. It is like supposing that when a finger held close to the eye covers up a distant mountain the finger is really larger than the mountain. Not *the* end—in the singular—justifies the means; for there is no such thing as the single all-important end. To suppose that there is such an end is like working over again, in behalf of our private wishes, the miracle of Joshua in arresting the course of nature. It is not possible adequately to characterize the presumption, the falsity and the deliberate perversion of intelligence involved in refusal to note the plural effects that flow from any act, a refusal adopted in order that we may justify an act by picking out that one consequence which will enable us to do what we wish to do and for which we feel the need of justification.

Yet this assumption is continually made. It is made by implication in the current view of purposes or ends-in-view as objects in themselves, instead of means to unification and liberation of present conflicting, confused habits and impulses. There is something almost sinister in the desire to label the doctrine that the end justifies the means with the name of some one obnoxious school. Politicians, especially if they have to do with the foreign affairs of a nation and are called statesmen, almost uniformly act upon the doctrine that the welfare of their own country justifies any measure irrespective of all the demoralization it works. Captains of industry, great executives in all lines, usually work upon this plan. But they are not the original offenders by any means. Every man works upon it so far as he permits himself to become so absorbed in one aspect of what he is doing that he loses a view of its varied consequences, hypnotizing his attention by consideration of just those consequences which in the abstract are desirable and slurring over other consequences equally real. Every man works upon this principle who becomes overinterested in any cause or project, and who uses its desirability in the abstract to justify himself in employing any means that will assist him in arriving, ignoring all the collateral "ends" of his behavior. It is frequently pointed out that there is a type of executive-man whose conduct seems to be as non-moral as the action of the forces of nature. We all tend to relapse into this non-moral condition whenever we want any one thing intensely. In general, the identification of the end prominent in conscious desire and effort with *the* end is part of the technique of avoiding a reasonable survey of consequences. The survey is avoided because of a subconscious recognition that it would reveal desire in its true worth and thus preclude action to satisfy it—or at all events give us an uneasy conscience in striving to realize it. Thus the doctrine of the isolated, complete or fixed end limits intelligent examination, encourages insincerity, and puts a pseudo-stamp of moral justification upon success at any price.

Moralistic persons are given to escaping this evil by falling into another pit. They deny that consequences have anything at all to do with the morality of acts. Not ends but motives they say justify or condemn acts. The thing to do, accordingly, is to cultivate certain motives or dispositions, benevolence, purity, love of perfection, loyalty. The denial of consequences thus turns out formal, verbal. In reality a consequence is set up at which to aim, only it is a subjective consequence. "Meaning well" is selected as *the* consequence or end to be cultivated at all hazards, an end which is all-justifying and to which everything else is offered up in sacrifice. The result is a sentimental futile complacency rather than the brutal efficiency of the executive. But the root of both evils is the same. One man selects some external consequence, the other man a state of internal feeling, to serve as the end. The doctrine of meaning well as *the* end is if anything the more contemptible of the two, for it shrinks from accepting any responsibility for actual results. It is negative, self-protective and sloppy. It lends itself to complete self-deception.

Why have men become so attached to fixed, external ends? Why is it not universally recognized that an end is a device of intelligence in guiding action, instrumental to freeing and harmonizing troubled and divided tendencies? The answer is virtually contained in what was earlier said about rigid habits and their effect upon intelligence. Ends are, in fact, literally endless, forever coming into existence as new activities occasion new consequences. "Endless ends" is a way of saying that there are no ends—that is no fixed self-enclosed finalities. While however we cannot actually prevent change from occurring we can and do regard it as evil. We strive to retain action in ditches already dug. We regard novelties as dangerous, experiments as illicit and deviations as forbidden. Fixed and separate ends reflect a projection of our own fixed and non-interacting compartmental habits. We see only consequences which correspond to our habitual courses. As we have said, men did not begin to shoot because there were ready-made targets to aim at. They made things into targets by shooting at them, and then made special targets to make shooting more significantly interesting. But if generation after generation were shown targets they had had no part in constructing, if bows and arrows were thrust into their hands, and pressure were brought to bear upon them to keep them shooting in season and out, some wearied soul would soon propound to willing listeners the theory that shooting was unnatural, that man was naturally wholly at rest, and that targets existed in order that men might be forced to be active; that the duty of shooting and the virtue of hitting are externally imposed and fostered, and that otherwise there would be no such thing as a shooting-activity—that is, morality.

The doctrine of fixed ends not only diverts attention from examination of consequences and the intelligent creation of purpose, but, since means and ends are two ways of regarding the same actuality, it also renders men careless in their inspection of existing conditions. An aim not framed on the basis of a survey of those present conditions which are to be employed as means of its realization simply throws us back upon past habits. We then do not do what we intended to do but what we have got used to doing, or else we thrash about in a blind ineffectual way. The result is failure. Discouragement follows, assuaged perhaps by the thought that in any case the end is too ideal, too noble and remote, to be capable of realization. We fall back on the consoling thought that our moral ideals are too good for this world and that we must accustom ourselves to a gap between aim and execution. Actual life is then thought of as a compromise with the best, an enforced second or third best, a dreary exile from our true home in the ideal, or a temporary period of troubled probation to be followed by a period of unending attainment and peace. At the same time, as has been repeatedly pointed out, persons of a more practical turn of mind accept the world "as it is," that is as past customs have made it to be, and consider what advantages for themselves may be extracted from it. They form aims on the basis of existing habits of life which may be turned to their own private account. They employ intelligence in framing ends and selecting and arranging means. But intelligence is confined to manipulation; it does not extend to construction. It is the intelligence of the politician, administrator and professional executive—the kind of intelligence which has given a bad meaning to a word that ought to have a fine meaning, opportunism For the highest task of intelligence is to grasp and realize genuine opportunity, possibility.

Roughly speaking, the course of forming aims is as follows. The beginning is with a wish, an emotional reaction against the present state of things and a hope for something different. Action fails to connect satisfactorily with surrounding conditions. Thrown back upon itself, it projects itself in an imagination of a scene which if it were present would afford satisfaction. This picture is often called an aim, more often an ideal. But in itself it is a fancy which may be only a phantasy, a dream, a castle in the air. In itself it is a romantic embellishment of the present; at its best it is material for poetry or the novel. Its natural home is not in the future but in the dim past or in some distant and supposedly better part of the present world. Every such idealized object is suggested by something actually experienced, as the flight of birds suggests the liberation of human beings from the restrictions of slow locomotion on dull earth. It becomes an aim or end only when it is worked out in terms of concrete conditions available for its realization, that is in terms of "means."

This transformation depends upon study of the conditions which generate or make possible the fact observed to exist already. The fancy of the delight of moving at will through the air became an actuality only after men carefully studied the way in which a bird although heavier than air actually sustains itself in air. A fancy becomes an aim, in short, when some past sequence of known cause-and-effect is projected into the future, and when by assembling its causal conditions we strive to generate a like result. We have to fall back upon what has already happened naturally without design, and study it to see *how* it happened, which is what is meant by causation. This knowledge joined to wish creates a purpose. Many men have doubtless dreamed of ability to have light in darkness without the trouble of oil, lamps and friction. Glow-worms, lightning, the sparks of cut electric conductors suggest such a possibility. But the picture remained a dream until an Edison studied all that could be found out about such casual phenomena of light, and then set to work to search out and gather together the means for reproducing their operation. The great trouble with what passes for moral ends and ideals is that they do not get beyond the stage of fancy of something agreeable and desirable based upon an emotional wish; very often, at that, not even an original wish, but the wish of some leader which has been conventionalized and transmitted through channels of authority. Every gain in natural science makes possible new aims. That is, the discovery of how things *do* occur makes it possible to conceive of their happening at will, and gives us a start on selecting and combining the conditions, the means, to command their happening. In technical matters, this lesson has been fairly well learned. But in moral matters, men still largely neglect the need of studying the way in which results similar to those which we desire actually happen. Mechanism is despised as of importance only in low material things. The consequent divorce of moral ends from scientific study of natural events renders the former impotent wishes, compensatory dreams in consciousness. In *fact* ends or consequences are still determined by fixed habit and the force of circumstance. The evils of idle dreaming and of routine are experienced in conjunction. "Idealism" must indeed come first—the imagination of some better state generated by desire. But unless ideals are to be dreams and idealism a synonym for romanticism and phantasy-building, there must be a most realistic study of actual conditions and of the mode or law of natural events, in order to give the imagined or ideal object definite form and solid substance—to give it, in short, practicality and constitute it a working end.

The acceptance of fixed ends in themselves is an aspect of man's devotion to an ideal of certainty. This affection was inevitably cherished as long as men believed that the highest things in physical nature are at rest, and that science is possible only by grasping immutable forms and species: in other words, for much the greater part of the intellectual history of mankind. Only reckless sceptics would have dared entertain any idea of ends except as fixed in themselves as long as the whole structure of science was erected upon the immobile. Behind however the conception of fixity whether in science or morals lay adherence to certainty of "truth," a clinging to something fixed, born of fear of the new and of attachment to possessions. When the classicist condemns concession to impulse and holds up to admiration the patterns tested in tradition, he little suspects how much he is himself affected by unavowed impulses—timidity which makes him cling to authority, conceit which moves him to be himself the authority who speaks in the name of authority, possessive impulse which fears to risk acquisition in new adventures. Love of certainty is a demand for guarantees in advance of action. Ignoring the fact that truth can be bought only by the adventure of experiment, dogmatism turns truth into an insurance company. Fixed ends upon one side and fixed "principles"—that is authoritative rules—on the other, are props for a feeling of safety, the refuge of the timid and the means by which the bold prey upon the timid.

WHAT IS FREEDOM? *

The place of natural fact and law in morals brings us to the problem of freedom. We are told that seriously to import empirical facts into morals is equivalent to an abrogation of freedom. Facts and laws mean necessity we are told. The way to freedom is to turn our back upon them and take flight to a separate ideal realm. Even if the flight could be successfully accomplished, the efficacy of the prescription may be doubted. For we need freedom in and among actual events, not apart from them. It is to be hoped therefore that there remains an alternative; that the road to freedom may be found in that knowledge of facts which enables us to employ them in connection with desires and aims. A physician or engineer is free in his thought and his action in the degree in which he knows what he deals with. Possibly we find here the key to any freedom.

What men have esteemed and fought for in the name of liberty is varied and complex—but certainly it has never been a metaphysical freedom of will. It seems to contain three elements of importance, though on their face not all of them are directly compatible with one another. (1) It includes efficiency in action, ability to carry out plans, the absence of cramping and thwarting obstacles. (2) It also includes capac-

---

* From *Human Nature and Conduct*, 1922.

ity to vary plans, to change the course of action, to experience novelties. And again (3) it signifies the power of desire and choice to be factors in events.

Few men would purchase even a high amount of efficient action along definite lines at the price of monotony, or if success in action were bought by all abandonment of personal preference. They would probably feel that a more precious freedom was possessed in a life of ill-assured objective achievement that contained undertaking of risks, adventuring in new fields, a pitting of personal choice against the odds of events, and a mixture of success and failures, provided choice had a career. The slave is a man who executes the wish of others, one doomed to act along lines predetermined to regularity. Those who have defined freedom as ability to act have unconsciously assumed that this ability is exercised in accord with desire, and that its operation introduces the agent into fields previously unexplored. Hence the conception of freedom as involving three factors.

Yet efficiency in execution cannot be ignored. To say that a man is free to choose to walk while the only walk he can take will lead him over a precipice is to strain words as well as facts. Intelligence is the key to freedom in act. We are likely to be able to go ahead properously in the degree in which we have consulted conditions and formed a plan which enlists their consenting cooperation. The gratuitous help of unforeseen circumstance we cannot afford to despise. Luck, bad if not good, will always be with us. But it has a way of favoring the intelligent and showing its back to the stupid. And the gifts of fortune when they come are fleeting except when they are made taut by intelligent adaptation of conditions. In neutral and adverse circumstances, study and foresight are the only roads to unimpeded action. Insistence upon a metaphysical freedom of will is generally at its most strident pitch with those who despise knowledge of matters-of-fact. They pay for their contempt by halting and confined action. Glorification of freedom in general at the expense of positive abilities in particular has often characterized the official creed of historic liberalism. Its outward sign is the separation of politics and law from economics. Much of what is called the "individualism" of the early nineteenth century has in truth little to do with the nature of individuals. It goes back to a metaphysics which held that harmony between man and nature can be taken for granted, if once certain artificial restrictions upon man are removed. Hence it neglected the necessity of studying and regulating industrial conditions so that a nominal freedom can be made an actuality. Find a man who believes that all men need is freedom *from* oppressive legal and political measures, and you have found a man who, unless he is merely obstinately maintaining his own private privileges, carries at the back of his head some heritage of the metaphysical doctrine of free-will, plus an optimistic confidence in natural harmony. He needs a philosophy that recognizes the objective character of freedom and its dependence upon a congruity of environment with human wants, an agreement which can be obtained only by profound thought and unremitting application. For freedom as a fact depends upon conditions of work which are socially and scientifically buttressed. Since industry covers the most pervasive relations of man with his environment, freedom is unreal which does not have as its basis an economic command of environment.

I have no desire to add another to the cheap and easy solutions which exist of the seeming conflict between freedom and organization. It is reasonably obvious that organization may become a hindrance to freedom; it does not take us far to say that the trouble lies not in organization but in overorganization. At the same time, it must be admitted that there is no effective or objective freedom without organization. It is easy to criticize the contract theory of the state which states that individuals surrender some at least of their natural liberties in order to make secure as civil liberties what they retain. Nevertheless there is some truth in the idea of surrender and exchange. A certain natural freedom is possessed by man. That is to say, in some respects harmony exists between a man's energies and his surroundings such that the latter support and execute his purposes. In so far he is free; without such a basic natural support, conscious contrivances of legislation, administration and deliberate human institution of social arrangements cannot take place. In this sense natural freedom is prior to political freedom and is its condition. But we cannot trust wholly to a freedom thus procured. It is at the mercy of accident. Conscious agreements among men must supplement and in some degree supplant freedom of action which is the gift of nature. In order to arrive at these agreements, individuals have to make concessions. They must consent to curtailment of some natural liberties in order that any of them may be rendered secure and enduring. They must, in short, enter into an organization with other human beings so that the activities of others may be permanently counted upon to assure regularity of action and far-reaching scope of plans and courses of action. The procedure is not, in so far, unlike surrendering a portion of one's income in order to buy insurance against future contingencies, and thus to render the future course of life more equably secure. It would be folly to maintain that there is no sacrifice; we can however contend that the sacrifice is a reasonable one, justified by results.

Viewed in this light, the relation of individual freedom to organization is seen to be an experimental affair. It is not capable of being settled by abstract theory. Take the question of labor unions and the closed or open shop. It is folly to fancy that no restrictions and surrenders of prior freedoms and possibilities of future freedoms are involved in the extension of this particular form of organization. But to condemn such organization on the theoretical ground that a restriction of liberty is entailed is to adopt a position which would have been fatal to every advance step in civilization, and to every net gain in effective freedom. Every such question is to be judged not on the basis of antecedent theory but on the basis of concrete consequences. The question is to the balance of freedom and security achieved, as compared with practicable alternatives. Even the question of the point where membership in an organization ceases to be a voluntary matter and becomes coercive or required, is also an experimental matter, a thing to be decided by scientifically conducted study of consequences, of pros and cons. It is definitely an affair of specific detail, not of wholesale theory.

It is equally amusing to see one man denouncing on grounds of pure theory the coercion of workers by a labor union while he avails himself of the increased power due to corporate action in business and praises the coercion of the political state; and to see another man denouncing the latter as pure tyranny, while lauding the power of industrial labor organizations. The position of one or the other may be justified in particular cases, but justification is due to results in practice not to general theory.

Organization tends, however, to become rigid and to limit freedom. In addition to security and energy in action, novelty, risk, change are ingredients of the freedom which men desire. Variety is more than the spice of life; it is largely of its essence, making a difference between the free and the enslaved. Invariant virtue appears to be as mechanical as uninterrupted vice, for true excellence changes with conditions. Unless character rises to overcome some new difficulty or conquer some temptation from an unexpected quarter we suspect its grain is only a veneer. Choice is an element in freedom and there can be no choice without unrealized and precarious possibilities. It is this demand for genuine contingency which is caricatured in the orthodox doctrine of a freedom of indifference, a power to choose this way or that apart from any habit or impulse, without even a desire on the part of will to show off. Such an indetermination of choice is not desired by the lover of either reason or excitement. The theory of arbitrary free choice represents indeterminateness of conditions grasped in a vague and lazy fashion and hardened into a desirable attribute of will. Under the title of freedom men prize such uncertainty of conditions as give deliberation and choice an opportunity. But uncertainty of volition which is more than a reflection of uncertainty of conditions is the mark of a person who has acquired imbecility of character through permanent weakening of his springs of action.

Whether or not indeterminateness, uncertainty, actually exists in the world is a difficult question. It is easier to think of the world as fixed, settled once for all, and man as accumulating all the uncertainty there is in his will and all the doubt there is in his intellect. The rise of natural science has facilitated this dualistic partitioning, making nature wholly fixed and mind wholly open and empty. Fortunately for us we do not have to settle the question. A hypothetical answer is enough. *If* the world is already done and done for, if its character is entirely achieved so that its behavior is like that of a man lost in routine, then the only freedom for which man can hope is one of efficiency in overt action. But *if* change is genuine, if accounts are still in process of making, and if objective uncertainty is the stimulus to reflection, then variation in action, novelty and experiment, have a true meaning. In any case the question is an objective one. It concerns not man in isolation from the world but man in his connection with it. A world that is at points and times indeterminate enough to call out deliberation and to give play to choice to shape its future is a world in which will is free, not because it is inherently vacillating and unstable, but because deliberation and choice are determining and stabilizing factors.

Upon an empirical view, uncertainty, doubt, hesitation, contingency and novelty, genuine change which is not mere disguised repetition, are facts. Only deductive reasoning from certain fixed premises creates a bias in favor of complete determination and finality. To say that these things exist only in human experience not in the world, and exist there only because of our "finitude" is dangerously like paying ourselves with words. Empirically the life of man seems in these respects as in others to express a culmination of facts in nature. To admit ignorance and uncertainty in man while denying them to nature involves a curious dualism. Variability, initiative, innovation, departure from routine, experimentation are empirically the manifestation of a genuine nisus in things. At all events it is these things that are precious to us under the name of freedom. It is their elimination from the life of a slave which makes his life servile, intolerable to the freeman who has once been on his own, no matter what his animal comfort and security. A free man would rather take his chance in an open world than be guaranteed in a closed world.

These considerations give point to the third factor in love

of freedom: the desire to have desire count as a factor, a force. Even if will chooses unaccountably, even if it be a capricious impulse, it does not follow that there are real alternatives, genuine possibilities, open in the future. What we want is possibilities open in the *world* not in the will, except as will or deliberate activity reflects the world. To foresee future objective alternatives and to be able by deliberation to choose one of them and thereby weight its chances in the struggle for future existence, measures our freedom. It is assumed sometimes that if it can be shown that deliberation determines choice and deliberation is determined by character and conditions, there is no freedom. This is like saying that because a flower comes from root and stem it cannot bear fruit. The question is not what are the antecedents of deliberation and choice, but what are their consequences. What do they do that is distinctive? The answer is that they give us all the control of future possibilities which is open to us. And this control is the crux of our freedom. Without it, we are pushed from behind. With it we walk in the light.

The doctrine that knowledge, intelligence rather than will, constitutes freedom is not new. It has been preached by moralists of many a school. All rationalists have identified freedom with action emancipated by insight into truth. But insight into necessity has by them been substituted for foresight of possibilities. Tolstoi for example expressed the idea of Spinoza and Hegel when he said that the ox is a slave as long as he refuses to recognize the yoke and chafes under it, while if he identifies himself with its necessity and draws willingly instead of rebelliously, he is free. But as long as the yoke is a yoke it is impossible that voluntary identification with it should occur. Conscious submission is then either fatalistic submissiveness or cowardice. The ox accepts in fact not the yoke but the stall and the hay to which the yoke is a necessary incident. But if the ox foresees the consequences of the use of the yoke, if he anticipates the possibility of harvest, and identifies himself not with the yoke but with the realization of its possibilities, he acts freely, voluntarily. He hasn't accepted a necessity as unavoidable; he has welcomed a possibility as a desirability.

Perception of necessary law plays, indeed, a part. But no amount of insight into necessity brings with it, as such, anything but a consciousness of necessity. Freedom is the "truth of necessity" only when we use one "necessity" to alter another. When we use the law to foresee consequences and to consider how they may be averted or secured, then freedom begins. Employing knowledge of law to enforce desire in execution gives power to the engineer. Employing knowledge of law in order to submit to it without further action constitutes fatalism, no matter how it be dressed up. Thus we recur to our main contention. Morality depends upon events, not upon commands and ideals alien to nature. But intelligence treats events as moving, as fraught with possibilities, not as ended, final. In forecasting their possibilities, the distinction between better and worse arises. Human desire and ability cooperates with this or that natural force according as this or that eventuality is judged better. We do not use the present to control the future. We use the foresight of the future to refine and expand present activity. In this use of desire, deliberation and choice, freedom is actualized.

ENDS AND VALUES *

It has been remarked more than once that the source of the trouble with theories which relate value to desire and interest, and then proceed to make a sharp division between prizing and appraisal, between ends and means, is the failure to make an empirical investigation of the actual conditions under which desires and interests arise and function, and in which end-objects, ends-in-view, acquire their actual contents. Such an analysis will now be undertaken.

When we inquire into the actual emergence of desire and its object and the value-property ascribed to the latter (instead of merely manipulating dialectically the general concept of desire), it is as plain as anything can be that desires arise only when "there is something the matter," when there is some "trouble" in an existing situation. When analyzed, this "something the matter" is found to spring from the fact that there is something lacking, wanting, in the existing situation as it stands, an absence which produces conflict in the elements that do exist. When things are going completely smoothly, desires do not arise, and there is no occasion to project ends-in-view, for "going smoothly" signifies that there is no need for effort and struggle. It suffices to let things take their "natural" course. There is no occasion to investigate

---

* This selection appeared originally in *Theory of Valuation*, 1939.

what it would be better to have happen in the future, and hence no projection of an end-object.

Now vital impulses and acquired habits often operate without the intervention of an end-in-view or a purpose. When someone finds that his foot has been stepped on, he is likely to react with a push to get rid of the offending element. He does not stop to form a definite desire and set up an end to be reached. A man who has started walking may continue walking from force of an acquired habit without continually interrupting his course of action to inquire what object is to be obtained at the next step. These rudimentary examples are typical of much of human activity. Behavior is often so direct that no desires and ends intervene and no valuations take place. Only the requirements of a preconceived theory will lead to the conclusion that a hungry animal seeks food because it has formed an idea of an end-object to be reached, or because it has evaluated that object in terms of a desire. Organic tensions suffice to keep the animal going until it has found the material that relieves the tension. But if and when *desire* and *an end-in-view* intervene between the occurrence of a vital impulse or a habitual tendency and the execution of an activity, then the impulse or tendency is to some degree modified and transformed: a statement which is purely tautological, since the occurrence of a desire related to an end-in-view *is* a transformation of a prior impulse or routine habit. It is only in such cases that valuation occurs. This fact, as we have seen, is of much greater importance than it might at first sight seem to be in connection with the theory which relates valuation to desire and interest, for it proves that valuation takes place only when there is something the matter; when there is some trouble to be done away with, some need, lack, or privation to be made good, some conflict of tendencies to be resolved by means of changing existing conditions. This fact in turn proves that there is present an intellectual factor—a factor of inquiry—whenever there is valuation, for the end-in-view is formed and projected as that which, if acted upon, will supply the existing need or lack and resolve the existing conflict.

It follows from this that the difference in different desires and their correlative ends-in-view depends upon two things. The first is the adequacy with which inquiry into the lacks and conflicts of the existing situation has been carried on. The second is the adequacy of the inquiry into the likelihood that the particular end-in-view which is set up will, if acted upon, actually fill the existing need, satisfy the requirements constituted by what is needed, and do away with conflict by directing activity so as to institute a unified state of affairs.

The case is empirically and dialectically so simple that it would be extremely difficult to understand why it has become so confused in discussion were it not for the influence of irrelevant theoretical preconceptions drawn in part from introspectionist psychology and in part from metaphysics. Empirically, there are two alternatives. Action may take place with or without an end-in-view. In the latter case, there is overt action with no intermediate valuation; a vital impulse or settled habit reacts directly to some immediate sensory stimulation. In case an end-in-view exists and is valued, or exists in relation to a desire or an interest, the (motor) activity engaged in is, tautologically, mediated by the anticipation of the consequences which *as a foreseen end* enter into the makeup of the desire or interest. Now, as has been so often repeated, things can be anticipated or foreseen *as ends* or outcomes only in terms of the conditions by which they are brought into existence. It is simply impossible to have an end-in-view or to anticipate the consequences of any proposed line of action save upon the basis of some, however slight, consideration of the means by which it can be brought into existence. Otherwise, there is no genuine desire but an idle fantasy, a futile wish. That vital impulses and acquired habits are capable of expending themselves in the channels of daydreaming and building castles in the air is unfortunately true. But by description the contents of dreams and air castles are *not* ends-in-view, and what makes them fantasies is precisely the fact that they are *not* formed in terms of actual conditions serving as means of their actualization. *Propositions in which things (acts and materials) are appraised as means enter necessarily into desires and interests that determine end-values.* Hence the importance of the inquiries that result in the appraisal of things as means.

The case is so clear that, instead of arguing it directly, it will prove more profitable to consider how it is that there has grown up the belief that there are such things as ends having value apart from valuation of the means by which they are reached.

1. The mentalistic psychology which operates "to reduce" affective-motor activities to mere *feelings* has also operated in the interpretations assigned to *ends-in-view, purposes,* and *aims.* Instead of being treated as anticipations of consequences of the same order as a prediction of future events and, in any case, as depending for their contents and validity upon such predictions, they have been treated as merely mental states; for, when they are so taken (and only then), ends, needs, and satisfactions are affected in a way that distorts the whole theory of valuation. An end, aim, or purpose as a *mental* state *is* independent of the biological and physical means by which it can be realized. The want, lack, or privation which exists wherever there is desire is then interpreted as a mere state of "mind" instead of as something lacking or absent *in the situation*—something that must be supplied if the empirical situation is to be complete. In its latter sense, the needful or required is that which is *existentially necessary* if an end-in-view is to be brought into actual existence. *What* is needed cannot in this case be told by examination of a state of mind but only by examination of actual conditions. With respect to interpretation of "satisfaction" there is an obvious difference between it as a state of mind and as fulfilment of conditions, i.e., as something that meets the conditions imposed by the conjoint potentialities and lacks of the situation in which desire arises and functions. Satisfaction of desire signifies that the lack, characteristic of the situation evoking desire, has been so met that the means used make sufficient, in the most literal sense, the conditions for accomplishing the end. Because of the subjectivistic interpretation of end, need, and satisfaction, the verbally correct statement that valuation is a *relation* between a personal attitude and

extra-personal things—a relation which, moreover, includes a motor (and hence physical) element—is so construed as to involve separation of means and end, of appraisal and prizing. A "value" is then affirmed to be a "feeling"—a feeling which is not, apparently, the feeling of anything but itself. If it were said that a "value" is *felt,* the statement *might* be interpreted to signify that a certain existing relation between a personal motor attitude and extra-personal environing conditions is a matter of direct experience.

2. The shift of ground between valuation as *desire-interest* and as *enjoyment* introduces further confusion in theory. The shift is facilitated because in fact there exist both enjoyments of things directly possessed *without* desire and effort and enjoyments of things that are possessed only *because* of activity put forth to obtain the conditions required to satisfy desire. In the latter case, the enjoyment is in functional relation to desire or interest, and there is no violation of the definition of valuation in terms of desire-interest. But since the same *word,* 'enjoyment,' is applied also to gratifications that arise quite independently of prior desire and attendant effort, the ground is shifted so that "valuing" is identified with any and every state of enjoyment no matter how it comes about—including gratifications obtained in the most casual and accidental manner, "accidental" in the sense of coming about apart from desire and intent. Take, for example, the gratification of learning that one has been left a fortune by an unknown relative. There is *enjoyment.* But if valuation is defined in terms of desire and interest, there is no valuation, and in so far no "value," the latter coming into being only when there arises some desire as to what shall be done with the money and some question as to formation of an end-in-view. The two kinds of enjoyment are thus not only different but their respective bearings upon the theory of valuation are incompatible with each other, since one is connected with direct possession and the other is conditioned upon prior lack of possession—the very case in which desire enters.

For sake of emphasis, let us repeat the point in a slightly varied illustration. Consider the case of a man gratified by the unexpected receipt of a sum of money, say money picked up while he is walking on the street, an act having nothing to do with his purpose and desire at the moment he is performing it. If values are connected with desire in such a way that the connection is involved in their definition, there is, so far, no valuation. The latter begins when the finder begins to consider *how* he shall prize and care for the money. Shall he prize it, for example, as a means of satisfying certain wants he has previously been unable to satisfy, or shall he prize it as something held in trust until the owner is found? In either case, there is, by definition, an act of valuation. But it is clear that the property of value is attached in the two cases to very different objects. Of course, the uses to which money is put, the ends-in-view which it will serve, are fairly standardized, and in so far the instance just cited is not especially well chosen. But take the case of a child who has found a bright smooth stone. His sense of touch and of sight is gratified. But there is no valuation because no desire and no end-in-view, until the question arises of what shall be done with it; until the child *treasures* what he has accidentally hit upon. The moment he begins to prize and care for it he puts it to some use and thereby employs it as a *means* to some end, and, depending upon his maturity, he estimates or values it *in that relation*, or as means to end.

The confusion that occurs in theory when shift is made from valuation related to desire and interest, to "enjoyment" independent of any relation to desire and interest is facilitated by the fact that attainment of the objectives of desire and interest (of valuation) is itself enjoyed. The nub of the confusion consists in isolating enjoyment from the conditions under which it occurs. Yet the enjoyment that is the consequence of fulfilment of a desire and realization of an interest is what it is because of satisfaction or making good of a need or lack—a satisfaction conditioned by effort directed by the idea of something as an end-in-view. In this sense "enjoyment" involves inherent connection with *lack* of possession; while, in the other sense, the "enjoyment" is that of sheer possession. Lack of possession and possession are tautologically incompatible. Moreover, it is a common experience that the object of desire when attained is *not* enjoyed, so common that there are proverbial sayings to the effect that enjoyment is in the seeking rather than in the obtaining. It is not necessary to take these sayings literally to be aware that the occurrences in question prove the existence of the difference between value as connected with desire and value as mere enjoyment. Finally, as matter of daily experience, enjoyments provide the primary material of *problems* of valuation. Quite independently of any "moral" issues, people continually ask themselves whether a given enjoyment is worth while or whether the conditions involved in its production are such as to make it a costly indulgence.

Reference was made earlier to the confusion in theory which results when "values" are *defined* in terms of vital impulses. (The ground offered is that the latter are conditions of the existence of values in the sense that they "spring from" vital impulse.) In the text from which the passage was quoted there occurs in close connection the following: "The ideal of rationality is itself as arbitrary, as much dependent upon the needs of a finite organization, as any other ideal." Implicit in this passage are two extraordinary conceptions. One of them is that an ideal is arbitrary if it is causally conditioned by actual existences and is relevant to actual needs of human beings. This conception is extraordinary because naturally it would be supposed that an ideal is arbitrary in the degree in which it is *not* connected with things which exist and is not related to concrete existential requirements. The other astounding conception is that the ideal of rationality is "arbitrary" because it is so conditioned. One would suppose it to be peculiarly true of the ideal of rationality that it is to be judged as to its reasonableness (versus its arbitrariness) on the ground of its function, of what it does, not on the ground of its origin. If rationality as an ideal or generalized end-in-view serves to direct conduct so that things experienced in consequence of conduct so directed are more reasonable in the concrete, nothing more can be asked of it. Both of the implied conceptions are so extraordinary that they can be understood only on the ground of some unexpressed preconceptions. As far as one can judge, these preconceptions are (1) that an ideal *ought* to be independent of existence, that is, a priori. The reference to the origin of ideals in vital impulses is in fact an effective criticism of this a priori view. But it provides a ground for calling ideas arbitrary only if the a priori view is accepted. (2) The other preconception would seem to be an acceptance of the view that there are or ought to be "ends-in-themselves"; that is to say, ends or ideals that are not also means, which, as we have already seen, is precisely what an ideal is, if it is judged and valued in terms of its function. The sole way of arriving at the conclusion that a generalized end-in-view or ideal is arbitrary because of existential and empirical origin is by first laying down as an ultimate criterion that an end should also *not* be a means. The whole passage and the views of which it is a typical and influential manifestation is redolent of the survival of belief in "ends-in-themselves" as the solely and finally legitimate kind of ends.

THE CONTINUUM OF ENDS-MEANS *

Those who have read and enjoyed Charles Lamb's essay on the origin of roast pork have probably not been conscious that their enjoyment of its absurdity was due to perception of the absurdity of any "end" which is set up apart from the means by which it is to be attained and apart from its own further function as means. Nor is it probable that Lamb himself wrote the story as a deliberate travesty of the theories that make such a separation. Nonetheless, that is the whole point of the tale. The story, it will be remembered, is that roast pork was first enjoyed when a house in which pigs were confined was accidentally burned down. While searching in the ruins, the owners touched the pigs that had been roasted in the fire and scorched their fingers. Impulsively bringing their fingers to their mouths to cool them, they experienced a new taste. Enjoying the taste, they henceforth set themselves to building houses, inclosing pigs in them, and then burning the houses down. Now, if ends-in-view are what they are entirely apart from means, and have their value independently of valuation of means, there is nothing absurd, nothing ridiculous, in this procedure, for the end attained, the *de facto* termination, *was* eating and enjoying roast pork, and that was just the end desired. Only when the end attained is

* This selection appeared originally in *Theory of Valuation*, 1939.

estimated in terms of the means employed—the building and burning-down of houses in comparison with other available means by which the desired result in view might be attained —is there anything absurd or unreasonable about the method employed.

The story has a direct bearing upon another point, the meaning of "intrinsic." *Enjoyment* of the taste of roast pork may be said to be immediate, although even so the enjoyment would be a somewhat troubled one, for those who have memory, by the thought of the needless cost at which it was obtained. But to pass from immediacy of enjoyment to something called "intrinsic value" is a leap for which there is no ground. The *value* of enjoyment of an object *as* an attained end is a value of something which in being an end, an outcome, stands in relation to the means of which it is the consequence. Hence if the object in question is prized *as* an end or "final" value, it is valued *in this relation* or as mediated. The first time roast pork was enjoyed, it was *not* an end-value, since by description it was not the result of desire, foresight, and intent. Upon subsequent occasions it was, by description, the outcome of prior foresight, desire, and effort, and hence occupied the position of an end-in-view. There are occasions in which previous effort enhances enjoyment of what is attained. But there are also many occasions in which persons find that, when they have attained something as an end, they have paid too high a price in effort and in sacrifice of other ends. In such situations *enjoyment* of the end attained is itself *valued,* for it is not taken in its immediacy but in terms of its cost—a fact fatal to its being regarded as "an end-in-itself," a self-contradictory term in any case.

The story throws a flood of light upon what is usually meant by the maxim "the end justifies the means" and also upon the popular objection to it. Applied in this case, it would mean that the value of the attained end, the eating of roast pork, was such as to warrant the price paid in the means by which it was attained—destruction of dwelling-houses and sacrifice of the values to which they contribute. The conception involved in the maxim that "the end justifies the means" is basically the same as that in the notion of ends-in-themselves; indeed, from a historical point of view, it is the fruit of the latter, for only the conception that certain things are ends-in-themselves can warrant the belief that the relation of ends-means is unilateral, proceeding exclusively from end to means. When the maxim is compared with empirically ascertained facts, it is equivalent to holding one of two views, both of which are incompatible with the facts. One of the views is that only the specially selected "end" held in view will actually be brought into existence by the means used, something miraculously intervening to prevent the means employed from having their other usual effects; the other (and more probable) view is that, as compared with the importance of the selected and uniquely prized end, other consequences may be completely ignored and brushed aside no matter how intrinsically obnoxious they are. This arbitrary selection of some one part of the attained consequences as *the* end and hence as the warrant of means used (no matter how objectionable are their *other* consequences) is the fruit of holding that *it*, as *the* end, is an end-in-itself, and hence possessed of "value" irrespective of all its existential relations. And this notion is inherent in *every* view that assumes that "ends" can be valued apart from appraisal of the things used as means in attaining them. The sole alternative to the view that *the* end is an arbitrarily selected part of actual consequences which *as* "the end" then justifies the use of means irrespective of the other consequences they produce, is that desires, ends-in-view, and consequences achieved be valued in turn as means of further consequences. The maxim referred to, under the guise of saying that ends, in the sense of actual consequences, provide the warrant for means employed—a correct position—actually says that some fragment of these actual consequences—a fragment arbitrarily selected because the heart has been set upon it—authorizes the use of means to obtain *it*, without the need of foreseeing and weighing other ends as consequences of the means used. It thus discloses in a striking manner the fallacy involved in the position that ends have value independent of appraisal of means involved and independent of their own further causal efficacy.

We are thus brought back to a point already set forth. In all the physical sciences (using "physical" here as a synonym for *nonhuman*) it is now taken for granted that all "effects" are also "causes," or, stated more accurately, that nothing happens which is *final* in the sense that it is not part of an ongoing stream of events. If this principle, with the accompanying discrediting of belief in objects that are ends but not means is, *in that connection,* an object of desire and an end-in-view, while the end actually reached is a means to future ends as well as a test of valuations previously made. Since the end attained is a condition of further existential occurrences, it must be appraised as a potential obstacle and potential resource. If the notion of some objects as ends-in-themselves were abandoned, not merely in words but in all practical implications, human beings would for the first time in history be in a position to frame ends-in-view and form desires on the basis of empirically grounded propositions of the temporal relations of events to one another.

At any given time an adult person in a social group has certain ends which are so standardized by custom that they are taken for granted without examination, so that the only problems arising concern the best means for attaining them. In one group money-making would be such an end; in another group, possession of political power; in another group, advancement of scientific knowledge; in still another group, military prowess, etc. But such ends in any case are (1) more or less blank frameworks where the nominal "end" sets limits within which definite ends will fall, the latter being determined by appraisal of things as means; while (2) as far as they simply express habits that have become established without critical examination of the relation of means and ends, they do not provide a model for a theory of valuation to follow. If a person moved by an experience of intense cold, which is highly objectionable, should momentarily judge it worth while to get warm by burning his house down, all that saves him from an act determined by a "compulsion neurosis" is the intellectual realization of what other consequences would ensue with the loss of his house. It is not necessarily a sign of insanity (as in the case cited) to isolate some event projected as an end out of the context of a world of moving changes in which it will in fact take place. But it is at least a sign of immaturity when an individual fails to view his end as also a moving condition of further consequences, thereby treating it as *final* in the sense in which "final" signifies that the course of events has come to a complete stop. Human beings do indulge in such arrests. But to treat them as models for forming a theory of ends is to substitute a manipulation of ideas, abstracted from the contexts in which they arise and function, for the conclusions of observation of concrete facts. It is a sign either of insanity, immaturity, indurated routine, or of a fanaticism that is a mixture of all three.

Generalized ideas of ends and values undoubtedly exist. They exist not only as expressions of habit and as uncritical and probably invalid ideas but also in the same way as valid general ideas arise in any subject. Similar situations recur; desires and interests are carried over from one situation to another and progressively consolidated. A schedule of general ends results, the involved values being "abstract" in the sense of not being directly connected with any particular existing case but not in the sense of independence of all empirically existent cases. As with general ideas in the conduct of any natural science, these general ideas are used as intellectual instrumentalities in judgment of particular cases as the latter arise; they are, in effect, tools that direct and facilitate examination of things in the concrete while they are also developed and tested by the results of their application in these cases. Just as the natural sciences began a course of sure development when the dialectic of concepts ceased to be employed to arrive at conclusions about existential affairs and was employed instead as a means of arriving at a hypothesis fruitfully applicable to particulars, so it will be with the theory of human activities and relations. There is irony in the fact that the very continuity of experienced activities which enables general ideas of value to function as rules for evaluation of particular desires and ends should have become the source of a belief that desires, by the bare fact of their occurrence, confer value upon objects as ends, entirely independent of their contexts in the continuum of activities.

In this connection there is danger that the idea of "finality" be manipulated in a way analogous to the manipulations of the concepts of "immediacy" and "intrinsic" previously remarked upon. A value is *final* in the sense that it represents the conclusion of a process of analytic appraisals of conditions operating in a concrete case, the conditions including impulses and desires on one side and external conditions on the other. Any conclusion reached by an inquiry that is taken to warrant the conclusion is "final" for that case. "Final" here has logical force. The quality or property of value that is correlated with the *last* desire formed in the process of valuation is, tautologically, ultimate for that particular situation. It applies, however, to a specifiable temporal *means-end relation* and not to something which is an end per se. There is a fundamental difference between a final property or quality and the property or quality of finality.

The objection always brought against the view set forth is that, according to it, valuation activities and judgments are involved in a hopeless *regressus ad infinitum*. If, so it is said, there is no end which is not in turn a means, foresight has no place at which it can stop, and no end-in-view can be formed except by the most arbitrary of acts—an act so arbitrary that it mocks the claim of being a genuine valuation-proposition.

This objection brings us back to the conditions under which desires take shape and foreseen consequences are projected as ends to be reached. These conditions are those of need, deficit, and conflict. Apart from a condition of tension between a person and environing conditions there is, as we have seen, no occasion for evocation of desire for something else; there is nothing to induce the formation of an end, much less the formation of one end rather than any other out of the indefinite number of ends theoretically possible. Control of transformation of active tendencies into a desire in which a particular end-in-view is incorporated, is exercised by the needs or privations of an actual situation as its requirements are disclosed to observation. The "value" of different ends that suggest themselves is estimated or measured by the capacity they exhibit to guide action in making good, *satisfying,* in its literal sense, existing lacks. Here is the factor which cuts short the process of foreseeing and weighing ends-in-view in their function as means. Sufficient unto the day is the evil thereof and sufficient also is the *good* of that which does away with the existing evil. Sufficient because it is the means of instituting a complete situation or an integrated set of conditions.

Two illustrations will be given. A physician has to determine the value of various courses of action and their results in the case of a particular patient. He forms ends-in-view having the value that justifies their adoption, on the ground of what his examination discloses is the "matter" or "trouble" with the patient. He estimates the worth of what he undertakes on the ground of its capacity to produce a condition in which these troubles will not exist, in which, as it is ordinarily put, the patient will be "restored to health." He does not have an idea of health as an absolute end-in-itself, an absolute good by which to determine what to do. On the contrary, he forms his general idea of health as an end and a good (value) for the patient on the ground of what his techniques of examination have shown to be the troubles from which patients suffer and the means by which they are overcome. There is no need to deny that a general and abstract conception of health finally develops. But it is the outcome of a great number of definite, empirical inquiries, not an a priori preconditioning "standard" for carrying on inquiries.

The other illustration is more general. In all inquiry, even the most completely scientific, what is proposed as a conclusion (the end-in-view in that inquiry) is evaluated as to its worth on the ground of its ability to resolve the *problem* presented by the conditions under investigation. There is no a priori standard for determining the value of a proposed solution in concrete cases. A hypothetical possible solution, as an end-in-view, is used as a methodological means to direct further observations and experiments. Either it performs the function of resolution of a problem for the sake of which it is adopted and tried or it does not. Experience has shown that problems for the most part fall into certain recurrent kinds so that there are general principles which, it is believed, proposed solutions must satisfy in a particular case. There thus develops a sort of reference which operates in an *empirically* regulative way in given cases. We may even say that it operates as an "a priori" principle, but in exactly the same sense in which rules for the conduct of a technological art are both empirically antecedent and controlling in a given case of the art. While there is no a priori standard of health with which the actual state of human beings can be compared so as to determine whether they are well or ill, or in what respect they are ill, there have developed, out of past experience, certain criteria which are operatively applicable in new cases as they arise. Ends in view are appraised or valued as *good* or *bad* on the ground of their serviceability in the direction of behavior dealing with states of affairs found to be objectionable because of some lack or conflict in them. They are appraised as fit or unfit, proper or improper, *right* or *wrong*, on the ground of their *requiredness* in accomplishing this end.

Considering the all but omnipresence of troubles and "evils" in human experience (evils in the sense of deficiencies, failures, and frustrations), and considering the amount of time that has been spent explaining them away, theories of human activity have been strangely oblivious of the concrete function troubles are capable of exercising when they are taken as *problems* whose conditions and consequences are explored with a view to finding methods of solution. The two instances just cited, the progress of medical art and of scientific inquiry, are most instructive on this point. As long as actual events were supposed to be judged by comparison with some absolute end-value as a standard and norm, no sure progress was made. When standards of health and of satisfaction of conditions of knowledge were conceived in terms of analytic observation of existing conditions, disclosing a trouble statable in a problem, criteria of judging were progressively self-corrective through the very process of use in observation to locate the source of the trouble and to indicate the effective means of dealing with it. These means form the content of the specific end-in-view, not some abstract standard or ideal.

This emphasis upon the function of needs and conflicts

as the controlling factor in institution of ends and values does not signify that the latter are themselves negative in content and import. While they are framed with reference to a negative factor, deficit, want, privation, and conflict, their function is positive, and the resolution effected by performance of their function is positive. To attempt to gain an end *directly* is to put into operation the very conditions that are the source of the experienced trouble, thereby strengthening them and at most changing the outward form in which they manifest themselves. Ends-in-view framed with a negative *reference* (i.e., to some trouble or problem) are means which inhibit the operation of conditions producing the obnoxious result; they enable positive conditions to operate as resources and thereby to effect a result which is, in the highest possible sense, positive in content. The content of the end as an object *held in view* is intellectual or methodological; the content of the attained outcome or the end *as consequence* is existential. It is positive in the degree in which it marks the doing-away of the need and conflict that evoked the *end-in-view*. The negative factor operates as a condition of forming the appropriate *idea* of an end; the idea when acted upon determines a positive outcome.

The attained end or consequence is always an organization of activities, where organization is a co-ordination of all activities which enter as factors. The *end-in-view* is that particular activity which operates as a co-ordinating factor of all other subactivities involved. Recognition of the end as a co-ordination or unified organization of activities, and of the end-in-view as the special activity which is the means of effecting this co-ordination, does away with any appearance of paradox that seems to be attached to the idea of a temporal continuum of activities in which each successive stage is equally end and means. The *form* of an attained end or consequence is always the same: that of adequate co-ordination. The content or involved matter of each successive result differs from that of its predecessors; for, while it is a *reinstatment* of a unified on-going action, after a period of interruption through conflict and need, it is also an *enactment* of a new state of affairs. It has the qualities and properties appropriate to its being the consummatory resolution of a previous state of activity in which there was a peculiar need, desire, and end-in-view. In the continuous temporal process of organizing activities into a co-ordinated and co-ordinating unity, a constituent activity is both an end and a means: an end, in so far as it is temporally and relatively a close; a means, in so far as it provides a condition to be taken into account in further activity.

Instead of there being anything strange or paradoxical in the existence of situations in which means are constituents of the very end-objects they have helped to bring into existence, such situations occur whenever behavior succeeds in intelligent projection of ends-in-view that direct activity to resolution of the antecedent trouble. The cases in which ends and means fall apart are the abnormal ones, the ones which deviate from activity which is intelligently conducted. Wherever, for example, there is sheer drudgery, there is separation of the required and necessary means from both the end-in-view and the end attained. Wherever, on the other side, there is a so-called "ideal" which is utopian and a matter of fantasy, the same separation occurs, now from the side of the so-called *end*. Means that do not become constituent elements of the very ends or consequences they produce form what are called "necessary evils," their "necessity" being relative to the existing state of knowledge and art. They are comparable to scaffoldings that had to be later torn down, but which were necessary in erection of buildings until elevators were introduced. The latter remained for use in the building erected and were employed as means of transporting materials that in turn became an integral part of the building. Results or consequences which at one time were necessarily waste products in the production of the particular thing desired were utilized in the light of the development of human experience and intelligence as means for further desired consequences. The generalized ideal and standard of economy-efficiency which operates in every advanced art and technology is equivalent, upon analysis, to the conception of means that are constituents of ends attained and of ends that are usable as means to further ends.

It must also be noted that *activity* and *activities,* as these words are employed in the foregoing account, involve, like any actual behavior, existential materials, as breathing involves air; walking, the earth; buying and selling, commodities; inquiry, things investigated, etc. No human activity operates in a vacuum; it acts in the world and has materials upon which and through which it produces results. On the other hand, no material—air, water, metal, wood, etc.—is *means* save as it is employed in some human activity to accomplish something. When "organization of activities" is mentioned, it always includes within itself organization of the materials existing in the world in which we live. That organizaton which is the "final" value for each concrete situation of valuation thus forms part of the existential conditions that have to be taken into account in further formation of desires and interests or valuations. In the degree in which a particular valuation is invalid because of inconsiderate shortsighted investigation of things in their relation of means-end, difficulties are put in the way of subsequent reasonable valuations. To the degree in which desires and interests are formed after critical survey of the conditions which as means determine the actual outcome, the more smoothly continuous become subsequent activities, for consequences attained are then such as are evaluated more readily as means in the continuum of action.

ETHICAL PRINCIPLES
UNDERLYING EDUCATION *

It is quite clear that there cannot be two sets of ethical principles, or two forms of ethical theory, one for life in the school, and the other for life outside of the school. As conduct is one, the principles of conduct are one also. The frequent tendency to discuss the morals of the school, as if the latter were an institution by itself, and as if its morale could be stated without reference to the general scientific principles of conduct, appears to me highly unfortunate. Principles are the same. It is the special points of contact and application which vary with different conditions. I shall make no apology, accordingly, for commencing with statements which seem to me of universal validity and scope, and afterwards considering the moral work of the school as a special case of these general principles. I may be forgiven also for adding that the limits of space forbid much in the way of amplification and qualification, and that, so far as form is concerned, the material will therefore be presented in somewhat dogmatic shape. I hope, however, it will not be found

* This selection appeared originally in National Herbart Society, *Third Yearbook*, 1897.

dogmatic in spirit, for the principles stated are all of them, in my judgment, capable of purely scientific justification.

All ethical theory is two faced. It requires to be considered from two different points of view, and stated in two different sets of terms. These are the social and the psychological. We do not have here, however, a division, but simply a distinction. Psychological ethics does not cover part of the field, and then require social ethics to include the territory left untouched. Both cover the entire sphere of conduct. Nor does the distinction mark a compromise, or a fusion, as if at one point the psychological view broke down, and needed to be supplemented by the sociological. Each theory is complete and coherent within itself, so far as its own end or purpose is concerned. But conduct is of such a nature as to require to be stated throughout from two points of view. How this distinction happens to exist may perhaps be guessed at by calling to mind that the individual and society are neither opposed to each other nor separated from each other. Society is a society of individuals and the individual is always a social individual. He has no existence by himself. He lives in, for, and by society, just as society has no existence excepting in and through the individuals who constitute it. But we can state one and the same process (as, for example, telling the truth) either from the standpoint of what it effects in society as a whole, or with reference to the particular individual concerned. The latter statement will be psychological; the former, social as to its purport and terms.

If, then, the difference is simply a point of view, we first need to find out what fixes the two points of view. Why are they necessary? Because conduct itself has two aspects. On one side conduct is a form of activity. It is a mode of operation. It is something which somebody does. There is no conduct excepting where there is an agent. From this standpoint conduct is a process having its own form or mode, having, as it were, its own running machinery. That is, it is something which the agent does in a certain way; something which is an outcome of the agent himself, and which effects certain changes within the agent considered as an agent or doer. Now when we ask how conduct is carried on, what sort of a *doing* it is, when, that is to say, we discuss it with reference to an agent from whom it springs, and whose powers it modifies, our discussion is necessarily psychological. Psychology thus fixes for us the *how* of conduct, the way in which it takes place. Consideration from this standpoint is necessary because it is obvious that modifications in results or products must flow from changes in the agent or doer. If we want to get different things done, we must begin with changing the machinery which does them.

I hope the term "machinery" here will not be misunderstood by being taken in too dead and mechanical a sense. All that is meant here is that the mode of action of the individual agent controls the product, or what is done, just as the way in which a particular machine works controls the output in that direction. The individual agent has a certain structure, and certain ways of operating. It is simply this which is referred to as machinery.

But conduct has a *what* as well as a how. There is something done as well as a way in which it is done. There are ends, outcomes, results, as well as ways, means, and processes. Now when we consider conduct from this standpoint (with reference, that is to say, to its actual filling, content, or concrete worth) we are considering conduct from a social standpoint—from the place which it occupies, not simply with reference to the person who does it, but with reference to the whole living situation into which it enters.

The psychological view of conduct has to do, then, with the question of agency, of how the individual operates; the social, with what the individual does and needs to do considered from the standpoint of his membership in a whole which is larger than himself.

We may illustrate by reference to business life. A man starts in a business of manufacturing cotton cloth. Now this occupation of his may be considered from two standpoints. The individual who makes the cloth does not originate the demand for it. Society needs the cloth, and thereby furnishes the end or aim to the individual. It needs a certain amount of cloth, and cloth of certain varying qualities and patterns. It is this situation outside the mere operations of the manufacturer which fixes the meaning and value of what he does. If it were not for these social needs and demands, the occupation of the manufacturer would be purely formal. He might as well go out into the wilderness and heap up and tear down piles of sand.

But on the other side society must have its needs met, its ends realized, through the activities of some specific individual or group of individuals. The needs will forever go unsatisfied unless somebody takes it as his special business to supply them. So we may consider the manufactory of cotton cloth, not only from the standpoint of the position which it occupies in the larger social whole, but also as a mode of operation which simply as a mode is complete in itself. After the manufacturer has determined the ends which he has to meet (the kinds and amounts of cloth he needs to produce) he has to go to work to consider the cheapest and best modes of producing them, and of getting them to the market. He has to transfer his attention from the ends to the means. He has to see how to make his factory, considered as a mode of activity, the best possible organized agency within itself. No amount of reflection upon how badly society needs cloth will help him here. He has to think out his problem in terms of the number and kind of machines which he will use, the number of men which he will employ, how much he will pay them, how and where he will buy his raw material, and through what instrumentalities he will get his goods to the market. Now while this question is ultimately only a means to the larger social end, yet in order that it may become a true means, and accomplish the work which it has to do, it must become, for the time being, an end in itself. It must be stated, in other words, in terms of the factory as a working agency.

I think this parallelism may be applied to moral conduct without the change of a single principle. It is not the mere individual as an individual who makes the final demand for moral action, who establishes the final end, or furnishes the final standards of worth. It is the constitution and development of the larger life into which he enters which settles these things. But when we come to the question of how the individual is to meet the moral demands, of how he is to realize the values within himself, the question is one which concerns the individual as an agent. Hence it must be answered in psychological terms.

Let us change the scene of discussion to the school. The child who is educated there is a member of society and must be instructed and cared for as such a member. The moral responsibility of the school, and of those who conduct it, is to society. The school is fundamentally an institution erected by society to do a certain specific work—to exercise a certain specific function in maintaining the life and advancing the welfare of society. The educational system which does not recognize this fact as entailing upon it an ethical responsibility is derelict and a defaulter. It is not doing what it was called into existence to do, and what it pretends to do. Hence the necessity of discussing the entire structure and the specific workings of the school system from the standpoint of its moral position and moral function to society.

The above is commonplace. But the idea is ordinarily taken in too limited and rigid a way. The social work of the school is often limited to training for citizenship, and citizenship is then interpreted in a narrow sense as meaning capacity to vote intelligently, a disposition to obey laws, etc. But it is futile to contract and cramp the ethical responsibility of the school in this way. The child is one, and he must either live his life as an integral unified being or suffer loss and create friction. To pick out one of the manifold social relations which the child bears, and to define the work of the school with relation to that, is like instituting a vast and complicated system of physical exercise which would have for its object simply the development of the lungs and the power of breathing, independent of other organs and functions. The child is an organic whole, intellectually, socially, and morally, as well as physically. The ethical aim which determines the work of the school must accordingly be interpreted in the most comprehensive and organic spirit. We must take the child as a member of society in the broadest sense and demand whatever is necessary to enable the child to recognize all his social relations and to carry them out.

The child is to be not only a voter and a subject of law; he is also to be a member of a family, himself responsible, in all probability, in turn, for rearing and training of future children, and thus maintaining the continuity of society. He is to be a worker, engaged in some occupation which will be of use to society, and which will maintain his own independence and self-respect. He is to be a member of some particular neighborhood and community, and must contribute to the values of life, add to the decencies and graces of civilization wherever he is. These are bare and formal statements, but if we let our imagination translate them into their concrete details we have a wide and varied scene. For the child properly to take his place with reference to these various functions means training in science, in art, in history; command of the fundamental methods of inquiry and the fundamental tools of intercourse and communication; it means a trained and sound body, skillful eye and hand; habits of industry, perseverance, and, above all, habits of serviceableness. To isolate the formal relationship of citizenship from the whole system of relations with which it is actually interwoven; to suppose that there is any one particular study or mode of treatment which can make the child a good citizen; to suppose, in other words, that a good citizen is anything more than a thoroughly efficient and serviceable member of society, one with all his powers of body and mind under control, is a cramped superstition which it is hoped may soon disappear from educational discussion.

One point more. The society of which the child is to be a member is, in the United States, a democratic and progressive society. The child must be educated for leadership as well as for obedience. He must have power of self-direction and power of directing others, powers of administration, ability to assume positions of responsibility. This necessity of educating for leadership is as great on the industrial as on the political side. The affairs of life are coming more and more under the control of insight and skill in perceiving and effecting combinations.

Moreover, the conditions of life are in continual change. We are in the midst of a tremendous industrial and commercial development. New inventions, new machines, new methods of transportation and intercourse are making over the whole scene of action year by year. It is an absolute impossibility to educate the child for any fixed station in life. So far as education is conducted unconsciously or consciously on this basis, it results in fitting the future citizen for no station in life, but makes him a drone, a hanger-on, or an actual retarding influence in the onward movement. Instead of caring for himself and for others, he becomes one who has himself to be cared for. Here, too, the ethical responsibility of the school on the social side must be interpreted in the broadest and freest spirit; it is equivalent to that training of the child which will give him such possession of himself that he may take charge of himself; may not only adapt himself to the changes which are going on, but have power to shape and direct those changes.

It is necessary to apply this conception of the child's membership in society more specifically to determining the ethical principles of education.

Apart from the thought of participation in social life the school has no end nor aim. As long as we confine ourselves to the school as an isolated institution we have no final directing ethical principles, because we have no object or ideal. But it is said the end of education may be stated in purely individual terms. For example, it is said to be the harmonious development of all the powers of the individual. Here we have no apparent reference to social life or membership, and yet it is argued we have an adequate and thoroughgoing definition of what the goal of education is. But if this definition is taken independently of social relationship we shall find that we have no standard or criterion for telling what is meant by any one of the terms concerned. We do not know what a power is; we do not know what development is; we do not know what harmony is; a power is a power with reference to the use to which it is put, the function it has to serve. There is nothing in the make-up of the human being, taken in an isolated way, which furnishes controlling ends and serves to mark out powers. If we leave out the aim supplied from social life we have nothing but the old "faculty psychology" to fall back upon to tell what is meant by power in general or what the specific powers are. The idea reduces itself to enumerating a lot of faculties like perception, memory, reasoning, etc., and then stating that each one of these powers needs to be developed. But this statement is barren and formal. It reduces training to an empty gymnastic.

Acute powers of observation and memory might be developed by studying Chinese characters; acuteness in reasoning might be got by discussion of the scholastic subtleties of the Middle Ages. The simple fact is that there is no isolated faculty of observation, or memory, or reasoning any more than there is an original faculty of blacksmithing, carpentering, or steam engineering. These faculties simply mean that particular impulses and habits have been coördinated and framed with reference to accomplishing certain definite kinds of work. Precisely the same thing holds of the so-called mental faculties. They are not powers in themselves, but are such only with reference to the ends to which they are put, the services which they have to perform. Hence they cannot be located nor discussed as powers on a theoretical, but only on a practical basis. We need to know the social situations with reference to which the individual will have to use ability to observe, recollect, imagine, and reason before we get any intelligent and concrete basis for telling what a training of mental powers actually means either in its general principles or in its working details.

We get no moral ideals, no moral standards for school life excepting as we so interpret in social terms. To understand what the school is actually doing, to discover defects in its practice, and to form plans for its progress means to have a clear conception of what society requires and of the relation of the school to these requirements. It is high time, however, to apply this general principle so as to give it a somewhat more definite content. What does the general principle signify when we view the existing school system in its light? What defects does this principle point out? What changes does it indicate?

The fundamental conclusion is that the school must be itself made into a vital social institution to a very much greater extent than obtains at present. I am told that there is a swimming school in the city of Chicago where youth are taught to swim without going into the water, being repeatedly drilled in the various movements which are necessary for swimming. When one of the young men so trained was asked what he did when he got into the water, he laconically replied, "Sunk." The story happens to be true; if it were not, it would seem to be a fable made expressly for the purpose of typifying the prevailing status of the school, as judged from the standpoint of its ethical relationship to society. The school cannot be a preparation for social life excepting as it reproduces, within itself, the typical conditions of social life. The school at present is engaged largely upon the futile task of Sisyphus. It is endeavoring to form practically an intellectual habit in children for use in a social life which is, it would almost seem, carefully and purposely kept away from any vital contact with the child who is thus undergoing training. The only way to prepare for social life is to engage in social life. To form habits of social usefulness and serviceableness apart from any direct social need and motive, and apart from any existing social situation, is, to the letter, teaching the child to swim by going through motions outside of the water. The most indispensable condition is left out of account, and the results are correspondingly futile.

The much and commonly lamented separation in the schools between intellectual and moral training, between acquiring information and growth of character, is simply one expression of the failure to conceive and construct the school as a social institution, having social life and value within itself. Excepting in so far as the school is an embryonic yet typical community life, moral training must be partly pathological inasmuch as the stress comes to be laid upon correcting wrongdoing instead of upon forming habits of positive service. The teacher is necessarily forced into a position where his concern with the moral life of the pupils takes largely the form of being on the alert for failures to conform to the school rules and routine. These regulations, judged from the standpoint of the development of the child at the time, are more or less conventional and arbitrary. They are rules which have to be made in order that the existing modes of school work may go on; but the lack of inherent necessity in the school work reflects itself in a feeling, on the part of the child, that the moral discipline of the school is somewhat arbitrary. Any conditions which compel the teacher to take note of failures rather than of healthy growth put the emphasis in the wrong place and result in distortion and perversion. Attending to wrongdoing ought to be an incident rather than the important phase. The child ought to have a positive consciousness of what he is about, and to be able to judge and criticise his respective acts from the standpoint of their reference to the work which he has to do. Only in this way does he have a normal and healthy standard, enabling him properly to appreciate his failures and to estimate them at their right value.

By saying that the moral training of the school is partly formal, I mean that the moral habits which are specially emphasized in the school are habits which are created, as it were, *ad hoc*. Even the habits of promptness, regularity, industry, non-interference with the work of others, faithfulness to tasks imposed, which are specially inculcated in the school, are habits which are morally necessary simply because the school system is what it is, and must be preserved intact. If we grant the inviolability of the school system as it is, these habits represent permanent and necessary moral ideas; but just in so far as the school system is itself isolated and mechanical, the insistence upon these moral habits is more or less unreal, because the ideal to which they relate is not itself necessary. The duties, in other words, are distinctly school duties, not life duties. If we compare this with the well-ordered home, we find that the duties and responsibilities which the child has to recognize and assume there are not such as belong to the family as a specialized and isolated institution, but flow from the very nature of the social life in which the family participates and to which it contributes. The child ought to have exactly the same motives for right doing, and be judged by exactly the same standard in the school, as the adult in the wider social life to which he belongs. Interest in the community welfare, an interest which is intellectual and practical, as well as emotional—an interest, that is to say, in perceiving whatever makes for social order and progress, and for carrying these principles into execution—is the ultimate ethical habit to which all the special school habits must be related if they are to be animated by the breath of moral life.

We may apply this conception of the school as a social community which reflects and organizes in typical form the fundamental principles of all community life, to both the methods and the subject-matter of instruction.

As to methods, this principle when applied means that the emphasis must be upon construction and giving out, rather than upon absorption and mere learning. We fail to recognize how essentially individualistic the latter methods are, and how unconsciously, yet certainly and effectively, they react into the child's ways of judging and of acting. Imagine forty children all engaged in reading the same books, and in preparing and reciting the same lessons day after day. Suppose that this constitutes by far the larger part of their work, and that they are continually judged from the standpoint of what they are able to take in in a study hour, and to reproduce in a recitation hour. There is next to no opportunity here for any social or moral division of labor. There is no opportunity for each child to work out something specifically his own, which he may contribute to the common stock, while he, in turn, participates in the productions of others. All are set to do exactly the same work and turn out the same results. The social spirit is not cultivated—in fact, in so far as this method gets in its work, it gradually atrophies for lack of use. It is easy to see, from the intellectual side, that one reason why reading aloud in school is as poor as it is is that the real motive for the use of language—the desire to communicate and to learn—is not utilized. The child knows perfectly well that the teacher and all his fellow pupils have exactly the same facts and ideas before them that he has; he is not giving them anything at all new. But it may be questioned whether the moral lack is not as great as the intellectual. The child is born with a natural desire to give out, to do, and that means to serve. When this tendency is not made use of, when conditions are such that other motives are substituted, the reaction against the social spirit is much larger than we have any idea of—especially when the burden of the work, week after week, and year after year, falls upon this side.

But lack of cultivation of the social spirit is not all. Positively individualistic motives and standards are inculcated. Some stimulus must be found to keep the child at his studies. At the best this will be his affection for his teacher, together with a feeling that in doing this he is not violating school rules, and this is negatively, if not positively, contributing to the good of the school. I have nothing to say against these motives as far as they go, but they are inadequate. The relation between the piece of work to be done and affection for a third person is external, not intrinsic. It is therefore liable to break down whenever the external conditions are changed. Moreover this attachment to a particular person, while in a way social, may become so isolated and exclusive as to be positively selfish in quality. In any case, it is necessary that the child should gradually grow out of this relatively external motive, into an appreciation of the social value of what he has to do for its own sake, and because of its relations to life as a whole, not as pinned down to two or three people.

But unfortunately the motive is not always at this relative best, while it is always mixed with lower motives which are distinctly individualistic. Fear is a motive which is almost sure to enter in—not necessarily physical fear, or of punishment, but fear of losing the approbation of others; fear of failure so extreme and sensitive as to be morbid. On the other side, emulation and rivalry enter in. Just because all are doing the same work, and are judged (both in recitation and in examination, with reference to grading and to promotion) not from the standpoint of their motives or the ends which they are trying to reach, the feeling of superiority is unduly appealed to. The children are judged with reference to their capacity to present the same external set of facts and ideas. As a consequence they must be placed in the hierarchy on the basis of this purely objective standard. The weaker gradually lose their sense of capacity, and accept a position of continuous and persistent inferiority. The effect of this upon both self-respect and respect for work need not be dwelt upon. The stronger grow to glory, not in their strength, but in the fact that they are stronger. The child is prematurely launched into the region of individualistic competition, and this in a direction where competition is least applicable, viz., in intellectual and spiritual matters, whose law is coöperation and participation.

I cannot stop to paint the other side. I can only say that the introduction of every method which appeals to the child's active powers, to his capacities in construction, production, and creation, marks an opportunity to shift the center of ethical gravity from an absorption which is selfish to a service which is social. I shall have occasion later on to speak of these same methods from the psychological side, that is, their relation to the development of the particular powers of the child. I am here speaking of these methods with reference to the relation which they bear to a sense of community life, to a feeling of a division of labor which enables each one to make his own contribution, and to produce results which are to be judged not simply as intellectual results but from the motive of devotion to work, and of usefulness to others.

Manual training is more than manual; it is more than intellectual; in the hands of any good teacher it lends itself easily, and almost as a matter of course, to development of social habits. Ever since the philosophy of Kant it has been a commonplace in the theory of art, that one of its indispensable features is that it be universal, that is, that it should not be the product of any purely personal desire or appetite, or be capable of merely individual appropriation, but should have its value participated in by all who perceive it.

The divorce between the intellectual and the moral must inevitably continue in our schools (in spite of the efforts of individual teachers) as long as there is a divorce between learning and doing. The attempt to attach genuine moral consideration to the mere processes of learning, and to the habits which go along with learning, can result only in a moral training which is infected with formality, arbitrariness, and an undue emphasis upon failure to conform. That as much is accomplished as actually is done only shows the possibilities which would go along with the more organic ethical relationships involved in methods of activity which would afford opportunity for reciprocity, coöperation, and mutual service.

The principle of the school as itself a representative social institution may be applied to the subject-matter of instruction —must be applied if the divorce between information and character is to be overcome.

A casual glance at pedagogical literature will show that we are much in need of an ultimate criterion for the values of studies, and for deciding what is meant by content value and by form value. At present we are apt to have two, three, or even four different standards set up, by which different values —as disciplinary, culture, and information values—are measured. There is no conception of any single unifying principle. The point here made is that the extent and way in which a study brings the pupil to consciousness of his social environment, and confers upon him the ability to interpret his own powers from the standpoint of their possibilities in social use, is this ultimate and unified standard.

The distinction of form and content value is becoming familiar, but, so far as I know, no attempt has been made to give it rational basis. I submit the following as the key to the distinction: A study from a certain point of view serves to introduce the child to a consciousness of the make-up or structure of social life; from another point of view, it serves to introduce him to a knowledge of, and command over, the instrumentalities through which the society carries itself along. The former is the content value; the latter is the form value. Form is thus in no sense a term of depreciation. Form is as necessary as content. Form represents, as it were, the technique, the adjustment of means involved in social action, just as content refers to the realized value or end of social action.

What is needed is not a depreciation of form, but a correct placing of it, that is, seeing that since it is related as means to end, it must be kept in subordination to an end, and taught in relation to the end. The distinction is ultimately an ethical one because it relates not to anything found in the study from a purely intellectual or logical point of view, but to the studies considered from the standpoint of the ways in which they develop a consciousness of the nature of social life, in which the child is to live.

I take up the discussion first from the side of content. The contention is that a study is to be considered as bringing the child to realize the social scene of action; that when thus considered it gives a criterion for the selection of material and for the judgment of value. At present, as already suggested, we have three independent values set up: one of culture, another of information, and another of discipline. In reality these refer only to three phases of social interpretation. Information is genuine or educative only in so far as it effects definite images and conceptions of material placed in social life. Discipline is genuine and educative only as it represents a reaction of the information into the individual's own powers so that he can bring them under control for social ends. Culture, if it is to be genuine and educative, and not an external polish or factitious varnish, represents the vital union of information and discipline. It designates the socialization of the individual in his whole outlook upon life and mode of dealing with it.

This abstract point may be illustrated briefly by reference to a few of the school studies. In the first place there is no line of demarkation within facts themselves which classifies them as belonging to science, history, or geography, respectively. The pigeonhole classification which is so prevalent at present (fostered by introducing the pupil at the outset into a number of different studies contained in different textbooks) gives an utterly erroneous idea of the relations of studies to each other, and to the intellectual whole to which they all belong. In fact these subjects have all to do with the same ultimate reality, namely, the conscious experience of man. It is only because we have different interests, or different ends, that we sort out the material and label part of it science, part history, part geography, and so on. Each of these subjects represents an arrangement of materials with reference to some one dominant or typical aim or process of the social life.

This social criterion is necessary not only to mark off the studies from each other, but also to grasp the reasons for the study of each and the motives in connection with which it should be presented. How, for example, shall we define geography? What is the unity in the different so-called divisions of geography—as mathematical geography, physical geography, political geography, commercial geography? Are these purely empirical classifications dependent upon the brute fact that we run across a lot of different facts which cannot be connected with one another, or is there some reason why they are all called geography, and is there some intrinsic principle upon which the material is distributed under these various heads? I understand by intrinsic not something which attaches to the objective facts themselves, for the facts do not classify themselves, but something in the interest and attitude of the human mind towards them. This is a large question and it would take an essay longer than this entire paper adequately to answer it. I raise the question partly to indicate the necessity of going back to more fundamental principles if we are to have any real philosophy of education, and partly to afford, in my answer, an illustration of the principle of social interpretation. I should say that geography has to do with all those aspects of social life which are concerned with the interaction of the life of man and nature; or, that it has to do with the world considered as the scene of social interaction. Any fact, then, will be a geographical fact in so far as it bears upon the dependence of man upon his natural environment, or with the changes introduced in this environment through the life of man.

The four forms of geography referred to above represent then four increasing stages of abstraction in discussing the mutual relation of human life and nature. The beginning must be the commercial geography. I mean by this that the essence of any geographical fact is the consciousness of two persons or two groups of persons, who are at once separated and connected by the physical environment, and that the interest is in seeing how these people are at once kept apart and brought together in their actions by the instrumentality of this physical environment. The ultimate significance of lake, river, mountain, and plain is not physical but social; it is the part which it plays in modifying and functioning human relationship. This evidently involves an extension of the term commercial. It has not to do simply with business, in the narrow sense, but includes whatever relates to human intercourse and intercommunication as affected by natural forms and properties. Political geography represents this same social interaction taken in a static instead of in a dynamic way; takes it, that is, as temporarily crystallized and fixed in certain forms. Physical geography (including under this not simply physiography, but also the study of flora and fauna) represents a further analysis or abstraction. It studies the conditions which determine human action, leaving out of account, temporarily, the ways in which they concretely do this. Mathematical geography simply carries the analysis back to more ultimate and remote conditions, showing that the physical conditions themselves are not ultimate, but depend upon the place which the world occupies in a larger system. Here, in other words, we have traced, step by step, the links which connect the immediate social occupations and interactions of man back to the whole natural system which ultimately conditioned them. Step by step the scene is enlarged and the image of what enters into the make-up of social action is widened and broadened, but at no time ought the chain of connection to be broken.

It is out of the question to take up the studies one by one and show that their meaning is similarly controlled by social consideration. But I cannot forbear a word or two upon history. History is vital or dead to the child according as it is or is not presented from the sociological standpoint. When treated simply as a record of what has passed and gone, it must be mechanical because the past, as the past, is remote. It no longer has existence and simply as past there is no motive for attending to it. The ethical value of history teaching will be measured by the extent to which it is treated as a matter of analysis of existing social relations—that is to say as affording insight into what makes up the structure and working of society.

This relation of history to comprehension of existing social forces is apparent whether we take it from the standpoint of social order or from that of social progress. Existing social structure is exceedingly complex. It is practically impossible for the child to attack it *en masse* and get any definite mental image of it. But type phases of historical development may be selected which will exhibit, as through a telescope, the essential constituents of the existing order. Greece, for example, represents what art and the growing power of individual expression stands for; Rome exhibits the political elements and determining forces of political life on a tremendous scale. Or, as these civilizations are themselves relatively complex, a study of still simpler forms of hunting, nomadic and agricultural life in the beginnings of civilization; a study of the effects of the introduction of iron, iron tools, and so forth, serves to reduce the existing complexity to its simple elements.

One reason historical teaching is usually not more effective is the fact that the student is set to acquire information in such a way that no epochs or factors stand out to his mind as typical; everything is reduced to the same dead level. The only way of securing the necessary perspective is by relating the past to the present, as if the past were a projected present in which all the elements are enlarged.

The principle of contrast is as important as that of similarity. Because the present life is so close to us, touching us at every point, we cannot get away from it to see it as it really is. Nothing stands out clearly or sharply as characteristic. In the study of past periods attention necessarily attaches itself to striking differences. Thus the child gets a locus in imagination, through which he can remove himself from the present pressure of surrounding circumstance and define it.

History is equally available as teaching the *methods* of social progress. It is commonly stated that history must be studied from the standpoint of cause and effect. The truth of this statement depends upon its interpretation. Social life is so complex and the various parts of it are so organically related to each other and to the natural environment that it is impossible to say that this or that thing is cause of some other particular thing. But what the study of history can effect is to reveal the main instruments in the way of discoveries, inventions, new modes of life, etc., which have initiated the great epochs of social advance, and it can present to the child's consciousness type illustrations of the main lines in which social progress has been made most easily and effectively and can set before him what the chief difficulties and obstructions have been. Progress is always rhythmic in its nature, and from the side of growth as well as from that of status or order it is important that the epochs which are typical should be selected. This once more can be done only in so far as it is recognized that social forces in themselves are always the same—that the same kind of influences were at work 100 and 1000 years ago that are now—and treating the particular historical epochs as affording illustration of the way in which the fundamental forces work.

Everything depends then upon history being treated from a social standpoint, as manifesting the agencies which have influenced social development, and the typical institutions in which social life has expressed itself. The culture-epoch theory, while working in the right direction, has failed to recognize the importance of treating past periods with relation to the present—that is, as affording insight into the representative factors of its structure; it has treated these periods too much as if they had some meaning or value in themselves. The way in which the biographical method is handled illustrates the same point. It is often treated in such a way as to exclude from the child's consciousness (or at least not sufficiently to emphasize) the social forces and principles involved in the association of the masses of men. It is quite true that the child is interested easily in history from the biographical standpoint; but unless the hero is treated in relation to the community life behind which he both sums up and directs, there is danger that the history will reduce itself to a mere story. When this is done moral instruction reduces itself to drawing certain lessons from the life of the particular personalities concerned, instead of having widened and deepened the child's imaginative consciousness of the social relationships, ideals, and means involved in the world in which he lives.

There is some danger, I presume, in simply presenting the illustrations without more development, but I hope it will be remembered that I am not making these points for their own sake, but with reference to the general principle that when history is taught as a mode of understanding social life it has positive ethical import. What the normal child continuously needs is not so much isolated moral lessons instilling in him the importance of truthfulness and honesty, or the beneficent results that follow from some particular act of patriotism, etc. It is the formation of habits of social imagination and conception. I mean by this it is necessary that the child should be forming the habit of interpreting the special incidents that occur and the particular situations that present themselves in terms of the whole social life. The evils of the present industrial and political situation, on the ethical side, are not due so much to actual perverseness on the part of individuals concerned, nor in mere ignorance of what constitutes the ordinary virtues (such as honesty, industry, purity, etc.) as to inability to appreciate the social environment in which we live. It is tremendously complex and confused. Only a mind trained to grasp social situations, and to reduce them to their simpler and typical elements, can get sufficient hold on the realities of this life to see what sort of action, critical and constructive, it really demands. Most people are left at the mercy of traditions, impulse, or the appeals of those who have special and class interests to serve. In relation to this highly complicated social environment, training for citizenship is formal and nominal unless it develops the power of observation, analysis, and inference with respect to what makes up a social situation and the agencies through which it is modified. Because history rightly taught is the chief instrumentality for accomplishing this, it has an ultimate ethical value.

I have been speaking so far of the school curriculum on the side of its content. I now turn to that of form; understanding by this term, as already explained, a consciousness of the instruments and methods which are necessary to the control of social movements. Studies cannot be classified into form studies and content studies. Every study has both sides. That is to say, it deals both with the actual make-up of society, and is concerned with the tools or machinery by which society maintains itself. Language and literature best illustrate the impossibility of separation. Through the ideas contained in language, the continuity of the social structure is effected. From this standpoint the study of literature is a content study. But language is also distinctly a means, a tool. It not simply has social value in itself, but is a social instrument. However, in some studies one side or the other predominates very much, and in this sense we may speak of specifically form studies. As, for example, mathematics.

My illustrative proposition at this point is that mathematics does, or does not, accomplish its full ethical purpose according as it is presented, or not presented, as such a social tool. The prevailing divorce between information and character, between knowledge and social action, stalks upon the scene here. The moment mathematical study is severed from the place which it occupies with reference to use in social life, it becomes unduly abstract, even from the purely intellectual side. It is presented as a matter of technical relations and formulae apart from any end or use. What the study of number suffers from in elementary education is the lack of motivation. Back of this and that and the other particular bad method is the radical mistake of treating number as if it were an end in itself instead of as a means of accomplishing some end. Let the child get a consciousness of what the use of number is, of what it really is for, and half the battle is won. Now this consciousness of the use or reason implies some active end in view which is always implicitly social since it involves the production of something which may be of use to others, and which is often explicitly social.

One of the absurd things in the more advanced study of arithmetic is the extent to which the child is introduced to numerical operations which have no distinctive mathematical principles characterizing them but which represent certain general principles found in business relationships. To train the child in these operations, while paying no attention to the business realities in which they will be of use, and the conditions of social life which make these business activities necessary, is neither arithmetic nor common sense. The child is called upon to do examples in interest, partnership, banking, brokerage, and so on through a long string, and no pains are taken to see that, in connection with the arithmetic, he has any sense of the social realities involved. This part of arithmetic is essentially sociological in its nature. It ought either to be omitted entirely or else taught in connection with a study of the relevant social realities. As we now manage the study it is the old case of learning to swim apart from the water over again, with correspondingly bad results on the practical and ethical side.[1]

I am afraid one question still haunts the reader. What has all this discussion about geography, history, and number, whether from the side of content or that of form, got to do with the underlying principles of education? The very reasons which induce the reader to put this question to himself, even in a half-formed way, illustrate the very point which I am trying to make. Our conceptions of the ethical in education have been too narrow, too formal, and too pathological. We have associated the term ethical with certain special acts which are labeled virtues and set off from the mass of other acts, and still more from the habitual images and motives in the agents performing them. Moral instruction is thus associated with teaching about these particular virtues, or with instilling certain sentiments in regard to them. The ethical has

---

[1] With increasing mental maturity, and corresponding specialization which naturally accompanies it, these various instrumentalities may become ends in themselves. That is, the child may, as he ripens into the period of youth, be interested in number relations for their own sake. What was once method may become an activity in itself. The above statement is not directed against this possibility. It is simply aimed at the importance of seeing to it that the preliminary period—that in which the form or means is kept in organic relationship to real ends and values—is adequately lived through.

been conceived in too goody-goody a way. But it is not such ethical ideas and motives as these which keep men at work in recognizing and performing their moral duty. Such teaching as this, after all is said and done, is external; it does not reach down into the depths of the character-making agency. Ultimate moral motives and forces are nothing more nor less than social intelligence—the power of observing and comprehending social situations—and social power—trained capacities of control—at work in the service of social interest and aims. There is no fact which throws light upon the constitution of society, there is no power whose training adds to social resourcefulness which is not ethical in its bearing.

I sum up, then, this part of the discussion by asking your attention to the moral trinity of the school. The demand is for social intelligence, social power, and social interests. Our resources are (1) the life of the school as a social institution in itself; (2) methods of learning and of doing work; and (3) the school studies or curriculum. In so far as the school represents, in its own spirit, a genuine community life; in so far as what are called school discipline, government, order, etc., are the expressions of this inherent social spirit; in so far as the methods used are those which appeal to the active and constructive powers, permitting the child to give out, and thus to serve; in so far as the curriculum is so selected and organized as to provide the material for affording the child a consciousness of the world in which he has to play a part, and the relations he has to meet; in so far as these ends are met, the school is organized on an ethical basis. So far as general principles are concerned, all the basic ethical requirements are met. The rest remains between the individual teacher and the individual child.

II

I pass over now to the other side of the discussion—the psychological. We have so far been concerned with the principle that the end and standard of the school work is to be found in its functional relation to social life. We have endeavored to apply this principle to some of the typical features of the school in order to give an illustration of what is meant by this statement. We now recur to the counterpart principle: These ends and aims are to be realized in the child as an individual, and by the child as an individual. The social values are abstract until they are taken up and manifested in the life of the individual pupils. We have to ask, therefore, what they mean when translated over into terms of individual conduct. These values are not only to be manifested in individual conduct, but they are to be worked out by individual effort and energy. We have to consider the child as an agent or doer—the methods by which he can reproduce in his own life the constituent values of social life.

The beginning has to be made with the observation of the individual child. We find in him certain dawning powers—instincts and impulses. We wish to know what these stand for —what they represent. This means an inquiry into the ends with respect to which they can function, or become organized instruments of action. This interpretation of the crude powers of the child takes us over into social life. We find there the answers to the questions which the child nature puts to us; we find the completed results which enable us to diagnose the symptoms and indications spontaneously exhibited in the child. Then we have to return again with this interpretation back to the individual in order to find out the easiest, most economical, and most effective points of attachment and relationship between the spontaneous activities of the child, and the aims which we expect these powers to realize. Our business is now to connect the two. This can be done only through the medium of the child himself; the teacher cannot really make the connection. He can only form the conditions in such a way that the child may make it for himself. Moreover, even if the teacher could make the connection, the result would not be ethical. The moral life is lived only as the individual appreciates for himself the ends for which he is working, and does his work in a personal spirit of interest and devotion to these ends. Consequently we are again thrown back upon a study of the individual; upon psychology in order to discover the means which are available to mediate the spontaneous and crude capacities of the child over into habits of social intelligence and responsiveness.

Now, it is psychology which reveals to us the nature and the working of the individual as such. Accordingly psychological study is absolutely required in education to help determine its ethical import and conduct in two specific directions. (1) In the first place, all conduct springs ultimately and radically out of native instincts and impulses. We must know what these instincts and impulses are and what they are at each particular stage of the child's development, in order to know what to appeal to and what to build upon. Neglect of this principle may give a mechanical imitation of moral conduct, but the imitation will be ethically dead because it is external and has its center without not within the individual. We must study the child, in other words, to get our indications, our symptoms, our suggestions. The more or less spontaneous acts of the child are not to be thought of as giving moral forms to which the efforts of the educator must conform—this would result simply in spoiling the child, but they are to be thought of as symptoms which require to be interpreted; as stimuli which need to be manifested in directed ways, as material which, in however transformed a shape, is the only ultimate constituent of future moral conduct and character.

(2) Our ethical principles need also to be stated in psychological terms because the child supplies us with the only means or instruments at command with which moral ideals are to be realized. The subject-matter of the curriculum, however important, however judiciously selected, is empty of conclusive moral content until it is made over into terms of the individual's own activities, habits, and desires. We must know what history, geography and mathematics mean in psychological terms, that is, as modes of personal experiencing, before we can get out of them their moral potentialities.

The psychological side of education sums itself up, of course, in a consideration of the nature of character, and of how character best grows. Some of the abstractness of the previous discussion may be relieved, if not removed, if we state it with reference to character.

It is a commonplace to say that this development of character is the ultimate end of all school work. The difficulty lies in the execution of this idea. And an underlying difficulty in this execution is the lack of any conception of what character means. This may seem an extreme and uncalled-for statement. If so, the idea may be better conveyed by saying that we conceive of character simply in terms of results; that we have no clear conception of it in psychological terms— that is, as a process, as working or dynamic. We know what character means in terms of the kinds of actions which proceed from character, but we have not a definite conception of it on its inner side, as a piece of running, psychical machinery.

I propose, then, to give a brief statement of the nature of character from this point of view. In general, character means power of social agency, organized capacity of social functioning. It means, as already suggested, social insight or intelligence, social executive power, and social interest or responsiveness. Stated in psychological terms, it means that there must be a training of the primary impulses and instincts, which organize them into habits which are reliable means of action.

(1) Force, efficiency in execution, or overt action, is the necessary constituent of character. In our moral books and lectures we may lay all the stress upon good intentions, etc. But we know practically that the kind of character we hope to build up through our education is one which not only has good intentions, but which insists upon carrying them out. Any other character is wishy-washy; it is goody, not good. The individual must have the power to stand up and count for something in the actual conflicts of life. He must have initiative, insistence, persistence, courage and industry. He must, in a word, have all that goes under a term, "force of character." Undoubtedly, individuals differ greatly in their native endowment in this respect. None the less, each has a certain primary equipment of impulse, of tendency forward, of innate urgency to do. The problem of education on this side is that of discovering what this native fund of power is, and then of utilizing it in such a way (affording conditions which both stimulate and control) as to organize it into definite conserved modes of action—habits.

(2) But something more is required than sheer force. Sheer

force may be brutal; it may override the interests of others. Even when aiming at right ends it may go at them in such a way as to violate the rights of others. More than this, in sheer force there is no guarantee for the right end itself. It may be directed towards mistaken ends, and result in positive mischief and destruction. Power, as already suggested, must be directed. It must be organized along certain channels of output or expression in such a way as to be attached to the valuable ends.

This involves training on both the intellectual and emotional side. On the intellectual side we must have judgment— what is ordinarily called good sense. The difference between mere knowledge, or information, and judgment is that the former is simply held, not used; judgment is ideas directed with reference to the accomplishment of ends. Good judgment is a sense of respective or proportionate values. The one who has judgment is the one who has ability to size up a situation. He is the one who can grasp the scene or situation before him, ignoring what is irrelevant, or what for the time being is unimportant, and can seize upon the factors which demand attention, and grade them according to their respective claims. Mere knowledge of what the right is in the abstract, mere intentions of following the right in general, however praiseworthy in themselves, are never a substitute for this power of trained judgment. Action is always in the concrete. It is definite and individualized. Except, therefore, as it is backed and controlled by a knowledge of the actual concrete factors in the situation demanding action, it must be relatively futile and waste.

(3) But the consciousness of end must be more than merely intellectual. We can imagine a person with most excellent judgment, who yet does not act upon his judgment. There must not only be force to insure effort in execution against obstacles, but there must also be a delicate personal responsiveness—there must be an emotional reaction. Indeed good judgment is impossible without this susceptibility. Unless there is a prompt and almost instinctive sensitiveness to the conditions about one, to the ends and interests of others, the intellectual side of judgment will not have its

proper material to work upon. Just as the material of objects of knowledge is related to the senses, so the material of ethical knowledge is related to emotional responsiveness. It is difficult to put this quality into words, but we all know the difference between the character which is somewhat hard and formal, and that which is sympathetic, flexible, and open. In the abstract the former may be as sincerely devoted to moral ideas as the latter, but as a practical matter we prefer to live with the latter, and we count upon it to accomplish more in the end by tact, by instinctive recognition of the claims of others, by skill in adjusting, than the former can accomplish by mere attachment to rules and principles which are intellectually justified.

We get here, then, the ethical standard upon the psychological side, by which to test the work of the school. (*a*) Does the school as a system, at present, attach sufficient importance to the spontaneous instincts and impulses? Does it afford sufficient opportunity for these to assert themselves and work out their own results? Omitting quantitative considerations, can we even say that the school in principle attaches itself, at present, to the active constructive powers rather than to processes of absorption and learning, acquiring information? Does not our talk about self-activity largely render itself meaningless because the self-activity we have in mind is purely intellectual, out of relation to the impulses of the child which work through hand and eye?

Just in so far as the present school methods fail to meet the test of these questions we must not be surprised if the ethical results attained are unsatisfactory. We cannot secure the development of positive force of character unless we are willing to pay the price psychologically required. We cannot smother and repress the child's powers, or gradually abort them (from failure to permit sufficient opportunity for exercise), and then expect to get a character with initiative and consecutive industry. I am aware of the importance attaching to inhibition, but mere inhibition is valueless. The only restraint, the only holding-in that is of any worth is that which comes through holding all the powers concentrated in devotion to a positive end. The end cannot be attained excepting as the instinct and impulses are kept from discharging at random and from running off on side tracks. In keeping the powers at work upon their relevant ends, there is sufficient opportunity for genuine inhibition. To say that inhibition is higher than power of direction, morally, is like saying that death is worth more than life, negation worth more than affirmation, sacrifice worth more than service. Morally educative inhibition is one of the factors of the power of direction.

(*b*) We must also test our school work as to whether it affords the conditions psychologically necessary for the formation of good judgment. Judgment as the sense of relative values involves ability to select, to discriminate, by reference to a standard. Acquiring information can therefore never develop the power of judgment. Whatever development the child gets is in spite of, not because of, those methods of instruction which emphasize simple learning. The test comes only when the information acquired has to be put to use. Will it do what we expect of it? I have heard an educator of large experience say that in her judgment the greatest defect of instruction today, on the intellectual side, is found in the fact that children leave school without a mental perspective. Facts seem to them all of the same importance. There is no foreground nor background. There is no instinctive habit of sorting out our facts upon any scale of worth, and of grading them accordingly. This may be an exaggerated statement, but in so far as there is any truth in it, it points to moral evils as serious as the intellectual ones.

The child cannot get power of judgment excepting as he is continually exercised in forming and testing judgment. He must have an opportunity to select for himself, and then to attempt to put his own selections into execution that he may submit them to the only final test, that of action. Only thus can he learn to discriminate that which promises success from that which promises failure; only thus can he form the habit of continually relating his otherwise isolated ideas to the conditions which determine their value. Does the school, as a system, afford, at present, sufficient opportunity for this sort of experimentation? Excepting in so far as the emphasis of the school work is upon the doing side, upon construction, upon active investigation, it cannot meet the psychological conditions necessary for the judgment which is an integral factor of good character.

(c) I shall be brief with respect to the other point, the need of susceptibility and responsiveness. The informal, social side of education, the aesthetic environment and influences, are all-important here. In so far as all the work is laid out in regular and formulated ways, in so far as there are lacking opportunities for casual and free social intercourse between the pupils, and between the pupils and the teacher, this side of the child's nature is either being starved or else left to find haphazard expression along more or less secret channels. When the school system under plea of the practical (meaning by the practical the narrowly utilitarian) confines the child to the three R's and the formal studies connected with them, and shuts him out from the vital sources of literature and history, and deprives him of his right to contact with what is best in architecture, music, sculpture and picture, it is hopeless to expect any definite results with respect to the training of this integral element in character.

What we need in education more than anything else is genuine, not merely nominal faith in the existence of moral principles which are capable of effective application. We believe that, so far as the mass of children are concerned, if we keep at them long enough we can teach reading and writing and figuring. We are practically, even if unconsciously, skeptical as to the possibility of anything like the same sort of assurance on the moral side. We believe in moral laws and rules, to be sure, but they are in the air. They are something set off by themselves. They are so *very* "moral" that there is no working contact between them and the average affairs of everyday life. What we need is to have these moral principles brought down to the ground through their statement in social and in psychological terms. We need to see that moral principles are not arbitrary, that they are not merely transcendental; that the term "moral" does not designate a special region or portion of life. We need to translate the moral into the actual conditions and working forces of our community life, and into the impulses and habits which make up the doing of the individual.

All the rest is mint, anise, and cummin. The one thing needful is that we recognize that moral principles are real in the same sense in which other forces are real; that they are inherent in community life, and in the running machinery of the individual. If we can secure a genuine faith in this fact, we shall have secured the only condition which is finally necessary in order to get from our educational system all the effectiveness there is in it. The teacher who operates in this faith will find every subject, every method of instruction, every incident of school life pregnant with ethical life.

III

Aesthetics
and
Education

AFFECTIVE THOUGHT IN LOGIC
AND PAINTING *

Traditional theories in philosophy and psychology have accustomed us to sharp separations between physiological and organic processes on the one hand and the higher manifestations of culture in science and art on the other. The separations are summed up in the common division made between mind and body. These theories have also accustomed us to draw rigid separations between the logical, strictly intellectual, operations which terminate in science, the emotional and imaginative processes which dominate poetry, music and to a lesser degree the plastic arts, and the practical doings which rule our daily life and which result in industry, business and political affairs. In other words, thought, sentiment or affectivity and volition have been marked off from one another. The result of these divisions has been the creation of a large number of problems which in their technical aspect are the special concern of philosophy, but which come home to everyone in his actual life in the segregation of the activities he carries on, the departmentalizing of life, the pigeonholing of interests. Between science's sake, art for art's sake, busi-

* This essay appeared originally in the *Journal of the Barnes Foundation,* 1926.

ness as usual or business for money-making, the relegation of religion to Sundays and holidays, the turning over of politics to professional politicians, the professionalizing of sports, and so on, little room is left for living, for the sake of living, a full, rich and free life.

Recent advances in some fundamental generalizations regarding biological functions in general and those of the nervous system in particular have made possible a definite conception of continuous development from the lower functions to the higher. Interestingly enough, this breaking-down of fixed barriers between physiological operations and the far reaches of culture in science and art has also removed the underpinning from beneath the separation of science, art and practical activity from one another. There has long been vague talk about the unity of experience and mental life, to the effect that knowledge, feeling and volition are all manifestations of the same energies, etc.; but there has now been put in our hands the means by which this talk may be made definite and significant.

Naturally, the variety of physiological details involved has not yet been adequately organized nor has there been time to digest them and get their net results. In any case, the writer is not an expert in this field, and even if he were this would hardly be the place to expound them. But some of their net results are easy of comprehension, and they have a definite bearing upon art and its connection with the normal processes of life.

We may begin with the field of reasoning, long supposed to be preëmpted by pure intellect, and to be completely severed, save by accident, from affectivity and desire and from the motor organs and habits by which we make our necessary practical adjustments to the world about us. But a recent writer, Rignano, working from a biological basis, has summed up his conclusions as follows: "The analysis of reasoning, the highest of our mental faculties, has led us to the view that it is constituted entirely by the reciprocal play of the two fundamental and primordial activities of our psyche, the intellectual and the affective. The first consist in simple mnemonic evocations of perceptions or images of the past; the second appear as tendencies or aspirations of our mind towards a certain end to be attained, towards which reasoning itself is directed." [1]

An isolated quotation fails, of course, to bring out the full force of the points made. But what is summed up here under the idea of "affectivity" is that an organism has certain basic needs which cannot be supplied without activity which modifies the surroundings; that when the organism is in any way disturbed in its "equilibration" with its environment, its needs show themselves as restless, craving, desiring activity which persists until the acts thus induced have brought about a new integration of the organism and its relation to the environment. Then it is shown that thinking falls within the scope of this principle; reasoning is a phase of the generic function of bringing about a new relationship between organisms and the conditions of life, and like other phases of the function is controlled by need, desire and progressive satisfactions.

Rignano calls the other phase "intellectual." But the context shows that the basic principle here is one of practical adjustments. Past experiences are retained so that they may be evoked and arranged when there is need to use them in attaining the new end set by the needs of our affective nature. But the retention is not intellectual. It is a matter of organic modifications, of change of disposition, attitude and habit. The "stuff" from which thinking draws its material in satisfying need by establishing a new relation to the surroundings is found in what, with some extension of the usual sense of the word, may be termed habits: namely, the changes wrought in our ways of acting and undergoing by prior experiences. Thus the material of thought all comes from the past; but its purpose and direction is future, the development of a new environment as the condition of sustaining a new and more fully integrated self.

It thus turns out, though the argument is too technical to be developed on this occasion, that the great gap which is

---

[1] Rignano, *The Psychology of Reasoning*, page 388 (Harcourt, Brace & Co., New York, N. Y., 1923).

traditionally made between the lower physiological functions and the higher cultural ones, is due first to isolating the organism from the environment, failing to see the necessity of its integration with environment, and secondly, to neglect of the function of needs in creating ends, or consequences to be attained. So when "ends" are recognized at all, it has been thought necessary to call in some higher and independent power to account for them. But the connection of ends with affectivities, with cravings and desires, is deepseated in the organism, and is constantly extended and refined through experience. Desire, interest, accomplishes what in the traditional theory a pure intellect was evoked to accomplish. More and more expansive desires and more varied and flexible habits build up more elaborate trains of thought and, finally, the harmonies, consistencies and comprehensive structures of logical systems result.

Reasoning and science are thus obviously brought nearer to art. The satisfaction of need requires that surroundings should be changed. In reasoning, this fact appears as the necessity for experimentation. In plastic art it is a commonplace. Art also explicitly recognizes what it has taken so long to discover in science: the control of re-shaping natural conditions exercised by emotion, and the place of the imagination, under the influence of desire, in re-creating the world into a more orderly place. When so-called non-rational factors are found to play a large part in the production of relations of consistency and order in logical systems, it is not surprising that they should operate in artistic structures. Indeed, it may be questioned whether any scientific systems extant, save perhaps those of mathematics, equal artistic structure in integrity, subtlety and scope, while the latter are evidently more readily and widely understood, and are the sources of a more widespread and direct satisfaction. These facts are explicable only when it is realized that scientific and artistic systems embody the same fundamental principles of the relationship of life to its surroundings, and that both satisfy the same fundamental needs. Probably a time will come when it will be universally recognized that the differences between coherent logical schemes and artistic structures in poetry, music and the plastic arts are technical and specialized, rather than deep-seated.

In the past we have had to depend mostly upon phrases to explain the production of artistic structures. They have been referred to genius or inspiration or the creative imagination. Contemporary appeal to the Unconscious and the Racial Unconscious are the same thing under a new name. Writing the word with a capital letter and putting "the" before it, as if it were a distinct force, gives us no more light than we had before. Yet unconscious activities are realities, and the newer biology is making it clear that such organic activities are just of the kind to re-shape natural objects in order to procure their adequate satisfaction, and that the re-shaped object will be marked by the features known to belong to works of art.

It is a commonplace that repetition in place and time, rhythm, symmetry, harmony, modulation, suspense and resolution, plot, climax and contrasting letdown, emphasis and intervals, action and retardation, unity, being "all of a piece," and inexhaustible variety, are marks, in varying ways, to meet the requirements of different media, of all artistic productions. These are just the traits which naturally characterize objects when the environment is made over in consonance with basic organic requirements. On the other hand, the fact that the spectator and auditor "clicks" so intimately and intensely in the face of works of art is accounted for. By their means there are released old, deep-seated habits or engrained organic "memories," yet these old habits are deployed in new ways, ways in which they are adapted to a more completely integrated world so that they themselves achieve a new integration. Hence the liberating, expansive power of art.

The same considerations explain the fact that works of art of a new style have to create their own audience. At first there is experienced largely the jar of dissonance with the superficial habits most readily called into play. But changes in the surroundings involve correlated changes in the organism, and so the eye and ear gradually become acclimatized. The organism is really made over, is reorganized in effecting an adequate perception of a work of art. Hence the proper effect of the latter is gradually realized, and then what was first condemned as *outré* falls into its serial place in the history of artistic achievement.

In *The Art in Painting,* Mr. Barnes has shown that plastic form is the *integration of all plastic means.* In the case of paintings, these are color, line, light and space. By means of their relations to one another, design is affected: design, namely, in line patterns, in surface masses, in three-dimensional solids, and in spatial intervals—the "room" about objects whether up and down, side to side, front and back. And Mr. Barnes has shown that it is the kind and degree of integration of plastic means in achieving each of the elements of design taken by itself, and also the integration of each with all the others, which constitutes the objective standard for value in painting. From the psychological standpoint, this integration in pictures means that a correlative integration is effected in the total set of organic responses; eye activities arouse allied muscular activities which in turn not merely harmonize with and support eye activities, but which in turn evoke further experiences of light and color, and so on. Moreover, as in every adequate union of sensory and motor actions, the background of visceral, circulatory, respiratory functions is also consonantly called into action. In other words, integration in the object permits and secures a corresponding integration in organic activities. Hence, the peculiar well-being and rest in excitation, vitality in peace, which is characteristic of aesthetic enjoyment.

Defective value can, of course, be judged by the same measure. Some one of the elements may be deficient; thereby adequate support is not given to the functioning of the other elements and a corresponding lack of vitality in response occurs or even a feeling of frustration and bafflement. Or, what is more likely to happen in pictures that may conventionally attain celebrity for a time, some factor is overaccentuated—so that while vision is captured and impressed for the moment, the final reaction is partial and one-sided, a fatiguing demand being made upon some organic activities which are not duly nourished and reinforced by the others.

Thus it is not too much to say that the statement of an objective criterion of value in paintings set forth for the first time by Mr. Barnes will make possible in time an adequate psychological, even physiological, analysis of aesthetic responses in spectators, so that the appreciation of paintings will no longer be a matter of private, absolute tastes and *ipse dixits*.

By the use of the same conception of integration of specified means, Mr. Barnes has also for the first time given us the clue to the historical development of modern painting in terms of paintings themselves. In the earlier period, integration is in considerable measure achieved by means extraneous to the painting itself, such as associated subject-matter in the religious or prior (academic) tradition, or by undue reliance upon familiar associations between light and shade and spatial positions. The history of art shows a tendency to secure variety and relationship in plastic form by means of the element most truly distinctive of painting, namely, color. Lines, for example, have ceased to be hard and fast clear-cut divisions (in which case they are more or less non-integrative), and are determined by subtle meetings of color-masses which upon close examination are found to melt into one another. Similarly, light and shade were long employed on the basis of everyday practical associations to give the impression of solidity. But artists capable of greater differentiation and integration of their experiences in terms of color itself experimented in conveying tri-dimensional relationships by means of variations and juxtapositions in color. Then color was employed to build up structural solidity and its variations in single objects. Painters have also learned to render action and movement, not by depending upon associations with extraneous experiences—which always lead to an overaccentuation of some one feature, light or line, as in depicting exaggerated muscular poses—but by use of the relations of forms to one another, in connection with spatial intervals, this end being attained by use of color as means. The fact that this more subtle and complete integration usually involves deformation or distortion of familiar forms —that is, conflicts with associations formed outside the realm of painting—accounts for the fact that they are greeted at first with disdainful criticism. But in time a new line of

organic associations is built up, formed on the basis of un-
alloyed aesthetic experiences, and deformations—that are
such from the practical everyday standpoint—cease to give
trouble and to be annoying. They become elements in a genuine and direct aesthetic grasp.

From the standpoint of the analysis of pictures, there is
nothing new in these remarks to anyone familiar with Mr.
Barnes' book. I have recurred to them only because the objective analysis of Mr. Barnes is in the first place so thoroughly in accord with the present trend of fundamental biological conceptions, and, secondly, because it makes possible
an application of these biological conceptions to the whole
field of artistic structures and aesthetic criticism. It then becomes possible to break down the traditional separation between scientific and intellectual systems and those of art, and
also to further the application of the principle of integration
to the relationship of those elements of culture which are so
segregated in our present life—to science, art, in its variety
of forms, industry and business, religion, sport and morals.
And it is daily being more evident that unless some integration can be attained, the always increasing isolations and oppositions consequent upon the growth of specialization in all
fields will in the end disrupt our civilization. That art and its
intelligent appreciation as manifested especially in painting
is itself an integrating experience is the constant implication
of the work of The Barnes Foundation as that is reflected in
The Art in Painting. For to make of paintings an educational
means is to assert that the genuine intelligent realization of
pictures is not only an integration of the specialized factors
found in the paintings as such, but is such a deep and abiding
experience of the nature of fully harmonized experience as
sets a standard or forms a habit for all other experiences. In
other words, paintings when taken out of their specialized
niche are the basis of an educational experience which coun-
teracts the disrupting tendencies of the hard-and-fast specializations, compartmental divisions and rigid segregations which
so confuse and nullify our present life.

INDIVIDUALITY
AND EXPERIENCE *

The methods of picture-making employed in the classes of Professor Cizek in Vienna raise a question that has to be dealt with in every branch of instruction. The question develops in two directions, one suggested by his statement that it is impossible to exclude outside influences, and the other by his report that upon the whole the more original constructions are those of younger pupils, that older students seem gradually to lose interest, so that no prominent artist has been produced. The problem thus defined consists in the relation of individuality and its adequate development to the work and responsibilities of the teacher, representing accumulated experience of the past.

Unfortunately, the history of schools not only in art but in all lines shows a swing of the pendulum between extremes, though it must be admitted that the simile of the pendulum is not a good one, for the schools remain, most of them, most of the time, near one extreme, instead of swinging periodically and evenly between the two. Anyway, the two extremes are external imposition and dictation, and "free-expression."

* This essay appeared originally in the *Journal of the Barnes Foundation*, 1926.

Revolt from the costly, nerve-taxing and inadequate results of mechanical control from without creates an enthusiasm for spontaneity and "development from within," as it is often phrased. It is found that children at first are then much happier in their work—anyone who has seen Cizek's class will testify to the wholesome air of cheerfulness, even of joy, which pervades the room—but gradually tend to become listless and finally bored, while there is an absence of cumulative, progressive development of power and of actual achievement in results. Then the pendulum swings back to regulation by the ideas, rules and orders of someone else, who being maturer, better informed and more experienced is supposed to know what should be done and how to do it.

The metaphor of the pendulum is faulty in another respect. It seems to suggest that the solution lies in finding a midpoint between the two extremes which would be at rest. But what is really wanted is a change in the direction of movement. As a general proposition no one would deny that personal mental growth is furthered in any branch of human undertaking by contact with the accumulated and sifted experience of others in that line. No one would seriously propose that all future carpenters should be trained by actually starting with a clean sheet, wiping out everything that the past has discovered about mechanics, about tools and their uses, and so on. It would not be thought likely that this knowledge would "cramp their style," limit their individuality, etc. But neither, on the other hand, have carpenters been formed by the methods often used in manual training shops where dinky tasks of a minute and technical nature are set, wholly independent of really making anything, having only specialized skill as their aim. As a rule carpenters are educated in their calling by working with others who have experience and skill, sharing in the simpler portions of the real undertakings, assisting in ways which enable them to observe methods and to see what results they are adapted to accomplish.

Such learning is controlled by two great principles: one is participation in something inherently worth while, or undertaken on its own account; the other is perception of the relation of means to consequences. When these two conditions are met, a third consideration usually follows as a matter of course. Having had an experience of the meaning of certain technical processes and forms of skill there develops an interest in skill and "technique": the meaning of the result is "transferred" to the means of its attainment. Boys interested in baseball as a game thus submit themselves voluntarily to continued practice in throwing, catching, batting, the separate elements of the game. Or boys, who get interested in the game of marbles, will practice to increase their skill in shooting and hitting. Just imagine, however, what would happen if they set these exercises as tasks in school, with no prior activity in the games and with no sense of what they were about or for, and without any such appeal to the social, or participating, impulses as takes place in games!

If we generalize from such a commonplace case as the education of artisans through their work, we may say that the customs, methods and *working* standards of the calling constitute a "tradition," and that initiation into the tradition is the means by which the powers of learners are released and directed. But we should also have to say that the urge or need of an individual to join in an undertaking is a necessary prerequisite of the tradition's being a factor in his personal growth in power and freedom; and also that he has to *see* on his own behalf and in his own way the relations between means and methods employed and results achieved. Nobody else can see for him, and he can't see just by being "told," although the right kind of telling may guide his seeing and thus help him see what he needs to see. And if he has no impelling desire of his own to become a carpenter, if his interest in being one is perfunctory, if it is not an interest in *being* a carpenter at all, but only in getting a pecuniary reward by doing jobs, the tradition will never of course really enter into and integrate with his own powers. It will remain, then, a mere set of mechanical and more or less meaningless rules that he is obliged to follow if he is to hold his job and draw his pay.

Supposing, again, that our imaginary pupil works for and with a master carpenter who believes in only one kind of house with a fixed design, and his aim is not only to teach his apprentice to make just that one kind of house, but to accept it with all his soul, heart and mind as the only kind of house that should ever be built, the very type and standard model of all houses. Then it is easy to see that limitation of personal powers will surely result, not merely, moreover, limitation of technical skill, but, what is more important, of his powers of observation, imagination, judgment, and even his emotions, since his appreciations will be warped to conform to the one preferred style. The imaginary case illustrates what often happens when we pass from the education of artisans to that of artists. As a rule a carpenter has to keep more or less open; he is exposed to many demands and must be flexible enough to meet them. He is in no position to set up a final authority about ends and models and standards, no matter how expert he may be in methods and means. But an architect in distinction from a builder is likely to be an "authority"; he can dictate and lay down what is right and wrong, and thus prescribe certain ends and proscribe others. Here is a case where tradition is not enhancing and liberating, but is restrictive and enslaving. If he has pupils, he is a "master" and not an advanced fellow worker; his students are disciples rather than learners. Tradition is no longer tradition but a fixed and absolute convention.

In short, the practical difficulty does not reside in any antagonism of methods and rules and results worked out in past experience to individual desire, capacity and freedom. It lies rather in the hard and narrow and, we may truly say, uneducated habits and attitudes of teachers who set up as authorities, as rulers and judges in Israel. As a matter of course they know that as bare individuals they are not "authorities" and will not be accepted by others as such. So they clothe themselves with some tradition as a mantle, and henceforth it is not just "I" who speaks, but some Lord speaks through me. The teacher then offers himself as the organ of the voice of a whole school, of a *finished* classic tradition, and arrogates to himself the prestige that comes from what he is the spokesman for. Suppression of the emotional and intellectual integrity of pupils is the result; their freedom is repressed and the growth of their own personalities stunted. But it is not because of any opposition between the wisdom and skill of the past and the individual capacities of learners; the trouble lies in the habits, standards and ideas of the teacher. It is analogous to another case. There is no inherent opposition between theory and practice; the former enlarges, releases and gives significance to the latter; while practice supplies theory with its materials and with the test and check which keep it sincere and vital. But there is a whole lot of opposition between human beings who set themselves up as practical and those who set themselves up as theorists, an irresolvable conflict because both have put themselves into a wrong position.

This suggests that the proponents of freedom are in a false position as well as the would-be masters and dictators. There is a present tendency in so-called advanced schools of educational thought (by no means confined to art classes like those of Cizek) to say, in effect, let us surround pupils with certain materials, tools, appliances, etc., and then let pupils respond to these things according to their own desires. Above all let us not suggest any end or plan to the students; let us not suggest to them what they shall do, for that is an unwarranted trespass upon their sacred intellectual individuality since the essence of such individuality is to set up ends and aims.

Now such a method is really stupid. For it attempts the impossible, which is always stupid; and it misconceives the conditions of independent thinking. There are a multitude of ways of reacting to surrounding conditions, and without some guidance from experience these reactions are almost sure to be casual, sporadic and ultimately fatiguing, accompanied by nervous strain. Since the teacher has presumably a greater background of experience, there is the same presumption of the right of a teacher to make suggestions as to what to do, as there is on the part of the head carpenter to suggest to apprentices something of what they are to do. Moreover, the theory literally carried out would be obliged to banish all artificial materials, tools and appliances. Being the product of the skill, thought and matured experience of others, they would also, by the theory, "interfere" with personal freedom.

Moreover, when the child proposes or suggests what to do,

some consequence to be attained, whence is the suggestion supposed to spring? There is no spontaneous germination in the mental life. If he does not get the suggestion from the teacher, he gets it from somebody or something in the home or the street or from what some more vigorous fellow pupil is doing. Hence the chances are great of its being a passing and superficial suggestion, without much depth and range—in other words, not specially conducive to the developing of freedom. If the teacher is really a teacher, and not just a master or "authority," he should know enough about his pupils, their needs, experiences, degrees of skill and knowledge, etc., to be able (not to dictate aims and plans) to share in a discussion regarding what is to be done and be as free to make suggestions as anyone else. (The implication that the teacher is the one and only person who has no "individuality" or "freedom" to "express" would be funny if it were not often so sad in its outworkings.) And his contribution, given the conditions stated, will presumably do more to getting something started which will really secure and increase the development of strictly individual capacities than will suggestions springing from uncontrolled haphazard sources.

The point is also worth dwelling upon, that the method of leaving the response entirely to pupils, the teacher supplying, in the language of the day, only the "stimuli," misconceives the nature of thinking. Any so-called "end" or "aim" or "project" which the average immature person can suggest in advance is likely to be highly vague and unformed, a mere outline sketch, not a suggestion of a definite result or consequence but rather a gesture which roughly indicates a field within which activities might be carried on. It hardly represents thought at all: it is a suggestion. The real intellectual shaping of the "end" or purpose comes during and because of the operations subsequently performed. This is as true of the suggestion which proceeds from the teacher as of those which "spontaneously" spring from the pupils, so that the former does not restrict thought. The advantage on the side of the teacher—if he or she has any business to be in that position—is the greater probability that it will be a suggestion which will permit and require thought in the subsequent activity which builds up a clear and organized conception of an end. There is no more fatal flaw in psychology than that which takes the original vague fore-feeling of some consequence to be realized as the equivalent of a *thought* of an end, a true purpose and directive plan. The thought of an end is strictly correlative to perception of means and methods. Only when, and as the latter becomes clear during the serial process of execution does the project and guiding aim and plan become evident and articulated. In the full sense of the word, a person becomes aware of what he wants to do and what he is about only when the work is actually complete.

The adjective "serial" is important in connection with the process of performance or execution. Each step forward, each "means" used, is a partial attainment of an "end." It makes clearer the character of that end, and hence suggests to an observing mind the next step to be taken, or the means and methods to be next employed. Originality and independence of thinking are therefore connected with the intervening process of execution rather than with the source of the initial suggestion. Indeed, genuinely fruitful and original suggestions are themselves usually the results of experience in the carrying out of undertakings. The "end" is not, in other words, an end or finality in the literal sense, but is in turn the starting point of new desires, aims and plans. By means of the process the mind gets power to make suggestions which are significant. There is now a past experience from which they can spring with an increased probability of their being worth while and articulate.

It goes without saying that a teacher may interfere and impose alien standards and methods during the operation. But as we have previously seen, this is not because of bringing to bear the results of previous experience, but because the habits of the teacher are so narrow and fixed, his imagination and sympathies so limited, his own intellectual horizon so bounded, that he brings them to bear in a wrong way. The fuller and richer the experience of the teacher, the more adequate his own knowledge of "traditions," the more likely is he, given the attitude of participator instead of that of master, to use them in a liberating way.

Freedom or individuality, in short, is not an original possession or gift. It is something to be achieved, to be wrought out. Suggestions as to things which may advantageously be taken, as to skill, as to methods of operation, are indispensable conditions of its achievement. These by the nature of the case must come from a sympathetic and discriminating knowledge of what has been done in the past and how it has been done.

EXPERIENCE, NATURE
AND ART *

Contemporary theories of art generally suffer from inconsistency. They are only in part interpretations of art and of experience as these are to be observed today; in part, they represent a survival of opinions and assumptions inherited from the Greeks. According to Greek theory, art is a form of practice, and so incurs the reproach of being concerned with a merely subjective, changing and imperfect world. This was true of all arts, of those now classified as "fine" as well as of the useful crafts practiced by the artisan. In contrast with both, science was regarded as a revelation—in fact, the only true revelation—of reality. It was thought to be through science alone that access is provided to the world as it is in itself, not colored or distorted by human wants or preferences. Art corresponded to production, science to "contemplation," and the productive was branded as inferior, an activity proper only to mechanics and slaves.

This view was a reflection in theory of the Greek social system, in which a menial class performed all necessary labor, and freeman and citizens alone enjoyed the fruits of

---

* This essay appeared originally in the *Journal of the Barnes Foundation*, 1925.

that labor. Since the leisure class held the position of power and honor, its part in life was regarded as intrinsically superior, and the artist, who by the labor of his hands shaped the objects which were the food of contemplation, belonged to the lower realm of nature and experience.

Contemporary opinion accepts, in the main, the Greek view that knowledge is contemplation, and that it alone reveals nature as nature is. The Greek disparagement of art, it partly accepts and partly rejects; accepts it as regards the useful arts, which are clearly modes of practice, but rejects it as regards the fine arts. In fine art it makes a distinction between the experience of the artist, which is considered to be creative, and the experience of the beholder or connoisseur, which is regarded as passive. Of these, it ranks the artist above the connoisseur, the producer above the consumer. At the same time, although it regards knowledge as contemplation, it recognizes that science, the systematic pursuit of knowledge, is active, an affair of making experiments, and so belongs to the realm of practice.

These notions are consistent neither with each other nor, as a whole, with experience. The Greek view was sound in recognizing the continuity of "useful" with "fine" art; it erred in neglecting the connection of knowledge with experiment, and so in isolating knowledge from practice. If knowledge is truly contemplation, and is on that account superior to mere practice, then all arts, that of the painter no less than that of the carpenter, are inferior to science, and the painter stands in rank below the dilettante who looks at paintings. If, however, not knowledge but art is the final flowering of experience, the crown and consummation of nature, and knowledge is only the means by which art, which includes all practice, is enabled to attain its richest development, then it is the artist who represents nature and life at their best.

Current discussion of aesthetics and art falls into inconsistency about the active and passive rôles of art largely because it confuses art as a process of execution, of creation of a type of material things, and art as the enjoyable appreciation of things so created. To avoid this inconsistency it is advantageous to use the word "artistic" to designate the activities by which works of art are brought into being, and to reserve the term "aesthetic" for the appreciation of them when created, the enhanced or heightened perceptions in which they result.

Although the view here defended asserts that there is no ultimate difference between the artist and the artisan, there is an obvious empirical difference between the activities and experience of the artist, as we actually find him, and those of the artisan. That the artist's life is the more humanly desirable, that it is the richer, more self-rewarding, more humane, none would deny. The difference, however, is not one between aesthetic contemplation and mere labor, but between those activities which are charged with intrinsic significance—which are both instrumental, means to more remote ends, and consummatory, immediately enjoyable—and those forms which are *merely* instrumental, and in themselves nothing but drudgery. This fact is due to nothing in the nature of experience or practice, but only to defects in the present economic and social order. To call the greater part of the productive activities now carried on "useful arts" is mere euphemism, by which the essential irrationality of the existing régime is concealed. Innumerable commodities which are manufactured by the "useful arts" are only apparently and superficially useful; their employment results not in satisfaction of intelligent desire, but in confusion and extravagance, bought at the price of a narrowed and embittered experience. There can be no true understanding of either practice or aesthetic appreciation while practice is in large measure slavery, and while "esthetic appreciation" is merely one of the forms of distraction by which intervals of respite from slavery are whiled away.

The degradation of labor is paralleled by a degradation of art. Most of what passes for art at present falls under three captions:

First, there is mere indulgence in emotional outpouring, without reference to the conditions of intelligibility. Such "expression of emotion" is largely futile—futile partly because of its arbitrary and willfully eccentric character, but partly also because the channels of expression currently accepted as permissible are so rigidly laid down that novelty can find acceptance only with the aid of violence.

In addition to this type—and frequently mingled with it—there is experimentation in new modes of craftsmanship, cases where the seemingly bizarre and over-individualistic character of the products is due to discontent with existing technique, and is associated with an attempt to find new modes of expression. It is aside from the point to treat these manifestations as if they constituted art for the first time in human history, or to condemn them as not art because of their violent departure from received canons and methods. Some movement in this direction has always been a condition of growth of new forms, a condition of salvation from that mortal arrest and decay called academic art.

Then there is that which in quantity bulks most largely as fine art: the production of buildings in the name of the art of architecture; of pictures in the name of painting; of novels, dramas, etc., in the name of literary art; a production which in reality is largely a form of commercialized industry in production of a class of commodities that find their sale among well-to-do persons desirous of maintaining a conventionally approved status. As the first two modes carry to disproportionate excess that factor of difference, particularity and contingency, which is indispensable in all art, deliberately flaunting avoidance of the repetitions and order of nature, so this mode celebrates the regular and finished. It is reminiscent rather than commemorative of the meanings of things. Its products remind their owner of things pleasant in memory though hard in direct undergoing, and remind others that their owner has achieved an economic standard which makes possible cultivation and decoration of leisure.

Obviously no one of these classes of activity and products, or all of them put together, mark off anything that can be called distinctively fine art. They share their qualities and defects with many other activities and objects. But, fortunately, there may be mixed with any of them, and, still more fortunately, there may occur without mixture, process and product which are characteristically excellent. *This occurs when activity is productive of an object which affords continuously renewed delight*. This condition requires that the object be, with its successive consequences, indefinitely instrumental to *new* satisfying events. For otherwise the object is quickly exhausted and satiety sets in. Anyone who reflects upon the commonplace that a measure of artistic products is their capacity to attract and retain observation with satisfaction under whatever conditions they are approached, has a sure demonstration that a genuinely aesthetic object is not exclusively consummatory, but is causally productive as well. A consummatory object that is not also instrumental turns in time to the dust and ashes of boredom. The "eternal" quality of great art is its renewed instrumentality for further consummatory experiences.

When this fact is noted it is also seen that limitation of fineness of art to paintings, statues, poems, songs and symphonies is conventional, or even verbal. Any activity that is productive of objects whose perception is an immediate good, and whose operation is a continual source of enjoyable perception of other events, exhibits fineness of art. There are acts of all kinds that directly refresh and enlarge the spirit and that are instrumental to the production of new objects and dispositions which are in turn productive of further refinements and replenishments. Frequently moralists make the acts *they* find excellent or virtuous wholly final, and treat art and affection as mere means. Aestheticians reverse the performance, and see in good *acts* means to an ulterior external happiness, while aesthetic appreciation is called a good in itself, or that strange thing, an end in itself. But on both sides it is true that in being predominantly fructifying, the things designated means are immediately satisfying. They are their own excuses for being just because they are charged with an office in quickening apprehension, enlarging the horizon of vision, refining discrimination, creating standards of appreciation which are confirmed and deepened by further experiences. It would almost seem that when their non-instrumental character is insisted on, what is meant were an indefinitely expansive and radiating instrumental efficacy.

It is the fact that art, so far as it is truly art, is a union of the serviceable and the immediately enjoyable, of the instrumental and the consummatory, that makes it impossible to institute a difference in kind between useful and fine art.

Many things are termed useful for reasons of social status, implying depreciation and contempt. Things are sometimes said to belong to the menial arts merely because they are cheap and used familiarly by common people. These things of daily use for ordinary ends may survive in later periods, or be transported to another culture, as from Japan and China to America, and being rare and sought by connoisseurs, rank forthwith as works of fine art. Other things may be called fine because their manner of use is decorative or socially ostentatious. It is tempting to make a distinction of degree and say that a thing belongs to the sphere of use when perception of its meaning is instrumental to something else; and that a thing belongs to fine art when its other uses are subordinate to its use in perception. The distinction has a rough practical value, but cannot be pressed too far. For in production of a painting or poem, as well as in making a vase or temple, a perception is also employed as a means for something beyond itself. Moreover, the perception of urns, pots and pans as commodities may be intrinsically enjoyable, although these things are primarily perceived with reference to some use to which they are put. The only *basic* distinction is that between bad art and good art, and this distinction between things that meet the requirements of art and those that do not applies equally to things of use and of beauty. Capacity to offer to perception meaning in which fruition and efficacy interpenetrate is met by different products in various degrees of fulness; it may be missed altogether by pans and poems alike. The difference between the ugliness of a meretriciously conceived and executed utensil and a meretricious and pretentious painting is one only of content or material; in form, both are articles, and bad articles.

The relation of the esthetic and the artistic, as above defined, may now be stated more precisely. Both are incidental to practice, to performance, but in the esthetic the attained vision with which the artist presents us releases energies which remain diffuse and inchoate, which raise the whole level of our existence, but do not find issue in any single or specific form. In the artistic the existing consummation is utilized to bring into existence further analogous perceptions.

A painter, for example, uses a picture not only to guide his perception of the world, but as a source of suggestions for painting additional pictures. Art in being, the active productive process, may thus be defined as an aesthetic perception, together with an *operative* perception of the efficiencies of the aesthetic object. A parallel contrast is to be found in scientific experience. The layman may by his knowledge of science understand the world about him much more clearly, and regulate his actions more effectively, than he could without it, but he is not called a scientist until he is able to utilize his knowledge to make fresh scientific discoveries. As to the scientist, knowledge is a means to more knowledge, so to the artist aesthetic insight is a means to further aesthetic insight, and not merely to enhancement of life in general. The distinction between the aesthetic and the artistic, important as it is, is thus, in the last analysis, a matter of degree.

The meaning of the view accepted here may be made clearer if it is contrasted with the theory of art prevalent today in one school of critics, that aesthetic qualities in works of fine art are unique, separate not only from everything that is existential in nature but from all other forms of good. In proclaiming that such arts as music, poetry, painting, have characteristics unshared by any natural things whatever, such critics carry to its conclusion the isolation of fine art from the useful, of the final from the efficacious.

As an example, we may consider that theory of art which makes the distinguishing quality of the esthetic object its possession of what is called "significant form." Unless the meaning of the term is so isolated as to be wholly occult, it denotes a selection, for the sake of emphasis, purity, subtlety, of those forms which give consummatory significance to everyday subject-matters of experience. "Forms" are not the peculiar property or creation of the aesthetic and artistic; they are characters in virtue of which anything meets the requirements of an enjoyable perception. "Art" does not create the forms; it is their selection and organization in such ways as to enhance, prolong and purify the perceptual experience. It is not by accident that some objects and situations afford marked perceptual satisfactions; they do so because of their structural properties and relations. An artist may work with a minimum of analytic recognition of these structures or "forms"; he may select them chiefly by a kind of sympathetic vibration. But they may also be discriminatively ascertained; and an artist may utilize his deliberate awareness of them to create works of art that are more formal and abstract than those to which the public is accustomed. Tendency to composition in terms of the formal characters marks much contemporary art, in poetry, painting, music, even sculpture and architecture. At their worst, these products are "scientific" rather than artistic; technical exercises, and of a new kind of pedantry. At their best, they assist in ushering in new modes of art and by education of the organs of perception in new modes of consummatory objects, they enlarge and enrich the world of human vision. But they do this, not by discarding altogether connection with the real world, but by a highly funded and generalized representation of the formal sources of ordinary emotional experience.

Thus we reach a conclusion regarding the relations of instrumental and fine art which is precisely the opposite of that intended by selective aestheticians; namely, that fine art consciously undertaken as such is peculiarly instrumental in quality. It is a device in experimentation carried on for the sake of education. It exists for a specialized use, use being a new training of modes of perception. The creators of such works of art are entitled, when successful, to the gratitude that we give to inventors of microscopes and microphones; in the end, they open new objects to be observed and enjoyed. This is a genuine service; but only an age of combined confusion and conceit will arrogate to works that perform this special utility the exclusive name of fine art.

Art is great in proportion as it is universal, that is, in proportion as the uniformities of nature which it reveals and utilizes are extensive and profound—provided, however, that they are freshly applied in concrete objects or situations. The only objects, insights, perceptions, which remain perennially unwithered and unstaled are those which sharpen our vision for new and unforeseen embodiments of the truth they convey. The "magic" of poetry—and pregnant experience has poetic quality—is precisely the revelation of meaning in the old effected by its presentation of the new. It radiates the light that never was on sea or land but that is henceforth an abiding illumination of objects.

IV

Science
and
Education

VI

PROGRESSIVE EDUCATION AND
THE SCIENCE OF EDUCATION *

What is Progressive Education? What is the meaning of experiment in education, of an experimental school? What can such schools as are represented here do for other schools, in which the great, indefinitely the greater, number of children receive their instruction and discipline? What can be rightfully expected from the work of these progressive schools in the way of a contribution to intelligent and stable educational practice; especially what can be expected in the way of a contribution to educational theory? Are there common elements, intellectual and moral, in the various undertakings here represented? Or is each school going its own way, having for its foundation the desires and preferences of the particular person who happens to be in charge? Is experimentation a process of trying anything at least once, of putting into immediate effect any "happy thought" that comes to mind, or does it rest upon principles which are adopted at least as a working hypothesis? Are actual results consistently observed and used to check an underlying hypothesis so that the latter develops intellectually? Can we be content if from the

* This selection appeared originally in *Progressive Education,* 1928.

various progressive schools there emanate suggestions which radiate to other schools to enliven and vitalize their work; or should we demand that out of the coöperative undertakings of the various schools a coherent body of educational principles shall gradually emerge as a distinctive contribution to the theory of education?

Such questions as these come to mind on the occasion of such a gathering as this. The interrogations expressed are far from all inclusive. They are one-sided, and intentionally so. They glide over the important questions that may be asked about what these schools are actually doing for the children who attend them; how they are meeting their primary responsibility to the children themselves and their families and friends. The one-sided emphasis is, as was said, intentional. The questions are shaped to take another slant; to direct attention to the intellectual contribution to be expected of progressive schools. The reasons for this one-sidedness are close at hand. It is natural that in your own exchange of experiences and ideas the question slurred over should be prominent. And that pupils in progressive schools are themselves progressing, and that the movement to establish more progressive schools is progressing, I have no doubt. Nor do I think that the old question, once a bugaboo, as to what will happen when the pupils go to college or out into life, is any longer an open one. Experience has proved that they give a good account of themselves; so it has seemed to me that the present is a fitting time to raise the intellectual, the theoretical problem´ of the relation of the progressive movement to the art and philosophy of education.

The query as to common elements in the various schools receives an easy answer up to a certain point. All of the schools, I take it for granted, exhibit as compared with traditional schools, a common emphasis upon respect for individuality and for increased freedom; a common disposition to build upon the nature and experience of the boys and girls that come to them, instead of imposing from without external subject-matter and standards. They all display a certain atmosphere of informality, because experience has proved that formalization is hostile to genuine mental activity and to sincere emotional expression and growth. Emphasis upon activity as distinct from passivity is one of the common factors. And again I assume that there is in all of these schools a common unusual attention to the human factors, to normal social relations, to communication and intercourse which is like in kind to that which is found in the great world beyond the school doors; that all alike believe that these normal human contacts of child with child and of child with teacher are of supreme educational importance, and that all alike disbelieve in those artificial personal relations which have been the chief factor in isolation of schools from life. So much at least of common spirit and purpose we may assume to exist. And in so far we already have the elements of a distinctive contribution to the body of educational theory: respect for individual capacities, interests and experience; enough external freedom and informality at least to enable teachers to become acquainted with children as they really are; respect for self-initiated and self-conducted learning; respect for activity as the stimulus and centre of learning; and perhaps above all belief in social contact, communication, and coöperation upon a normal human plane as all-enveloping medium.

These ideas constitute no mean contribution: It is a contribution to educational theory as well as to the happiness and integrity of those who come under the influence of progressive schools. But the elements of the contribution are general, and like all generalities subject to varied and ambiguous interpretations. They indicate the starting point of the contribution that progressive schools may make to the theory or science of education, but only the starting point. Let us then reduce our questions to a single one and ask, What is the distinctive relation of progressive education to the science of education, understanding by science a body of verified facts and tested principles which may give intellectual guidance to the practical operating of schools?

Unless we beg the question at the outset assuming that it is already known just what education is, just what are its aims and what are its methods, there is nothing false nor extravagant in declaring that at the present time different sciences of education are not only possible but also much needed. Of course such a statement goes contrary to the idea that science by its very nature is a single and universal system of truths. But this idea need not frighten us. Even in the advanced sciences, like those of mathematics and physics, advance is made by entertaining different points of view and hypotheses, and working upon different theories. The sciences present no fixed and closed orthodoxy.

And certainly in such an undertaking as education, we must employ the word "science" modestly and humbly; there is no subject in which the claim to be strictly scientific is more likely to suffer from pretence, and none in which it is more dangerous to set up a rigid orthodoxy, a standardized set of beliefs to be accepted by all. Since there is no one *thing* which is beyond question, education, and since there is no likelihood that there will be until society and hence schools have reached a dead monotonous uniformity of practice and aim, there cannot be one single science. As the working operations of schools differ, so must the intellectual theories devised from those operations. Since the practice of progressive education differs from that of the traditional schools, it would be absurd to suppose that the intellectual formulation and organization which fits one type will hold for the other. To be genuine, the science which springs from schools of the older and traditional type, must work upon that foundation, and endeavor to reduce its subject-matter and methods to principles such that their adoption will eliminate waste, conserve resources, and render the existing type of practice more effective. In the degree in which progressive schools mark a departure in their emphasis from old standards, as they do in freedom, individuality, activity, and a coöperative social medium the intellectual organization, the body of facts and principles which they may contribute must of necessity be different. At most they can only occasionally borrow from the "science" that is evolved on the basis of a different type of practice, and they can even then borrow only what is appropriate to their own special aims and processes. To discover how much is relevant is of course a real problem. But this is a very different thing from assuming

that the methods and results obtained under traditional scholastic conditions from the standard of science to which progressive schools must conform.

For example it is natural and proper that the theory of the
practices found in traditional schools should set great store by
tests and measurements. This theory reflects modes of school
administration in which marks, grading, classes, and promotions are important. Measurement of I.Q.'s and achievements are ways of making these operations more efficient.
It would not be hard to show that need for classification underlies the importance of testing for I.Q.'s. The aim
is to establish a norm. The norm, omitting statistical refinements, is essentially an average found by taking a sufficiently
large number of persons. When this average is found, any
given child can be rated. He comes up to it, falls below it,
or exceeds it, by an assignable quantity. Thus the application
of the results make possible a more precise classification than
did older methods which were by comparison hit and miss.
But what has all this to do with schools where individuality is
a primary object of consideration, and wherein the so-called
"class" becomes a grouping for social purposes and wherein
diversity of ability and experience rather than uniformity is
prized?

In the averaging and classificatory scheme some special
capacity, say in music, dramatics, drawing, mechanical skill
or any other art, appears only one along with a large number
of other factors, or perhaps does not appear at all in the list
of things tested. In any case, it figures in the final result
only as smoothed down, ironed out, against a large number
of other factors. In the progressive school, such an ability is a
distinctive resource to be utilized in the coöperative experience
of a group; to level it down by averaging it with other qualities until it simply counts in assigning to the individual child a
determinate point on a curve is simply hostile to the aim and
spirit of progressive schools.

Nor need the progressive educator be unduly scared by the
idea that science is constituted by quantitative results, and,
as it is often said, that whatever exists can be measured, for
all subjects pass through a qualitative stage before they arrive

at a quantitative one; and if this were the place it could be shown that even in the mathematical sciences quantity occupies a secondary place as compared with ideas of order which verge on the qualitative. At all events, *quality* of activity and of consequence is more important for the teacher than any quantitative element. If this fact prevents the development of a certain kind of science, it may be unfortunate. But the educator cannot sit down and wait till there are methods by which quality may be reduced to quantity; he must operate here and now. If he can organize his qualitative processes and results into some connected intellectual form, he is really advancing scientific method much more than if, ignoring what is actually most important, he devotes his energies to such unimportant by-products as may now be measured.

Moreover, even if it be true that everything which exists could be measured—if only we knew how—that which does *not* exist cannot be measured. And it is no paradox to say that the teacher is deeply concerned with what does not exist. For a progressive school is primarily concerned with growth, with a moving and changing process, with *transforming* existing capacities and experiences; what already exists by way of native endowment and past achievement is subordinate to what it may become. Possibilities are more important than what already exists, and knowledge of the latter counts only in its bearing upon possibilities. The place of measurement of achievements as a theory of education is very different in a static educational system from what it is in one which is dynamic, or in which the ongoing process of growing is the important thing.

The same principle applies to the attempt to determine objectives and select subject-matter of studies by wide collection and accurate measurement of data. If we are satisfied upon the whole with the aims and processes of existing society, this method is appropriate. If you want schools to perpetuate the present order, with at most an elimination of waste and with such additions as enable it to do better what it is already doing, then one type of intellectual method or "science" is indicated. But if one conceives that a social order different in quality and direction from the present is desirable and that schools should strive to educate with social change in view by producing individuals not complacent about what already exists, and equipped with desires and abilities to assist in transforming it, quite a different method and content is indicated for educational science.

While what has been said may have a tendency to relieve educators in progressive schools from undue anxiety about the criticism that they are unscientific—a criticism levelled from the point of view of theory appropriate to schools of quite a different purpose and procedure—it is not intended to exempt them from responsibility for contributions of an organized, systematic, intellectual quality. The contrary is the case. All new and reforming movements pass through a stage in which what is most evident is a negative phase, one of protest, of deviation, and innovation. It would be surprising indeed if this were not true of the progressive educational movement. For instance, the formality and fixity of traditional schools seemed oppressive, restrictive. Hence in a school which departs from these ideals and methods, freedom is at first most naturally conceived as removal of artificial and benumbing restrictions. Removal, abolition, are, however, negative things, so in time it comes to be seen that such freedom is no end in itself, nothing to be satisfied with and to stay by, but marks at most an opportunity to do something of a positive and constructive sort.

Now I wonder whether this earlier and more negative phase of progressive education has not upon the whole run its course, and whether the time has not arrived in which these schools are undertaking a more constructively organized function. One thing is sure: in the degree in which they enter upon organized constructive work, they are bound to make definite contributions to building up the theoretical or intellectual side of education. Whether this be called science or philosophy of education, I for one, care little; but if they do not *intellectually* organize their own work, while they may do much in making the lives of the children committed to them more joyous and more vital, they contribute only incidental scraps to the science of education.

The word organization has been freely used. This word

suggests the nature of the problem. Organization and administration are words associated together in the traditional scheme, hence organization conveys the idea of something external and set. But reaction from this sort of organization only creates a demand for another sort. Any genuine intellectual organization is flexible and moving, but it does not lack its own internal principles of order and continuity. An experimental school is under the temptation to improvise its subject-matter. It must take advantage of unexpected events and turn to account unexpected questions and interests. Yet if it permits improvisation to dictate its course, the result is a jerky, discontinuous movement which works against the possibility of making any important contribution to educational subject-matter. Incidents are momentary, but the use made of them should not be momentary or short-lived. They are to be brought within the scope of a developing whole of content and purpose, which is a whole because it has continuity and consecutiveness in its parts. There is no single subject-matter which all schools must adopt, but in every school there should be some significant subject-matters undergoing growth and formulation.

An illustration may help make clearer what is meant. Progressive schools set store by individuality, and sometimes it seems to be thought that orderly organization of subject-matter is hostile to the needs of students in their individual character. But individuality is something developing and to be continuously attained, not something given all at once and ready-made. It is found only in life-history, in its continuing growth; it is, so to say, a career and not just a fact discoverable at a particular cross section of life. It is quite possible for teachers to make such a fuss over individual children, worrying about their peculiarities, their likes and dislikes, their weaknesses and failures, so that they miss perception of real individuality, and indeed tend to adopt methods which show no faith in the power of individuality. A child's individuality cannot be found in what he does or in what he consciously likes at a given moment; it can be found only in the connected course of his actions. Consciousness of desire and purpose can be genuinely attained only toward the close of some fairly prolonged sequence of activities. Consequently some organization of subject-matter reached through a serial or consecutive course of doings, held together within the unity of progressively growing occupation or project, is the only means which corresponds to real individuality. So far is organization from being hostile to the principle of individuality.

Thus much of the energy that sometimes goes to thinking about individual children might better be devoted to discovering some worthwhile activity and to arranging the conditions under which it can be carried forward. As a child engages in this consecutive and cumulative occupation, then in the degree in which it contains valuable subject-matter, the realization or building up of his individuality comes about as a consequence, one might truly say, as a natural by-product. He finds and develops himself in what he does, not in isolation but by interaction with the conditions which contain and carry subject-matter. Moreover a teacher can find out immensely more about the real needs, desires, interests, capacities, and weaknesses of a pupil by observing him throughout the course of such consecutive activity than by any amount of direct prodding or of merely cross-sectional observation. And all observations are of necessity cross-sectional when made of a child engaged in a succession of disconnected activities.

Such a succession of unrelated activities does not provide, of course, the opportunity or content of building up an organized subject-matter. But neither do they provide for the development of a coherent and integrated self. Bare doing, no matter how active, is not enough. An activity or project must, of course, be within the range of the experience of pupils and connected with their needs—which is very far from being identical with any likes or desires which they can consciously express. This negative condition having been met, the test of a good project is whether it is sufficiently full and complex to demand a variety of responses from different children and permit each to go at it and make his contribution in a way which is characteristic of himself. The further test or mark of a good activity, educationally speaking, is that it have a sufficiently long time-span so that a series of endeavors and explorations are involved in it, and included in such a way that each step opens up a new field, raises new questions, arouses a demand for further knowledge, and suggests what to do next on the basis of what has been accomplished and the knowledge thereby gained. Occupational activities which meet these two conditions will of necessity result in not only amassing known subject-matter but in its organization. They simply cannot be carried on without resulting in some orderly collection and systematization of related facts and principles. So far is the principle of working toward organization of knowledge not hostile to the principles of progressive education that the latter cannot perform its functions without reaching out into such organization.

An exaggerated illustration, amounting to a caricature, may perhaps make the point clearer. Suppose there is a school in which pupils are surrounded with a wealth of material objects, apparatus, and tools of all sorts. Suppose they are simply asked what they would like to do and then told in effect to "go to it," the teacher keeping hands—and mind, too—off. *What* are they going to do? What assurance is there that what they do is anything more than the expression, and exhaustion, of a momentary impulse and interest? The supposition does not, you may say, correspond to any fact. But what are the implications of the opposite principle? Where can we stop as we get away from the principle contained in the illustration? Of necessity—and this is as true of the traditional school as of a progressive—the start, the first move, the initial impulse in action, must proceed from the pupil. You can lead a horse to water but you can't make him drink. But whence comes his idea of *what* to do? That must come from what he has already heard or seen; or from what he sees some other child doing. It comes as a suggestion from beyond himself, from the environment, he being not an originator of the idea and purpose but a vehicle through which his surroundings past and present suggest something to him. That such suggestions are likely to be chance ideas, soon exhausted, is highly probable. I think observation will show that when a child enters upon a really fruitful and consecutively developing activity, it is because, and in as far as, he has previously engaged in some complex and gradually unfolding activity which has left him a question he wishes to prove further or with the idea of some piece of work still to be accomplished to bring his occupation to completion. Otherwise he is at the mercy of chance suggestion, and chance suggestions are not likely to lead to anything significant or fruitful.

While in outward form, these remarks are given to show that the teacher, as the member of the group having the riper and fuller experience and the greater insight into the possibilities of continuous development found in any suggested project, has not only the right but the duty to suggest lines of activity, and to show that there need not be any fear of adult imposition provided the teacher knows children as well as subjects, their import is not exhausted in bringing out this fact. Their basic purport is to show that progressive schools by virtue of being progressive, and not in spite of that fact, are under the necessity of finding projects which involve an orderly development and inter-connection of subject-matter, since otherwise there can be no sufficiently complex and long-span undertaking. The opportunity and the need impose a responsibility. Progressive teachers may and can work out and present to other teachers for trial and criticism definite and organized bodies of knowledge, together with a listing of sources from which additional information of the same sort can be secured. If it is asked how the presentation of such bodies of knowledge would differ from the standardized texts of traditional schools, the answer is easy. In the first place, the material would be associated with and derived from occupational activities or prolonged courses of action undertaken by the pupils themselves. In the second place, the material presented would not be something to be literally followed by other teachers and students, but would be indications of the intellectual possibilities of this and that course of activity—statements on the basis of carefully directed and observed experience of the questions that have arisen in connection with them and of the kind of information found useful in answering them, and of where that knowledge can be had. No second experience would exactly duplicate the course of the first; but the presentation of material of this kind would liberate and direct the activities of any teacher in dealing with the distinctive emergencies and needs that would arise in re-undertaking the same general type of project. Further material thus developed would be added, and a large and yet free body of related subject-matter would gradually be built up.

As I have touched in a cursory manner upon the surface of a number of topics, it may be well in closing to summarize. In substance, the previous discussion has tried to elicit at least two contributions which progressive schools may make to that type of a science of education which corresponds to their own type of procedure. One is the development of organized subject-matter just spoken of. The other is a study of the conditions favorable to learning. As I have already said there are certain traits characteristic of progressive schools which are not ends in themselves but which are opportunities to be used. These reduce themselves to opportunities for *learning,* for gaining knowledge, mastering definite modes of skill or techniques, and acquiring socially desirable attitudes and habits—the three chief aspects of learning, I should suppose. Now of necessity the contribution from the side of traditional schools to this general topic is concerned chiefly with methods of teaching, or, if it passes beyond that point, to the methods of study adopted by students. But from the standpoint of progressive education, the question of method takes on a new and still largely untouched form. It is no longer a question of how the teacher is to instruct or how the pupil is to study. The problem is to find what conditions must be fulfilled in order that study and learning will naturally and necessarily take place, what conditions must be present so that pupils will make the responses which cannot help having learning as their consequence. The pupil's mind is no longer to be on study or learning. It is given to doing the things that the situation calls for, while learning is the result. The method of the teacher, on the other hand, becomes a matter of finding the conditions which call out self-educative activity, or learning, and of coöperating with the activities of the pupils so that they have learning as their consequence.

A series of constantly multiplying careful reports on conditions which experience has shown in actual cases to be favorable and unfavorable to learning would revolutionize the whole subject of method. The problem is complex and difficult. Learning involves, as just said, at least three factors: knowledge, skill, and character. Each of these must be studied. It requires judgment and art to select from the total circumstances of a case just what elements are the casual conditions of learning, which are influential, and which secondary or irrelevant. It requires candor and sincerity to keep track of failures as well as successes and to estimate the relative degree of success obtained. It requires trained and acute observation to note the indications of progress in learning, and even more to detect their causes—a much more highly skilled kind of observation than is needed to note the results of mechanically applied tests. Yet the progress of a science of education depends upon the systematic accumulation of just this sort of material. Solution of the problem of discovering the causes of learning is an endless process. But no advance will be made in the solution till a start is made, and the freer and more experimental character of progressive schools places the responsibility for making the start squarely upon them.

I hardly need remind you that I have definitely limited the field of discussion to one point: the relation of progressive education to the development of a science of education. As I began with questions, I end with one: Is not the time here when the progressive movement is sufficiently established so that it may now consider the intellectual contribution which it may make to the art of education, to the art which is the most difficult and the most important of all human arts?

SCIENCE AS SUBJECT-MATTER
AND AS METHOD *

One who, like myself, claims no expertness in any branch of natural science can undertake to discuss the teaching of science only at some risk of presumption. At present, however, the gap between those who are scientific specialists and those who are interested in science on account of its significance in life, that is to say, on account of its educational significance, is very great. Therefore I see no other way of promoting that mutual understanding so requisite for educational progress than for all of us frankly to state our own convictions, even if thereby we betray our limitations and trespass where we have no rights save by courtesy.

I suppose that I may assume that all who are much interested in securing for the sciences the place that belongs to them in education feel a certain amount of disappointment at the results hitherto attained. The glowing predictions made respecting them have been somewhat chilled by the event. Of course, this relative shortcoming is due in part to the unwillingness of the custodians of educational traditions and ideals to give scientific studies a fair show. Yet in view of the relatively equal opportunity accorded to science to-day compared with

* This selection appeared originally in *Science*, 1910.

its status two generations ago, this cause alone does not explain the unsatisfactory outcome. Considering the opportunities, students have not flocked to the study of science in the numbers predicted, nor has science modified the spirit and purport of all education in a degree commensurate with the claims made for it. The causes for this result are many and complex. I make no pretense of doing more than singling out what seems to me one influential cause, the remedy for which most lies with scientific men themselves. I mean that science has been taught too much as an accumulation of ready-made material with which students are to be made familiar, not enough as a method of thinking, an attitude of mind, after the pattern of which mental habits are to be transformed.

Among the adherents of a literary education who have contended against the claims of science, Matthew Arnold has, I think, been most discreetly reasonable. He freely admitted the need of men knowing something, knowing a good deal, about the natural conditions of their own lives. Since, so to say, men have to breathe air, it is advisable that they should know something of the constitution of air and of the mechanism of the lungs. Moreover, since the sciences have been developed by human beings, an important part of humanistic culture, of knowing the best that men have said and thought, consists in becoming acquainted with the contributions of the great historic leaders of science.

These concessions made, Matthew Arnold insisted that the important thing, the indispensable thing in education, is to become acquainted with human life itself, its art, its literature, its politics, the fluctuations of its career. Such knowledge, he contended, touches more closely our offices and responsibilities as human beings, since these, after all, are to human beings and not to physical things. Such knowledge, moreover, lays hold of the emotions and the imagination and modifies character, while knowledge about things remains an inert possession of speculative intelligence.

Those who believe, nevertheless, that the sciences have a part to play in education equal—at the least—to that of literature and language, have perhaps something to learn from this contention. If we regard science and literary culture as just so much subject-matter, is not Mr. Arnold's contention essentially just? Conceived from this standpoint, knowledge of human affairs couched in personal terms seems more important and more intimately appealing than knowledge of physical things conveyed in impersonal terms. One might well object to Arnold that he ignored the place of natural forces and conditions *in* human life and thereby created an impossible dualism. But it would not be easy to deny that knowledge of Thermopylae knits itself more readily into the body of emotional images that stir men to action than does the formula for the acceleration of a flying arrow; or that Burns's poem on the daisy enters more urgently and compellingly into the moving vision of life than does information regarding the morphology of the daisy.

The infinitely extensive character of natural facts and the universal character of the laws formulated about them is sometimes claimed to give science an advantage over literature. But viewed from the standpoint of education, this presumed superiority turns out a defect; that is to say, so long as we confine ourselves to the point of view of subject-matter. Just because the facts of nature are multitudinous, inexhaustible, they begin nowhere and end nowhere in particular, and hence are not, just as facts, the best material for the education of those whose lives are centered in quite local situations and whose careers are irretrievably partial and specific. If we turn from multiplicity of detail to general laws, we find indeed that the laws of science are universal, but we also find that for educational purposes their universality means abstractness and remoteness. The conditions, the interests, the ends of conduct are irredeemably concrete and specific. We do not live in a medium of universal principles, but by means of adaptations, through concessions and compromises, struggling as best we may to enlarge the range of a concrete here and now. So far as acquaintance is concerned, it is the individualized and the humanly limited that helps, not the bare universal and the inexhaustibly multifarious.

These considerations are highly theoretical. But they have very practical counterparts in school procedure. One of the most serious difficulties that confronts the educator who wants in good faith to do something worth while with the sciences is their number, and the indefinite bulk of the material in each. At times, it seems as if the educational availability of science were breaking down because of its own sheer mass. There is at once so much of science and so many sciences that educators oscillate, helpless, between arbitrary selection and teaching a little of everything. If any one questions this statement, let him consider in elementary education the fortunes of nature-study for the last two decades.

Is there anything on earth, or in the waters under the earth or in the heavens above, that distracted teachers have not resorted to? Visit schools where they have taken nature study conscientiously. This school moves with zealous bustle from leaves to flowers, from flowers to minerals, from minerals to stars, from stars to the raw materials of industry, thence back to leaves and stones. At another school you find children energetically striving to keep up with what is happily termed the "rolling year." They chart the records of barometer and thermometer; they plot changes and velocities of the winds; they exhaust the possibilities of colored crayons to denote the ratio of sunshine and cloud in successive days and weeks; they keep records of the changing heights of the sun's shadows; they do sums in amounts of rainfalls and atmospheric humidities—and at the end, the rolling year, like the rolling stone, gathers little moss.

Is it any wonder that after a while teachers yearn for the limitations of the good old-fashioned studies—for English grammar, where the parts of speech may sink as low as seven but never rise above nine; for text-book geography, with its strictly inexpansive number of continents; even for the war campaigns and the lists of rulers in history since they can not be stretched beyond a certain point, and for "memory gems" in literature, since a single book will contain the "Poems Every Child Should Know."

There are many who do not believe it amounts to much one way or the other what children do in science in the elementary school. I do not agree, for upon the whole, I believe the attitude toward the study of science is, and should be, fixed during the earlier years of life. But in any case, how far does the situation in the secondary schools differ from that just described? Any one who has followed the discussions of college faculties for the last twenty-five years concerning entrance requirements in science, will be able to testify that the situation has been one of highly unstable equilibrium between the claims of a little of a great many sciences, a good deal (comparatively) of one, a combination of one biological and one exact science, and the arbitrary option of the pupil of one, two or three out of a list of six or seven specified sciences. The only safe generalization possible is that whatever course a given institution pursues, it changes that course at least as often as the human organism proverbially renews its issues. The movement has probably tended in the direction of reduction, but every one who has followed the history of pedagogical discussion will admit that every alteration of opinion as to what subjects should be taught has been paralleled by a modification of opinion as to the portions of any subject to be selected and emphasized.

All this change is to some extent a symptom of healthy activity, change being especially needed in any group of studies so new that they have to blaze their own trail, since they have no body of traditions upon which to fall back as is the case with study of language and literature. But this principle hardly covers the whole field of change. A considerable part of it has been due not to intelligent experimentation and exploration, but to blind action and reaction, or to the urgency of some strenuous soul who has propagated some emphatic doctrine.

Imagine a history of the teaching of the languages which should read like this: "The later seventies and early eighties of the nineteenth century witnessed a remarkable growth in the attention given in high schools to the languages. Hundreds of schools adopted an extensive and elaborate scheme by means of which almost the entire linguistic ground was covered. Each of the three terms of the year was devoted to a language. In the first year, Latin and Greek and Sanskrit were covered; in the next, French, German and Italian; while the last year was given to review and to Hebrew and Spanish as optional studies."

This piece of historic parallelism raises the question as to the real source of the educational value of, say, Latin. How much is due to its being a "humanity," its giving insight into the best the world has thought and said, and how much to its being pursued continuously for at least four years? How much to the graded and orderly arrangement that this long period both permitted and compelled? How much to the cumulative effort of constant recourse to what had earlier been learned, not by way of mere monotonous repetition, but as a necessary instrument of later achievement? Are we not entitled to conclude that the method demanded by the study is the source of its efficacy rather than anything inhering in its content?

Thus we come around again to the primary contention of the paper: that science teaching has suffered because science has been so frequently presented just as so much ready-made knowledge, so much subject-matter of fact and law, rather than as the effective method of inquiry into any subject-matter.

Science might well take a leaf from the book of the actual, as distinct from the supposititious, pursuit of the classics in the schools. The claim for their worth has professedly rested upon their cultural value; but imaginative insight into human affairs has perhaps been the last thing, save *per accidens,* that the average student has got from his pursuit of the classics. His time has gone of necessity to the mastering of a language, not to appreciation of humanity. To some extent just because of this enforced simplification (not to say meagerness) the student acquires, if he acquires anything, a certain habitual method. Confused, however, by the tradition that the subject-matter is the efficacious factor, the defender of the sciences has thought that he could make good his case only on analogous grounds, and hence has been misled into resting his claim upon the superior significance of his special subject-matter; even into efforts to increase still further the scope of scientific subject-matter in education. The procedure of Spencer is typical. To urge the prerogative of science, he raised the question what knowledge, what facts, are of most utility for life, and, answering the question by this criterion of the value of subject-matter, decided in favor of the sciences. Having thus identified education with the amassing of information, it is not a matter of surprise that for the rest of his life he taught that comparatively little is to be expected from education in the way of moral training and social reform, since the motives of conduct lie in the affections and the aversions, not in the bare recognition of matters of fact.

Surely if there is any knowledge which is of most worth it is knowledge of the ways by which anything is entitled to be called knowledge instead of being mere opinion or guesswork or dogma.

Such knowledge never can be learned by itself; it is not information, but a mode of intelligent practise, an habitual disposition of mind. Only by taking a hand in the making of knowledge, by transferring guess and opinion into belief authorized by inquiry, does one ever get a knowledge of the method of knowing. Because participation in the making of knowledge has been scant, because reliance on the efficacy of acquaintance with certain kinds of facts has been current, science has not accomplished in education what was predicted for it.

We define science as systematized knowledge, but the definition is wholly ambiguous. Does it mean the body of facts, the subject-matter? Or does it mean the processes by which something fit to be called knowledge is brought into existence, and order introduced into the flux of experience? That science means both of these things will doubtless be the reply, and rightly. But in the order both of time and of importance, science as method precedes science as subject-matter. Systematized knowledge is science only because of the care and thoroughness with which it has been sought for, selected and arranged. Only by pressing the courtesy of language beyond what is decent can we term such information as is acquired ready-made, without active experimenting and testing, science.

The force of this assertion is not quite identical with the

commonplace of scientific instruction that text-book and lecture are not enough; that the student must have laboratory exercises. A student may acquire laboratory methods as so much isolated and final stuff, just as he may so acquire material from a text-book. One's mental attitude is not necessarily changed just because he engages in certain physical manipulations and handles certain tools and materials. Many a student has acquired dexterity and skill in laboratory methods without its ever occurring to him that they have anything to do with constructing beliefs that are alone worthy of the title of knowledge. To do certain things, to learn certain modes of procedure, are to him just a part of the subject-matter to be acquired; they belong, say, to chemistry, just as do the symbols H_2SO_4 or the atomic theory. They are part of the arcana in process of revelation to him. In order to proceed in the mystery one has, of course, to master its ritual. And how easily the laboratory becomes liturgical! In short, it is a problem and a difficult problem to conduct matters so that the technical methods employed in a subject shall become conscious instrumentalities of realizing the meaning of knowledge—what is required in the way of thinking and of search for evidence before anything passes from the realm of opinion, guess work and dogma into that of knowledge. Yet unless this perception accrues, we can hardly claim that an individual has been instructed in science. This problem of turning laboratory technique to intellectual account is even more pressing than that of utilization of information derived from books. Almost every teacher has had drummed into him the inadequacy of mere book instruction, but the conscience of most is quite at peace if only pupils are put through some laboratory exercises. Is not this the path of experiment and induction by which science develops?

I hope it will not be supposed that, in dwelling upon the relative defect and backwardness of science teaching I deny its absolute achievements and improvements, if I go on to point out to what a comparatively slight extent the teaching of science has succeeded in protecting the so-called educated public against recrudescences of all sorts of corporate superstitions and silliness. Nay, one can go even farther and say that science teaching not only has not protected men and women who have been to school from the revival of all kinds of occultism, but to some extent has paved the way for this revival. Has not science revealed many wonders? If radio-activity is a proved fact, why is not telepathy highly probable? Shall we, as a literary idealist recently pathetically inquired, admit that mere brute matter has such capacities and deny them to mind? When all allowance is made for the unscrupulous willingness of newspapers and magazines to publish any marvel of so-called scientific discovery that may give a momentary thrill of sensation to any jaded reader, there is still, I think, a large residuum of published matter to be accounted for only on the ground of densely honest ignorance. So many things have been vouched for by science; so many things that one would have thought absurd have been substantiated, why not one more, and why not *this* one more? Communication of science as subject-matter has so far outrun in education the construction of a scientific habit of mind that to some extent the natural common sense of mankind has been interfered with to its detriment.

Something of the current flippancy of belief and quasi-scepticism must also be charged to the state of science teaching. The man of even ordinary culture is aware of the rapid changes of subject-matter, and taught so that he believes subject-matter, not method, constitutes science, he remarks to himself that if this is science, then science is in constant change, and there is no certainty anywhere. If the emphasis had been put upon method of attack and mastery, from this change he would have learned the lesson of curiosity, flexibility and patient search; as it is, the result too often is a blasé satiety.

I do not mean that our schools should be expected to send forth their students equipped as judges of truth and falsity in specialized scientific matters. But that the great majority of those who leave school should have some idea of the kind of evidence required to substantiate given types of belief does not seem unreasonable. Nor is it absurd to expect that they should go forth with a lively interest in the ways in which knowledge is improved and a marked distaste for all conclusions reached in disharmony with the methods of scientific inquiry. It would be absurd, for example, to expect any large number to master the technical methods of determining distance, direction and position in the arctic regions; it would perhaps be possible to develop a state of mind with American people in general in which the supposedly keen American sense of humor would react when it is proposed to settle the question of reaching the pole by aldermanic resolutions and straw votes in railway trains or even newspaper editorials.

If in the foregoing remarks I have touched superficially upon some aspects of science teaching rather than sounded its depths, I can not plead as my excuse failure to realize the importance of the topic. One of the only two articles that remain in my creed of life is that the future of our civilization depends upon the widening spread and deepening hold of the scientific habit of mind; and that the problem of problems in our education is therefore to discover how to mature and make effective this scientific habit. Mankind so far has been ruled by things and by words, not by thought, for till the last few moments of history, humanity has not been in possession of the conditions of secure and effective thinking. Without ignoring in the least the consolation that has come to men from their literary education, I would even go so far as to say that only the gradual replacing of a literary by a scientific education can assure to man the progressive amelioration of his lot. Unless we master things, we shall continue to be mastered by them: the magic that words cast upon things may indeed disguise our subjection or render us less dissatisfied with it, but after all science, not words, casts the only compelling spell upon things.

Scientific method is not just a method which it has been found profitable to pursue in this or that abstruse subject for purely technical reasons. It represents the only method of thinking that has proved fruitful in any subject—that is what we mean when we call it scientific. It is not a peculiar development of thinking for highly specialized ends; it is thinking so far as thought has become conscious of its proper ends and of the equipment indispensable for success in their pursuit.

The modern warship seems symbolic of the present position of science in life and education. The warship could not exist were it not for science: mathematics, mechanics, chemistry, electricity supply the technique of its construction and management. But the aims, the ideals in whose service this marvelous technique is displayed are survivals of a pre-scientific age, that is, of barbarism. Science has as yet had next to nothing to do with forming the social and moral ideals for the sake of which she is used. Even where science has received its most attentive recognition, it has remained a servant of ends imposed from alien traditions. If ever we are to be governed by intelligence, not by things and by words, science must have something to say about *what* we do, and not merely about *how* we may do it most easily and economically. And if this consummation is achieved, the transformation must occur through education, by bringing home to men's habitual inclination and attitude the significance of genuine knowledge and the full import of the conditions requisite for its attainment. Actively to participate in the making of knowledge is the highest prerogative of man and the only warrant of his freedom. When our schools truly become laboratories of knowledge-making, not mills fitted out with information-hoppers, there will no longer be need to discuss the place of science in education.

V

Psychology
and
Education

WHAT PSYCHOLOGY
CAN DO FOR THE TEACHER *

The value of any fact or theory as bearing on human activity is, in the long run, determined by practical application—that is, by using it for accomplishing some definite purpose. If it works well—if it removes friction, frees activity, economizes effort, makes for richer results—it is valuable as contributing to a perfect adjustment of means to end. If it makes no such contribution it is practically useless, no matter what claims may be theoretically urged in its behalf. To this the question of the relation between psychology and education presents no exception. The value of a knowledge of psychology in general, or of the psychology of a particular subject, will be best made known by its fruits. No amount of argument can settle the question once for all and in advance of any experimental work. But, since education is a rational process, that is a process in harmony with the laws of psychical development, it is plain that the educator need not and should not depend upon vague inductions from a practice not grounded upon principles. Psychology can not dispense with experience, nor can experience, if it is to be rational, dispense

* This selection appeared originally in a book by John Dewey and James A. McLellan, *The Psychology of Number*, 1895.

with psychology. It is possible to make actual practice less a matter of mere experiment and more a matter of reason; to make it contribute directly and economically to a rich and ripe, because rational, experience. And this the educational psychologist attempts to do by indicating in what directions help is likely to be found; by indicating what kind of psychology is likely to help and what is not likely; and, finally, by indicating what valid reasons there are for anticipating any help at all.

I. As to the last point suggested, that psychology *ought* to help the educator, there can be no disagreement. In the *first place* the study of psychology has a high *disciplinary* value for the teacher. It develops the power of connected thinking and trains to logical habits of mind. These qualities, essential though they are in thorough teaching, there is a tendency to undervalue in educational methods of the present time when so much is made of the accumulation of facts and so little of their organization. In our eager advocacy of "facts and things" we are apparently forgetting that these are comparatively worthless, either as stored knowledge or for developing power, till they have been subjected to the discriminating and formative energy of the intelligence. Unrelated facts are not knowledge any more than the words of a dictionary are connected thoughts. And so the work of getting "things" may be carried to such an extent as to burden the mind and check the growth of its higher powers. There may be a surfeit of things with the usual consequence of an impaired mental digestion. It is pretty generally conceded that the number of facts memorized is by no means a measure of the amount of power developed; indeed, unless reflection has been exercised step by step with observation, the mass of power gained may turn out to be inversely proportional to the multitude of facts. This does not mean that there is any opposition between reflection and true observation. There can not be observation in the best sense of the word without reflection, nor can reflection fail to be an effective preparation for observation.

It will be readily admitted that this tendency to exalt facts unduly may be checked by the study of psychology. Here, in a comparatively abstract science, there *must* be reflec-tion—abstraction and generalization. In nature study we gather the facts, and we *may* reflect upon the facts: in mind study we must reflect in order to get the facts. To observe the subtle and complex facts of mind, to discriminate the elements of a consciousness never the same for two successive moments, to give unity of meaning to these abstract mental phenomena, demands such concentration of attention as must secure the growth of mental power—power to master, and not be mastered by, the facts and ideas of whatever kind which may be crowding in upon the mind; to resolve a com-plex subject into its component parts, seizing upon the most important and holding them clearly defined and related in consciousness; to take, in a word, any "chaos" of experience and reduce it to harmony and system. This analytic and relat-ing power, which is an essential mark of the clear thinker, is the prime qualification of the clear teacher.

But, in the *second place,* the study of psychology is of still more value to the teacher in its bearing upon his *practical* or strictly professional training.

Every one grants that the primary aim of education is the training of the powers of intelligence and will—that the ob-ject to be attained is a certain quality of character. To say that the purpose of education is "an increase of the powers of the mind rather than an enlargement of its possessions"; that education is a science, the science of the formation of char-acter; that character means a measure of mental power, mas-tery of truths and laws, love of beauty in nature and in art, strong human sympathy, and unswerving moral rectitude; that the teacher is a trainer of mind, a former of character; that he is an artist above nature, yet in harmony with nature, who applies the science of education to help another to the full realization of his personality in a character of strength, beauty, freedom—to say this is simply to proclaim that the problem of education is essentially an ethical and psychologi-cal problem. This problem can be solved only as we know the true nature and destination of man as a rational being, and the rational methods by which the perfection of his na-ture may be realized. Every aim proposed by the educator which is not in harmony with the intrinsic aim of human nature itself, every method or device employed by the teacher that is not in perfect accord with the mind's own workings, not only wastes time and energy, but results in positive and permanent harm; running counter to the true activities of the mind, it certainly distorts and may possibly destroy them. To the educator, therefore, the only solid ground of assurance that he is not setting up impossible or artificial aims, that he is not using ineffective and perverting methods, is a clear and definite knowledge of the normal end and the normal forms of mental action. To know these things is to be a true psychologist and a true moralist, and to have the essential qualifications of the true educationist. Briefly, only psychology and ethics can take education out of its purely empirical and rule-of-thumb stage. Just as a knowledge of mathematics and mechanics have wrought marvelous improvements in all the arts of construction; just as a knowledge of steam and electricity has made a revolution in modes of communication, travel, and transportation of commodities; just as a knowledge of anatomy, physiology, pathology has transformed medicine from empiricism to applied science, so a knowledge of the structure and functions of the human being can alone elevate the school from the position of a mere workshop, a more or less cumbrous, uncertain, and even baneful institution, to that of a vital, certain, and effective instrument in the greatest of all constructions—the building of a free and powerful character.

Without the assured methods and results of science there are just three resources available in the work of education.

1. The first is *native tact and skill,* the intuitive power that comes mainly from sympathy. For this personal power there is absolutely no substitute. "Any one can keep school," perhaps, but not every one can teach school any more than every one can become a capable painter, or an able engineer, or a skilled artist in any direction. To ignore native aptitude, and to depend wholly, or even chiefly, upon the knowledge and use of "methods," is an error fatal to the best interests of education; and there can be no question that many schools are suffering frightfully from ignoring or undervaluing this

paramount qualification of the true teacher. But in urging the need of psychology in the preparation of the teacher there is no question of ignoring personal power or of finding a substitute for personal magnetism. It is only a question of providing the best opportunities for the exercise of native capacity—for the fullest development and most fruitful application of endowments of heart and brain. Training and native outfit, culture and nature, are never opposed to each other. It is always a question, not of suppressing or superseding, but of cultivating native instinct, of training natural equipment to its ripest development and its richest use. A Pheidias does not despise learning the principles necessary to the mastery of his art, nor a Beethoven disregard the knowledge requisite for the complete technical skill through which he gives expression to his genius. In a sense it is true that the great artist is born, not made; but it is equally true that a scientific insight into the technics of his art *helps* to make him. And so it is with the artist teacher. The greater and more scientific his knowledge of human nature, the more ready and skilful will be his application of principles to varying circumstances, and the larger and more perfect will be the product of his artistic skill.

But the genius in education is as rare as the genius in other realms of human activity. Education is, and forever will be, in the hands of ordinary men and women; and if psychology—as the basis of scientific insight into human nature—is of high value to the few who possess genius, it is indispensable to the many who have not genius. Fortunately for the race, most persons, though not "born" teachers, are endowed with some "genial impulse," some native instinct and skill for education; for the cardinal requisite in this endowment is, after all, sympathy with human life and its aspirations. We are all born to be educators, to be parents, as we are not born to be engineers, or sculptors, or musicians, or painters. Native capacity for education is therefore much more common than native capacity for any other calling. Were it not so, human society could not hold together at all. But in most people this native sympathy is either dormant or blind and irregular in its action; it needs to be awakened, to be cultivated, and above all to be intelligently directed. The instinct to walk, to speak, and the like are imperious instincts, and yet they are not wholly left to "nature"; we do not assume that they will take care of themselves; we stimulate a guide, we supply them with proper conditions and material for their development. So it must be with this instinct, so common yet at present so comparatively ineffective, which lies at the heart of all educational efforts, the instinct to help others in their struggle for self-mastery and self-expression. The very fact that this instinct is so strong, and all but universal, and that the happiness of the individual and of the race so largely depends upon its development and intelligent guidance, gives greater force to the demand that its growth may be fostered by favourable conditions; and that it may be made certain and reasonable in its action, instead of being left blind and faltering, as it surely will be without rational cultivation.

To this it may be added that native endowment can work itself out in the best possible results only when it works under right conditions. Even if scientific insight were not a necessity for the true educator himself, it would still remain a necessity for others in order that they might not obstruct and possibly drive from the profession the teacher possessed of the inborn divine light, and restrict or paralyze the efforts of the teacher less richly endowed. It is the mediocre and the bungler who can most readily accommodate himself to the conditions imposed by ignorance and routine; it is the higher type of mind and heart which suffers most from its encounter with incapacity and ignorance. One of the greatest hindrances to true educational progress is the reluctance of the best class of minds to engage in educational work precisely because the general standard of ethical and psychological knowledge is so low that too often high ideals are belittled and efforts to realize them even vigorously opposed. The educational genius, the earnest teacher of any class, has little to expect from an indifference, or a stolidity, which is proof alike against the facts of experience and the demonstrations of science.

2. The Second Resource is *experience*. This, again, is necessary. Psychology is not a short and easy path that renders

personal experience superfluous. The real question is: What kind of experience shall it be? It is in a way perfectly true that only by teaching can one become a teacher. But not any and every sort of thing which passes for teaching or for "experience" will make a teacher any more than simply sawing a bow across violin strings will make a violinist. It is a certain quality of practice, not mere practice, which produces the expert and the artist. Unless the practice is based upon rational principles, upon insight into facts and their meaning, "experience" simply fixes incorrect acts into wrong habits. Nonscientific practice, even if it finally reaches sane and reasonable results—which is very unlikely—does so by unnecessarily long and circuitous routes; time and energy are wasted that might easily be saved by wise insight and direction at the outset.

The worst thing about empiricism in every department of human activity is that it leads to a blind observance of rule and routine. The mark of the empiric is that he is helpless in the face of new circumstances; the mark of the scientific worker is that he has power in grappling with the new and the untried; he is master of principles which he can effectively apply under novel conditions. The one is a slave of the past, the other is a director of the future. This attachment to routine, this subservience to empiric formula, always reacts into the character of the empiric; he becomes hour by hour more and more a mere routinist and less and less an artist. Even that which he has once learned and applied with some interest and intelligence tends to become more and more mechanical, and its application more and more an unintelligent and unemotional procedure. It is never brightened and quickened by adaptation to new ends. The machine teacher, like the empiric in every profession, thus becomes a stupefying and corrupting influence in his surroundings; he himself becomes a mere tradesman, and makes his school a mere machine shop.

3. The Third Resource is *authoritative instruction in methods and devices*. At present, the real opposition is not between native skill and experience on the one side, and psychological methods on the other; it is rather between devices

picked up no one knows how, methods inherited from a crude past, or else invented, *ad hoc,* by educational quackery—and methods which can be rationally justified—devices which are the natural fruit of knowing the mind's powers and the ways in which it works and grows in assimilating its proper nutriment. The mere fact that there are so many methods current, and constantly pressed upon the teacher as the acme of the educational experience of the past, or as the latest and best discovery in pedagogy, makes an absolute demand for some standard by which they may be tested. Only knowledge of the principles upon which all methods are based can free the teacher from dependence upon the educational nostrums which are recommended like patent medicines, as panaceas for all educational ills. If a teacher is one fairly initiated into the real workings of the mind, if he realizes its normal aims and methods, false devices and schemes can have no attraction for him; he will not swallow them "as silly people swallow empirics' pills"; he will reject them as if by instinct. All new suggestions, new methods, he will submit to the infallible test of science; and those which will further his work he can adopt and rationally apply, seeing clearly their place and bearings, and the conditions under which they can be most effectively employed. The difference between being overpowered and used by machinery and being able to use the machinery is precisely the difference between methods externally inculcated and methods freely adopted, because of insight into the psychological principles from which they spring.

Summing up, we may say that the teacher requires a sound knowledge of ethical and psychological principles—first, because such knowledge, besides its indirect value as forming logical habits of mind, is necessary to secure the full use of native skill; secondly, because it is necessary in order to attain a perfected experience with the least expenditure of time and energy; and thirdly, in order that the educator may not be at the mercy of every sort of doctrine and device, but may have his own standard by which to test the many methods and expedients constantly urged upon him, selecting those which stand the test and rejecting those which do not, no matter by what authority or influence they may be supported.

II. We may now consider more positively how psychology is to perform this function of developing and directing native skill, making experience rational and hence prolific of the best results, and providing a criterion for suggested devices.

Education has two main phases which are never separated from each other, but which it is convenient to distinguish. One is concerned with the organization and workings of the school as part of an organic whole; the other, with the adaptation of this school structure to the individual pupil. This difference may be illustrated by the difference in the attitude of the school board or minister of education or superintendent, whether state, county, or local, to the school, and that of the individual teacher within the school. The former (the administrators of an organized system) are concerned more with the constitution of the school as a whole; their survey takes in a wide field, extending in some cases from the kindergarten to the university throughout an entire country, in other cases from the primary school to the high or academic school in a given town or city. Their chief business is with the organization and management of the school, or system of schools, upon certain general principles. What shall be the end and means of the entire institution? What subjects shall be studied? At what stage shall they be introduced, and in what sequence shall they follow one another—that is, what shall be the arrangement of the school as to its various parts in time? Again, what shall be the correlation of studies and methods at every period? Shall they be taught as different subjects? in departments? or shall methods be sought which shall work them into an organic whole? All this lies, in a large measure, outside the purview of the individual teacher; once within the institution he finds its purpose, its general lines of work, its constitutional structure, as it were, fixed for him. An individual may choose to live in France, or Great Britain, or the United States, or Canada; but after he has made his choice, the general conditions under which he shall exercise his citizenship are decided for him. So it is, in the main, with the individual teacher.

But the citizen who lives within a given system of institutions and laws finds himself constantly called upon to act. He must adjust his interests and activities to those of others in the same country. There is, at the same time, scope for purely individual selection and application of means to ends, for unfettered action of strong personality, as well as opportunity and stimulus for the free play and realization of individual equipment and acquisition. The better the constitution, the system which he can not directly control, the wider and freer and more potent will be this sphere of individual action. Now, the individual teacher finds his duties within the school as an entire institution; he has to adapt this organism, the subjects taught, the modes of discipline, etc., to the individual pupil. Apart from this personal adaptation on the part of the individual teacher, and the personal assimilation on the part of the individual pupil, the general arrangement of the school is purely meaningless; it has its object and its justification in this individual realm. Geography, arithmetic, literature, etc., may be provided in the curriculum, and their order, both of sequence and coexistence, laid down; but this is all dead and formal until it comes to the intelligence and character of the individual pupil, and the individual teacher is *the medium through which it comes.*

Now, the bearing of this upon the point in hand is that psychology and ethics have to subserve these two functions. These functions, as already intimated, can not be separated from each other; they are simply the general and the individual aspects of school life; but for purposes of study, it is convenient and even important to distinguish them. We may consider psychology and ethics from the standpoint of the light they throw upon the organization of the school as a whole—its end, its chief methods, the order and correlation of studies—and we may consider from the standpoint of the service they can perform for the individual teacher in qualifying him to use the prescribed studies and methods intelligently and efficiently, the insight they can give him into the workings of the individual mind, and the relation of any given subject to that mind.

Next to positive doctrinal error within the pedagogy itself, it may be said that the chief reason why so much of current pedagogy has been either practically useless or even practically harmful is the failure to distinguish these two functions of psychology. Considerations, principles, and maxims that derive their meaning, so far as they have any meaning, from their reference to the organization of the whole institution, have been presented as if somehow the individual teacher might derive from them specific information and direction as to how to teach particular subjects to particular pupils; on the other hand, methods that have their value (if any) as simple suggestions to the individual teacher as to how to accomplish temporary ends at a particular time have been presented as if they were eternal and universal laws of educational polity. As a result the teacher is confused; he finds himself expected to draw particular practical conclusions from very vague and theoretical educational maxims (e.g., proceed from the whole to the part, from the concrete to the abstract), or he finds himself expected to adopt as rational principles what are mere temporary expedients. It is, indeed, advisable that the teacher should understand, and even be able to criticise, the general principles upon which the whole educational system is formed and administered. He is not like a private soldier in an army, expected merely to obey, or like a cog in a wheel, expected merely to respond to and transmit external energy; he must be an intelligent medium of action. But only confusion can result from trying to get principles or devices to do what they are not intended to do—to adapt them to purposes for which they have no fitness.

In other words, the existing evils in pedagogy, the prevalence of merely vague principles upon one side and of altogether too specific and detailed methods (expedients) upon the other, are really due to failure to ask what psychology is called upon to do, and upon failure to present it in such a form as will give it undoubted value in practical applications.

III. This brings us to the positive question: In what forms can psychology best do the work which it ought to do?

1. *The Psychical Functions Mature in a Certain Order.*— When development is normal the appearance of a certain impulse or instinct, the ripening of a certain interest, always prepares the way for another. A child spends the first six months of his life in learning a few simple adjustments; his

instincts to reach, to see, to sit erect assert themselves, and
are worked out. These at once become tools for further activities; the child has now to use these acquired powers as
means for further acquisitions. Being able, in a rough way, to
control the eye, the arm, the hand, and the body in certain
positions in relation to one another, he now inspects, touches,
handles, throws what comes within reach; and thus getting a
certain amount of physical control, he builds up for himself
a simple world of objects.

But his instinctive bodily control goes on asserting itself;
he continues to gain in ability to balance himself, to co-
ordinate, and thus control, the movements of his body. He
learns to manage the body, not only at rest, but also in mo-
tion—to creep and to walk. Thus he gets a further means of
growth; he extends his acquaintance with things, daily widening his little world. He also, through moving about, goes from
one thing to another—that is, makes simple and crude *connection*s of objects, which become the basis of subsequent relating and generalizing activities. This carries the child to the
age of twelve or fifteen months. Then another instinct, already in occasional operation, ripens and takes the lead—
that of imitation. In other words, there is now the attempt to
adjust the activities which the child has already mastered to
the activities which he sees exercised by others. He now en-
deavours to make the simple movements of hand, of vocal
organs, etc., already in his possession the instruments of reproducing what his eye and his ear report to him of the world
about him. Thus he learns to talk and to repeat many of the
simple acts of others. This period lasts (roughly) till about
the thirtieth month. These attainments, in turn, become the
instruments of others. The child has now control of all his
organs, motor and sensory. The next step, therefore, is to relate these activities to one another consciously, and not simply unconsciously as he has hitherto done. When, for example,
he sees a block, he now sees in it the possibility of a whole
series of activities, of throwing, building a house, etc. The
head of a broken doll is no longer to him the mere thing directly before his senses. It symbolizes "some fragment of his
dream of human life." It arouses in consciousness an entire

group of related actions; the child strokes it, talks to it, sings it to sleep, treats it, in a word, as if it were the perfect doll. When this stage is reached, that of ability to see in a partial activity or in a single perception, a whole system or circuit of relevant actions and qualities, the imagination is in active operation; the period of symbolism, of recognition of meaning, of significance, has dawned.

But the same general process continues. Each function as it matures, and is vigorously exercised, prepares the way for a more comprehensive and a deeper conscious activity. All education consists in seizing upon the dawning activity and in presenting the material, the conditions, for promoting its best growth—in making it work freely and fully towards its proper end. Now, even in the first stages, the wise foresight and direction of the parent accomplish much, far more indeed than most parents are ever conscious of; yet the activities at this stage are so simple and so imperious that, given any chance at all, they work themselves out in some fashion or other. But when the stage of conscious recognition of meaning, of conscious direction of action, is reached, the process of development is much more complicated; many more possibilities are opened to the parent and the teacher, and so the demand for proper conditions and direction becomes indefinitely greater. Unless the right conditions and direction are supplied, the activities do not freely express themselves; the weaker are thwarted and die out; among the stronger an unhappy conflict wages and results in abnormal growth; some one impulse, naturally stronger than others, asserts itself out of all proportion, and the person "runs wild," becomes wilful, capricious, irresponsible in action, and unbalanced and irregular in his intellectual operations.

Only knowledge of the order and connection of the stages in the development of the psychical functions can, negatively, guard against these evils, or, positively, insure the full meaning and free, yet orderly or law-abiding, exercise of the psychical powers. In a word, education itself is precisely the work of supplying the conditions which will enable the psychical functions, as they successively arise, to mature and pass into higher functions in the freest and fullest manner, and this result can be secured only by knowledge of the process—that is, only by a knowledge of psychology.

The so-called psychology, or pedagogical psychology, which fails to give this insight, evidently fails of its value for educational purposes. This failure is apt to occur for one or the other of two reasons: either because the psychology is too vague and general, not bearing directly upon the actual evolution of psychical life, or because, at the other extreme, it gives a mass of crude, particular, undigested facts, with no indicated bearing or interpretations:

1. The psychology based upon a doctrine of "faculties" of the soul is a typical representative of the first sort, and educational applications based upon it are necessarily mechanical and formal; they are generally but plausible abstractions, having little or no direct application to the practical work of the classroom. The mind having been considered as split up into a number of independent powers, pedagogy is reduced to a set of precepts about the "cultivation" of these powers. These precepts are useless, in the first place, because the teacher is confronted not with abstract faculties, but with living individuals. Even when the psychology teaches that there is a unity binding together the various faculties, and that they are not really separate, this unity is presented in a purely external way. It is not shown in what way the various so-called faculties are the expressions of one and the same fundamental process. But, in the second place, this "faculty" psychology is not merely negatively useless for the educator, it is positively false, and therefore harmful in its effects. The psychical reality is that continuous growth, that unfolding of a single functional principle already referred to. While perception, memory, imagination and judgment are not present in complete form from the first, one physical activity is present, which, as it becomes more developed and complex, manifests itself in these processes as stages of its growth. What the educator requires, therefore, is not vague information about these mental powers in general, but a clear knowledge of the underlying single activity and of the conditions under which it differentiates into these powers.

2. The value for educational purposes of the mere presen-

tation of unrelated facts, of anecdotes of child life, or even of particular investigations into certain details, may be greatly exaggerated. A great deal of material which, even if intelligently collected, is simply data for the scientific specialist, is often presented as if educational practice could be guided by it. Only *interpreted* material, that which reveals general principles or suggests the lines of growth to which the educator has to adapt himself, can be of much practical avail; and the interpreter of the facts of the child mind must begin with knowing the facts of the adult mind. Equally in mental evolution as in physical, nature makes no leaps. "The child is father of the man" is the poetic statement of a psychologic fact.

3. *Every Subject Has Its Own Psychological Place and Method.*—Every special subject, geography, for instance, represents a certain grouping of facts, classified on the basis of *the mind's attitude towards these facts.* In the thing itself, in the actual world, there is organic unity; there is no division in the facts of geology, geography, zoölogy, and botany. These facts are not externally sorted out into different compartments. They are all bound up together; the facts are many, but the thing is *one*. It is simply some interest, some urgent need of man's activities, which discriminates the facts and unifies them under different heads. *Unless the fundamental interest and purpose which underlie this classification are discovered and appealed to, the subject which deals with it can not be presented along the lines of least resistance and in the most fruitful way.* This discovery is the work of psychology. In geography, for example, we deal with certain classes of facts, not merely in themselves, but from the standpoint of their influence in the development and modification of human activities. A mountain range or a river, treated simply as mountain range or river, gives us geology; treated in relation to the distribution of genera of plants and animals, it has a biological interpretation; treated as furnishing conditions which have entered into and modified human activities—grazing, transportation of commodities, fixing political boundaries, etc.—it acquires a geographical significance.

In other words, the unity of geography is a certain unity of human action, a certain human interest. Unless, therefore, geographical data are presented in such a way as to appeal to this interest, the method of teaching geography is uncertain, vacillating, confusing; it throws the movement of the child's mind into lines of great, rather than of least, resistance, and leaves him with a mass of disconnected facts and a feeling of unreality in presence of which his interest dies out. All method means adaptation of means to a certain end; if the end is not grasped there is no rational principle for the selection of means; the method is haphazard and empirical—a chance selection from a bundle of expedients. But the elaboration of this interest, the discovery of the concrete ways in which the mind realizes it, is unquestionably the province of psychology. There are certain definite modes in which the mind images to itself the relation of environment and human activity in production and exchange; there is a certain order of growth in this imagery; to know this is psychology; and, once more, to know this is to be able to direct the teaching of geography rationally and fruitfully, and to secure the best results, both in culture and discipline, that can be had from the study of the subject.

Application to Arithmetic.—In the following pages an attempt has been made to present the psychology of number from this point of view. Number represents a certain interest, a certain psychical demand; it is not a bare property of facts, but is a certain way of interpreting and arranging them —a certain method of construing them. What is the interest, the demand, which gives rise to the psychical activity by which objects are taken as numbered or measured? And how does this activity develop? In so far as we can answer these questions we have a sure guide to methods of instruction in dealing with number. We have a positive basis for testing and criticising various proposed methods and devices; we have only to ask whether they are true to this specific activity, whether they build upon it and further it. In addition to this we have a standard at our disposal for setting forth correct methods; we have but to translate the theory of mental activity in this direction—the psychical nature of number and the problem of its origin—over into its practical meaning.

Knowing the nature and origin of number and numerical properties as psychological facts, the teacher knows how the mind works in the construction of number, and is prepared to help the child to think number: is prepared to use a method, helpful to the normal movement of the mind. In other words, rational method in arithmetic must be based on the psychology of number.

WHY REFLECTIVE THINKING
MUST BE AN EDUCATIONAL AIM *

I. The Values of Thinking

IT MAKES POSSIBLE ACTION WITH A CONSCIOUS AIM

We all acknowledge, in words at least, that ability to think is highly important; it is regarded as the distinguishing power that marks man off from the lower animals. But since our ordinary notions of how and why thinking is important are vague, it is worth while to state explicitly the values possessed by reflective thought. In the first place, it emancipates us from merely impulsive and merely routine activity. Put in positive terms, thinking enables us to direct our activities with foresight and to plan according to ends-in-view, or purposes of which we are aware. It enables us to act in deliberate and intentional fashion to attain future objects or to come into command of what is now distant and lacking. By putting the consequences of different ways and lines of action before the mind, it enables us to *know what we are about* when we act. *It converts action that is merely appetitive, blind, and impulsive into intelligent action.* A brute animal, as far as we know, is pushed on from behind; it is moved in accordance with its present physiological state by some present external stimulus. The being who can think is moved

* From *How We Think: A Restatement of the Relation of Reflective Thinking to the Educative Process*, 1933.

by remote considerations, by results that can be attained perhaps only after a lapse of years—as when a young person sets out to gain a professional education to fit himself for a career in years to come.

For example, an animal without thought will go into its hole when rain threatens, because of some immediate stimulus to its organism. But a thinking being will perceive that certain given facts are probable signs of a future rain and will take steps in the light of this anticipated future. To plant seeds, to cultivate the soil, to harvest grain, are intentional acts, possible only to a being who has learned to subordinate the immediately felt elements of an experience to those values which these elements hint at and prophesy. Philosophers have made much of the phrases 'book of nature,' 'language of nature.' Well, it is in virtue of thought that given things are significant of absent things and that nature speaks a language which may be interpreted. To a being who thinks, things are records of their past, as fossils tell of the prior history of the earth, and are prophetic of their future, as from the present positions of heavenly bodies remote eclipses are foretold. Shakespeare's "tongues in trees, books in the running brooks," expresses literally enough the power superadded to existences when they are used by a thinking being. Only when things about us have meaning for us, only when they signify consequences that can be reached by using them in certain ways, is any such thing as intentional, deliberate control of them possible.

IT MAKES POSSIBLE SYSTEMATIC PREPARATIONS AND INVENTIONS

By thought man also develops and arranges artificial signs to remind him in advance of consequences and of ways of securing and avoiding them. As the trait just mentioned makes the difference between savage man and brute; so this trait makes the difference between civilized man and savage. A savage who has been shipwrecked on a river may note certain things that serve him as signs of danger in the future. But civilized man deliberately *makes* such signs; he sets up in ad-

vance of any particular shipwreck warning buoys, and builds
lighthouses where he sees signs that such an event may occur.
A savage reads weather signs with great expertness; civilized man institutes a weather service by which signs are artificially secured and information is distributed in advance of
the appearance of any signs that could be detected without
special methods. A savage finds his way skillfully through a
wilderness by reading certain obscure indications; civilized
man builds a highway that shows the road to all. The savage
learns to detect the signs of fire and thereby to invent methods of producing flame; civilized man discovers illuminating
gas and oils, and invents lamps, electric lights, stoves, fur-
naces, central heating plants, etc. The very essence of civilized culture is that we deliberately erect monuments and
memorials, lest we forget; and deliberately institute, in advance of the happening of various contingencies and emergencies of life, devices for detecting their approach and regis-
tering their nature, for warding off what is unfavorable, or
at least for protecting ourselves from its full impact and for
making more secure and extensive what is favorable. All
forms of artificial apparatus are intentional modifications of
natural things so designed that they may serve better than
in their natural estate to indicate the hidden, the absent, and
the remote.

IT ENRICHES THINGS WITH MEANINGS

Finally, thought confers upon physical events and objects a
very different status and value from those which they possess
to a being that does not reflect. These words are mere
scratches, curious variations of light and shade, to one to
whom they are not linguistic signs. To him for whom they are
signs of other things, the collection of marks stands for some
idea or object. We are so used to the fact that things have
meaning for us, that they are not mere excitations of sense
organs, that we fail to recognize that they are charged with
the significance they have only because in the past absent
things have been suggested to us by what is present and these
suggestions have been confirmed in subsequent experience. If

we stumble against something in the dark, we may react to it and get out of the way to save ourselves a bruise or a tumble without recognizing what particular *object* it is. We react almost automatically to many stimuli; they have no meaning for us or are not definite individual objects. For an *object* is more than a mere *thing;* it is a thing having a definite significance.

The distinction we are making can be most readily understood if the reader will call to mind things and events that are strange to him and compare them with the same things and events as they appear to persons having expert knowledge of them; or if he will compare a thing or event as it is *before,* with what it is *after,* he has obtained intellectual mastery over it. To a layman a particular body of water may signify only something to wash with or to drink; to another person it may stand for a union of two chemical elements, themselves not liquids but gases; or it may signify something that should *not* be drunk because of danger of typhoid fever. To a baby things are at first only patterns of color and light, sources of sound; they acquire meaning only as they become signs of possible, but not yet present and actual, experiences. To the learned scientific man, the range of meanings possessed by ordinary things is much widened. A stone is not merely a stone; it is a stone of a given mineralogical type, from a particular geological stratum, etc. It tells him something about what happened millions of years ago, and helps paint the picture of the earth's history.

CONTROL AND ENRICHED VALUE

The first two values mentioned are of a practical sort; they give increased power of *control*. The value just mentioned is an enrichment of meaning apart from added control—a certain event in the heavens cannot be warded off just because we know it is an eclipse and how it is produced, but it does have a significance for us that it did not have before. We may not need to do any thinking now when some event occurs, but if we have thought about it before, the outcome of that thinking is funded as a directly added and deepened meaning of the event. The great reward of exercising the power of thinking is that there are no limits to the possibility of carrying over into the objects and events of life, meanings originally acquired by thoughtful examination, and hence no limit to the continual growth of meaning in human life. A child to-day may see meanings in things that were hidden from Ptolemy and Copernicus because of the results of reflective investigations that have occurred in the meantime.

Various values of the power of thought are summed up in the following quotation from John Stuart Mill.

> To draw inferences has been said to be the great business of life. Every one has daily, hourly, and momentary need of ascertaining facts which he has not directly observed: not from any general purpose of adding to his stock of knowledge, but because the facts themselves are of importance to his interests or to his occupations. The business of the magistrate, of the military commander, of the navigator, of the physician, of the agriculturist, *is merely to judge of evidence and to act accordingly.* . . . As they do this well or ill, so they discharge well or ill the duties of their several callings. *It is the only occupation in which the mind never ceases to be engaged.*[1]

TWO REASONS FOR TRAINING THOUGHT

These three values, in their cumulative effect, make the difference between a truly human and rational life and the existence lived by those animals that are immersed in sensation and appetite. Beyond a somewhat narrow limit, enforced by the necessities of life, the values that have been described do not, however, automatically realize themselves. For anything approaching their adequate realization, thought needs careful and attentive educational direction. Nor is that the whole story. Thinking may develop in positively wrong ways and lead to false and harmful beliefs. The need of systematic training would be less than it is if the only danger to be

---

[1] Mill, *System of Logic,* Introduction, § 5.

feared were lack of any development; the evil of the wrong kind of development is even greater.

An earlier writer than Mill, John Locke (1632-1704), brings out the importance of thought for life and the need of training so that its best and not its worst possibilities will be realized, in the following words:

> No man ever sets himself about anything but upon some view or other, which serves him for a reason for what he does; and whatsoever faculties he employs, the understanding with such light as it has, well or ill informed, constantly leads; and by that light, true or false, all his operative powers are directed. . . . Temples have their sacred images, and we see what influence they have always had over a great part of mankind. But in truth the ideas and images in men's minds are the invisible powers that constantly govern them, and to these they all, universally, pay a ready submission. It is therefore of the highest concernment that great care should be taken of the understanding, to conduct it aright in the search of knowledge and in judgments it makes.[2]

While the power of thought, then, frees us from servile subjection to instinct, appetite, and routine, it also brings with it the occasion and possibility of error and mistake. In elevating us above the brute, it opens the possibility of failures to which the animal, limited to instinct, cannot sink.

II. Tendencies Needing Constant Regulation

PHYSICAL AND SOCIAL SANCTIONS
OF CORRECT THINKING

Up to a certain point, the necessities of life enforce a fundamental and persistent discipline of thought for which the most cunningly devised artifices would be ineffective substitutes. The burnt child dreads the fire; a painful consequence emphasizes the need of correct inference much more than

---

[2] Locke, *The Conduct of the Understanding*, first paragraph.

would learned discourses on the properties of heat. Social conditions also put a premium on correct inference in matters where action based on valid thought is socially important. These sanctions of proper thinking may affect life itself, or at least a life reasonably free from perpetual discomfort. The signs of enemies, of shelter, of food, of the main social conditions, have to be correctly apprehended.

But this disciplinary training, efficacious as it is within certain limits, does not carry us far. Logical attainment in one direction is no bar to extravagant conclusions in another. A savage who is expert in judging the movements and location of the animals that he hunts will accept and gravely narrate the most preposterous yarns concerning the origin of their habits and peculiarities of structure. When there is no direct appreciable reaction of the inference upon the security and prosperity of life, there are no natural checks to the acceptance of wrong beliefs. Conclusions may be accepted merely because the suggestions are vivid and interesting, while a large accumulation of dependable data may fail to suggest a proper conclusion because of opposition from existing customs. Then there is a 'primitive credulity,' a natural tendency to believe anything that is suggested unless there is overpowering evidence to the contrary. It sometimes seems, upon surveying the history of thought, that men exhausted pretty much all wrong forms of belief before they hit upon the right conceptions. The history of scientific beliefs also shows that when a wrong theory once gets general acceptance, men will expend ingenuity of thought in buttressing it with additional errors rather than surrender it and start in a new direction: witness for example the elaborate pains taken to preserve the Ptolemaic theory of the solar system. Even today correct beliefs about the constitution of nature are held by the great multitude merely because they are current and popular rather than because the multitude understands the reasons upon which they rest.

SUPERSTITION IS AS NATURAL AS SCIENCE

As to the mere function of suggestion, there is no difference between the power of a column of mercury to portend rain and that of the entrails of an animal or the flight of birds to foretell the fortunes of war. For all anybody can tell in advance, the spilling of salt is as likely to import bad luck as the bite of a mosquito to import malaria. Only systematic regulation of the conditions under which observations are made and severe discipline of the habits of entertaining suggestions can secure a decision that one type of belief is vicious and the other sound. The substitution of scientific for superstitious habits of inference has not been brought about by any improvement in the acuteness of the senses or in the natural workings of the function of suggestion. It is the result of regulation *of the conditions* under which observation and inference take place. When such regulation is absent, dreams, the position of stars, the lines of the hand, are regarded as valuable signs, and the fall of cards as an inevitable omen, while natural events of the most crucial significance go disregarded. Hence beliefs in portents of various kinds, now mere nook-and-cranny superstitions, were once universal. A long discipline in exact science was required for their conquest.

THE GENERAL CAUSES OF
BAD THINKING: BACON'S "IDOLS"

It is instructive to note some of the attempts that have been made to classify the main sources of error in reaching beliefs. Francis Bacon, for example, at the beginning of modern scientific inquiry, enumerated four such classes, under the somewhat fantastic title of "idols" (Gr. $\epsilon\check{\iota}\delta\omega\lambda\alpha$, images), spectral forms that allure the mind into false paths. These he called the idols, or phantoms, of (*a*) the tribe, (*b*) the market place, (*c*) the cave or den, and (*d*) the theatre; or, less metaphorically, (*a*) standing erroneous methods (or at least temptations to error) that have their roots in human nature generally, (*b*) those that come from intercourse and language,

(c) those that are due to causes peculiar to a specific individual, and finally, (d) those that have their sources in the fashion or general current of a period. Classifying these causes of fallacious belief somewhat differently, we may say that two are intrinsic and two are extrinsic. Of the intrinsic, one is common to all men alike (such as the universal tendency to notice instances that corroborate a favorite belief more readily than those that contradict it), while the other resides in the specific temperament and habits of the given individual. Of the extrinsic, one proceeds from generic social conditions—like the tendency to suppose that there is a fact wherever there is a word, and no fact where there is no linguistic term—while the other proceeds from local and temporary social currents.

LOCKE ON TYPICAL FORMS OF WRONG BELIEF

Locke's method of dealing with typical forms of wrong belief is less formal and may be more enlightening. We can hardly do better than quote his forcible and quaint language, when, enumerating different classes of men, he shows different ways in which thought goes wrong.

(a) The first is of those who seldom reason at all, but do and think according to the example of others, whether parents, neighbors, ministers, or who else they are pleased to make choice of to have an implicit faith in, for the saving of themselves the pains and troubles of thinking and examining for themselves.

(b) This kind is of those who put passion in the place of reason, and being resolved that shall govern their actions and arguments, neither use their own, nor hearken to other people's reason, any farther than it suits their humor, interest, or party.[3]

---

[3] In another place Locke says: "Men's prejudices and inclinations impose often upon themselves. . . . Inclination suggests and slides into discourse favorable terms, which introduce favorable ideas; till at last by this means that is concluded clear and evident, thus dressed up, which, taken in its native state, by making use of none but precise determined ideas, would find no admittance at all."

(*c*) The third sort is of those who readily and sincerely follow reason, but for want of having that which one may call large, sound, roundabout sense, have not a full view of all that relates to the question. . . . They converse but with one sort of men, they read but one sort of books, they will not come in the hearing but of one sort of notions. . . . They have a pretty traffic with known correspondents in some little creek . . . but will not venture out into the great ocean of knowledge. [Men of originally equal natural parts may finally arrive at very different stores of knowledge and truth] when all the odds between them has been the different scope that has been given to their understandings to range in, for the gathering up of information and furnishing their heads with ideas and notions and observations, whereon to employ their mind.[4]

In another portion of his writings,[5] Locke states the same ideas in slightly different form.

1. That which is inconsistent with our *principles* is so far from passing for probable with us that it will not be allowed possible. The reverence borne to these principles is so great, and their authority so paramount to all other, that the testimony, not only of other men, but the evidence of our own senses are often rejected, when they offer to vouch anything contrary to these *established rules*. . . . There is nothing more ordinary than children's receiving into their minds propositions . . . from their parents, nurses, or those about them; which being insinuated in their unwary as well as unbiased understandings, and fastened by degrees, are at last (and this whether true or false) riveted there by long custom and education, beyond all possibility of being pulled out again. For men, when they are grown up, reflecting upon their opinions and finding those of this sort to be as ancient in their minds as their very memories, not having observed their early insinuation, nor by what means they got them,

---

[4] *The Conduct of the Understanding,* § 3.
[5] *Essay Concerning Human Understanding,* Bk. IV, Ch. XX, "Of Wrong Assent or Error."

they are apt to reverence them as sacred things, and not to suffer them to be profaned, touched, or questioned. [They take them as standards] to be the great and unerring deciders of truth and falsehood, and the judges to which they are to appeal in all manner of controversies.

2. Secondly, next to these are men whose understandings are cast into a mold, and fashioned just to the size of a received hypothesis. [Such men, while not denying the existence of facts and evidence, cannot be convinced even by the evidence that would decide them if their minds were not so closed by adherence to fixed belief.]

3. Predominant Passions. Thirdly, probabilities which cross men's appetites and prevailing passions run the same fate. Let ever so much probability hang on one side of a covetous man's reasoning, and money on the other, it is easy to foresee which will outweigh. Earthly minds, like mud walls, resist the strongest batteries.

4. Authority. The fourth and last wrong measure of probability I shall take notice of, and which keeps in ignorance or error more people than all the others together, is the giving up our assent to the common received opinions, either of our friends or party, neighborhood or country.

IMPORTANCE OF ATTITUDES

We have quoted from influential thinkers of the past. But the facts to which they refer are familiar in our everyday experience. Any observant person can note any day, both in himself and in others, the tendency to believe that which is in harmony with desire. We take that to be true which we should like to have so, and ideas that go contrary to our hopes and wishes have difficulty in getting lodgment. We all jump to conclusions; we all fail to examine and test our ideas because of our personal attitudes. When we generalize, we tend to make sweeping assertions; that is, from one or only a few facts we make a generalization covering a wide field. Observation also reveals the powerful influence wielded by social influences that have actually nothing to do with the truth or falsity of what is asserted and denied. Some of the dispositions that give these irrelevant influences power to limit and mislead thought are good in themselves, a fact that renders the need of training the more important. Reverence for parents and regard for those placed in authority are in the abstract surely valuable traits. Yet, as Locke points out, they are among the chief forces that determine beliefs apart from and even contrary to the operations of intelligent thought. The desire to be in harmony with others is in itself a desirable trait. But it may lead a person too readily to fall in with the prejudices of others and may weaken his independence of judgment. It even leads to an extreme partisanship that regards it as disloyal to question the beliefs of a group to which one belongs.

Because of the importance of attitudes, ability to train thought is not achieved merely by knowledge of the best forms of thought. Possession of this information is no guarantee for ability to think well. Moreover, there are no set exercises in correct thinking whose repeated performance will cause one to be a good thinker. The information and the exercises are both of value. But no individual realizes their value except as he is personally animated by certain dominant attitudes in his own character. It was once almost universally believed that the mind had faculties, like memory and attention, that could be developed by repeated exercise, as gymnastic exercises are supposed to develop the muscles. This belief is now generally discredited in the large sense in which it was once held. Similarly it is highly questionable whether the practice of thinking in accordance with some logical formula results in creation of a general habit of thinking; namely, one applicable over a wide range of subjects. It is a matter of common notice that men who are expert thinkers in their own special fields adopt views on other matters without doing the inquiring that they know to be necessary for substantiating simpler facts that fall within their own specialties.

THE UNION OF ATTITUDE AND SKILLED METHOD

What can be done, however, is to cultivate those *attitudes* that are favorable to the use of the best methods of inquiry and testing. Knowledge of the methods alone will not suffice; there must be the desire, the will, to employ them. This desire is an affair of personal disposition. But on the other hand the disposition alone will not suffice. There must also be understanding of the forms and techniques that are the channels through which these attitudes operate to the best advantage. Since these forms and techniques will be taken up for discussion later, we shall here mention the attitudes that need to be cultivated in order to secure their adoption and use.

   a. Open-mindedness. This attitude may be defined as freedom from prejudice, partisanship, and such other habits as close the mind and make it unwilling to consider new problems and entertain new ideas. But it is something more active and positive than these words suggest. It is very different from empty-mindedness. While it *is* hospitality to new themes, facts, ideas, questions, it is not the kind of hospitality that would be indicated by hanging out a sign: "Come right in; there is nobody at home." It includes an active desire to listen to more sides than one; to give heed to facts from whatever source they come; to give full attention to alternative possibilities; to recognize the possibility of error even in the beliefs that are dearest to us. Mental sluggishness is one great factor in closing the mind to new ideas. The path of least resistance and least trouble is a mental rut already made. It requires troublesome work to undertake the alteration of old beliefs. Self-conceit often regards it as a sign of weakness to admit that a belief to which we have once committed ourselves is wrong. We get so identified with an idea that it is literally a 'pet' notion and we rise to its defense and stop our mental eyes and ears to anything different. Unconscious fears also drive us into purely defensive attitudes that operate like a coat of armor not only to shut out new conceptions but even to prevent us from making a new observation. The cumulative effect of these forces is to shut in the mind, and to create a withdrawal from new intellectual contacts that are needed for learning. They can best be fought by cultivating that alert curiosity and spontaneous outreaching for the new which is the essence of the open mind. The mind that is open merely in the sense that it passively permits things to trickle in and through will not be able to resist the factors that make for mental closure.

b. Whole-heartedness. When anyone is thoroughly interested in some object and cause, he throws himself into it; he does so, as we say, 'heartily,' or with a whole heart. The importance of this attitude or disposition is generally recognized in practical and moral affairs. But it is equally important in intellectual development. There is no greater enemy of effective thinking than divided interest. This division unfortunately is often produced in school. A pupil gives an external, perfunctory attention to the teacher and to his book and lesson while his inmost thoughts are concerned with matters more attractive to him. He pays attention with ear or eye, but his brain is occupied with affairs that make an immediate appeal. He feels obliged to study because he has to recite, to pass an examination, to make a grade, or because he wishes to please his teacher or his parents. But the material does not hold him by its own power. His approach is not straightforward and single-minded. This point may in some cases seem trivial. But in others it may be very serious. It then contributes to the formation of a general habit or attitude that is most unfavorable to good thinking.

When a person is absorbed, the subject carries him on. Questions occur to him spontaneously; a flood of suggestions pour in on him; further inquiries and readings are indicated and followed; instead of having to use his energy to hold his mind to the subject (thereby lessening that which is available for the subject, itself, and creating a divided state of mind), the material holds and buoys his mind up and gives an onward impetus to thinking. A genuine enthusiasm is an attitude that operates as an intellectual force. A teacher who arouses such an enthusiasm in his pupils has done something that no amount of formalized method, no matter how correct, can accomplish.

c. Responsibility. Like sincerity or whole-heartedness, responsibility is usually conceived as a moral trait rather than as an intellectual resource. But it is an attitude that is necessary to win the adequate support of desire for new points of view and new ideas and of enthusiasm for and capacity for absorption in subject matter. These gifts may run wild, or at least they may lead the mind to spread out too far. They do not of themselves ensure that centralization, that unity, which is essential to good thinking. To be intellectually responsible is to consider the consequences of a projected step; it means to be willing to adopt these consequences when they follow reasonably from any position already taken. Intellectual responsibility secures integrity; that is to say, consistency and harmony in belief. It is not uncommon to see persons continue to accept beliefs whose logical consequences they refuse to acknowledge. They profess certain beliefs but are unwilling to commit themselves to the consequences that flow from them. The result is mental confusion.The 'split' inevitably reacts upon the mind to blur its insight and weaken its firmness of grasp; no one can use two inconsistent mental standards without losing some of his mental grip. When pupils study subjects that are too remote from their experience, that arouse no active curiosity, and that are beyond their power of understanding, they begin to use a measure of value and of reality for school subjects different from the measure they employ for affairs of life that make a vital appeal. They tend to become intellectually irresponsible; they do not ask for the *meaning* of what they learn, in the sense of what difference it makes to the rest of their beliefs and to their actions.

The same thing happens when such a multitude of subjects or disconnected facts is forced upon the mind that the student does not have time and opportunity to weigh their meaning. He fancies he is accepting them, is believing them, when in fact his belief is of a totally different kind and implies a different measure of reality from that which operates in his life and action out of school. He then becomes mentally mixed; mixed not only about particular things but also about the basic reasons that make things worthy of belief. Fewer subjects and fewer facts and more responsibility for thinking the material of those subjects and facts through to realize what they involve would give better results. To carry something through to completion is the real meaning of thoroughness, and power to carry a thing through to its end or conclusion is dependent upon the existence of the attitude of intellectual responsibility.

THE BEARING OF THESE PERSONAL ATTITUDES
UPON THE READINESS TO THINK

The three attitudes that have been mentioned, openmindedness, whole-hearted or absorbed interest, responsibility in facing consequences, are of themselves personal qualities, traits of character. They are not the only attitudes that are important in order that the *habit* of thinking in a reflective way may be developed. But the other attitudes that might be set forth are also traits of character, attitudes that, in the proper sense of the word, are *moral,* since they are traits of personal character that have to be cultivated. Any person thinks at times on particular subjects that arouse him. Other persons have habits of thinking quite persistently in special fields of interest; on matters, for example, that are their professional concern. A thoroughgoing habit of thinking is, however, more extended in its scope. No one can think about everything, to be sure; no one can think about *any*thing without experience and information about it. Nevertheless, there is such a thing as *readiness* to consider in a thoughtful way the subjects that do come within the range of experience—a readiness that contrasts strongly with the disposition to pass judgment on the basis of mere custom, tradition, prejudice, etc., and thus shun the task of thinking. The personal attitudes that have been named are essential constituents of this general readiness.

If we were compelled to make a choice between these personal attitudes and knowledge about the principles of logical reasoning together with some degree of technical skill in manipulating special logical processes, we should decide for the former. Fortunately no such choice has to be made, because there is no opposition between personal attitudes and logical processes. We only need to bear in mind that, with respect to the aims of education, no separation can be made between impersonal, abstract principles of logic and moral qualities of character. What is needed is to weave them into unity.

SCHOOL CONDITIONS AND THE
TRAINING OF THOUGHT *

I. Introductory: Methods and Conditions

FORMAL DISCIPLINE *versus* REAL THINKING

The so-called "faculty psychology" went hand in hand with the vogue of the formal-discipline idea in education. If thought is a distinct piece of mental machinery, separate from observation, memory, imagination, and common-sense judgments of persons and things, then thought should be trained by special exercises designed for the purpose, as one might devise special exercises for developing the biceps muscles. Certain subjects are then to be regarded as intellectual or logical subjects *par excellence,* possessed of a predestined fitness to exercise the thought faculty, just as certain machines are better than others for developing arm power. With these three notions goes the fourth, that method consists of a set of operations by which the machinery of thought is set going and kept at work upon any subject matter.

We have tried to make it clear in the previous chapters that there is no single and uniform power of thought, but a multitude of different ways in which specific things—things observed, remembered, heard of, read about—evoke suggestions or ideas that are pertinent to a problem or question

---

* From *How We Think: A Restatement of the Relation of Reflective Thinking to the Educative Process,* 1933.

and that carry the mind forward to a justifiable conclusion. Training is that development of curiosity, suggestion, and habits of exploring and testing, which increases sensitiveness to questions and love of inquiry into the puzzling and unknown; which enhances the fitness of suggestions that spring up in the mind, and controls their succession in a developing and cumulative order; which makes more acute the sense of the force, the *proving* power, of every fact observed and suggestion employed. Thinking is not a separate mental process; it is an affair of the *way* in which the vast multitude of objects that are observed and suggested are employed, the way they run together and are *made* to run together, the way they are handled. Consequently any subject, topic, question, is intellectual not *per se* but because of the part it is made to play in directing thought in the life of any particular person.

THE TRAINING OF THOUGHT IS INDIRECT

For these reasons, the problem of *method* in forming habits of reflective thought is the problem of establishing *conditions* that will arouse and guide *curiosity;* of setting up the connections in things experienced that will on later occasions promote the flow of *suggestions,* create problems and purposes that will favor *consecutiveness* in the succession of ideas. These topics will be considered more at length later, but an illustration or two drawn from failure to secure proper conditions will indicate more clearly what is meant. Children are hushed up when they ask questions; their exploring and investigating activities are inconvenient and hence they are treated like nuisances; pupils are taught to memorize things so that merely one-track verbal associations are set up instead of varied and flexible connections with things themselves; no plans and projects are provided that compel the student to look ahead and foresee and in the execution of which the accomplishment of one thing sets up new questions and suggests new undertakings. The teacher may devise special exercises intended to train thinking directly, but when these wrong conditions exist, special exercises are doomed to be futile. The training of thought can be attained only by regulating the causes that evoke and guide it.

With respect to the training of habits of thought, the teacher's problem is thus twofold. On the one side, he needs (as we saw in the last chapter) to be a student of individual traits and habits; on the other side, he needs to be a student of the conditions that modify for better or worse the directions in which individual powers habitually express themselves. He needs to recognize that method covers not only what he intentionally devises and employs for the purpose of mental training, but also what he does without any conscious reference to it—anything in the atmosphere and conduct of the school that reacts in any way upon the curiosity, the responsiveness, and the orderly activity of children. The teacher who is an intelligent student both of individual mental operations and of the effects of school conditions upon those operations can largely be trusted to select for himself methods of instruction in their narrower and more technical sense—those best adapted to achieve results in particular subjects, such as reading, geography, or algebra. In the hands of one who is not intelligently aware of individual capacities and of the influence unconsciously exerted upon them by the entire environment, even the best of technical methods are likely to get an immediate result at the expense of forming deepseated and persistent *bad* habits.

GENERIC AND SPECIFIC CONDITIONS

There is always a temptation for the teacher to keep attention fixed upon a limited field of the pupil's activity. Is the student progressing in the particular topic in arithmetic, history, geography, etc., that is under consideration? When the teacher fixes his attention exclusively on such matters as these, the process of forming underlying and permanent habits, attitudes, and interests is overlooked. Yet the formation of the latter is the more important for the future. The other side of this fact is that the teacher, while fixing attention upon the *specific* conditions that seem to affect learning of the immedi-

ate lesson before the class, ignores the more general conditions that influence the creation of permanent attitudes,
especially the traits of character, open-mindedness, whole-
heartedness, and responsibility, mentioned in an earlier chapter. Postponing consideration of special points, we shall, accordingly, in the present chapter take up some of the more
generic conditions of the schoolroom that affect the development of effective mental habits.

II. The Influence of the Habits of Others

Bare reference to the imitativeness of human nature is
enough to suggest how profoundly the mental habits of others affect the attitude of the one being trained. Example is
more potent than precept, and a teacher's best conscious efforts may be more than counteracted by the influence of
personal traits that he is unaware of or that he regards as
unimportant. Methods of instruction and discipline that are
technically faulty may be rendered practically innocuous by
the inspiration of the personal method that lies back of them.

THE TEACHER A STIMULUS TO RESPONSE
IN INTELLECTUAL MATTERS

To confine, however, the conditioning influence of the educator, whether parent or teacher, to imitation is to get a
very superficial view of the intellectual influence of others.
Imitation is but one case of a deeper principle—that of stimulus and response. *Everything the teacher does, as well as the
manner in which he does it, incites the child to respond in
some way or other, and each response tends to set the child's
attitude in some way or other.* Even the inattention of the
child to the adult is often a response that is the result of
unconscious training.[1] The teacher is rarely (and even then
never entirely) a transparent medium of the access of an-

---

[1] A child of four or five who had been repeatedly called to the
house by his mother with no apparent response on his own part,
was asked if he did not hear her. He replied quite judicially, "Oh,
yes, but she doesn't call very mad yet."

other mind to a subject. With the young, the influence of the teacher's personality is intimately fused with that of the subject; the child does not separate or even distinguish the two. And as the child's response is *toward* or *away from* anything presented, he keeps up a running commentary, of which he himself is hardly distinctly aware, of like and dislike, of sympathy and aversion, not merely upon the acts of the teacher, but also upon the subject with which the teacher is occupied.

The extent and power of this influence upon morals and manners, upon character, upon habits of speech and social bearing, are almost universally recognized. But the tendency to conceive of thought as an isolated faculty often blinds teachers to the fact that this influence is just as real and pervasive in intellectual concerns. Teachers, as well as children, stick more or less to the main points, have more or less wooden and rigid methods of response, and display more or less intellectual curiosity about matters that come up. And every trait of this kind is an inevitable part of the teacher's method of teaching. Merely to accept without notice slipshod habits of speech, slovenly inferences, unimaginative and literal response, is to indorse these tendencies and to ratify them into habits—and so it goes throughout the whole range of contact between teacher and student. In this complex and intricate field, two or three points may well be singled out for special notice.

a. *Judging Others by Ourselves.* Most persons are quite unaware of the distinguishing peculiarities of their own mental habits. They take their own mental operations for granted and unconsciously make them the standard for judging the mental processes of others.[2] Hence there is a tendency to encourage whatever in the pupil agrees with this attitude and to neglect or fail to understand whatever is incongruous with it. The prevalent overestimation of the value, for mind

---

[2] People who have *number-forms*—i.e., who project number series into space and see them arranged in certain shapes—when asked why they have not mentioned the fact before, often reply that it never occurred to them; they supposed that everybody had the same habit.

training, of *theoretic* subjects as compared with practical pursuits, is doubtless due partly to the fact that the teacher's calling tends to select those persons in whom the theoretic interest is specially strong and to repel those in whom executive abilities are marked. Teachers sifted out on this basis judge pupils and subjects by a like standard, encouraging an intellectual one-sidedness in those to whom it is naturally congenial, and repelling from study those in whom practical instincts are more urgent.

b. Undue Reliance upon Personal Influence. Teachers— and this holds especially of the stronger and better teachers— tend to rely upon their personal strong points to hold a child to his work, and thereby to substitute their personal influence for that of subject matter as a motive for study. The teacher finds by experience that his own personality is often effective where the power of the subject to command attention is almost nil; then he utilizes the former more and more, until the pupil's relation to the teacher almost takes the place of his relation to the subject. In this way the teacher's personality may become for the pupil a source of personal dependence and weakness, an influence that renders the pupil indifferent to the value of the subject for its own sake.

c. Satisfying the Teacher instead of the Problem. The operation of the teacher's own mental habit tends, unless carefully watched and guided, to make the child a student of the teacher's peculiarities rather than of the subjects that he is supposed to study. His chief concern is to accommodate himself to what the teacher expects of him, rather than to devote himself energetically to the problems of subject matter. "Is this right?" comes to mean "Will this answer or this process satisfy the teacher?"—instead of meaning "Does it satisfy the inherent conditions of the problem?" It would be folly to deny the legitimacy or the value of the study of human nature that children carry on in school, but it is obviously undesirable that their chief intellectual problem should be to produce the answer approved by the teacher, and that their standard of success should be successful adaptation to the requirements of another person.

III. The Influence of the Nature of Studies

Studies are conventionally and conveniently grouped under these heads: (1) those especially involving the acquisition of skill in performance—the school arts, such as reading, writing, figuring, and music; (2) those mainly concerned with acquiring knowledge—"informational" studies, such as geography and history; and (3) those in which skill in doing and bulk of information are relatively less important, and appeal to abstract thinking, to "reasoning," is most marked—"disciplinary" studies, such as arithmetic and formal grammar.[3] Each of these groups of subjects has its own special pitfalls.

DISCIPLINARY STUDIES LIABLE TO LOSE CONTACT WITH THE PRACTICAL

In the case of the so-called disciplinary or preëminently logical studies, there is danger of the isolation of intellectual activity from the ordinary affairs of life. Teacher and student alike tend to set up a chasm between logical thought, as something abstract and remote, and the specific and concrete demands of everyday events. The abstract tends to become so aloof, so far away from application, as to be cut loose from practical and moral bearing. The gullibility of specialized scholars when out of their own lines, their extravagant habits of inference and speech, their ineptness in reaching conclusions in practical matters, their egotistical engrossment in their own subjects, are extreme examples of the bad effects of severing studies completely from their ordinary connections in life.

[3] Of course, any one subject has all three aspects; *e.g.,* in arithmetic, counting, reading and writing numbers, rapid adding, etc., are cases of skill in doing; the tables of weights and measures are a matter of information, etc.

SKILL STUDIES LIABLE TO BECOME
PURELY MECHANICAL

The danger in those studies where the main emphasis is upon acquisition of skill is just the reverse. The tendency is to take the shortest cuts possible to gain the required end. This makes the subjects *mechanical,* and thus restrictive of intellectual power. In the mastery of reading, writing, drawing, laboratory technique, etc., the need for economy of time and material, of neatness and accuracy, for promptness and uniformity, is so great that these things tend to become ends in themselves, irrespective of their influence upon general mental attitude. Sheer imitation, dictation of steps to be taken, mechanical drill, may give results most quickly and yet strengthen traits likely to be fatal to reflective power. The pupil is enjoined to do this and that specific thing, with no knowledge of any reason except that by so doing he gets his result most speedily; his mistakes are pointed out and corrected for him; he is kept at pure repetition of certain acts till they become automatic. Later, teachers wonder why the pupil reads with so little expression, and figures with so little intelligent consideration of the terms of his problem. In some educational dogmas and practices, the very idea of training the mind seems to be hopelessly confused with that of a drill which hardly touches *mind* at all—or touches it for the worse—since it is wholly taken up with training skill in external execution. This method reduces the "training" of human beings to the level of animal training. Practical skills, modes of effective technique, can be intelligently, nonmechanically *used* only when intelligence has played a part in their *acquisition.*

INFORMATIONAL STUDIES MAY FAIL
TO DEVELOP WISDOM

A false opposition is often set up also, especially in higher education, between information and understanding. One party insists that the acquisition of scholarship must come first, since intelligence can operate only on the basis of actual subject matter that is under control. The other party holds that scholarship for and by itself is at best an end only for the specialist, the graduate student, etc., and that the development of power to think is the chief thing. The real desideratum is getting command of scholarship—or skill—under conditions that *at the same time* exercise thought. The distinction between information and wisdom is old, and yet requires constantly to be redrawn. Information is knowledge that is merely acquired and stored up; wisdom is knowledge operating in the direction of powers to the better living of life. Information, merely as information, implies no special training of intellectual capacity; wisdom is the finest fruit of that training. In school, amassing information always tends to escape from the ideal of wisdom or good judgment. The aim often seems to be—especially in such a subject as geography —to make the pupil what has been called a "cyclopedia of useless information." "Covering the ground" is the primary necessity; the nurture of mind a bad second. Thinking cannot, of course, go on in a vacuum; suggestions and inferences can occur only to a mind that possesses information as to matters of fact.

But there is all the difference in the world whether the acquisition of information is treated as an end in itself, or is made an integral portion of the training of thought. The assumption that information that has been accumulated apart from use in the recognition and solution of a problem may later on be, at will, freely employed by thought is quite false. The skill at the ready command of intelligence is the skill acquired with the aid of intelligence; the only information which, otherwise than by accident, can be put to logical use is that acquired in the course of thinking. Because their knowledge has been achieved in connection with the needs of specific situations, men of little book-learning are often able to put to effective use every ounce of knowledge they possess; while men of vast erudition are often swamped by the mere bulk of their learning, because memory, rather than thinking, has been operative in obtaining it.

IV. The Influence of Current Aims and Ideals

It is, of course, impossible to separate this somewhat intangible condition from the points just dealt with; for automatic skill and quantity of information are educational ideals that pervade the whole school. We may distinguish, however, certain tendencies, such as that of judging education from the standpoint of external results, instead of from that of the development of personal attitudes and habits. The ideal of the *product*, as against that of the mental *process* by which the product is attained, shows itself both in instruction and in moral discipline.

THE EXALTATION OF EXTERNAL STANDARDS

a. In Instruction. In instruction, the external standard manifests itself in the importance attached to the "correct answer." No one other thing, probably, works so fatally against focussing the attention of teachers upon the training of mind as the domination of *their* minds by the idea that the chief thing is to get pupils to recite their lessons correctly. As long as this end is uppermost (whether consciously or unconsciously), training of mind remains an incidental and secondary consideration. There is no great difficulty in understanding why this ideal has such vogue. The large number of pupils to be dealt with and the tendency of parents and school authorities to demand speedy and tangible evidence of progress conspire to give it authority. Knowledge of subject matter—not of children—is alone exacted of teachers by this aim; and moreover, knowledge of subject matter only in portions definitely prescribed and laid out, and hence mastered with comparative ease. Education that takes as its standard the improvement of the intellectual attitude and method of students demands more serious preparatory training, for it exacts sympathetic and intelligent insight into the workings of individual minds and a very wide and flexible command of subject matter—so as to be able to select and apply just what is needed when it is needed. Finally, the securing of external results is an aim that lends itself naturally to the mechanics of school administration—to examinations, marks, gradings, promotions, and so on.

b. In Behavior. With reference to behavior also, the external ideal has a great influence. Conformity of acts to precepts and rules is the easiest, because most mechnical, standard to employ. It is no part of our present task to tell just how far dogmatic instruction, or strict adherence to custom, convention, and the commands of a social superior, should extend in moral training; but since problems of conduct are the deepest and most common of all the problems of life, the ways in which they are met have an influence that radiates into every other mental attitude, even those far remote from any direct or conscious moral consideration. Indeed, the *deepest plane of the mental attitude of everyone is fixed by the way in which problems of behavior are treated.* If the function of thought, of serious inquiry and reflection, is reduced to a minimum in dealing with them, it is not reasonable to expect habits of thought to exercise great influence in less important matters. On the other hand, habits of active inquiry and careful deliberation in the significant and vital problems of conduct afford the best guarantee that the general structure of mind will be reasonable.

IS THERE TRANSFER OF TRAINING IN THINKING?

The point just made leads to the question that is sometimes raised as to whether the rejection of the idea of special faculties that can be trained by formal exercises does not demand the rejection also of the possibility of training thought. The question has been partly answered in the conception of the nature of thinking that has been set forth (that it is not a "faculty," but an organization of materials and activities) and its relation to objective conditions. But there is another aspect of the question that is suggested by the term "transfer." The question is asked whether the ability to think gained in dealing with one situation or subject will prove itself equally efficient in dealing with another subject and situation; that it does not do so necessarily is indicated by the fact that a scientific specialist may be a child in practical affairs of business; that he may violate in matters of politics or religious belief every principle that he scrupulously observes in his special field of inquiry. It is now generally recognized that common elements are the basis of so-called "transfer." That is, the carrying over of skill and understanding from one experience to another is dependent upon the existence of like elements in both experiences. The simplest sort of example is found in the extended application given by children to ideas and words. A young child whose acquaintance with quadrupeds is limited to a dog will tend to call any four-footed animal of a similar size "doggie." Similar qualities are always the bridge over which the mind passes in going from a former experience to a new one. Now thinking, as we shall see later in detail, is a process of *grasping in a conscious way* the common elements. It thus adds greatly to the availability of common elements for purposes of transfer. Unless these elements are seized and held by the mind (as they are in a rudimentary way by the symbol "dog"), any transfer occurs only blindly, by sheer accident. The first answer to the objection that the building up of a general habit of thinking is impossible is, therefore, that thinking is precisely the factor that makes transfer possible and that brings it under control.

The more technical a subject, the fewer common elements it provides for thinking to work with. In fact, we might almost set up this test for the technical nature of any subject, theme, or undertaking: in what degree is it isolated from the material of everyday experiences because of absence of elements common to both? To the person just beginning algebra and physics, the ideas of "exponent" and "atom" are technical; they stand alone. He is not aware of these meanings in connection with the objects and acts of his ordinary experience; they do not seem to be contained in even the materials of his school experience. To the mature scientist, on the contrary, the ideas are much less technical because they enter into so many experiences that have become familiar to him as a scientific inquirer. During the early stages of experience and for the greater part of *all* experience, save that of specialists, the common elements are the *human* elements, those connected with the relations of persons to one another and to groups. The most important things to a child are his connections with father and mother, brother and sister. Elements connected with them recur in most of the experiences he has. They saturate the greater number of his experiences and supply them with their meaning. These human and social factors are accordingly those that carry over and can be carried over most readily from one experience to another. They furnish the material best suited for developing generalized abilities of thinking. One reason why much of elementary schooling is so useless for the development of reflective attitudes is that, on entering school life, a break is suddenly made in the life of the child, a break with those of his experiences that are saturated with social values and qualities. Schooling is then technical because of its isolation, and the child's thinking cannot operate because school has nothing in common with his earlier experiences.

THE PROCESS AND PRODUCT OF REFLECTIVE ACTIVITY: PSYCHOLOGICAL PROCESS AND LOGICAL FORM *

I. Thinking as a Formal and as an Active Occurrence

THE LOGIC OF THE TEXTBOOKS

When you look into a treatise on Logic, you find in it a classification of terms, such as particular, general, denotative, connotative, etc.; of propositions, such as positive, negative, universal, particular; and of arguments in the form of syllogisms. A familiar example of the latter is: All men are mortal; Scorates is a man; therefore, Socrates is mortal. It is characteristic of a formal statement that particular specific objects may be eliminated and a blank substituted which may be filled in with any material. The form of the syllogism just cited is: All M (human beings in this case) is P; all S is M; therefore, all S is P. In this formulation S stands for the subject of the conclusion, P for its predicate, and M for the *middle* term. The middle term appears in both premises and is the connecting link by which S and P, otherwise logically disconnected, are locked into unity. It is the ground

---

* From *How We Think: A Restatement of the Relation of Reflective Thinking to the Educative Process*, 1933.

and justification of the assertion at the close that *S* is *P*. In invalid reasonings the middle term fails to bind together tightly and exclusively the subject and predicate of the conclusion. It is possible to state a number of rules setting forth the forms in which syllogisms, positive and negative, are valid, and ruling out incorrect forms.

HOW ACTUAL THINKING DIFFERS FROM FORMAL LOGIC

Inspection shows important differences between formal reasoning and thinking as it actually goes on in the mind of any person. (1) The subject matter of formal logic is strictly impersonal, as much so as the formulae of algebra. The forms are thus independent of the attitude taken by the thinker, of his desire and intention. Thought carried on by anyone depends, on the other hand, as we have already seen, upon his habits. It is likely to be good when he has attitudes of carefulness, thoroughness, etc., and bad in the degree in which he is headlong, unobservant, lazy, moved by strong passion, tending to favor himself, etc. (2) The forms of logic are constant, unchanging, indifferent to the subject matter with which they are filled. They exclude change as much as does the fact that 2 plus 2 equals 4. Actual thinking is a *process;* it occurs, goes on; in short, it is in continual change as long as a person thinks. It has at every step to take account of subject matter; for parts of the material dealt with offer obstacles, pose problems and perplexities, while other portions indicate solutions and make the road out of intellectual difficulties. (3) Because forms are uniform and hospitable to any subject matter whatever, they pay no attention to context. Actual thinking, on the other hand, always has reference to some context. It occurs, as we have seen, because of some unsettled situation that itself lies outside of thinking. We may compare the formal syllogism about Socrates with the state of mind of his disciples when they were considering at the time of his trial the prospects of Socrates' continuing to live.

THOUGHT AS LOGICAL FORM, OR PRODUCT,
AND AS PSYCHOLOGICAL PROCESS

It follows from these contrasts that thought is looked at from two different points of view. These two points of view are indicated in the title of this chapter. We call them product and process; logical form and existent, or psychological, process. They may also be termed the historical, or chronological, and the timeless. Forms are constant; thinking takes time. It is evident that education is primarily concerned with thinking as it actually takes place in individual human beings. It is concerned to create attitudes favorable to effective thought, and it has to select and arrange subject matter and the activities dealing with subject matter so as to promote these attitudes.

It does not follow, however, that formal treatment lacks all value for education. It has value, provided it is put and kept in its place. That place is suggested by giving it the name "product." It sets forth forms into which the result of actual thinking is thrown in order to help test its worth. Consider, as an analogy, the relation that a map sustains to the explorations and surveys of which it is the outcome. The latter correspond to processes. The map is the product. *After* it is constructed, it can be used without any reference to the journeys and expeditions of which it is the fruit, although it would not exist if it had not been for them. When you look at a map of the United States, you do not have, in order to use it, to think of Columbus, Champlain, Lewis and Clark, and the thousands of others whose trials and labors are embodied in it.

Now the map is all there before you at once. It may with propriety be called the *form* of all the special journeyings from place to place that can be undertaken by any number of persons. Moreover, when a person is traveling, it serves, if he knows how to use it, as a check on his position and a guide to his movements. But it does not tell him where to go; his own desires and plans determine his goal, as his own past determines where he is now and where he must start from.

LOGICAL FORMS NOT USED IN ACTUAL THINKING, BUT TO SET FORTH RESULTS OF THINKING

Logical forms such as one finds in a logical treatise do not pretend to tell *how* we think or even how we *should* think. No one ever arrived at the idea that Socrates, or any other creature, was mortal by following the form of the syllogism. If, however, one who has arrived at that notion by gathering and interpreting evidence wishes to expound to another person the *grounds* of his belief, he might use the syllogistic form and would do so if he wished to state the proof in its most compact form. A lawyer, for example, who knows in advance what he wants to prove, who has a conclusion already formed in his mind, and who wishes to impress others with it, is quite likely to put his reasonings into syllogistic form.

In short, these forms apply not to *reaching* conclusions, not to *arriving* at beliefs and knowledge, but to the most effective way in which to set forth what has already been concluded, so as to convince others (or oneself if one wishes to recall to mind its grounds) of the soundness of the result. In the thinking by which a conclusion is actually reached, observations are made that turn out to be aside from the point; false clues are followed; fruitless suggestions are entertained; superfluous moves are made. Just because you do not know the solution of your problem, you have to grope toward it and grope in the dark or at least in an obscure light; you start on lines of inquiry that in the end you give up. When you are only seeking the truth and of necessity seeking somewhat blindly, you are in a radically different position from the one you are in when you are already in possession of truth.

The logical forms that characterize conclusions reached and adopted cannot therefore prescribe the way in which we should attempt to arrive at a conclusion when we are still in a condition of doubt and inquiry. Yet partial conclusions emerge during the course of reflection. There are temporary stopping places, landings of past thought that are also stations of departure for subsequent thought. We do not reach *the* conclusion at a single jump. At every such landing stage it is useful to retrace the processes gone through and to state to oneself how much and how little of the material previously thought about really bears on the conclusion reached and *how* it bears. Thus premises and conclusions are formulated at the same time in definite relation to one another, and *forms* belong to such formulations.

ACTUAL THINKING HAS ITS OWN LOGIC; IT IS ORDERLY, REASONABLE, REFLECTIVE

The distinction between process and product of reflective inquiry is thus not fixed and absolute. In calling the process "psychological" and the product "logical," we do not mean that only the final outcome is logical or that the activity that goes in a series of steps in time and that involves personal desire and purpose is not logical. Rather, we must distinguish between the logical *form,* which applies to the product, and the logical *method,* which may and should belong to the process.

We speak of the "logic" of history; that is, of the orderly movement of events to a concluding climax. We say that one person acts or talks "logically," another person "illogically." We do not mean that the first person acts, thinks, or talks in syllogisms, but that there is *order,* consecutiveness, in what he says and does; that the means he uses are well calculated to reach the end he has in mind. "Logically" in such cases is a synonym for "reasonably." The illogical person wanders aimlessly; he shifts his topic without being aware of it; he skips about at random; he not only jumps to a conclusion (all of us have to do that at some point), but he fails to retrace his steps to see whether the conclusion to which he has jumped is supported by evidence; he makes contradictory, inconsistent statements without being sensitive to what he is doing.

A person, on the other hand, thinks logically when he is careful in the conduct of his thinking, when he takes pains to make sure he has evidence to go upon, and when, after reaching a conclusion, he checks it by the evidence he can offer in its support. In short, "logical," as applied to the process of thinking, signifies that the course of thoughts is carried on *reflectively*, in the sense in which reflection was discriminated from other kinds of thinking. A bungler can make a box, but the joints will not fit exactly; the edges will not be even. A skilled person will do the work in a way that does not waste time or material, and the result is firm and neat. So it is with thinking.

When we say a person is *thoughtful*, we mean something more than that he merely indulges in thoughts. To be really thoughtful is to be logical. Thoughtful persons are heedful, not rash; they look about, are circumspect instead of going ahead blindly. They weigh, ponder, deliberate—terms that imply a careful comparing and balancing of evidence and suggestions, a process of evaluating what occurs to them in order to decide upon its force and weight for their problem. Moreover, the thoughtful person looks into matters; he scrutinizes, inspects, examines. He does not, in other words, take observations at their face value, but probes them to see whether they are what they seem to be. "Skim milk masquerades as cream"; a fungus looks like an edible mushroom, but is poisonous; "fool's gold" seems like gold, but is only iron pyrites. There are comparatively few cases in which we can accept without questioning the so-called "evidence of the senses"; the sun does not really travel around the earth; the moon does not actually change its own form, and so on. The logical person inspects to make sure of his data. Finally, the thoughtful person "puts two and two together." He reckons, calculates, casts up an account. The word "reason" is connected etymologically with the word "ratio." The underlying idea here is *exactness of relationship*. All reflective thinking is a process of detecting relations; the terms just used indicate that *good* thinking is not contented with finding "any old kind" of relation but searches until a relation is found that is as accurately defined as conditions permit.

IN SUMMARY

The "psychological," as we use the term, is not, then, opposed to the "logical." As far as an actual process of thought is truly reflective, it is alert, careful, thorough, definite, and accurate, pursuing an orderly course. In short, it is then logical. When we use the term "logical" in distinction from the actual process (when the latter is controlled), we have in mind the *formal* arrangement of the final *product* of a particular process of thinking, the arrangement being such as to sum up the net conclusion and to extract the exact grounds on which that conclusion rests. Loose thought leaves the result hanging in the air, with only a vague sense of just what has been proved or arrived at. A genuinely reflective activity terminates in declaring just what the outcome is. By formulating that outcome as definitely as possible, it is converted into a true *conclusion*. Reflective activity also makes a survey, a review, of the material upon which *alone* this conclusion rests, and thus formulates the *premises* upon which it rests. A geometrical demonstration, for example, always states at its close just what has been proved; and if the reasoning is understood and not merely memorized, the mind grasps the demonstrated proposition as a conclusion; it is aware of the prior points that prove it.

II. Education in Relation to Form

LEARNING IS LEARNING TO THINK

From what has been said, however, it is evident that education, *upon its intellectual side,* is vitally concerned with cultivating the attitude of reflective thinking, preserving it where it already exists, and changing looser methods of thought into stricter ones whenever possible. Of course, education is not exhausted in its intellectual aspect; there are practical attitudes of efficiency to be formed, moral dispositions to be strengthened and developed, aesthetic appreciations to be cultivated. But in all these things there is at least an element of conscious meaning and hence of thought. Otherwise, practical activity is mechanical and routine, morals are blind and arbitrary, and aesthetic appreciation is sentimental gush. In what follows we shall confine ourselves, however, to the intellectual side. We state emphatically that, *upon its intellec-*

tual side education consists in the formation of wide-awake, careful, thorough habits of thinking.

Of course intellectual learning includes the amassing and retention of information. But information is an undigested burden unless it is understood. It is *knowledge* only as its material is *comprehended*. And understanding, comprehension, means that the various parts of the information acquired are grasped in their relations to one another—a result that is attained only when acquisition is accompanied by constant reflection upon the meaning of what is studied. There is an important distinction between verbal, mechanical memory and what older writers called "judicious memory." The latter seizes the *bearings* of what is retained and recalled; it can, therefore, use the material in new situations where verbal memory would be completely at a loss.

What we have called "psychological thinking" is just the actual process that takes place. This, in particular cases, may be random and disorderly or else a mere play of fantasy. But if it were *always* nothing but that, not only would thinking be of no use, but life could hardly be even maintained. If thought had nothing to do with real conditions and if it did not move logically from these conditions to the thought of ends to be reached, we should never invent, or plan, or know how to get out of any trouble or predicament. As we have already noted, there are both intrinsic elements and pressure of circumstances that introduce into thinking genuinely logical or reflective qualities.

THE CONNECTION BETWEEN PROCESS
AND PRODUCT OF THINKING
OVERLOOKED BY TWO EDUCATIONAL SCHOOLS

Curiously enough, the internal and necessary connection between the actual process of thinking and its intellectual product is overlooked by two opposite educational schools.

One of these schools thinks that the mind is naturally so illogical in its processes that logical form must be impressed upon it from without. It assumes that logical quality belongs only to organized knowledge and that the operations of the mind become logical only through absorption of logically formulated, ready-made material. In this case, the logical formulations are not the outcome of any process of thinking that is personally undertaken and carried out; the formulation has been made by another mind and is presented in a finished form, apart from the processes by which it was arrived at. Then it is assumed that by some magic its logical character will be transferred into the minds of pupils.

An illustration or two will make clear what is meant by the foregoing statements. Suppose the subject is geography. The first thing is to give its definition, marking it off from every other subject. Then the various abstract terms upon which depends the scientific development of the science are stated and defined one by one—pole, equator, ecliptic, zone—from the simpler units to the more complex that are formed out of them; then the more concrete elements are taken in similar series—continent, island, coast, promontory, cape, isthmus, peninsula, ocean, lake, coast, gulf, bay, and so on. In acquiring this material the pupil's mind is supposed not only to gain important information, but, by accommodating itself to ready-made logical definitions, generalizations, and classifications, gradually also to acquire logical habits.

This type of method has been applied to every subject taught in the schools—reading, writing, music, physics, grammar, arithmetic. Drawing, for example, has been taught on the theory that, since all pictorial representation is a matter of combining straight and curved lines, the simplest procedure is to have the pupil acquire the ability first to draw straight lines in various positions (horizontal, perpendicular, diagonals at various angles), then typical curves; and finally, to combine straight and curved lines in various permutations to construct actual pictures. This seemed to give the ideal "logical" method, beginning with analysis into elements, and then proceeding in regular order to more and more complex syntheses, each element being defined when used, and thereby clearly understood.

Even when this method in its extreme form is not followed, few schools (especially of the middle or upper elementary grades) are free from an exaggerated attention to forms supposedly necessary for the pupil to use if he is to get his result logically. It is held that there are certain steps, arranged in a certain order, that express preëminently an understanding of the subject, and the pupil is made to "analyze" his procedure into these steps; *i.e.,* to learn a certain routine formula of statement. While this method is usually at its height in grammar and arithmetic, it invades also history and even literature, which are then reduced, under plea of intellectual training, to outlines, diagrams, and other schemes of division and subdivision. In memorizing this simulated cut-and-dried copy of the logic of an adult, the child is generally made to stultify his own vital logical movement. The adoption by teachers of this misconception of logical method has probably done more than anything else to bring pedagogy into disrepute, for to many persons "pedagogy" means precisely a set of mechanical, self-conscious devices for replacing by some cast-iron external scheme the personal mental movement of the individual.

It is evident from these examples that in such a scheme of instruction, the logical is identified exclusively with certain formal properties of subject matter; with subject matter defined, refined, subdivided, classified, organized according to certain principles of connection that have been worked out by persons who are expert in that particular field. It conceives the method of instruction to be the devices by which similar traits are imported into the mind by careful reproduction of the given material in arithmetic, geography, grammar, physics, biology, or whatnot. The natural operations of the mind are supposed to be indifferent or even averse to all logical achievement. Hence the mottoes of this school are "discipline," "restraint," "conscious effort," "the necessity of tasks," and so on. From this point of view studies, rather than attitudes and habits, embody the logical factor in education. The mind becomes logical only by learning to conform to an external subject matter. To produce this conformity, the study should first be analyzed (by textbook or teacher) into its logical elements; then each of these elements should be defined; finally, all the elements should be arranged in series or classes according to logical formulae or general principles. Then the pupil learns the definitions one by one and, progressively adding one to another, builds up the logical system, and thereby is himself imbued, from without, with logical quality.

A reaction inevitably occurs from the poor results that accrue from these professedly "logical" methods. Lack of interest in study, habits of inattention and procrastination, positive aversion to intellectual application, dependence upon sheer memorizing and mechanical routine with only a modicum of understanding by the pupil of what he is about, show that the theory of logical definition, division, gradation, and system does not work out practically as it is theoretically supposed to do. The consequent disposition—as in every reaction—is to go to the opposite extreme. The "logical" is thought to be wholly artificial and extraneous; teacher and pupil alike are to turn their backs upon it, and to give free rein to the expression of existing aptitudes and tastes. Emphasis upon natural tendencies and powers as the only possible starting point of development is indeed wholesome. But the reaction is false, and hence misleading, in what it ignores and denies: the presence of genuinely intellectual factors in existing powers and interests.

The other type of school really accepts the underlying premise of the opposite educational theory. It also assumes that the mind is naturally averse to logical form; it grounds this conviction upon the fact that many minds *are* rebellious to the particular logical forms in which a certain type of textbook presents its material. From this fact it is inferred that logical order is so foreign to the natural operations of the mind that it is of slight importance in education, at least in that of the young, and that the main thing is just to give free play to impulses and desires without regard to any definitely *intellectual* growth. Hence the mottoes of this school are "freedom," "self-expression," "individuality," "spontaneity," "play," "interest," "natural unfolding," and so on. In its emphasis upon individual attitude and activity, it sets slight store upon organized subject matter. It conceives *method* to consist of various devices for stimulating and evoking, in their natural order of growth, the native potentialities of individuals.

THE BASIC ERROR OF THE TWO SCHOOLS
IS THE SAME

Thus the basic error of the two schools is the same. Both ignore and virtually deny the fact that tendencies toward a reflective and truly logical activity are native to the mind, and that they show themselves at an early period, since they are demanded by outer conditions and stimulated by native curiosity. There is an innate disposition to draw inferences, and an inherent desire to experiment and test. The mind at every stage of growth has its own logic. It entertains suggestions, tests them by observation of objects and events, reaches conclusions, tries them in action, finds them confirmed or in need of correction or rejection. A baby, even at a comparatively early period, makes inferences in the way of expectations from what is observed, interpreting what it sees as a sign or evidence of something it does not observe with the senses. The school of so-called "free self-expression" thus fails to note that one thing that is urgent for expression in the spontaneous activity of the young is *intellectual* in character. Since this factor is predominantly the *educative* one, as far as instruction is concerned, other aspects of activity should be made means to its effective operation.

Any teacher who is alive to the modes of thought operative in the natural experience of the normal child will have no difficulty in avoiding the identification of the logical with a ready-made organization of subject matter, as well as the notion that the way to escape this error is to pay no attention to logical considerations. Such a teacher will have no difficulty in seeing that the real problem of intellectual education is the *transformation* of natural powers into expert, tested powers: the transformation of more or less casual curiosity and sporadic suggestion into attitudes of alert, cautious, and thorough inquiry. He will see that the *psychological* and the *logical*, instead of being opposed to each other (or even independent of each other), are connected as the earlier and the terminal, or concluding, stages of the same process. He will recognize, moreover, that the kind of logical arrangement that marks subject matter at the stage of maturity is not the only kind possible; that the kind found in scientifically organized material is actually undesirable until the mind has reached a point of maturity where it is capable of understanding just *why* this form, rather than some other, is adopted.

That which is strictly logical from the standpoint of subject matter really represents the conclusions of an expert, trained mind. The definitions, divisions, and classifications of the conventional text represent these conclusions boiled down. The only way in which a person can reach ability to make accurate definitions, penetrating classifications, and comprehensive generalizations is by thinking alertly and carefully on his own *present* level. Some kind of intellectual organization must be required, or else habits of vagueness, disorder, and incoherent "thinking" will be formed. But the organization need not be that which would satisfy the mature expert. For the immature mind is still in process of gaining the intellectual skill that the latter has already achieved. It is absurd to suppose that the beginner can commence where the adept stops. But the beginner should be trained to demand from himself careful examination, consecutiveness, and some sort of summary and formulation of *his* conclusions, together with a statement of the reasons for them.

IN SUMMARY

We may summarize by saying that "logical" has at least three different meanings. In its widest sense, any thinking that is intended, to reach a conclusion that is to be accepted and believed in is logical, even though the actual operations are *il*-logical. In the narrowest sense, "logical" signifies that which is demonstrated, according to certain approved forms, to follow from premises the terms of which have clear and definite meanings; it signifies *proof of a stringent character*. Between the two lies the meaning, which is educationally vital: systematic care to safeguard the processes of thinking so that it is truly reflective. In this connection "logical" signifies the *regulation* of natural and spontaneous processes of observation, suggestion, and testing; that is, thinking as an *art*.

III. Discipline and Freedom

THE CONCEPTION OF DISCIPLINE

It was remarked in the foregoing discussion that two schools of educational thought have opposing mottoes, or slogans. One of them makes *discipline* primary; the other, *freedom*. The position we have taken implies, however, that each school has a wrong notion of the meaning of its own professed principle. If the natural, or "psychological," processes are lacking in all inherent logical quality, so that the latter has to be imposed from without, then discipline must be something negative. It will be a painfully disagreeable forcing of mind away from channels congenial to it into channels of constraint, a process grievous at the time but necessary as preparation for a more or less remote future. Discipline is then generally identified with drill; and drill is conceived after the mechanical analogy of driving, by unremitting blows, a foreign substance into a resistant material; or imaged after the analogy of the mechanical routine by which raw recruits are trained to a soldierly bearing and habits that are naturally wholly foreign to their possessors. Training of this latter sort, whether it be called "discipline" or not, is not *mental* discipline. Its aim and result are not *habits* of thinking, but uniform *external modes of action*. By failing to ask what he means by discipline, many a teacher is misled into supposing that he is engaged in disciplining the mind of pupils, when in reality he is creating an aversion to study and a belief that using the mind is a disagreeable, instead of a delightful operation.

In truth, discipline is positive and constructive. It is power, power of control of the means necessary to achieve ends and also power to value and test ends. A painter is disciplined in his art in the degree in which he can manage and use effectively all the elements that enter into his art—externally, canvas, colors, and brush; internally, his power of vision and imagination. Practice, exercise, are involved in the acquisition of power, but they do not take the form of meaningless drill, but of practicing the *art*. They occur as part of the operation of attaining a desired end, and they are not mere repetition. Discipline is a product, an outcome, an achievement, not something applied from without. All genuine education *terminates* in discipline, but it *proceeds* by engaging the mind in activities worth while for their own sake.

THE CONCEPTION OF FREEDOM

This fact enables us to see the error in the conception of freedom held by the opposite school of educational theory. The discipline that is identical with trained power is also identical with *freedom*. For freedom is power to act and to execute independent of external tutelage. It signifies mastery capable of independent exercise, emancipated from the leading strings of others, not mere unhindered external operation. When spontaneity or naturalness is identified with more or less casual discharge of transitory impulses, the tendency of the educator is to supply a multitude of stimuli in order that spontaneous activity may be kept up. All sorts of interesting materials, equipments, tools, modes of activity, are provided in order that there may be no flagging of free self-expression. This method overlooks some of the essential conditions of the attainment of genuine freedom.

FREEDOM IS ACHIEVED BY CONQUERING OBSTACLES

Direct immediate discharge or expression of an impulsive tendency is fatal to thinking. Only when the impulse is to some extent checked and thrown back upon itself does reflection ensue. It is, indeed, a stupid error to suppose that arbitrary tasks must be imposed from without in order to furnish the factor of perplexity and difficulty that is the necessary cue to thought. Every vital activity of any depth and range inevitably meets obstacles in the course of its effort to realize itself—a fact that renders the search for artificial or external problems quite superfluous. The difficulties that present themselves within the development of an experience are, however, to be cherished by the educator, not minimized, for they are the natural stimuli to reflective inquiry. Freedom does not consist in keeping up an uninterrupted and unimpeded external activity, but is something achieved through conquering, by personal reflection, the difficulties that prevent immediate overflow into action and spontaneous success.

THINKING DEMANDS A NATURAL DEVELOPMENT
FROM EARLY CHILDHOOD

A method that emphasizes the psychological and natural, yet fails to see what an important part of natural tendencies is constituted at every period of growth by curiosity, inference, and the desire to test, cannot secure a *natural development*. In natural growth each successive stage of activity prepares unconsciously, but thoroughly, the conditions for the manifestation of the next stage—as in the cycle of a plant's growth. There is no ground for assuming that thinking is a special, isolated natural tendency that will bloom inevitably in due season simply because various sense and motor activities have been freely manifested before; or because observation, memory, imagination, and manual skill have been previously exercised without thought. Only when thinking is constantly employed in using the senses and muscles for the guidance and application of observations and movements is the way prepared for subsequent higher types of thinking.

At present, the notion is current that childhood is almost entirely unreflective—a period of mere sensory, motor, and memory development, while adolescence suddenly brings the manifestation of thought and reason.

Adolescence is not, however, a synonym for magic. Doubtless youth should bring with it an enlargement of the horizon of childhood, a susceptibility to larger concerns and issues, a more generous and a more general standpoint toward nature and social life. This development affords an opportunity for thinking of a more comprehensive and abstract type than has previously obtained. But thinking itself remains just what it has been all the time, a matter of following up and testing the conclusions suggested by the facts and events of life. Thinking begins as soon as the baby who has lost the ball that he is playing with begins to foresee the possibility of something not yet existing—its recovery—and begins to forecast steps toward the realization of this possibility, and, by experimentation, to guide his acts by his ideas and thereby also test the ideas. Only by making the most of the thought factor already active in the experiences of childhood, is there any promise or warrant for the emergence of superior reflective power at adolescence or at any later period.

MENTAL HABITS, WHETHER GOOD OR BAD, ARE CERTAIN TO BE FORMED

In any case *positive habits are being formed:* if not habits of careful looking into things, then habits of hasty, heedless impatient glancing over the surface; if not habits of consecutively following up the suggestions that occur, then habits of haphazard, grasshopper-like guessing; if not habits of suspending judgment till inferences have been tested by the examination of evidence, then habits of credulity alternating with flippant incredulity, belief or unbelief being based, in either case, upon whim, emotion, or accidental circumstances. The only way to achieve traits of carefulness, thoroughness, and continuity (traits that are, as we have seen, the elements of the "logical") is by exercising these traits from the beginning, and by seeing to it that conditions call for their exercise.

GENUINE FREEDOM IS INTELLECTUAL

Genuine freedom, in short, is intellectual; it rests in the trained *power of thought*, in ability to "turn things over," to look at matters deliberately, to judge whether the amount and kind of evidence requisite for decision is at hand, and if not, to tell where and how to seek such evidence. If a man's actions are not guided by thoughtful conclusions, then they are guided by inconsiderate impulse, unbalanced appetite, caprice, or the circumstances of the moment. To cultivate unhindered unreflective external activity is to foster enslavement, for it leaves the person at the mercy of appetite, sense, and circumstance.

INTEREST IN RELATION
TO TRAINING OF THE WILL *

There is much the same difficulty in isolating any educational topic for discussion that there is in the case of philosophy. The issues are so interdependent that any one of them can be selected only at the risk of ignoring important considerations, or else of begging the question by bringing in the problem under discussion under cover of some other subject. Yet limits of time and space require that some one field be entered and occupied by itself. Under such circumstances about all one can do is to pursue a method which shall at least call attention to the problems involved, and to indicate the main relations of the matters discussed to relevant topics. The difficulty is particularly great in the discussion of interest. Interest is in the closest relation to the emotional life, on one side; and, through its close relation, if not identity with attention, to the intellectual life, on the other side. Any adequate explanation of it, therefore, would require the development of the complete psychology both of feeling and of knowledge, and of their relations to each other, and the dis-

* This selection appeared originally in National Herbart Society, *Second Supplement to the Herbart Year Book for 1895*, 1896.

cussion of their connection or lack of connection with volition.

Accordingly, I can only hope to bring out what seem to
me to be the salient points, and if my results do not command
agreement, to help at least define the problem for further discussion.

While it would be sanguine to anticipate agreement upon
any important educational doctrine, there is perhaps more
hope of reaching a working consensus by beginning with the
educational side. If we can lay down some general principle
regarding the place and function of Interest in the school, we
shall have a more or less sure basis on which to proceed to
the psychological analysis of interest in its relation to the
other factors and aspects of volition. At all events, we shall
have limited the field and fixed the boundaries within which
the psychological discussion may proceed. After this we
may with more promise of success proceed to the discussion
of some of the chief attitudes assumed toward the problem
of interest in historic and current investigations. Finally,
we may return with the results reached by this psychological
and critical consideration to the educational matter. We may
restate and reinterpret the part played by interest in instruction with deeper insight and more definite emphasis upon
the question of moral training.

I

At first sight the hope of gaining a working consensus regarding
interest on the educational side seems futile. The first thing
that strikes us is the profound contradiction sometimes expressed, more often latent, in current educational ideas
and standards regarding precisely this matter of interest. On
the one hand, we have the school which insists that interest
is the keynote both of instruction and of moral training, that
the essential problem of the teacher is to make the material
presented so interesting that it shall command and retain attention. On the other hand, we have the assertion that the
putting forth of effort from within is alone truly educative;
that to rely upon the principle of interest is to distract the
child intellectually and to weaken him morally.

In this educational law-suit of interest versus effort let us consider the respective briefs of plaintiff and defendant. In behalf of interest it is claimed that it is the sole guarantee of attention; that, if we can secure interest in a given set of facts or ideas, we may be perfectly sure that the pupil will direct his energies towards mastering them; that if we can secure interest in a certain moral train or line of conduct, we are equally safe in assuming that the child's activities are responding in that direction; that if we have not secured interest we have no safeguard as to what will be done in any given case. As matter of fact the doctrine of discipline has not succeeded. It is absurd to suppose that a child gets more intellectual or mental discipline when he goes at a matter unwillingly than when he goes at it with complete interest and out of the fullness of his heart. The theory of effort simply says that unwilling attention (doing something which is disagreeable and because it is disagreeable) should take precedence over spontaneous attention.

Practically the theory of effort amounts to nothing. When a child feels that his work is a task it is only under compulsion that he gives himself to it. At the least let-up of external pressure we find his attention at once directed to what interests him. The child brought up on the basis of the theory of effort simply acquires marvelous skill in appearing to be occupied with an uninteresting subject, while the real heart and core of his energies are otherwise engaged. Indeed, the theory contradicts itself. It is psychologically impossible to call forth any activity without some interest. The theory of effort simply substitutes one interest for another. It substitutes the impure interest of fear of the teacher or hope of future reward for pure interest in the material presented. The type of character induced is that illustrated by Emerson at the beginning of his essay on Compensation, where he holds up the current doctrine of compensation as virtually implying that if you only sacrifice yourself enough now, you will be permitted to indulge yourself a great deal more in the future; or that if you are only good now (goodness consisting in attention to what is uninteresting) you will have a great many more pleasing interests at some future time;—that is, may then be bad.

While the theory of effort is always holding up to us a strong, vigorous character as the outcome of its method of education, practically we do not get this character. We get either the narrow, bigoted man who is obstinate and irresponsible save in the line of his own preconceived aims and beliefs; or else we get a character dull, mechanical, unalert, because the vital juice of the principle of spontaneous interest has been squeezed out of it.

We may now hear the defendant's case. Life, says the other theory, is full of things not interesting, but which have to be faced none the less. Demands are continually made, situations have to be dealt with which present no features of interest. Unless the individual has had previous training in devoting himself to uninteresting work, unless habits have been formed of attending to matters simply because they have to be attended to, irrespective of the personal satisfaction gotten out of them, character will either break down, or avoid the issue, when confronted with the more serious matters of life. Life is too serious to be degraded to a merely pleasant affair, or reduced to the continual satisfaction of personal interests. The concerns of future life, therefore, imperatively demand such continual exercise of effort in the performance of tasks as to form the habit of recognizing the real labors of life. Anything else eats out the fiber of character and reduces the person to a wishy washy, colorless being; or else to a state of moral dependence, with over-reliance upon others and with continual demand for amusement and distraction.

Apart from the question of the future, continually to appeal in childhood days even to the principle of interest is eternally to excite, that is distract the child. Continuity of activity is destroyed. Everything is made play, amusement. This means over-stimulation; it means dissipation of energy. Will is never called into action at all. The reliance is upon external attractions and amusements. Everything is sugar-coated for the child, and he soon learns to turn from everything which is not artificially surrounded with diverting circumstances. The spoiled child who does only what he likes is the inevitable outcome of the theory of interest in education.

The theory is intellectually as well as morally harmful. Attention is never directed to the essential and important facts. It is directed simply to the wrappings of attraction with which the facts are surrounded. If a fact is repulsive or uninteresting, it has to be faced in its own naked character sooner or later. Putting a fringe of fictitious interest around it does not bring the child any nearer to it than he was at the outset. The fact that two and two make four is a naked fact which has to be mastered in and of itself. The child gets no greater hold upon the fact by having attached to it amusing stories of birds or dandelions than he would if the simple naked fact were presented to him. It is self-deception to suppose that the child is being interested in the numerical relation. His attention is going out to and taking in only the amusing images associated with this relation. The theory thus defeats its own end. It would be more direct and straightforward to recognize at the outset that certain facts have to be learned which have little or no interest, and that the only way to deal with these facts is through the power of effort, the internal power of putting forth activity wholly independent of any external inducement. Moreover, in this way the discipline, the habit of responding to serious matters, is formed which is necessary to equip the child for the life that lies ahead of him.

I have attempted to set forth the respective claims of each side as we find them, not only in current discussions but in the old controversy, as old as Plato and Aristotle. A little reflection will convince one that the strong point in each argument is not so much what it says in its own behalf, as in its attacks on the weak places of the opposite theory. Each theory is strong in its negations rather than in its position. It is a common, though somewhat surprising, fact that there is generally a common principle unconsciously assumed at the basis of two theories which to all outward appearances are the extreme opposites of each other. Such a common principle is presupposed by the theories of effort and interest in the one-sided forms in which they have already been stated.

This identical assumption is the externality of the object or idea to be mastered, the end to be reached, the act to be performed, to the self. It is because the object or end is assumed to be outside self that it has to be *made* interesting, that it has to be surrounded with artificial stimuli and with fictitious inducements to attention. It is equally because the object lies outside the sphere of self that the sheer power of "will," the putting forth of effort without interest, has to be appealed to. The genuine principle of interest is the principle of the recognized identity of the fact or proposed line of action with the self; that it lies in the direction of the agent's own self-expression and is therefore, imperiously demanded, if the agent is to be himself. Let this condition of identification once be secured, and we neither have to appeal to sheer strength of will nor do we have to occupy ourselves with making things interesting to the child.

The theory of effort, as already stated, means a virtual division of attention and the corresponding disintegration of character, intellectually and morally. The great fallacy of the so-called effort theory is that it identifies the exercise and training of will with certain external activities and certain external results. It is supposed that because a child is occupied at some outward task and because he succeeds in exhibiting the required product, that he is really putting forth will, and that definite intellectual and moral habits are in process of formation. But as a matter of fact, the moral exercise of the will is not found in the external assumption of any posture, and the formation of moral habit can not be identified with the ability to show up results at the demand of another. The exercise of the will is manifest in the direction of attention, and depends upon the spirit, the motive, the disposition in which work is carried on.

A child may be externally entirely occupied with mastering the multiplication table, and be able to reproduce that table when asked to do so by his teacher. The teacher may congratulate himself that the child has been so exercising his will power as to be forming right intellectual and moral habits. Not so, unless moral habit be identified with this ability to show certain results when required. The question of moral training has not been touched until we know what the child has been internally occupied with, what the predominating direction of his attention, his feelings, his disposition has been while engaged upon this task. If the task has appealed to him merely as a task, it is as certain, psychologically, as the law of action and reaction is, physically, that the child is simply engaged in acquiring the habit of divided attention; that he is getting the ability to direct eye and ear, lips and mouth, to what is present before him in such a way as to impress those things upon his memory, while at the same time getting his mental imagery free to work upon matters of real interest to him.

No account of the actual moral training secured is adequate unless it recognizes this division of attention into which the child is being educated, and faces the question of what the moral worth of such a division may be. External mechanical attention to a task conceived as a task is the inevitable correlate of an internal random mind-wandering along the lines of the pleasurable.

The spontaneous power of the child, his demand for self-expression, can not by any possibility be suppressed. If the external conditions are such that the child cannot put his spontaneous activity into the work to be done, if he finds that he cannot express himself in that, he learns in a most miraculous way the exact amount of attention that has to be given to this external material to satisfy the requirements of the teacher, while saving up the rest of his mental powers for following out lines of imagery that appeal to him. I do not say that there is absolutely no moral training involved in forming these habits of external attention, but I do say that there is a question of moral import involved in the formation of the habits of internal inattention.

While we are congratulating ourselves upon the well disciplined habits which the pupil is acquiring, judged by his ability to reproduce a lesson when called upon, we forget to commiserate ourselves because the deeper intellectual and moral nature of the child has secured absolutely no discipline at all, but has been left to follow its own caprices, the disordered suggestions of the moment, or of past experience. I do not see how anyone can deny that the training of this internal imagery is at least equally important with the development of certain outward habits of action. For myself, when it comes to the mere moral question and not a question of practical convenience, I think it is infinitely more important. Nor do I see how anyone at all familiar with the great mass of existing school work can deny that the greater part of the pupils are gradually forming habits of divided attention. If the teacher is skillful and wide-awake, if she is what is termed a good disciplinarian, the child will indeed learn to keep his senses intent in certain ways, but he will also learn to direct the fruitful imagery, which constitutes the value of what is before his senses, in totally other directions. I do not think it would be well for us to have to face the actual psychological condition of the majority of the pupils that leave our schools. We should find this division of attention and the resulting disintegration so great that we might be discouraged from all future endeavor. None the less, it is well for us to recognize that this state of things exists, and that it is the inevitable outcome of those conditions which require the simulation of attention without requiring its essence.

The principle of making objects and ideas interesting implies the same divorce between object and self as does the theory of "effort." When things have to be *made* interesting it is because interest itself is wanting. Moreover, the phrase is a misnomer. The thing, the object is no more interesting than it was before. The appeal is simply made to the child's love of pleasure. He is excited in a given direction with the hope that somehow or rather during this excitation he will assimilate something otherwise repulsive. There are two types of pleasure. One is the accompaniment of activity. It is found wherever there is self-expression. It is simply the internal realization of the outgoing energy. This sort of pleasure is always absorbed in the activity itself. It has no separate existence in consciousness. This is the type of pleasure found in legitimate interest. Its stimulus is found in the needs of the organism. The other sort of pleasure arises from contact. It marks receptivity. Its stimuli are external. We take interest; we get pleasure. The type of pleasure which arises from external stimulation is isolated. It exists by itself in consciousness as a pleasure, not as the pleasure of activity.

When objects are made interesting it is this latter type of pleasure that comes into play. Advantage is taken of the fact that a certain amount of excitation of any organ is pleasurable. The pleasure arising is employed to cover the gap between self and some fact not in itself arousing interest.

The result here also is division of energies. In the case of disagreeable effort the division is simultaneous. In this case it is successive. Instead of having a mechanical external activity and a random internal activity at the same time there is oscillation of excitement and apathy. The child alternates between periods of over-stimulation and of inertness. It is a condition realized in some so-called kindergartens. Moreover, this excitation of any particular organ, as eye or ear by itself, creates an abiding demand for such stimulation. It is as possible to create an appetite on the part of the eye or the ear for pleasurable stimulation as it is on the part of the taste. Some kindergarten children are as dependent upon the recurrent presence of bright colors or agreeable sounds as the drunkard is upon his dram. It is this which accounts for the distraction and dissipation of energy so characteristic of such children, and for their dependence upon external suggestion.

Before attempting a more specific psychological analysis, the discussion up to this point may be summarized as follows: Genuine interest in education is the accompaniment of the identification, through action, of the self with some object or idea, because of the necessity of that object or idea for the maintenance of self-expression. Effort, in the sense in which it may be opposed to interest, implies a separation between the self and the fact to be mastered or task to be performed, and sets up an habitual division of activities. Externally, we have mechanical habits with no psychical end or value. Internally, we have random energy or mind-wandering, a sequence of ideas with no end at all because not brought to a focus in action. Interest, in the sense in which it is opposed to effort, means simply an excitation of the sense organ to give pleasure, resulting in strain on one side and list-lessness on the other.

Self-expression in which the psychical energy assimilates material because of the recognized value of this material in aiding the self to reach its end, does not find it necessary to oppose interest to effort. Effort is the result of interest, and indicates the persistent outgo of activities in attaining an end felt as valuable; while interest is the consciousness of the value of this end, and of the means necessary to realize it.

II

We come now to our second main topic, the psychology of interest. It should be obvious from the preceding educational discussion that the points upon which we particularly need enlightenment are its relation to desire and pleasure on one side, to ideas and effort on the other.

I begin with a brief descriptive account of interest. Interest is first active, projective, or propulsive. We take interest. To be interested in any matter is to be actively concerned with it. The mere feeling regarding a subject may be static or inert, but interest is dynamic. Second, it is objective. We say a man has many interests to care for or look after. We talk about the range of a man's interests, his business interests, local interests, etc. We identify interests with concerns or affairs. Interest does not end simply in itself as bare feelings may, but always has some object, end, or aim to which it attaches itself. Third, interest is subjective; it signifies an *internal* realization, or feeling, of worth. It has its emotional, as well as its active and objective sides. Wherever there is interest there is response in the way of feeling.

These are the various meanings in which common sense employs the term interest. The root idea of the term seems to be that of being engaged, engrossed, or entirely taken up with some activity because of its recognized worth. The etymology of the term inter-esse, "to be between," points in the same direction. Interest marks the annihilation of the distance between subject and object; it is the instrument which effects their organic union.

It is true that the term interest is also used in a definitely disparaging sense. We speak of interest as opposed to principle, of self-interest as a motive to action which regards only one's personal advantage; but these are neither the only nor the controlling senses in which the term is used. It may fairly be questioned whether this is anything but a narrowing or degrading of the legitimate sense of the term. However that may be, it appears to me certain that much of the controversy regarding the moral use of interest arises because one party is using the term in the larger objective sense of recognized value or engrossing activity, while the other is using it as equivalent to selfish motive.

We have now to deal more in detail with each of the three phases mentioned. (1) First, the active or propulsive phase of interest takes us back to the consideration of impulse and the spontaneous urgencies or tendencies of activity. There is no such thing as absolutely diffuse, impartial impulse. Impulse is always differentiated along some more or less specific channel. Impulse has its own special lines of discharge. The old puzzle about the ass between two bundles of hay is only too familiar, but the recognition of its fundamental fallacy is not so common. If the self were purely passive or purely indifferent, waiting upon stimulation from without, then the self illustrated in this supposed example would remain forever helpless, starving to death, because of its equipoise between two sources of food. The error is in the supposition of this balanced internal condition. The self is always already doing something, intent on something urgent. And this ongoing activity always gives it a bent in one direction rather than another. The ass, in other words, is always already moving toward one bundle rather than the other. No amount of physical cross-eyedness could induce such psychical cross-eyedness that the animal would be in a condition of equal stimulation from both sides.

In this primitive condition of spontaneous impulsive activity, we have the basis for natural interest. Interest is no more passively waiting around to be excited from the outside than is impulse. In the selective or preferential quality of impulse we have the basis of the fact that at any given time, if we are psychically awake at all, we are always interested in one direction rather than another. The condition of total lack of interest, or of absolutely impartially distributed interest, is as mythical as the story of the ass in scholastic ethics.

An equally great fallacy is the oft-made assumption of some chasm between impulse and the self. Impulse is spoken of as if it were a force swaying the self in this direction or that; as if the self were an indifferent, passive something waiting to be moved by the pressure of impulse; in reality, impulse is simply the impetus or outgoing of the self in one direction or other. This point is mentioned now because the connection of impulse and interest is so close that any assumption, at this point, of impulse as external to self is sure to manifest itself later on in the assumption that interest is of the nature of an external inducement or attraction to self, instead of being an absorption of the activities of the self in the object that allows these activities to function.

(2) Second, the objective side of interest. Every interest, as already said, attaches itself to an object. The artist is interested in his brushes, in his colors, in his technique. The business man is interested in the play of supply and demand, in the movement of markets, etc. Take whatever instance of interest we choose and we shall find that, if we cut out the factor of the object about which interest clusters, interest itself disappears, relapsing into mere subjective feeling.

The question of psychological import is the relationship existing between activity and idea or object. The object arises as the definition or interpretation of the impulsive activity. The objects exhibit the bringing to consciousness of the quality of the impulsive activity.

Error begins in supposing the object already there, and then calling the activity into being. Canvas, brushes, and paints interest the artist, for example, only because they help him find his existing artistic capacity. There is nothing in a wheel and a piece of string to arouse a child's activity save as they set before him, in objective shape, some capacity which he already possesses and of whose mode of translation into action he is thereby made conscious. The object, in other words, transfers the impulsive activity into intellectual terms.

The impulse itself is blind. This only means that it does not know what it wants, what it is after. But as it finds outlet and expression, it reveals itself. The object of interest is that which gives the spontaneous activity filling or content. The object which supplies means and ends to an impulse brings it to consciousness and thus transforms it into an abiding interest.

(3) We now come to the emotional phase. Value is not only objective but subjective. That is, there is not only the thing which is projected as valuable or worth while, but there is also the feeling of its worth. It is, of course, impossible to define feeling. We can only say that it is the purely individual consciousness of worth and recognize that wherever we have interest there we have internal realization of value.

The gist of the psychology of interest may, accordingly, be stated as follows: An interest is primarily a form of self-expressive activity. If we examine this activity on the side of the content of expression, of what is done, we get its objective features, the ideas, objects, etc., to which the interest is attached, about which it clusters. If we take into account that it is self-expression, that self finds itself, is reflected back to itself, in this content, we get its emotional or feeling side. Any account of genuine interest must, therefore, grasp it as outgoing activity holding within its grasp an intellectual content, and reflecting itself in felt value.

At this point, it is necessary to distinguish two typical phases into which the one activity of self-expression, at the basis of all interest, differentiates itself, as this differentiation gives us also two types of interest. These two types of self-expression arise according as the end and means of expression do, or do not, coincide in time. In the former case we have immediate interest, in the latter mediate. It is all-important to carry our analysis over into an examination of these points, because it is in the matter of mediate interest that the one-sided theories arise, which, on one side (isolating the emotional phase), identify pleasure with interest; or, on the other (isolating the intellectual or ideal phase), deny interest and identify volition with effort.

There are cases where self-expression is direct and immedi-

ate. It puts itself forth with no thought of anything beyond.
The present activity is the only ultimate in consciousness. It
satisfies in and of itself. The end *is* the present activity, and so
there is no gap in space nor time between means and end.
All play is of this immediate character. All purely aesthetic
appreciation approximates this type. The existing experience holds us for its own sake and we do not demand of it
that it take us into something beyond itself. With the child
and his ball, the amateur and the hearing of a symphony, the
immediate engrosses. Its value is there, and is there in what
is directly present.

We may, if we choose, say that the interest is in the object
present to the senses, but we must beware how we interpret this saying. The object has no conscious existence, at
the time, save *in* the activity. The ball to the child is his game,
his game is his ball. The music has no existence save in the
rapt hearing of the music—so long as the interest is immediate or aesthetic. It is frequently said to be the object which
attracts attention, which calls forth interest to itself by its
own inherent qualities. But this is a psychological impossibility. The bright color, the sweet sound, that interest the
child are themselves phases of his organic activity. To say the
child attends to the color does not mean that he gives himself
up to an external object, but rather that he continues the activity which results in the presence of the color. His own activity so engrosses him that he endeavors to maintain it. But
when the object or end exists in idea or symbol, then the end,
the object to be reached and the means, the energies at command for reaching it, fall apart. A period of adjustment is
required. We do things in which we would not be interested
if they were ultimates; in which we are interested because they
are conceived as necessary to an end.

It is a mistake, however, to suppose that we regard these
intermediates *merely* as means;—as *lacking* in interest. In a
case of sheer drudgery we feel that we have to go through
things merely in order to reach a final end. But these intermediate steps are not recognized as in any sense *really* means;
and hence interest in the end is never transferred over into
them. If we felt they were in reality means to the end, we

should feel them so organically bound up with the end as to share in its value. The fact that they are repulsive indicates that we do not consider them intrinsically connected with the desired end. They are necessary evils, accidentally and externally attached to something we want, so that we can't get one without the other. They are not regarded as in the same process of self-expression as is the end. If we take the example of a man doing a day's work utterly repulsive to him simply for the sake of getting his wage, it is obvious that the day's task is to him only incidentally, accidentally, not intrinsically, a means to the end. The wage is an end simply in the sense that it comes last or afterwards; it is a physical, not a psychical, end. So the day's work is a means simply in the sense that it must precede getting pay, not in the sense that it organically aids in realizing the end.

The all-important point then in the consideration of mediate interest or voluntary attention is the kind of relationship which exists between the putting forth of energy considered as means, and the idea or object to be reached considered as end. If the two fall apart, if the means are not identified with the end, interest is not really mediated. The intervening steps are regarded simply as necessary evils to be gotten over with as soon as possible for the sake of the final outcome.

Here self-contradiction emerges. If the interest is wholly in the end and not at all in the means, there is nothing to insure attention being kept upon the means, and hence no way to guarantee the reaching of the end. The mind is not really on the work. The agent is not taken up with what he is doing. He is not psychically, but only externally, engaged. Hence, so far as he is concerned, it is a mere accident whether or not the end be reached. The break in interest between means and end marks, in other words, a break in the self.

On the other hand, if the means are recognized truly as means, if they are felt to be simply the way in which the end presents itself at the particular moment, then the full interest in the end is at once transferred to the so-called means. For the time being that becomes the end. As we illustrated the other case by an instance of drudgery, we may illustrate this by one of artistic construction. The sculptor has his end, his ideal, in view. To realize that end he must go through a series of intervening steps which are not, on the face of it, equivalent to the end. He must model and mould and chisel in a series of particular acts, no one of which is the beautiful form he has in mind, and every one of which represents the putting forth of personal energy on his own part. But because these are to him necessary means for the end, the ideal, the finished form is completely transferred over into these special acts. Each moulding of the clay, each stroke of the chisel, is for him at the time the whole end in process of realization. Whatever interest or value attaches to the end attaches to each of these steps. He is as much absorbed in one as in the other. Any failure in this complete identification means an inartistic product, means that he is not really interested in his ideal. A genuine interest in the ideal indicates of necessity an equal interest in all the conditions of its expression.

We are now in position to deal with the question of the relation of interest to desire and to effort. Desire and effort in their legitimate meaning are both of them phases of this mediated interest. They are correlatives, not opposites. Both effort and desire exist only when the end is somewhat remote. When energy is put forth purely for its own sake, there is no question of effort and equally no question of desire. Effort and desire both imply a state of tension. There is a certain amount of opposition existing between the ideal in view and the present actual state of things. We call it effort when we are thinking of the necessity of a decided transformation of the actual state of things in order to make it conform to the ideal—when we are thinking of the process from the side of the idea and interested in the question how to get it realized. We call it desire when we think of the tendency of the existing energies to push themselves forward so as to secure this transformation, or change the idea into a fact—when we think of the process from the side of the means at hand. But in either case, obstacles delaying us, and the continued persistence of activity against them, are implied. The only sure evidence of desire as against mere vague wishing, is effort,

and desire is aroused only when the exercise of effort is required.

In discussing the condition of mediate interest we may emphasize either the end in view, the idea, or we may start with
the consideration of the present means, the active side urgent for expression. The former is the intellectual side, the
latter the emotional. The tendency of the end to realize itself
through the process of mediation, overcoming resistance, is
effort. The tendency of the present powers to continue a
struggle for complete expression in an end remote in time is
desire.

According to the previous account, there is absolutely one
and the same psychical process at the basis of both desire and
effort. The distinction is not in the facts themselves, but simply in the attitude which the psychologist or observer takes
toward the facts. Both desire and effort are phases of self-
expression arising whenever it becomes so complex that the
end, the self to be expressed, and the powers at hand, the
means of expression, do not directly coincide with each other.
The errors previously discussed on the educational side arise
from abstracting either desire or effort from the active process of self-expression. Separated from activity, one may be
set over against the other. For the sake of dealing with these
educational errors at their root, it becomes necessary, accordingly, to discuss both desire and effort somewhat more
in detail.

We often speak of appetite as blind and lawless. We conceive it as insisting upon its own satisfaction, irrespective of
circumstances or of the good to the self. This means that the
appetite is only felt; it is not known. It is not considered from
the standpoint of its bearings or relationships. It is not translated over into terms of its results. Consequently, it is not
made intelligent. It is not rationalized. As a result energy is
wasted. In any strong appetite there is an immense amount
of power, physical and psychical, stirred up; but where the
agent does not anticipate the ends corresponding to this
power it is undirected. The energy expends itself in chance
channels or according to some accidental stimulus. The organism is exhausted, and nothing positive or objective is

accomplished. The disturbance or agitation is out of proportion to any ends reached. All there is to show for such a vast excitation of energy is the momentary satisfaction felt in its stimulation and expenditure.

Even as regards this blind appetite, there is, however, a decided difference of type between the lower animals and man. In the animals, while the appetite is not conscious of its own end, it none the less seeks that end by a sort of harmony pre-established in the animal structure. Fear serves the animal as a stimulus to flight or to seeking cover. Anger serves it for purposes of attack and defence. It is a very unusual occurrence when the feeling gets the better of the animal and causes it to waste its powers uselessly. But of the blind feelings in the human being, it is to be said that most of them require adjustment before they are of any regular permanent service. There is no doubt that fear or anger may be rendered useful to the man as they are to the animal. But in the former case they have to be trained to this use; in the latter they originally possess it. The ultimate function of anger is undoubtedly to do away with obstacles hindering the process of self-expression, but in a child the exhibition of anger is almost sure to leave the object, the obstacle, untouched and to exhaust the child. The blind feeling needs to be rationalized. The agent has to become conscious of the end or object and control his aroused powers by conscious reference to it.

For the process of self-expression to be effective and mechanical, there must, in other words, be a consciousness of both end and means. Whenever there is difficulty in effecting adjustment of means and ends the agent is thrown into a condition of emotion. Whenever we have on one side the idea corresponding to some end or object, and whenever we have on the other side a stirring up of the active impulses and habits, together with a tendency of the latter to focus themselves at once upon the former, there we have a disturbance or agitation, known on its psychical side as emotion. It is a common-place that as fast as habit gets definitely formed in relation to its own special end the feeling element drops out. But now let the usual end to which the habit is adapted be taken away and a sudden demand be made for the old habit to become a means towards a new end, and emotional stress at once becomes urgent. The active side is all stirred up, but neither discharges itself at once, without any end, nor yet directs itself towards any accustomed end. The result is tension between habit and aim, between impulse and idea, between means and end. This tension is the essential feature of emotion.

It is obvious from this account that the function of emotion is to secure a sufficient arousing of energy in critical periods of the life of the agent. When the end is new or unusual and there is great difficulty in attending to it, the natural tendency would be to let it go or turn away from it. But the very newness of the end often represents the importance of the demand that is being made. To neglect the end would be a serious, if not fatal, matter for the agent. The very difficulty in effecting the adjustment sends out successive waves of stimuli, which call into play more impulses and habits, thus reinforcing the powers, resources at the agent's command. The function of emotion is thus to brace or reinforce the agent in coping with the novel element in unexpected and immediate situations.

The normal moral outcome is found in a balance between the excitation and the ideal. If the former is too weak or diffused, the agent lacks in motor power. If it is relatively too strong, the agent is not able to handle the powers which have been stirred up. He is more or less beside himself. He is carried away by the extent of his own agitation. He relapses, in other words, into the phase of blind feeling.

Desire is a phase of this excitation or disturbance in the adjustment of active impulses or habits as means to an object considered as end or ideal. Desire cannot be identified with mere impulse or with blind feeling. Desire differs from the appetite of the animal in that it is always conscious, at least dimly, of its own end. When the agent is in the condition known as desire, he is conscious of some object ahead of him, and the consciousness of this object serves to reinforce his active tendencies. The thought of the desired object serves, in a word, to stimulate the means necessary to its attainment.

While desire is thus not a purely impulsive state, neither, of course, is it a purely intellectual one. The object may be present in consciousness, but it is simply contemplated as an object; if it does not serve as stimulus to activity, it occupies a purely aesthetic or theoretic place. At most, it will arouse only a pious wish or a vague sentimental longing, not an active desire.

The true moral function of desire is thus identical with that of emotion, of which, indeed, it is only one special phase. Its place in the moral life is to arouse energy, to stimulate the means necessary to accomplish the realization of ends otherwise purely theoretic or aesthetic. Our desires in a given direction simply measure the hold which certain ends or ideals have upon us. They *exhibit* the force of character, the *Drang* in that direction. They *test* the sincerity of character. A produced end which does not awaken desire is a mere pretension. It indicates a growing division of character, a threatening hypocrisy.

The moral treatment of desire, like that of emotion, involves securing a balance. Desire tends continually to overdo itself. It marks energy stirred up to serve as means; but the energy once stirred up tends to express itself on its own account independently of the end. Desire is greedy, lends itself to overhastiness, and unless watched makes the agent overhasty. It runs away with him. It is not enough that the contemplation of the end stir up the impulses and habits; the consciousness of the end must also abide, after they are excited, to direct the energy called into being.

The question, in other words, is whether the desire is made to contribute to the realization of the end, whether it has held strictly to its function as instrument, or whether the end gets subordinated to the desire. In the latter case we have self-indulgence. The end is thought of in order to get the impulses into play; but the moment this is secured the end is dropped or pushed out of sight, and the satisfaction got out of the excitation is substituted for it. The object, end, in other words, is prostituted to be an instrument of excitation only. Its claim to direct the powers which it has stimulated is ignored or willfully denied. Hence, the contradiction involved in the immoral use of emotion and desire. The end, the ideal, cannot be entirely absent from consciousness, as it is in the case of purely brute appetite. The end or aim has to be in consciousness to stir up or reinforce the active tendencies. It must be admitted, therefore, as end, but no sooner has it done the work of stimulation than it is denied to be an end and is reduced purely to the place of means.

We thus get a criterion for the normal position of pleasure in relation to desire. There can be no doubt that desire is always more or less pleasurable. It is pleasurable in so far as the end of self-expression is present in consciousness. For the end defines satisfaction, and any conception of it awakens, therefore, an image of satisfaction, which, so far as it goes, is itself pleasurable. The use of this pleasure is to give the end such a hold upon the agent that it may pass over from its ideal condition into one of actualization. Normal pleasure has a strictly instrumental place. It is *due* to the thought of the end on one side, and it *contributes* to the practical efficiency of the end on the other. In the case of self-indulgence the end is used simply to excite the pleasurable state of consciousness, and having done this, is thereafter denied. Pleasure, instead of serving to hold the mind to the end, is now made itself the end.

What, it may be asked, is the connection of this with the question of interest? Precisely this. In the analysis of desire we are brought back exactly to the question of mediate interest. Normal desire is simply a case of properly mediated interest. The problem of attaining the proper balance between the impulses on one side and an ideal or end on the other is just the question of getting enough interest in the end to prevent a too sudden expenditure of the waste energy—to direct this excited energy so that it shall be tributary to realizing the end. Here the interest in the end is taken over into the means. Interest, in other words, marks the fact that the emotional force aroused is functioning. This is our definition of interest; it is impulse functioning with reference to an idea of self-expression.

Interest in the end indicates that desire is both calmed and steadied. Over-greedy desire, like over-anxious aversion, defeats itself. The youthful hunter is so anxious to kill his game, he is so stimulated by the thought of reaching his end, that he can not control himself sufficiently to take steady aim. He shoots wild. The successful hunter is not the one who has lost interest in his end, in killing the game, but the one who is able to translate this interest completely over into the means necessary to accomplish his purpose. It is no longer the killing of the game that occupies his consciousness by itself, but the thought of the steps he has to perform. The means, once more, have been identified with the end; the desire has become mediate interest. The ideal dies as bare ideal to live again in instrumental powers.

We are thus able to see the error in those theories which hold that pleasure is the end of desire. As is well known, these theories divide themselves into two types. On one hand, one school of moralists holds that since pleasure is the object of desire it is the ideal and standard of conduct. The other school, accepting the same theory of the relation of pleasure and desire, holds that, on this very account, desire must be eliminated from the moral will; that the presence of desire in the motivation of conduct indicates a purely selfish or pleasure-seeking factor. Once recognized, however, that pleasure marks the satisfaction taken in the ideal of self-expression, and we see the falsity of both these theories. The real object of desire is not pleasure, but self-expression. The presence of desire marks simply the tension in the stage of self-expression reached. The pleasure felt is simply the reflex of the satisfaction which the self is anticipating in its own expression.

The fundamental mistake, in other words, lies in considering desire as a process prior to or outside of volition. It marks one stage in the development of volition—that stage in which the end, the purpose, the ideal, is sufficiently present to arouse and reinforce active impulses, and when there is still enough conflict within the self, as ideal on one side and as actual on the other, to make it a problem whether the end will succeed in directing the active powers as well as in exciting them. The development of desire into interest marks the happy solution of this problem.

So far we have been discussing the process of mediated self-expression from the standpoint of the means. We have now to consider the same process, throwing the emphasis of intellectual analysis on the side of the end. Because of the length of the foregoing discussion we may here briefly consider the end or ideal, on the sides, respectively, of its origin and its function.

First, its origin. The ideal is normally a projection of the active powers. It is not generated in a vacuum nor introduced into the mind from outside impulses and habits actually striving for expression. It is simply these active powers getting off and looking at themselves to see what they are like; to see what they are upon the whole, permanently, in their final bearings, and not simply as they are at the moment and in their relative isolation. The ideal, in other words, is the self-consciousness of the impulse. It is its self-interpretation; its value in terms of objective self-expression.

Second, hence its function. If the ideal had its genesis independent of the active powers, it is impossible to see how it could ever get to work. The psychical machinery by which it should cease to be barely an ideal, and become an actuality, would be wanting. But just because the ideal is normally the projection of the active powers into intellectual terms the ideal inevitably possesses active quality. This dynamic factor is present to stay. Its appearance as motive is not anything different in kind from its appearance as ideal. Motivation is just the realization of the active value originally attaching to it.

In other words, when the ideal has the function of motive (a power inducing to activity), we have precisely the same fact, viewed from the standpoint of the end, that we have just now considered as the passing over of desire into mediate interest when viewing it from the side of the means. So long as the ideal does not become a motive it indicates that the ideal itself is not yet definitely formed. There is conflict of ideals. The agent has two possible ends before him, one corresponding to one set of his active powers and another to another set of impulses or habits. Thought, reflection, is not focused, accordingly, in any single direction. The self has not yet found itself. It does not know what it really wants. It is in process of tentative self-expression, first trying on one self and then another to see how they fit. The attainment of a single purpose or the defining of one final ideal indicates the self has found its unity of expression. At this exact point the ideal, having no longer any opposition to hold it back, begins to show itself in overt action. The ideal has become a motive. The interest in the end is now taken over into the impulses and habits, and they become the present ends. Motive is the interest in the ideal mediated into impulse and habit.

Normal effort is precisely this self-realizing tendency of the ideal—its struggle to pass over into motive. The empty or formal ideal is the end which is not suggested by, or does not grow out of, the agent's active powers. Lacking any dynamic qualities, it does not assert itself; it does not become a motor, a motive. But whenever the ideal is really a projection or translation of self-expression, it must strive to assert itself. It must persist through obstacles, and endeavor to transform obstacles into means of its own realization. The degree of its persistency simply marks the extent to which it is in reality and not simply in name a true ideal or conceived form of self-expression.

The matter of good intentions or "meaning well" affords a good illustration of this principle. When a person who has outwardly failed in his duty offers his good intentions as a justification or palliation of conduct, what determines whether or no his excuse shall be accepted? Is it not precisely whether he can or not show effort on the part of his intention, his ideal, to realize itself, and can show obstacles intervening from without which have prevented its expression up to the point of overt realization? If he cannot show such overwhelming interference from without, we have a right to conclude either that the agent is attempting to deceive us or else is self-deceived—that his so-called good intention was in reality but a vague sentimental wish or else a second-handed reference to some conventional ideal which had no real hold upon him. We always use the persistence of an end against obstacles as a test of its vitality, its genuineness.

On the other hand, effort in the sense of strain because of

lack in interest is evidence of the abnormal use of effort. The necessity of effort in this sense indicates that the end nominally held up is not recognized as a form of self-expression—that it is external to the self and hence fails in interest. The *conscious* stirring up of effort marks simply the unreal strain necessarily involved in any attempt to reach an end which is not part and parcel of the self's own process. The strain is always artificial; it requires external stimulation of some sort or other to keep it going and always leads to exhaustion. Not only does effort in its true sense play no part in moral training, but it plays a distinctly immoral part. The externality of the end as witnessed in its failure to arouse the active impulses and to persist towards its own realization makes it impossible that any strain to attain this end should have any other than a relatively immoral motive. Only selfish fear, the dread of some external power, or else purely mechanical habit, or else the hope of some external reward, some more or less subtle form of bribery, can be really a motive in any such instance.

We thus see how the theories of pleasure as a motive and artificial effort as a motive have the same practical outcome. The theory of strain always involves some reference to either pleasure or pain as the real controlling motive. And the theory of pleasure, because of its lack of an intrinsic end which holds and directs the powers, has continually to fall back upon some external inducement to excite the flagging powers. It is a common-place in morals that no one puts forth more effort with less avail than the habitual seeker after pleasure.

The outcome of our psychological analysis is thus identical with the results reached by consideration of the practical educational side. There we found that the appeal to making things interesting, to stirring up pleasure in things not of themselves interesting, leads as a matter of common experience to alternation of over-stimulation and dull apathy. Here we find that the desire for pleasure as an end leads necessarily to the stirring up of energies uselessly on one side, and the undirected wasteful expenditure of energies on the other.

On the educational side we saw that the appeal to the sheer

force of "will," so-called, apart from any interest in the object, means the formation of habits of divided attention—the mechanical doing of certain things in a purely external way on the one side and the riotous uncontrolled play of imagery on the other. On the psychological side we find that interest in an end or object simply means that the self is finding its own expression in a certain direction; that, therefore, the effort to realize an end where such interest is wanting means necessarily a division of the self. On one side, its natural tendency to self-expression cannot be got rid of by being ignored. On the other, external circumstances force it to utilize some of its energies in ways which to it are valueless.

On the educational side we were led to assume that normal interest and effort are identical with the process of self-expression. We have now through the process of mediated self-expression secured a fairly adequate psychological justification for that practical postulate of education.

VI

Society
and
Education

AMERICAN EDUCATION
AND CULTURE *

One can foretell the derision which will be awakened in certain quarters by a statement that the central theme of the current meeting of the National Educational Association is cultural education. What has culture to do with the quotidian tasks of millions of harassed pupils and teachers preoccupied with the routine of alphabetic combinations and figuring? What bond is there between culture and barren outlines of history and literature? So far the scene may be called pathetic rather than an occasion for satire. But one foresees the critics, the self-elected saving remnant, passing on to indignant condemnation of the voluntary surrender of our educational system to utilitarian ends, its prostitution to the demands of the passing moment and the cry for the practical. Or possibly the selection of cultural education as a theme of discourse will be welcome as a sign of belated repentance, while superior critics sorrowingly wonder whether the return to the good old paths is sought out too late.

To those who are in closer contact with the opinions which hold conscious sway in the minds of the great mass of teachers and educational leaders there is something humorous in

* From *Characters and Events*, 1929.

the assumption that they are given over to worship of the vocational and industrial. The annual pilgrimage of the teachers of the country to European cathedral and art gallery is the authentic indication of the conscious estimate of the older ideal of culture. Nothing gets a hand so quickly in any gathering of teachers as precisely the sort of talk in which the critics engage. The shibboleths and the sentimentalities are held in common by critic and the workers criticized. "Culture and discipline" serve as emblems of a superiority hoped for or attained, and as catchwords to save the trouble of personal thought. Behind there appears a sense of some deficiency in our self-conscious devotion to retrospective culture. We protest too much. Our gestures betray the awkwardness of a pose maintained laboriously against odds. In contrast there is grace in the spontaneous uncouthness of barbarians whole-heartedly abandoned in their barbarism.

While the critics are all wrong about the conscious attitude and intent of those who manage our educational system, they are right about the powerful educational currents of the day. These cannot be called cultural:—not when measured by any standard drawn from the past. For these standards concern the past—what *has* been said and thought—while what is alive and compelling in our education moves toward some undiscovered future. From this contrast between our conscious ideals and our tendencies in action spring our confusion and our blind uncertainties. We think we think one thing while our deeds require us to give attention to a radically different set of considerations. This intellectual constraint is the real foe to our culture. The beginning of culture would be to cease plaintive eulogies of a past culture, eulogies which carry only a few yards before they are drowned in the noise of the day, and essay an imaginative insight into the possibilities of what is going on so assuredly although so blindly and crudely.

The disparity between actual tendency and backward-looking loyalty carries within itself the whole issue of cultural education. Measured in other terms than that of some as yet unachieved possibility of just the forces from which sequestered culture shrinks in horror, the cause of culture is doomed so far as public education is concerned. Indeed, it hardly exists anywhere outside the pages of Mr. Paul Elmer More, and his heirs and assigns. The serious question is whether we may assist the vital forces into new forms of thought and sensation. It would be cruel were it not so impotent to assess stumbling educational efforts of the day by ideas of archaic origin when the need is for an idealized interpretation of facts which will reveal mind in those concerns which the older culture thought of as purely material, and perceive human and moral issues in what seem to be the purely physical forces of industry.

The beginning of a culture stripped of egoistic illusions is the perception that we have as yet no culture: that our culture is something to achieve, to create. This perception gives the national assembly of teachers representative dignity. Our school men and women are seen as adventuring for that which is not but which may be brought to be. They are not in fact engaged in protecting a secluded culture against the fierce forays of materialistic and utilitarian America. They are endeavoring, so far as they are not rehearsing phrases whose meaning is forgot, to turn these very forces into thought and sentiment. The enterprise is of heroic dimensions. To set up as protector of a shrinking classicism requires only the accidents of a learned education, the possession of leisure and a reasonably apt memory for some phrases, and a facile pen for others. To transmute a society built on an industry which is not yet humanized into a society which wields its knowledge and its industrial power in behalf of a democratic culture requires the courage of an inspired imagination.

I am one of those who think that the only test and justification of any form of political and economic society is its contribution to art and science—to what may roundly be called culture. That America has not yet so justified itself is too obvious for even lament. The explanation that the physical conquest of a continent had first to be completed is an inversion. To settle a continent is to put in order, and this is a work which comes after, not before, great intelligence and great art. The accomplishment of the justification is then hugely difficult. For it means nothing less than the discovery and application of a method of subduing and settling nature in the interests of a democracy, that is to say of masses who shall form a community of directed thought and emotion in spite of being the masses. That this has not yet been effected goes without saying. It has never even been attempted before. Hence the puny irrelevancy that measures our strivings with yard sticks handed down from class cultures of the past.

That the achievement is immensely difficult means that it may fail. There is no inevitable predestined success. But the failure, if it comes, will be the theme of tragedy and not of complacent lamentation nor wilful satire. For while success is not predestined, there are forces at work which are like destiny in their independence of conscious choice or wish. Not conscious intent, either perverse or wise, is forcing the realistic, the practical, the industrial, into education. Not conscious deliberation causes college presidents who devote commencement day to singing the praises of pure culture to spend their working days in arranging for technical and professional schools. It is not conscious preference which leads school superintendents who deliver orations at teachers' meetings upon the blessings of old-fashioned discipline and culture to demand from their boards new equipment, new courses and studies of a more "practical" and appealing kind. Political and economic forces quite beyond their control are compelling these things. And they will remain beyond the control of any of us save as men honestly face the actualities and busy themselves with inquiring what education they impart and what culture may issue from *their* cultivation.

It is as elements in this heroic undertaking that current tendencies in American education can be appraised. Since we can neither beg nor borrow a culture without betraying both it and ourselves, nothing remains save to produce one. Those who are too feeble or too finicky to engage in the enterprise will continue their search for asylums and hospitals which they idealize into palaces. Others will either go their way still caught in the meshes of a mechanical industrialism, or will subdue the industrial machinery to human ends until the nation is endowed with soul.

Certain commonplaces must be reiterated till their import

is acknowledged. The industrial revolution was born of the new science of nature. Any democracy which is more than an imitation of some archaic republican government must issue from the womb of our chaotic industrialism. Science makes democracy possible because it brings relief from depending upon massed human labor, because of the substitution it makes possible of inanimate forces for human muscular energy, and because of the resources for excess production and easy distribution which it effects. The old culture is doomed for us because it was built upon an alliance of political and spiritual powers, an equilibrium of governing and leisure classes, which no longer exists. Those who deplore the crudities and superficialities of thought and sensation which mark our day are rarely inhuman enough to wish the old régime back. They are merely unintelligent enough to want a result without the conditions which produced it, and in the face of conditions making the result no longer possible.

In short, our culture must be consonant with realistic science and with machine industry, instead of a refuge from them. And while there is no guaranty that an education which uses science and employs the controlled processes of industry as a regular part of its equipment will succeed, there is every assurance that an educational practice which sets science and industry in opposition to its ideal of culture will fail. Natural science has in its applications to economic production and exchange brought an industry and a society where quantity alone seems to count. It is for education to bring the light of science and the power of work to the aid of every soul that it may discover its quality. For in a spiritually democratic society every individual would realize distinction. Culture would then be for the first time in human history an individual achievement and not a class possession. An education fit for our ideal uses is a matter of actual forces not of opinions.

Our public education is the potential means for effecting the transfiguration of the mechanics of modern life into sentiment and imagination. We may, I repeat, never get beyond the mechanics. We may remain burly, merely vigorous, expending energy riotously in making money, seeking pleasure and winning temporary victories over one another. Even such an estate has a virility lacking to a culture whose method is reminiscence, and whose triumph is finding a place of refuge. But it is not enough to justify a democracy as against the best of past aristocracies even though return to them is forever impossible. To bring to the consciousness of the coming generation something of the potential significance of the life of to-day, to transmute it from outward fact into intelligent perception, is the first step in the creation of a culture. The teachers who are facing this fact and who are trying to use the vital unspiritualized agencies of to-day as means of effecting the perception of a human meaning yet to be realized are sharing in the act of creation. To perpetuate in the name of culture the tradition of aloofness from realistic science and compelling industry is to give them free course in their most unenlightened form. Not chiding but the sympathy and direction of understanding is what the harsh utilitarian and prosaic tendencies of present education require.

THE SCHOOL AND SOCIETY *

The School and Social Progress

We are apt to look at the school from an individualistic standpoint, as something between teacher and pupil, or between
teacher and parent. That which interests us most is naturally
the progress made by the individual child of our acquaintance, his normal physical development, his advance in ability
to read, write, and figure, his growth in the knowledge of
geography and history, improvement in manners, habits of
promptness, order, and industry—it is from such standards
as these that we judge the work of the school. And rightly so.
Yet the range of the outlook needs to be enlarged. What the
best and wisest parent wants for his own child, that must the
community want for all of its children. Any other ideal for
our schools is narrow and unlovely; acted upon, it destroys
our democracy. All that society has accomplished for itself is
put, through the agency of the school, at the disposal of its
future members. All its better thoughts of itself it hopes to
realize through the new possibilities thus opened to its future
self. Here individualism and socialism are at one. Only by being true to the full growth of all the individuals who make it
up, can society by any chance be true to itself. And in the
self-direction thus given, nothing counts as much as the

---

* This was published originally as a pamphlet by University of
Chicago Press, 1899.

school, for, as Horace Mann said, "Where anything is growing, one former is worth a thousand re-formers."

Whenever we have in mind the discussion of a new movement in education, it is especially necessary to take the
broader, or social, view. Otherwise, changes in the school institution and tradition will be looked at as the arbitrary inventions of particular teachers, at the worst transitory fads,
and at the best merely improvements in certain details—and
this is the plane upon which it is too customary to consider
school changes. It is as rational to conceive of the locomotive or the telegraph as personal devices. The modification
going on in the method and curriculum of education is as
much a product of the changed social situation, and as much
an effort to meet the needs of the new society that is forming,
as are changes in modes of industry and commerce.

It is to this, then, that I especially ask your attention: the
effort to conceive what roughly may be termed the "New
Education" in the light of larger changes in society. Can we
connect this "New Education" with the general march of
events? If we can, it will lose its isolated character; it will
cease to be an affair which proceeds only from the over-
ingenious minds of pedagogues dealing with particular pupils.
It will appear as part and parcel of the whole social evolution, and, in its more general features at least, as inevitable.
Let us then ask after the main aspects of the social movement; and afterward turn to the school to find what witness
it gives of effort to put itself in line. And since it is quite impossible to cover the whole ground, I shall for the most part
confine myself to one typical thing in the modern school
movement—that which passes under the name of manual
training—hoping, if the relation of that to changed social
conditions appears, we shall be ready to concede the point
as well regarding other educational innovations.

I make no apology for not dwelling at length upon the social changes in question. Those I shall mention are writ so
large that he who runs may read. The change that comes first
to mind, the one that overshadows and even controls all others, is the industrial one—the application of science resulting in the great inventions that have utilized the forces of

nature on a vast and inexpensive scale: the growth of a world-wide market as the object of production, of vast manufacturing centers to supply this market, of cheap and rapid means of communication and distribution between all its parts. Even as to its feebler beginnings, this change is not much more than a century old; in many of its most important aspects it falls within the short span of those now living. One can hardly believe there has been a revolution in all history so rapid, so extensive, so complete. Through it the face of the earth is making over, even as to its physical forms; political boundaries are wiped out and moved about, as if they were indeed only lines on a paper map; population is hurriedly gathered into cities from the ends of the earth; habits of living are altered with startling abruptness and thoroughness; the search for the truths of nature is infinitely stimulated and facilitated, and their application to life made not only practicable, but commercially necessary. Even our moral and religious ideas and interests, the most conservative because the deepest-lying things in our nature, are profoundly affected. That this revolution should not affect education in some other than a formal and superficial fashion is inconceivable.

Back of the factory system lies the household and neighborhood system. Those of us who are here today need go back only one, two, or at most three generations, to find a time when the household was practically the center in which were carried on, or about which were clustered, all the typical forms of industrial occupation. The clothing worn was for the most part not only made in the house, but the members of the household were usually familiar with the shearing of the sheep, the carding and spinning of the wool, and the plying of the loom. Instead of pressing a button and flooding the house with electric light, the whole process of getting illumination was followed in its toilsome length from the killing of the animal and the trying of fat to the making of wicks and dipping of candles. The supply of flour, of lumber, of foods, of building materials, of household furniture, even of metal ware, of nails, hinges, hammers, etc., was in the immediate neighborhood, in shops which were constantly open to inspection and often centers of neighborhood congregation. The entire industrial process stood revealed, from the production on the farm of the raw materials till the finished article was actually put to use. Not only this, but practically every member of the household had his own share in the work. The children, as they gained in strength and capacity, were gradually initiated into the mysteries of the several processes. It was a matter of immediate and personal concern, even to the point of actual participation.

We cannot overlook the factors of discipline and of character-building involved in this: training in habits of order and of industry, and in the idea of responsibility, of obligation to do something, to produce something, in the world. There was always something which really needed to be done, and a real necessity that each member of the household should do his own part faithfully and in coöperation with others. Personalities which became effective in action were bred and tested in the medium of action. Again, we cannot overlook the importance for educational purposes of the close and intimate acquaintance got with nature at first hand, with real things and materials, with the actual processes of their manipulation, and the knowledge of their social necessities and uses. In all this there was continual training of observation, of ingenuity, constructive imagination, of logical thought, and of the sense of reality acquired through first-hand contact with actualities. The educative forces of the domestic spinning and weaving, of the sawmill, the gristmill, the cooper shop, and the blacksmith forge, were continuously operative.

No number of object-lessons, got up as object-lessons for the sake of giving information, can afford even the shadow of a substitute for acquaintance with the plants and animals of the farm and garden acquired through actual living among them and caring for them. No training of sense-organs in school, introduced for the sake of training, can begin to compete with the alertness and fulness of sense-life that comes through daily intimacy and interest in familiar occupations. Verbal memory can be trained in committing tasks, a certain discipline of the reasoning powers can be acquired through lessons in science and mathematics; but, after all, this is somewhat remote and shadowy compared with the training of attention and of judgment that is acquired in having to do things with a real motive behind and a real outcome ahead. At present, concentration of industry and division of labor have practically eliminated household and neighborhood occupations—at least for educational purposes. But it is useless to bemoan the departure of the good old days of children's modesty, reverence, and implicit obedience, if we expect merely by bemoaning and by exhortation to bring them back. It is radical conditions which have changed, and only an equally radical change in education suffices. We must recognize our compensations—the increase in toleration, in breadth of social judgment, the larger acquaintance with human nature, the sharpened alertness in reading signs of character and interpreting social situations, greater accuracy of adaptation to differing personalities, contact with greater commercial activities. These considerations mean much to the city-bred child of today. Yet there is a real problem: how shall we retain these advantages, and yet introduce into the school something representing the other side of life—occupations which exact personal responsibilities and which train the child in relation to the physical realities of life?

When we turn to the school, we find that one of the most striking tendencies at present is toward the introduction of so-called manual training, shopwork, and the household arts —sewing and cooking.

This has not been done "on purpose," with a full consciousness that the school must now supply that factor of training formerly taken care of in the home, but rather by instinct, by experimenting and finding that such work takes a vital hold of pupils and gives them something which was not to be got in any other way. Consciousness of its real import is still so weak that the work is often done in a half-hearted, confused, and unrelated way. The reasons assigned to justify it are painfully inadequate or sometimes even positively wrong.

If we were to cross-examine even those who are most favorably disposed to the introduction of this work into our school system, we should, I imagine, generally find the main reasons to be that such work engages the full spontaneous interest and attention of the children. It keeps them alert and active, instead of passive and receptive; it makes them more useful, more capable, and hence more inclined to be helpful at home; it prepares them to some extent for the practical duties of later life—the girls to be more efficient house managers, if not actually cooks and sempstresses; the boys (were our educational system only adequately rounded out into trade schools) for their future vocations. I do not underestimate the worth of these reasons. Of those indicated by the changed attitude of the children I shall indeed have something to say in the next chapter, when speaking directly of the relationship of the school to the child. But the point of view is, upon the whole, unnecessarily narrow. We must conceive of work in wood and metal, of weaving, sewing, and cooking, as methods of life, not as distinct studies.

We must conceive of them in their social significance, as types of the processes by which society keeps itself going, as agencies for bringing home to the child some of the primal necessities of community life, and as ways in which these needs have been met by the growing insight and ingenuity of man; in short, as instrumentalities through which the school itself shall be made a genuine form of active community life, instead of a place set apart in which to learn lessons.

A society is a number of people held together because they are working along common lines, in a common spirit, and with reference to common aims. The common needs and aims demand a growing interchange of thought and growing unity of sympathetic feeling. The radical reason that the present school cannot organize itself as a natural social unit is because just this element of common and productive activity is absent. Upon the playground, in game and sport, social organization takes place spontaneously and inevitably. There is something to do, some activity to be carried on, requiring natural divisions of labor, selection of leaders and followers, mutual coöperation and emulation. In the schoolroom the motive and the cement of social organization are alike wanting. Upon the ethical side, the tragic weakness of the present school is that it endeavors to prepare future members of the social order in a medium in which the conditions of the social spirit are eminently wanting.

The difference that appears when occupations are made the articulating centers of school life is not easy to describe in words; it is a difference in motive, of spirit and atmosphere. As one enters a busy kitchen in which a group of children are actively engaged in the preparation of food, the psychological difference, the change from more or less passive and inert recipiency and restraint to one of buoyant outgoing energy, is so obvious as fairly to strike one in the face. Indeed, to those whose image of the school is rigidly set the change is sure to give a shock. But the change in the social attitude is equally marked. The mere absorption of facts and truths is so exclusively individual an affair that it tends very naturally to pass into selfishness. There is no obvious social motive for the acquirement of mere learning, there is no clear social gain in success thereat. Indeed, almost the only measure for success is a competitive one, in the bad sense of that term—a comparison of results in the recitation or in the examination to see which child has succeeded in getting ahead of others in storing up, in accumulating, the maximum of information. So thoroughly is this the prevalent atmosphere that for one child to help another in his task has become a school crime. Where the school work consists in simply learning lessons, mutual assistance, instead of being the most natural form of coöperation and association, becomes a clandestine effort to relieve one's neighbor of his proper duties. Where active work is going on, all this is changed. Helping others, instead of being a form of charity which impoverishes the recipient, is simply an aid in setting free the powers and furthering the impulse of the one helped. A spirit of free communication, of interchange of ideas, suggestions, results, both successes and failures of previous experiences, becomes the dominating note of the recitation. So far as emulation enters in, it is in the comparison of individuals, not with regard to the quantity of information personally absorbed, but with reference to the quality of work done—the genuine community standard of value. In an in-

formal but all the more pervasive way, the school life organizes itself on a social basis.

Within this organization is found the principle of school
discipline or order. Of course, order is simply a thing which
is relative to an end. If you have the end in view of forty
or fifty children learning certain set lessons, to be recited to a
teacher, your discipline must be devoted to securing that result. But if the end in view is the development of a spirit of
social coöperation and community life, discipline must grow
out of and be relative to this. There is little order of one sort
where things are in process of construction; there is a certain
disorder in any busy workshop; there is not silence; persons
are not engaged in maintaining certain fixed physical postures;
their arms are not folded; they are not holding their books
thus and so. They are doing a variety of things, and there is
the confusion, the bustle, that results from activity. But out
of the occupation, out of doing things that are to produce
results, and out of doing these in a social and coöperative
way, there is born a discipline of its own kind and type. Our
whole conception of school discipline changes when we get
this point of view. In critical moments we all realize that the
only discipline that stands by us, the only training that becomes intuition, is that got through life itself. That we learn
from experience, and from books or the sayings of others
only as they are related to experience, are not mere phrases.
But the school has been so set apart, so isolated from the ordinary conditions and motives of life, that the place where
children are sent for discipline is the one place in the world
where it is most difficult to get experience—the mother of all
discipline worth the name. It is only when a narrow and fixed
image of traditional school discipline dominates that one is
in any danger of overlooking that deeper and infinitely wider
discipline that comes from having a part to do in constructive
work, in contributing to a result which, social in spirit, is none
the less obvious and tangible in form—and hence in a form
with reference to which responsibility may be exacted and
accurate judgment passed.

The great thing to keep in mind, then, regarding the introduction into the school of various forms of active occupa-

tion, is that through them the entire spirit of the school is renewed. It has a chance to affiliate itself with life, to become the child's habitat, where he learns through directed living, instead of being only a place to learn lessons having an abstract and remote reference to some possible living to be done in the future. It gets a chance to be a miniature community, an embryonic society. This is the fundamental fact, and from this arise continuous and orderly sources of instruction. Under the industrial *régime* described, the child, after all, shared in the work, not for the sake of the sharing, but for the sake of the product. The educational results secured were real, yet incidental and dependent. But in the school the typical occupations followed are freed from all economic stress. The aim is not the economic value of the products, but the development of social power and insight. It is this liberation from narrow utilities, this openness to the possibilities of the human spirit, that makes these practical activities in the school allies of art and centers of science and history.

The unity of all the sciences is found in geography. The significance of geography is that it presents the earth as the enduring home of the occupations of man. The world without its relationship to human activity is less than a world. Human industry and achievement, apart from their roots in the earth, are not even a sentiment, hardly a name. The earth is the final source of all man's food. It is his continual shelter and protection, the raw material of all his activities, and the home to whose humanizing and idealizing all his achievement returns. It is the great field, the great mine, the great source of the energies of heat, light, and electricity; the great scene of ocean, stream, mountain, and plain, of which all our agriculture and mining and lumbering, all our manufacturing and distributing agencies, are but the partial elements and factors. It is through occupations determined by this environment that mankind has made its historical and political progress. It is through these occupations that the intellectual and emotional interpretation of nature has been developed. It is through what we do in and with the world that we read its meaning and measure its value.

In educational terms, this means that these occupations in the school shall not be mere practical devices or modes of routine employment, the gaining of better technical skill as cooks, sempstresses, or carpenters, but active centers of scientific insight into natural materials and processes, points of departure whence children shall be led out into a realization of the historic development of man. The actual significance of this can be told better through one illustration taken from actual school work than by general discourse.

There is nothing which strikes more oddly upon the average intelligent visitor than to see boys as well as girls of ten, twelve, and thirteen years of age engaged in sewing and weaving. If we look at this from the standpoint of preparation of the boys for sewing on buttons and making patches, we get a narrow and utilitarian conception—a basis that hardly justifies giving prominence to this sort of work in the school. But if we look at it from another side, we find that this work gives the point of departure from which the child can trace and follow the progress of mankind in history, getting an insight also into the materials used and the mechanical principles involved. In connection with these occupations the historic development of man is recapitulated. For example, the children are first given the raw material—the flax, the cotton plant, the wool as it comes from the back of the sheep (if we could take them to the place where the sheep are sheared, so much the better). Then a study is made of these materials from the standpoint of their adaptation to the uses to which they may be put. For instance, a comparison of the cotton fiber with wool fiber is made. I did not know, until the children told me, that the reason for the late development of the cotton industry as compared with the woolen is that the cotton fiber is so very difficult to free by hand from the seeds. The children in one group worked thirty minutes freeing cotton fibers from the boll and seeds, and succeeded in getting out less than one ounce. They could easily believe that one person could only gin one pound a day by hand, and could understand why their ancestors wore woolen instead of cotton clothing. Among other things discovered as affecting their relative utilities was the shortness of the cotton fiber as

compared with that of wool, the former being one-tenth of
an inch in length, while that of the latter is an inch in length;
also that the fibers of cotton are smooth and do not cling together, while the wool has a certain roughness which makes
the fibers stick, thus assisting the spinning. The children worked
this out for themselves with the actual material, aided by questions and suggestions from the teacher.

They then followed the processes necessary for working
the fibers up into cloth. They reinvented the first frame for
carding the wool—a couple of boards with sharp pins in them
for scratching it out. They redevised the simplest process for
spinning the wool—a pierced stone or some other weight
through which the wool is passed, and which as it is twirled
draws out the fiber; next the top, which was spun on the
floor, while the children kept the wool in their hands until it
was gradually drawn out and wound upon it. Then the children are introduced to the invention next in historic order,
working it out experimentally, thus seeing its necessity, and
tracing its effects, not only upon that particular industry, but
upon modes of social life—in this way passing in review the
entire process up to the present complete loom, and all that
goes with the application of science in the use of our present
available powers. I need not speak of the science involved in
this—the study of the fibers, of geographical features, the
conditions under which raw materials are grown, the great
centers of manufacture and distribution, the physics involved in the machinery of production; nor, again, of the
historical side—the influence which these inventions have
had upon humanity. You can concentrate the history of all
mankind into the evolution of the flax, cotton, and wool
fibers into clothing. I do not mean that this is the only, or the
best, center. But it is true that certain very real and important avenues to the consideration of the history of the race
are thus opened—that the mind is introduced to much more
fundamental and controlling influences than usually appear in
the political and chronological records that usually pass for
history.

Now, what is true of this one instance of fibers used in
fabrics (and, of course, I have only spoken of one or two

elementary phases of that) is true in its measure of every material used in every occupation, and of the processes employed. The occupation supplies the child with a genuine motive; it gives him experience at first hand; it brings him into contact with realities. It does all this, but in addition it is liberalized throughout by translation into its historic and social values and scientific equivalencies. With the growth of the child's mind in power and knowledge it ceases to be a pleasant occupation merely and becomes more and more a medium, an instrument, an organ—and is thereby transformed.

This, in turn, has its bearing upon the teaching of science. Under present conditions, all activity, to be successful, has to be directed somewhere and somehow by the scientific expert—it is a case of applied science. This connection should determine its place in education. It is not only that the occupations, the so-called manual or industrial work in the school, give the opportunity for the introduction of science which illuminates them, which makes them material, freighted with meaning, instead of being mere devices of hand and eye; but that the scientific insight thus gained becomes an indispensable instrument of free and active participation in modern social life. Plato somewhere speaks of the slave as one who in his actions does not express his own ideas, but those of some other man. It is our social problem now, even more urgent than in the time of Plato, that method, purpose, understanding, shall exist in the consciousness of the one who does the work, that his activity shall have meaning to himself.

When occupations in the school are conceived in this broad and generous way, I can only stand lost in wonder at the objections so often heard, that such occupations are out of place in the school because they are materialistic, utilitarian, or even menial in their tendency. It sometimes seems to me that those who make these objections must live in quite another world. The world in which most of us live is a world in which everyone has a calling and occupation, something to do. Some are managers and others are subordinates. But the great thing for one as for the other is that each shall have had the education which enables him to see within his daily work all there is in it of large and human significance. How many of the employed are today mere appendages to the machines which they operate! This may be due in part to the machine itself or the *régime* which lays so much stress upon the products of the machine; but it is certainly due in large part to the fact that the worker has had no opportunity to develop his imagination and his sympathetic insight as to the social and scientific values found in his work. At present, the impulses which lie at the basis of the industrial system are either practically neglected or positively distorted during the school period. Until the instincts of construction and production are systematically laid hold of in the years of childhood and youth, until they are trained in social directions, enriched by historical interpretation, controlled and illuminated by scientific methods, we certainly are in no position even to locate the source of our economic evils, much less to deal with them effectively.

If we go back a few centuries, we find a practical monopoly of learning. The term *possession* of learning was, indeed, a happy one. Learning was a class matter. This was a necessary result of social conditions. There were not in existence any means by which the multitude could possibly have access to intellectual resources. These were stored up and hidden away in manuscripts. Of these there were at best only a few, and it required long and toilsome preparation to be able to do anything with them. A high-priesthood of learning, which guarded the treasury of truth and which doled it out to the masses under severe restrictions, was the inevitable expression of these conditions. But, as a direct result of the industrial revolution of which we have been speaking, this has been changed. Printing was invented; it was made commercial. Books, magazines, papers were multiplied and cheapened. As a result of the locomotive and telegraph, frequent, rapid, and cheap intercommunication by mails and electricity was called into being. Travel has been rendered easy; freedom of movement, with its accompanying exchange of ideas, indefinitely facilitated. The result has been an intellectual revolution. Learning has been put into circulation. While there still is, and probably always will be, a particular class having the special business of inquiry in hand, a distinctively learned class is henceforth out of the question. It is an anachronism. Knowledge is no longer an immobile solid; it has been liquefied. It is actively moving in all the currents of society itself.

It is easy to see that this revolution, as regards the materials of knowledge, carries with it a marked change in the attitude of the individual. Stimuli of an intellectual sort pour in upon us in all kinds of ways. The merely intellectual life, the life of scholarship and of learning, thus gets a very altered value. Academic and scholastic, instead of being titles of honor, are becoming terms of reproach.

But all this means a necessary change in the attitude of the school, one of which we are as yet far from realizing the full force. Our school methods, and to a very considerable extent our curriculum, are inherited from the period when learning and command of certain symbols, affording as they did the only access to learning, were all-important. The ideals of this period are still largely in control, even where the outward methods and studies have been changed. We sometimes hear the introduction of manual training, art, and science into the elementary, and even the secondary, schools deprecated on the ground that they tend toward the production of specialists—that they detract from our present scheme of generous, liberal culture. The point of this objection would be ludicrous if it were not often so effective as to make it tragic. It is our present education which is highly specialized, one-sided, and narrow. It is an education dominated almost entirely by the mediaeval conception of learning. It is something which appeals for the most part simply to the intellectual aspect of our natures, our desire to learn, to accumulate information, and to get control of the symbols of learning; not to our impulses and tendencies to make, to do, to create, to produce, whether in the form of utility or of art. The very fact that manual training, art, and science are objected to as technical, as tending toward mere specialism, is of itself as good testimony as could be offered to the specialized aim which controls current education. Unless education had been virtually identified with the exclusively intellectual pursuits, with learning as such, all these materials and methods would be welcome, would be greeted with the utmost hospitality.

While training for the profession of learning is regarded as the type of culture, as a liberal education, that of a mechanic, a musician, a lawyer, a doctor, a farmer, a merchant, or a railroad manager is regarded as purely technical and professional. The result is that which we see about us everywhere —the division into "cultured" people and "workers," the separation of theory and practice. Hardly 1 per cent of the entire school population ever attains to what we call higher education; only 5 per cent to the grade of our high school; while much more than half leave on or before the completion of the fifth year of the elementary grade. The simple facts of the case are that in the great majority of human beings the distinctively intellectual interest is not dominant. They have the so-called practical impulse and disposition. In many of those in whom by nature intellectual interest is strong, social conditions prevent its adequate realization. Consequently by far the larger number of pupils leave school as soon as they have acquired the rudiments of learning, as soon as they have enough of the symbols of reading, writing, and calculating to be of practical use to them in getting a living. While our educational leaders are talking of culture, the development of personality, etc., as the end and aim of education, the great majority of those who pass under the tuition of the school regard it only as a narrowly practical tool with which to get bread and butter enough to eke out a restricted life. If we were to conceive our educational end and aim in a less exclusive way, if we were to introduce into educational processes the activities which appeal to those whose dominant interest is to do and to make, we should find the hold of the school upon its members to be more vital, more prolonged, containing more of culture.

But why should I make this labored presentation? The obvious fact is that our social life has undergone a thorough and radical change. If our education is to have any meaning for life, it must pass through an equally complete transformation. This transformation is not something to appear suddenly, to be executed in a day by conscious purpose. It is already in progress. Those modifications of our school system which often appear (even to those most actively concerned with them, to say nothing of their spectators) to be mere changes of detail, mere improvement within the school mechanism, are in reality signs and evidences of evolution. The introduction of active occupations, of nature-study, of elementary science, of art, of history; the relegation of the merely symbolic and formal to a secondary position; the change in the moral school atmosphere, in the relation of pupils and teachers—of discipline; the introduction of more active, expressive, and self-directing factors—all these are not mere accidents, they are necessities of the larger social evolution. It remains but to organize all these factors, to appreciate them in their fulness of meaning, and to put the ideas and ideals involved into complete, uncompromising possession of our school system. To do this means to make each one of our schools an embryonic community life, active with types of occupations that reflect the life of the larger society and permeated throughout with the spirit of art, history, and science. When the school introduces and trains each child of society into membership within such a little community, saturating him with the spirit of service, and providing him with the instruments of effective self-direction, we shall have the deepest and best guaranty of a larger society which is worthy, lovely, and harmonious.

VII

Principles
of
Pedagogy

THE RELATION OF THEORY TO
PRACTICE IN EDUCATION * ¹

It is difficult, if not impossible, to define the proper relationship of theory and practice without a preliminary discussion, respectively, (1) of the nature and aim of theory; (2) of practice.

A. I shall assume without argument that adequate professional instruction of teachers is not exclusively theoretical, but involves a certain amount of practical work. The primary question as to the latter is the aim with which it shall be conducted. Two controlling purposes may be entertained so different from each other as radically to alter the amount, conditions, and method of practice work. On one hand, we may carry on the practical work with the object of giving teachers in training working command of the necessary tools of their profession; control of the technique of class instruction and management; skill and proficiency in the work of teaching. With this aim in view, practice work is, as far as it

* This selection appeared originally in National Society for the Scientific Study of Education, *Third Yearbook,* Part I, 1904.
¹ This paper is to be taken as representing the views of the writer, rather than those of any particular institution in an official way; for the writer thought it better to discuss certain principles that seem to him fundamental, rather than to define a system of procedure.

goes, of the nature of apprenticeship. On the other hand, we may propose to use practice work as an instrument in making real and vital theoretical instruction; the knowledge of subject-matter and of principles of education. This is the laboratory point of view.

The contrast between the two points of view is obvious; and the two aims together give the limiting terms within which all practice work falls. From one point of view, the aim is to form and equip the actual teacher; the aim is immediately as well as ultimately practical. From the other point of view, the *immediate* aim, the way of getting at the ultimate aim, is to supply the intellectual method and material of good workmanship, instead of making on the spot, as it were, an efficient workman. Practice work thus considered is administered primarily with reference to the intellectual reactions it incites, giving the student a better hold upon the educational significance of the subject-matter he is acquiring, and of the science, philosophy, and history of education. Of course, the *results* are not exclusive. It would be very strange if practice work in doing what the laboratory does for a student of physics or chemistry in way of securing a more vital understanding of its principles, should not at the same time insure some skill in the instruction and management of a class. It would also be peculiar if the process of acquiring such skill should not also incidentally serve to enlighten and enrich instruction in subject-matter and the theory of education. None the less, there is a fundamental difference in the conception and conduct of the practice work according as one idea or the other is dominant and the other subordinate. If the primary object of practice is acquiring skill in performing the duties of a teacher, then the amount of time given to practice work, the place at which it is introduced, the method of conducting it, of supervising, criticising, and correlating it, will differ widely from the method where the laboratory ideal prevails; and *vice versa*.

In discussing this matter, I shall try to present what I have termed the laboratory, as distinct from the apprentice idea. While I speak primarily from the standpoint of the college, I should not be frank if I did not say that I believe what I am going to say holds, *mutatis mutandis,* for the normal school as well.

I. I first adduce the example of other professional schools. I doubt whether we, as educators, keep in mind with sufficient constancy the fact that the problem of training teachers is one species of a more generic affair—that of training for professions. Our problem is akin to that of training architects, engineers, doctors, lawyers, etc. Moreover, since (shameful and incredible as it seems) the vocation of teaching is practically the last to recognize the need of specific professional preparation, there is all the more reason for teachers to try to find what they may learn from the more extensive and matured experience of other callings. If now we turn to what has happened in the history of training for other professions, we find the following marked tendencies:

1. The demand for an increased amount of scholastic attainments as a prerequisite for entering upon professional work.

2. Development of certain lines of work in the applied sciences and arts, as centers of professional work; compare, for example, the place occupied by chemistry and physiology in medical training at present, with that occupied by chairs of "practice" and of *"materia medica"* a generation ago.

3. Arrangement of the practical and quasi-professional work upon the assumption that (limits of time, etc., being taken into account) the professional school does its best for its students when it gives them typical and intensive, rather than extensive and detailed, practice. It aims, in a word, at *control of the intellectual methods* required for personal and independent mastery of practical skill, rather than at turning out at once masters of the craft. This arrangement necessarily involves considerable postponement of skill in the routine and technique of the profession, until the student, after graduation, enters upon the pursuit of his calling.

These results are all the more important to us because other professional schools mostly started from the same position which training schools for teachers have occupied. Their history shows a period in which the idea was that students ought from the start to be made as proficient as possible in practical skill. In seeking for the motive forces which have caused professional schools to travel so steadily away from this position and toward the idea that practical work should be conducted for the sake of vitalizing and illuminating *intellectual* methods two reasons may be singled out:

a) First, the limited time at the disposal of the schools, and the consequent need of economy in its employ. It is not necessary to assume that apprenticeship is of itself a bad thing. On the contrary, it may be admitted to be a good thing; but the time which a student spends in the training school is short at the best. Since short, it is an urgent matter that it be put to its most effective use; and, relatively speaking, the wise employ of this short time is in laying scientific foundations. These cannot be adequately secured when one is doing the actual work of the profession, while professional life does afford time for acquiring and perfecting skill of the more technical sort.

b) In the second place, there is inability to furnish in the school adequate conditions for the best acquiring and using of skill. As compared with actual practice, the best that the school of law or medicine can do is to provide a somewhat remote and simulated copy of the real thing. For such schools to attempt to give the skill which comes to those adequately prepared, insensibly and unavoidably in actual work, is the same sort of thing as for grammar schools to spend months upon months in trying to convey (usually quite unsuccessfully) that skill in commercial arithmetic which comes, under penalty of practical failure, in a few weeks in the bank or counting-house.

It may be said that the analogy does not hold good for teachers' training schools, because such institutions have model or practice departments, supplying conditions which are identical with those which the teacher has to meet in the' actual pursuit of his calling. But this is true at most only in such normal schools as are organized after the Oswego pattern—schools, that is to say, where the pupil-teacher is given for a considerable period of time the entire charge of instruction and discipline in the class-room, and does not come under a room critic-teacher. In all other cases, some of the most fundamentally significant features of the real school are reduced or eliminated. Most "practice schools" are a compromise. In theory they approximate ordinary conditions. As matter of fact, the "best interests of the children" are so safeguarded and supervised that the situation approaches learning to swim without going *too* near the water.

There are many ways that do not strike one at first glance, for removing the conditions of "practice work" from those of actual teaching. Deprivation of responsibility for the discipline of the room; the continued presence of an expert ready to suggest, to take matters into his own hands; close supervision; reduction of size of group taught; etc., etc., are some of these ways. The topic of "lesson plans" will be later referred to in connection with another topic. Here they may be alluded to as constituting one of the modes in which the conditions of the practice-teacher are made unreal. The student who prepares a number of more or less set lessons; who then has those lesson plans criticised; who then has his actual teaching criticised from the standpoint of success in carrying out the prearranged plans, is in a totally different attitude from the teacher who has to build up and modify his teaching plans as he goes along from experience gained in contact with pupils.

It would be difficult to find two things more remote from each other than the development of subject-matter under such control as is supplied from actual teaching, taking effect through the teacher's own initiative and reflective criticism, and its development with an eye fixed upon the judgment, presumed and actual, of a superior supervisory officer. Those phases of the problem of practice teaching which relate more distinctly to responsibility for the discipline of the room, or of the class, have received considerable attention in the past; but the more delicate and far-reaching matter of intellectual responsibility is too frequently ignored. Here enters the problem of securing conditions which will make practice work a genuine apprenticeship.

II. To place the emphasis upon the securing of proficiency in teaching and discipline *puts the attention of the student*

*teacher in the wrong place, and tends to fix it in the wrong
direction*—not wrong absolutely, but relatively as regards
perspective of needs and opportunities. The would-be teacher
has some time or other to face and solve two problems, each
extensive and serious enough by itself to demand absorbing
and undivided attention. These two problems are:

1. Mastery of subject-matter from the standpoint of its
educational value and use; or, what is the same thing, the
mastery of educational principles in their application to that
subject-matter which is at once the material of instruction
and the basis of discipline and control;

2. The mastery of the technique of class management.

This does not mean that the two problems are in any way
isolated or independent. On the contrary, they are strictly
correlative. *But the mind of a student cannot give equal attention to both at the same time.*

The difficulties which face a beginning teacher, who is set
down for the first time before a class of from thirty to sixty
children, in the responsibilities not only of instruction, but of
maintaining the required order in the room as a whole, are
most trying. It is almost impossible for an old teacher who
has acquired the requisite skill of doing two or three distinct
things simultaneously—skill to see the room as a whole
while hearing one individual in one class recite, of keeping
the program of the day and, yes, of the week and of the
month in the fringe of consciousness while the work of the
hour is in its center—it is almost impossible for such a
teacher to realize all the difficulties that confront the average
beginner.

There is a technique of teaching, just as there is a technique
of piano-playing. The technique, if it is to be educationally
effective, is dependent upon principles. But it is possible for a
student to acquire outward form of method without capacity
to put it to genuinely educative use. As every teacher knows,
children have an inner and an outer attention. The inner attention is the giving of the mind without reserve or qualification
to the subject in hand. It is the first-hand and personal play of
mental powers. As such, it is a fundamental condition of mental growth. To be able to keep track of this mental play, to rec-

ognize the signs of its presence or absence, to know how it is initiated and maintained, how to test it by results attained, and to test *apparent* results by it, is the supreme mark and criterion of a teacher. It means insight into soul-action, ability to discriminate the genuine from the sham, and capacity to further one and discourage the other.

External attention, on the other hand, is that given to the book or teacher as an independent object. It is manifested in certain conventional postures and physical attitudes rather than in the movement of thought. Children acquire great dexterity in exhibiting in conventional and expected ways the *form* of attention to school work, while reserving the inner play of their own thoughts, images, and emotions for subjects that are more important to them, but quite irrelevant.

Now, the teacher who is plunged prematurely into the pressing and practical problem of keeping order in the schoolroom has almost of necessity to make supreme the matter of external attention. The teacher has not yet had the training which affords psychological insight—which enables him to judge promptly (and therefore almost automatically) the kind and mode of subject-matter which the pupil needs at a given moment to keep his attention moving forward effectively and healthfully. He does know, however, that he must maintain order; that he must keep the attention of the pupils fixed upon his own questions, suggestions, instructions, and remarks, and upon their "lessons." The inherent tendency of the situation therefore is for him to acquire his technique in relation to the outward rather than the inner mode of attention.

III. Along with this fixation of attention upon the secondary at the expense of the primary problem, *there goes the formation of habits of work which have an empirical, rather than a scientific, sanction.* The student adjusts his actual methods of teaching, not to the principles which he is acquiring, but to what he sees succeed and fail in an empirical way from moment to moment: to what he sees other teachers doing who are more experienced and successful in keeping order than he is; and to the injunctions and directions given him by others. In this way the controlling habits of the teacher finally gets fixed with comparatively little reference to principles in the psychology, logic, and history of education. In theory, these latter are dominant; in practice, the moving forces are the devices and methods which are picked up through blind experimentation; through examples which are not rationalized; through precepts which are more or less arbitrary and mechanical; through advice based upon the experience of others. Here we have the explanation, in considerable part at least, of the dualism, the unconscious duplicity, which is one of the chief evils of the teaching profession. There is an enthusiastic devotion to certain principles of lofty theory in the abstract—principles of self-activity, self-control, intellectual and moral—and there is a school practice taking little heed of the official pedagogic creed. Theory and practice do not grow together out of and into the teacher's personal experience.

Ultimately there are two bases upon which the habits of a teacher as a teacher may be built up. They may be formed under the inspiration and constant criticism of intelligence, applying the best that is available. This is possible only where the would-be teacher has become fairly saturated with his subject-matter, and with his psychological and ethical philosophy of education. Only when such things have become incorporated in mental habit, have become part of the working tendencies of observation, insight, and reflection, will these principles work automatically, unconsciously, and hence promptly and effectively. And this means that practical work should be pursued primarily with reference to its reaction upon the professional pupil in making him a thoughtful and alert student of education, rather than to help him get immediate proficiency.

For immediate skill may be got at the cost of power to go on growing. The teacher who leaves the professional school with power in managing a class of children may appear to superior advantage the first day, the first week, the first month, or even the first year, as compared with some other teacher who has a much more vital command of the psychology, logic, and ethics of development. But later "progress" may with such consist only in perfecting and refining skill already possessed. Such persons seem to know how to teach, but they are not students of teaching. Even though they go on studying books of pedagogy, reading teachers' journals, attending teachers' institutes, etc., yet the root of the matter is not in them, unless they continue to be students of subject-matter, and students of mind-activity. Unless a teacher is such a student, he may continue to improve in the mechanics of school management, but he can not grow as a teacher, an inspirer and director of soul-life. How often do candid instructors in training schools for teachers acknowledge disappointment in the later career of even their more promising candidates! They seem to strike twelve at the start. There is an unexpected and seemingly unaccountable failure to maintain steady growth. Is this in some part due to the undue premature stress laid in early practice work upon securing immediate capability in teaching?

I might go on to mention other evils which seem to me to be more or less the effect of this same cause. Among them are the lack of intellectual independence among teachers, their tendency to intellectual subserviency. The "model lesson" of the teachers' institute and of the educational journal is a monument, on the one hand, of the eagerness of those in authority to secure immediate practical results at any cost; and, upon the other, of the willingness of our teaching corps to accept without inquiry or criticism any method or device which seems to promise good results. Teachers, actual and intending, flock to those persons who give them clear-cut and definite instructions as to just how to teach this or that.

The tendency of educational development to proceed by reaction from one thing to another, to adopt for one year, or for a term of seven years, this or that new study or method of teaching, and then as abruptly to swing over to some new educational gospel, is a result which would be impossible if teachers were adequately moved by their own independent intelligence. The willingness of teachers, especially of those occupying administrative positions, to become submerged in the routine detail of their callings, to expend the bulk of their energy upon forms and rules and regulations, and reports and percentages, is another evidence of the absence of intellectual vitality. If teachers were possessed by the spirit of an abiding student of education, this spirit would find some way of breaking through the mesh and coil of circumstance and would find expression for itself.

B. Let us turn from the practical side to the theoretical. What must be the aim and spirit of theory in order that practice work may really serve the purpose of an educational laboratory? We are met here with the belief that instruction in theory is merely theoretical, abstruse, remote, and therefore relatively useless to the teacher as a teacher, unless the student is at once set upon the work of teaching; that only "practice" can give a motive to a professional learning, and supply material for educational courses. It is not infrequently claimed (or at least unconsciously assumed) that students will not have a professional stimulus for their work in subject-matter and in educational psychology and history, will not have any outlook upon their relation to education, unless these things are immediately and simultaneously reinforced by setting the student upon the work of teaching. But is this the case? Or are there practical elements and bearings already contained in theoretical instruction of the proper sort?

I. Since it is impossible to cover in this paper all phases of the philosophy and science of education, I shall speak from the standpoint of psychology, believing that this may be taken as typical of the whole range of instruction in educational theory as such.

In the first place, beginning students have without any reference to immediate teaching a very large capital of an exceedingly practical sort in their own experience. The argument that theoretical instruction is merely abstract and in the air unless students are set at once to test and illustrate it by practice-teaching of their own, *overlooks the continuity of the class-room mental activity with that of other normal experience*. It ignores the tremendous importance for educational purposes of this continuity. Those who employ this argument seem to isolate the psychology of learning that goes on in the schoolroom from the psychology of learning found elsewhere.

This isolation is both unnecessary and harmful. It is unnecessary, tending to futility, because it throws away or makes light of the greatest asset in the student's possession— the greatest, moreover, that ever will be in his possession— his own direct and personal experience. There is every pre- sumption (since the student is not an imbecile) that he has been learning all the days of his life, and that he is still learn- ing from day to day. He must accordingly have in his own ex- perience plenty of practical material by which to illustrate and vitalize theoretical principles and laws of mental growth in the process of learning. Moreover, since none of us is brought up under ideal conditions, each beginning student has plenty of practical experience by which to illustrate cases of arrested development—instances of failure and maladaptation and ret- rogression, or even degeneration. The material at hand is path- ological as well as healthy. It serves to embody and illustrate both achievement and failure, in the problem of learning.

But it is more than a serious mistake (violating the prin- ciple of proceeding from the known to the unknown) to fail to take account of this body of practical experience. Such ig- noring tends also to perpetuate some of the greatest evils of current school methods. Just because the student's attention is not brought to the point of recognizing that *his own* past and present growth is proceeding in accordance with the very laws that control growth in the school, and that there is no psychology of the schoolroom different from that of the nursery, the playground, the street, and the parlor, he comes unconsciously to assume that education in the class-room is a sort of unique thing, having its own laws.[2] Unconsciously, but none the less surely, the student comes to believe in certain "methods" of learning, and hence of teaching which are somehow especially appropriate to the school—which some- how have their particular residence and application there. Hence he comes to believe in the potency for schoolroom purposes of materials, methods, and devices which it never occurs to him to trust to in his experience outside of school.

---

[2] There is where the plea for "adult" psychology has force. The person who does not know himself is not likely to know others. The adult psychology ought, however, to be just as genetic as that of childhood.

I know a teacher of teachers who is accustomed to say that when she fails to make clear to a class of teachers some point relative to children, she asks these teachers to stop thinking of their own pupils and to think of some nephew, niece, cousin, some child of whom they have acquaintance in the unformalities of home life. I do not suppose any great argument is needed to prove that breach of continuity between learning within and without the school is the great cause in education of wasted power and misdirected effort. I wish rather to take advantage of this assumption (which I think will be generally accepted) to emphasize the danger of bringing the would-be teacher into an abrupt and dislocated contact with the psychology of the schoolroom—abrupt and dislocated because not prepared for by prior practice in selecting and organizing the relevant principles and data contained within the experience best known to him, his own.[3]

From this basis, a transition to educational psychology may be made in observation of the teaching of others—visiting classes. I should wish to note here, however, the same principle that I have mentioned as regards practice work, specifically so termed. The first observation of instruction given by model- or critic-teachers should not be too definitely practical in aim. The student should not be observing to find out how the good teacher does it, in order to accumulate a store of methods by which he also may teach successfully. He should rather observe with reference to seeing the interaction of mind, to see how teacher and pupils react upon each other—how mind answers to mind. Observation should at first be conducted from the psychological rather than from the "practical" standpoint. If the latter is emphasized before the student has an independent command of the former, the principle of imitation is almost sure to play an exaggerated part in the observer's future teaching, and hence

---

[3] It may avoid misapprehension if I repeat the word *experience*. It is not a *metaphysical* introspection that I have in mind, but the process of turning back upon one's own experiences, and turning them over to see how they were developed, what helped and hindered, the stimuli and the inhibitions both within and without the organism.

at the expense of personal insight and initiative. What the student needs most at this stage of growth is ability to see what is going on in the minds of a group of persons who are in intellectual contact with one another. He needs to learn to observe psychologically—a very different thing from simply observing how a teacher gets "good results" in presenting any particular subject.

It should go without saying that the student who has acquired power in psychological observation and interpretation may finally go on to observe more technical aspects of instruction, namely, the various methods and instrumentalities used by a good teacher in giving instruction in any subject. If properly prepared for, this need not tend to produce copiers, followers of tradition and example. Such students will be able to translate the practical devices which are such an important part of the equipment of a good teacher over into their psychological equivalents; to know not merely as a matter of brute fact that they do work, but to know how and why they work. Thus he will be an independent judge and critic of their proper use and adaptation.

In the foregoing I have assumed that educational psychology is marked off from general psychology simply by the emphasis which it puts upon two factors. The first is the stress laid upon a certain end, namely, growth or development—with its counterparts, arrest and adaptation. The second is the importance attached to the social factor—to the mutual interaction of different minds with each other. It is, I think, strictly true that no educational procedure nor pedagogical maxim can be derived directly from pure psychological data. The psychological data taken without qualification (which is what I mean by their being pure) cover everything and anything that may take place in a mind. Mental arrest and decay occur according to psychological laws, just as surely as do development and progress.

We do not make practical maxims out of physics by telling persons to move according to laws of gravitation. If people move at all, they *must* move in accordance with the conditions stated by this law. Similarly, if mental operations take place at all, they *must* take place in accordance with the principles stated in correct psychological generalizations. It is superfluous and meaningless to attempt to turn these psychological principles directly into rules of teaching. But the person who knows the laws of mechanics knows the conditions of which he must take account when he wishes to reach a certain end. He knows that *if* he aims to build a bridge, he must build it in a certain way and of certain materials, or else he will not have a bridge, but a heap of rubbish. So in psychology. Given an end, say promotion of healthy growth, psychological observations and reflection put us in control of the conditions concerned in that growth. We know that if we are to get that *end,* we must do it in a certain way. It is the subordination of the psychological material to the problem of effecting growth and avoiding arrest and waste which constitutes a distinguishing mark of educational psychology.

I have spoken of the importance of the social factor as the other mark. I do not mean, of course, that general theoretical psychology ignores the existence and significance of the reaction of mind to mind—though it would be within bounds to say that till recently the social side was an unwritten chapter of psychology. I mean that considerations of the ways in which one mind responds to the stimuli which another mind is consciously or unconsciously furnishing possess a relative importance for the educator which they have not for the psychologist as such. From the teacher's standpoint, it is not too much to say that every habit which a pupil exhibits is to be regarded as a reaction to stimuli which some persons or group of persons have presented to the child. It is not too much to say that the most important thing for the teacher to consider, as regards his present relations to his pupils, is the attitudes and habits which his own modes of being, saying, and doing are fostering or discouraging in them.

Now, if these two assumptions regarding educational psychology be granted, I think it will follow as a matter of course, that only by beginning with the values and laws contained in the student's own experience of his own mental growth, and by proceeding gradually to facts connected with other persons of whom he can know little; and by proceeding still more gradually to the attempt actually to influence the mental operations of others, can educational theory be made most effective. Only in this way can the most essential trait of the mental habit of the teacher be secured—that habit which looks upon the internal, not upon the external; which sees that the important function of the teacher is direction of the mental movement of the student, and that the mental movement must be known before it can be directed.

II. I turn now to the side of subject-matter, or scholarship, with the hope of showing that here too the material, when properly presented, is not so *merely* theoretical, remote from the practical problems of teaching, as is sometimes supposed. I recall that once a graduate student in a university made inquiries among all the leading teachers in the institution with which he was connected as to whether they had received any professional training, whether they had taken courses in pedagogy. The inquirer threw the results, which were mostly negative, into the camp of the local pedagogical club. Some may say that this proves nothing, because college teaching is proverbially poor, considered simply as teaching. Yet no one can deny that there is *some* good teaching, and some teaching of the very first order, done in colleges, and done by persons who have never had any instruction in either the theory or the practice of teaching.

This fact cannot be ignored any more than can the fact that there were good teachers before there was any such thing as pedagogy. Now, I am not arguing for not having pedagogical training—that is the last thing I want. But I claim the facts mentioned prove that scholarship *per se* may itself be a most effective tool for training and turning out good teachers. If it has accomplished so much when working unconsciously and without set intention, have we not good reason to believe that, when acquired in a training school for teachers—with the end of making teachers held definitely in view and with conscious reference to its relation to mental activity—it may prove a much more valuable pedagogical asset than we commonly consider it?

Scholastic knowledge is sometimes regarded as if it were something quite irrelevant to method. When this attitude is even unconsciously assumed, method becomes an external attachment to knowledge of subject-matter. It has to be elaborated and acquired in relative independence from subject-matter, and *then* applied.

Now the body of knowledge which constitutes the subject-matter of the student-teacher must, by the nature of the case, be organized subject-matter. It is not a miscellaneous heap of separate scraps. Even if (as in the case of history and literature), it be not technically termed "science," it is none the less material which has been subjected to method—has been selected and arranged with reference to controlling intellectual principles. There is, therefore, method in subject-matter itself—method indeed of the highest order which the human mind has yet evolved, scientific method.

It cannot be too strongly emphasized that this scientific method is the method of mind itself.[4] The classifications, interpretations, explanations, and generalizations which make subject-matter a branch of study do not lie externally in facts apart from mind. They reflect the attitudes and workings of mind in its endeavor to bring raw material of experience to a point where it at once satisfies and stimulates the needs of active thought. Such being the case, there is something wrong in the "academic" side of professional training, if by means of it the student does not constantly get object-lessons of the finest type in the kind of mental activity which characterizes mental growth and, hence, the educative process.

It is necessary to recognize the importance for the teacher's equipment of his own habituation to superior types of method of mental operation. The more a teacher in the future is likely to have to do with elementary teaching, the more, rather than the less, necessary is such exercise. Otherwise, the current traditions of elementary work with their tendency to talk and write down to the supposed intellectual level of children, will be likely to continue. Only a teacher thoroughly trained in the higher levels of intellectual method and who thus has constantly in his own mind a sense of what

---

[4] Professor Ella F. Young's "Scientific Method in Education" (*University of Chicago Decennial Publications*) is a noteworthy development of this conception, to which I am much indebted.

adequate and genuine intellectual activity means, will be likely, in deed, not in mere word, to respect the mental integrity and force of children.

Of course, this conception will be met by the argument that the scientific organization of subject-matter, which constitutes the academic studies of the student-teacher is upon such a radically different basis from that adapted to less mature students that too much pre-occupation with scholarship of an advanced order is likely actually to get in the way of the teacher of children and youth. I do not suppose anybody would contend that teachers really can know more than is good for them, but it may reasonably be argued that continuous study of a specialized sort forms mental habits likely to throw the older student out of sympathy with the type of mental impulses and habits which are found in younger persons.

Right here, however, I think normal schools and teachers' colleges have one of their greatest opportunities—an opportunity not merely as to teachers in training, but also for reforming methods of education in colleges and higher schools having nothing to do with the training of teachers. It is the business of normal schools and collegiate schools of education to present subject-matter in science, in language, in literature and the arts, in such a way that the student both sees and feels that these studies *are* significant embodiments of mental operations. He should be led to realize that they are not products of technical methods, which have been developed for the sake of the specialized branches of knowledge in which they are used, but represent fundamental mental attitudes and operations—that, indeed, particular scientific methods and classifications simply express and illustrate in their most concrete form that of which simple and common modes of thought-activity are capable when they work under satisfactory conditions.

In a word, it is the business of the "academic" instruction of future teachers to carry back subject-matter to its common psychical roots.[5] In so far as this is accomplished, the gap be-

---

[5] It is hardly necessary to refer to Dr. Harris's continued conten-

tween the higher and the lower treatment of subject-matter, upon which the argument of the supposed objector depends, ceases to have the force which that argument assigns to it. This does not mean, of course, that exactly the same subject-matter, in the same mode of presentation, is suitable to a student in the elementary or high schools that is appropriate to the normal student. But it does mean that a mind which is habituated to viewing subject-matter from the standpoint of the function of that subject-matter in connection with *mental* responses, attitudes, and methods will be sensitive to *signs of intellectual activity* when exhibited in the child of four, or the youth of sixteen, and will be trained to a spontaneous and unconscious appreciation of the subject-matter which is fit to call out and direct mental activity.

We have here, I think, the explanation of the success of some teachers who violate every law known to and laid down by pedagogical science. They are themselves so full of the spirit of inquiry, so sensitive to every sign of its presence and absence, that no matter what they do, nor how they do it, they succeed in awakening and inspiring like alert and intense mental activity in those with whom they come in contact.

This is not a plea for the prevalence of these irregular, inchoate methods. But I feel that I may recur to my former remark: if some teachers, by sheer plenitude of knowledge, keep by instinct in touch with the mental activity of their pupils, and accomplish so much without, and even in spite of, principles which are theoretically sound, then there must be in this same scholarship a tremendous resource when it is more consciously used—that is, employed in clear connection with psychological principles.

When I said above that schools for training teachers have here an opportunity to react favorably upon general education, I meant that no instruction in subject-matter (wherever it is given) is adequate if it leaves the student with just acquisition of certain information about external facts and

---

tion that normal training should give a higher view or synthesis of even the most elementary subjects.

laws, or even a certain facility in the intellectual manipulation of this material. It is the business of our higher schools in all lines, and not simply of our normal schools, to furnish the student with the realization that, after all, it is the human mind, trained to effective control of its natural attitudes, impulses, and responses, that is the significant thing in all science and history and art so far as these are formulated for purposes of study.

The present divorce between scholarship and method is as harmful upon one side as upon the other—as detrimental to the best interests of higher academic instruction as it is to the training of teachers. But the only way in which this divorce can be broken down is by so presenting all subject-matter, for whatever ultimate, practical, or professional purpose, that it shall be apprehended as an objective embodiment of methods of mind in its search for, and transactions with, the truth of things.

Upon the more practical side, this principle requires that, so far as students appropriate new subject-matter (thereby improving their own scholarship and realizing more consciously the nature of method), they should finally proceed to organize this same subject-matter with reference to its use in teaching others. The curriculum of the elementary and the high school constituting the "practice" or "model" school ought to stand in the closest and most organic relation to the instruction in subject-matter which is given by the teachers of the professional school. If in any given school this is not the case, it is either because in the *training class* subject-matter is presented in an isolated way, instead of as a concrete expression of methods of mind, or else because the *practice school* is dominated by certain conventions and traditions regarding material and the methods of teaching it, and hence is not engaged in work of an adequate educational type.

As a matter of fact, as everybody knows, both of these causes contribute to the present state of things. On the one hand, inherited conditions impel the elementary school to a certain triviality and poverty of subject-matter, calling for mechanical drill, rather than for thought-activity, and the high school to a certain technical mastery of certain conventional culture subjects, taught as independent branches of the same tree of knowledge! On the other hand traditions of the different branches of science (the academic side of subject-matter) tend to subordinate the teaching in the normal school to the attainment of certain facilities, and the acquirement of certain information, both in greater or less isolation from their value as exciting and directing mental power.

The great need is convergence, concentration. Every step taken in the elementary and the high school toward intelligent introduction of more worthy and significant subject-matter, one requiring consequently for its assimilation thinking rather than "drill," must be met by a like advance step in which the mere isolated specialization of collegiate subject-matter is surrendered, and in which there is brought to conscious and interested attention its significance in expression of fundamental modes of mental activity—so fundamental as to be common to both the play of the mind upon the ordinary material of everyday experience and to the systematized material of the sciences.

III. As already suggested, this point requires that training students be exercised in making the connections between the course of study of the practice or model school, and the wider horizons of learning coming within their ken. But it is consecutive and systematic exercise in the consideration of the subject-matter of the elementary and high schools that is needed. The habit of making isolated and independent lesson plans for a few days' or weeks' instruction in a separate grade here or there not only does not answer this purpose, but is likely to be distinctly detrimental. Everything should be discouraged which tends to put the student in the attitude of snatching at the subject-matter which he is acquiring in order to see if by some hook or crook it may be made immediately available for a lesson in this or that grade. What is needed is the habit of viewing the entire curriculum as a continuous growth, reflecting the growth of mind itself. This in turn demands, so far as I can see, consecutive and longitudinal consideration of the curriculum of the elementary and high school rather than a cross-sectional view of it. The student should be led to see that the same subject-matter in geography, nature-study, or art develops not merely day to day in a given grade, but from year to year throughout the entire movement of the school; and he should realize this before he gets much encouragement in trying to adapt subject-matter in lesson plans for this or that isolated grade.

C. If we attempt to gather together the points which have been brought out, we should have a view of practice work something like the following—though I am afraid even this formulates a scheme with more appearance of rigidity than is desirable:

At first, the practice school would be used mainly for purposes of observation. This observation, moreover, would not be for the sake of seeing how good teachers teach, or for getting "points" which may be employed in one's own teaching, but to get material for psychological observation and reflection, and some conception of the educational movement of the school as a whole.

Secondly, there would then be more intimate introduction to the lives of the children and the work of the school through the use as assistants of such students as had already got psychological insight and a good working acquaintance with educational problems. Students at this stage would not undertake much direct teaching, but would make themselves useful in helping the regular class instructor. There are multitudes of ways in which such help can be given and be of real help—that is, of use to the school, to the children, and not merely of putative value to the training student.[6] Special attention to backward children, to children who have been out of school, assisting in the care of material, in forms of handwork, suggest some of the avenues of approach.

This kind of practical experience enables, in the third place, the future teacher to make the transition from his more psychological and theoretical insight to the observation of the more technical points of class teaching and management. The informality, gradualness, and familiarity of the earlier con-

---

[6] This question of some real need in the practice school itself for the work done is very important in its moral influence and in assimilating the conditions of "practice work" to those of real teaching.

tact tend to store the mind with material which is unconsciously assimilated and organized, and thus supplies a background for work involving greater responsibility.

As a counterpart of this work in assisting, such students might well at the same time be employed in the selection and arrangement of subject-matter, as indicated in the previous discussion. Such organization would at the outset have reference to at least a group of grades, emphasizing continuous and consecutive growth. Later it might, without danger of undue narrowness, concern itself with finding supplementary materials and problems bearing upon the work in which the student is giving assistance; might elaborate material which could be used to carry the work still farther, if it were desirable; or, in case of the more advanced students, to build up a scheme of possible alternative subjects for lessons and studies.

Fourthly, as fast as students are prepared through their work of assisting for more responsible work, they could be given actual teaching to do. Upon the basis that the previous preparation has been adequate in subject-matter, in educational theory, and in the kind of observation and practice already discussed, such practice teachers should be given the maximum amount of liberty possible. They should not be too closely supervised, nor too minutely and immediately criticised upon either the matter or the method of their teaching. Students should be given to understand that they not only are *permitted* to act upon their own intellectual initiative, but that they are *expected* to do so, and that their ability to take hold of situations for themselves would be a more important factor in judging them than their following any particular set method or scheme.

Of course, there should be critical discussion with persons more expert of the work done, and of the educational results obtained. But sufficient time should be permitted to allow the practice-teacher to recover from the shocks incident to the newness of the situation, and also to get enough experience to make him capable of seeing the *fundamental* bearings of criticism upon work done. Moreover, the work of the expert or supervisor should be directed to getting the student to judge his own work critically, to find out for himself in what respects he has succeeded and in what failed, and to find the probable reasons for both failure and success, rather than to criticising him too definitely and specifically upon special features of his work.

It ought to go without saying (unfortunately, it does not in all cases) that criticism should be directed to making the professional student thoughtful about his work in the light of principles, rather than to induce in him a recognition that certain special methods are good, and certain other special methods bad. At all events, no greater travesty of real intellectual criticism can be given than to set a student to teaching a brief number of lessons, have him under inspection in practically all the time of every lesson, and then criticise him almost, if not quite, at the very end of each lesson, upon the particular way in which that particular lesson has been taught, pointing out elements of failure and of success. Such methods of criticism may be adapted to giving a training-teacher command of some of the knacks and tools of the trade, but are not calculated to develop a thoughtful and independent teacher.

Moreover, while such teaching (as already indicated) should be extensive or continuous enough to give the student time to become at home and to get a body of funded experience, it ought to be intensive in purpose rather than spread out miscellaneously. It is much more important for the teacher to assume responsibility for the consecutive development of some one topic, to get a feeling for the movement of that subject, than it is to teach a certain number (necessarily smaller in range) of lessons in a larger number of subjects. What we want, in other words, is not so much technical skill, as a realizing sense in the teacher of what the educational development of a subject means, and, in some typical case, command of a method of control, which will then serve as a standard for self-judgment in other cases.

Fifthly, if the practical conditions permit—if, that is to say, the time of the training course is sufficiently long, if the practice schools are sufficiently large to furnish the required number of children, and to afford actual demand for the work to be done—students who have gone through the stages already referred to should be ready for work of the distinctly apprenticeship type.

Nothing that I have said heretofore is to be understood as ruling out practice-teaching which is designed to give an individual mastery of the actual technique of teaching and management, provided school conditions permit it in reality and not merely in external form—provided, that is, the student has gone through a training in educational theory and history, in subject-matter, in observation, and in practice work of the laboratory type, before entering upon the latter. The teacher must acquire his technique some time or other; and if conditions are favorable, there are some advantages in having this acquisition take place in cadetting or in something of that kind. By means of this probation, persons who are unfit for teaching may be detected and eliminated more quickly than might otherwise be the case and before their cases have become institutionalized.

Even in this distinctly apprenticeship stage, however, it is still important that the student should be given as much responsibility and initiative as he is capable of taking, and hence that supervision should not be too unremitting and intimate, and criticism not at too short range or too detailed. The advantage of this intermediate probationary period does not reside in the fact that thereby supervisory officers may turn out teachers who will perpetuate their own notions and methods, but in the inspiration and enlightenment that come through prolonged contact with mature and sympathetic persons. If the conditions in the public schools were just what they ought to be, if all superintendents and principals had the knowledge and the wisdom which they should have, and if they had time and opportunity to utilize their knowledge and their wisdom in connection with the development of the younger teachers who come to them, the value of this apprenticeship period would be reduced, I think, very largely to its serving to catch in time and to exclude persons unfitted for teaching.

In conclusion, I may say that I do not believe that the principles presented in this paper call for anything utopian.

The present movement in normal schools for improvement of range and quality of subject-matter is steady and irresistible. All the better classes of normal schools are already, in effect, what are termed "junior colleges." That is, they give two years' work which is almost, and in many cases quite, of regular college grade. More and more, their instructors are persons who have had the same kind of scholarly training that is expected of teachers in colleges. Many of these institutions are already of higher grade than this; and the next decade will certainly see a marked tendency on the part of many normal schools to claim the right to give regular collegiate bachelor degrees.

The type of scholarship contemplated in this paper is thus practically assured for the near future. If two other factors co-operate with this, there is no reason why the conception of relation of theory and practice here presented should not be carried out. The second necessary factor is that the elementary and high schools, which serve as schools of observation and practice, should represent an advanced type of education properly corresponding to the instruction in academic subject-matter and in educational theory given to the training classes. The third necessity is that work in psychology and educational theory make concrete and vital the connection between the normal instruction in subject-matter and the work of the elementary and high schools.

If it should prove impracticable to realize the conception herein set forth, it will not be, I think, because of any impossibility resident in the outward conditions, but because those in authority, both within and without the schools, believe that the true function of training schools is just to meet the needs of which people are already conscious. In this case, of course, training schools will be conducted simply with reference to perpetuating current types of educational practice, with simply incidental improvement in details.

The underlying assumption of this paper is, accordingly, that training schools for teachers do not perform their full duty in accepting and conforming to present educational standards, but that educational leadership is an indispensable part of their office. The thing needful is improvement of education, not simply by turning out teachers who can do better the things that are now necessary to do, but rather by changing the conception of what constitutes education.

THE CHILD
AND THE CURRICULUM *

Profound differences in theory are never gratuitous or invented. They grow out of conflicting elements in a genuine
problem—a problem which is genuine just because the elements, taken as they stand, are conflicting. Any significant
problem involves conditions that for the moment contradict
each other. Solution comes only by getting away from the
meaning of terms that is already fixed upon and coming to
see the conditions from another point of view, and hence in a
fresh light. But this reconstruction means travail of thought.
Easier than thinking with surrender of already formed ideas
and detachment from facts already learned is just to stick by
what is already said, looking about for something with which
to buttress it against attack.

Thus sects arise: schools of opinion. Each selects that set
of conditions that appeals to it; and then erects them into a
complete and independent truth, instead of treating them as a
factor in a problem, needing adjustment.

The fundamental factors in the educative process are an
immature, undeveloped being; and certain social aims, mean-

---

* This was published originally as a pamphlet by the University
of Chicago Press, 1902.

ings, values incarnate in the matured experience of the adult. The educative process is the due interaction of these forces. Such a conception of each in relation to the other as facilitates completest and freest interaction is the essence of educational theory.

But here comes the effort of thought. It is easier to see the conditions in their separateness, to insist upon one at the expense of the other, to make antagonists of them, than to discover a reality to which each belongs. The easy thing is to seize upon something in the nature of the child, or upon something in the developed consciousness of the adult, and insist upon *that* as the key to the whole problem. When this happens a really serious practical problem—that of interaction—is transformed into an unreal, and hence insoluble, theoretic problem. Instead of seeing the educative steadily and as a whole, we see conflicting terms. We get the case of the child *vs.* the curriculum; of the individual nature *vs.* social culture. Below all other divisions in pedagogic opinion lies this opposition.

The child lives in a somewhat narrow world of personal contacts. Things hardly come within his experience unless they touch, intimately and obviously, his own well-being, or that of his family and friends. His world is a world of persons with their personal interests, rather than a realm of facts and laws. Not truth, in the sense of conformity to external fact, but affection and sympathy, is its keynote. As against this, the course of study met in the school presents material stretching back indefinitely in time, and extending outward indefinitely into space. The child is taken out of his familiar physical environment, hardly more than a square mile or so in area, into the wide world—yes, and even to the bounds of the solar system. His little span of personal memory and tradition is overlaid with the long centuries of the history of all peoples.

Again, the child's life is an integral, a total one. He passes quickly and readily from one topic to another, as from one spot to another, but is not conscious of transition or break. There is no conscious isolation, hardly conscious distinction. The things that occupy him are held together by the unity of the personal and social interests which his life carries along. Whatever is uppermost in his mind constitutes to him, for the time being, the whole universe. That universe is fluid and fluent; its contents dissolve and re-form with amazing rapidity. But, after all, it is the child's own world. It has the unity and completeness of his own life. He goes to school, and various studies divide and fractionize the world for him. Geography selects, it abstracts and analyzes one set of facts, and from one particular point of view. Arithmetic is another division, grammar another department, and so on indefinitely.

Again, in school each of these subjects is classified. Facts are torn away from their original place in experience and re-arranged with reference to some general principle. Classification is not a matter of child experience; things do not come to the individual pigeonholed. The vital ties of affection, the connecting bonds of activity, hold together the variety of his personal experiences. The adult mind is so familiar with the notion of logically ordered facts that it does not recognize— it cannot realize—the amount of separating and reformulating which the facts of direct experience have to undergo before they can appear as a "study," or branch of learning. A principle, for the intellect, has had to be distinguished and defined; facts have had to be interpreted in relation to this principle, not as they are in themselves. They have had to be regathered about a new center which is wholly abstract and ideal. All this means a development of a special intellectual interest. It means ability to view facts impartially and objectively; that is, without reference to their place and meaning in one's own experience. It means capacity to analyze and to synthesize. It means highly matured intellectual habits and the command of a definite technique and apparatus of scientific inquiry. The studies as classified are the product, in a word, of the science of the ages, not of the experience of the child.

These apparent deviations and differences between child and curriculum might be almost indefinitely widened. But we have here sufficiently fundamental divergences: first, the narrow but personal world of the child against the impersonal but infinitely extended world of space and time; second, the unity, the single wholeheartedness of the child's life, and the specializations and divisions of the curriculum; third, an abstract principle of logical classification and arrangement, and the practical and emotional bonds of child life.

From these elements of conflict grow up different educational sects. One school fixes its attention upon the importance of the subject-matter of the curriculum as compared with the contents of the child's own experience. It is as if they said: Is life petty, narrow, and crude? Then studies reveal the great, wide universe with all its fulness and complexity of meaning. Is the life of the child egoistic, self-centered, impulsive? Then in these studies is found an objective universe of truth, law, and order. Is his experience confused, vague, uncertain, at the mercy of the moment's caprice and circumstance? Then studies introduce a world arranged on the basis of eternal and general truth; a world where all is measured and defined. Hence the moral: ignore and minimize the child's individual peculiarities, whims, and experiences. They are what we need to get away from. They are to be obscured or eliminated. As educators our work is precisely to substitute for these superficial and casual affairs stable and well-ordered realities; and these are found in studies and lessons.

Subdivide each topic into studies; each study into lessons; each lesson into specific facts and formulae. Let the child proceed step by step to master each one of these separate parts, and at last he will have covered the entire ground. The road which looks so long when viewed in its entirety is easily traveled, considered as a series of particular steps. Thus emphasis is put upon the logical subdivisions and consecutions of the subject-matter. Problems of instruction are problems of procuring texts giving logical parts and sequences, and of presenting these portions in class in a similar definite and graded way. Subject-matter furnishes the end, and it determines method. The child is simply the immature being who is to be matured; he is the superficial being who is to be deepened; his is narrow experience which is to be widened. It is his to receive, to accept. His part is fulfilled when he is ductile and docile.

Not so, says the other sect. The child is the starting-point, the center, and the end. His development, his growth, is the ideal. It alone furnishes the standard. To the growth of the child all studies are subservient; they are instruments valued as they serve the needs of growth. Personality, character, is more than subject-matter. Not knowledge or information, but self-realization, is the goal. To possess all the world of knowledge and lose one's own self is as awful a fate in education as in religion. Moreover, subject-matter never can be got into the child from without. Learning is active. It involves reaching out of the mind. It involves organic assimilation starting from within. Literally, we must take our stand with the child and our departure from him. It is he and not the subject-matter which determines both quality and quantity of learning.

The only significant method is the method of the mind as it reaches out and assimilates. Subject-matter is but spiritual food, possible nutritive material. It cannot digest itself; it cannot of its own accord turn into bone and muscle and blood. The source of whatever is dead, mechanical, and formal in schools is found precisely in the subordination of the life and experience of the child to the curriculum. It is because of this that "study" has become a synonym for what is irksome, and a lesson identical with a task.

This fundamental opposition of child and curriculum set up by these two modes of doctrine can be duplicated in a series of other terms. "Discipline" is the watchword of those who magnify the course of study; "interest" that of those who blazon "The Child" upon their banner. The standpoint of the former is logical; that of the latter psychological. The first emphasizes the necessity of adequate training and scholarship on the part of the teacher; the latter that of need of sympathy with the child, and knowledge of his natural instincts. "Guidance and control" are the catchwords of one school; "freedom and initiative" of the other. Law is asserted here; spontaneity proclaimed there. The old, the conservation of what has been achieved in the pain and toil of the ages, is dear to the one; the new, change, progress, wins the affection of the other. Inertness and routine, chaos and anarchism, are accusations bandied back and forth. Neglect of the sacred authority of duty is charged by one side, only to be met by counter-charges of suppression of individuality through tyrannical despotism.

Such oppositions are rarely carried to their logical conclusion. Common-sense recoils at the extreme character of these results. They are left to theorists, while common-sense vibrates back and forward in a maze of inconsistent compromise. The need of getting theory and practical common-sense into closer connection suggests a return to our original thesis: that we have here conditions which are necessarily related to each other in the educative process, since this is precisely one of interaction and adjustment.

What, then, is the problem? It is just to get rid of the prejudicial notion that there is some gap in kind (as distinct from degree) between the child's experience and the various forms of subject-matter that make up the course of study. From the side of the child, it is a question of seeing how his experience already contains within itself elements—facts and truths—of just the same sort as those entering into the formulated study; and, what is of more importance, of how it contains within itself the attitudes, the motives, and the interests which have operated in developing and organizing the subject-matter to the plane which it now occupies. From the side of the studies, it is a question of interpreting them as outgrowths of forces operating in the child's life, and of discovering the steps that intervene between the child's present experience and their richer maturity.

Abandon the notion of subject-matter as something fixed and ready-made in itself, outside the child's experience; cease thinking of the child's experience as also something hard and fast; see it as something fluent, embryonic, vital; and we realize that the child and the curriculum are simply two limits which define a single process. Just as two points define a straight line, so the present standpoint of the child and the facts and truths of studies define instruction. It is continuous reconstruction, moving from the child's present experience out into that represented by the organized bodies of truth that we call studies.

On the face of it, the various studies, arithmetic, geography, language, botany, etc., are themselves experience—they are that of the race. They embody the cumulative outcome of the efforts, the strivings, and the successes of the human generation after generation. They present this, not as a mere accumulation, not as a miscellaneous heap of separate bits of experience, but in some organized and systematized way—that is, as reflectively formulated.

Hence, the facts and truths that enter into the child's present experience, and those contained in the subject-matter of studies, are the initial and final terms of one reality. To oppose one to the other is to oppose the infancy and maturity of the same growing life; it is to set the moving tendency and the final result of the same process over against each other; it is to hold that the nature and the destiny of the child war with each other.

If such be the case, the problem of the relation of the child and the curriculum presents itself in this guise: Of what use, educationally speaking, is it to be able to see the end in the beginning? How does it assist us in dealing with the early stages of growth to be able to anticipate its later phases? The studies, as we have agreed, represent the possibilities of development inherent in the child's immediate crude experience. But, after all, they are not parts of that present and immediate life. Why, then, or how, make account of them?

Asking such a question suggests its own answer. To see the outcome is to know in what direction the present experience is moving, provided it move normally and soundly. The faraway point, which is of no significance to us simply as far away, becomes of huge importance the moment we take it as defining a present direction of movement. Taken in this way it is no remote and distant result to be achieved, but a guiding method in dealing with the present. The systematized and defined experience of the adult mind, in other words, is of value to us in interpreting the child's life as it immediately shows itself, and in passing on to guidance or direction.

Let us look for a moment at these two ideas: interpretation and guidance. The child's present experience is in no way self-explanatory. It is not final, but transitional. It is nothing complete in itself, but just a sign or index of certain growth-tendencies. As long as we confine our gaze to what the child here and now puts forth, we are confused and misled. We cannot read its meaning. Extreme depreciations of the child morally and intellectually, and sentimental idealizations of him, have their root in a common fallacy. Both spring from taking stages of a growth or movement as something cut off and fixed. The first fails to see the promise contained in feelings and deeds which, taken by themselves, are uncompromising and repellent; the second fails to see that even the most pleasing and beautiful exhibitions are but signs, and that they begin to spoil and rot the moment they are treated as achievements.

What we need is something which will enable us to interpret, to appraise, the elements in the child's present puttings forth and fallings away, his exhibitions of power and weakness, in the light of some larger growth-process in which they have their place. Only in this way can we discriminate. If we isolate the child's present inclinations, purposes, and experiences from the place they occupy and the part they have to perform in a developing experience, all stand upon the same level; all alike are equally good and equally bad. But in the movement of life different elements stand upon different planes of value. Some of the child's deeds are symptoms of a waning tendency; they are survivals in functioning of an organ which has done its part and is passing out of vital use. To give positive attention to such qualities is to arrest development upon a lower level. It is systematically to maintain a rudimentary phase of growth. Other activities are signs of a culminating power and interest; to them applies the maxim of striking while the iron is hot. As regards them, it is perhaps a matter of now or never. Selected, utilized, emphasized, they may mark a turning-point for good in the child's whole career; neglected, an opportunity goes, never to be recalled. Other acts and feelings are prophetic; they represent the dawning of flickering light that will shine steadily only in the far future. As regards them there is little at present to do but give them fair and full chance, waiting for the future for definite direction.

Just as, upon the whole, it was the weakness of the "old

education" that it made invidious comparisons between the immaturity of the child and the maturity of the adult, regarding the former as something to be got away from as soon as possible and as much as possible; so it is the danger of the "new education" that it regard the child's present powers and interests as something finally significant in themselves. In truth, his learnings and achievements are fluid and moving. They change from day to day and from hour to hour.

It will do harm if child-study leave in the popular mind the impression that a child of a given age has a positive equipment of purposes and interests to be cultivated just as they stand. Interests in reality are but attitudes toward possible experiences; they are not achievements; their worth is in the leverage they afford, not in the accomplishment they represent. To take the phenomena presented at a given age as in any way self-explanatory or self-contained is inevitably to result in indulgence and spoiling. Any power, whether of child or adult, is indulged when it is taken on its given and present level in consciousness. Its genuine meaning is in the propulsion it affords toward a higher level. It is just something to do with. Appealing to the interest upon the present plane means excitation; it means playing with a power so as continually to stir it up without directing it toward definite achievement. Continuous initiation, continuous starting of activities that do not arrive, is, for all practical purposes, as bad as the continual repression of initiative in conformity with supposed interests of some more perfect thought or will. It is as if the child were forever tasting and never eating; always having his palate tickled upon the emotional side, but never getting the organic satisfaction that comes only with digestion of food and transformation of it into working power.

As against such a view, the subject-matter of science and history and art serves to reveal the real child to us. We do not know the meaning either of his tendencies or of his performances excepting as we take them as germinating seed, or opening bud, of some fruit to be borne. The whole world of visual nature is all too small an answer to the problem of the meaning of the child's instinct for light and form. The entire science of physics is none too much to interpret adequately to us what is involved in some simple demand of the child for explanation of some casual change that has attracted his attention. The art of Raphael or of Corot is none too much to enable us to value the impulses stirring in the child when he draws and daubs.

So much for the use of the subject-matter in interpretation. Its further employment in direction or guidance is but an expansion of the same thought. To interpret the fact is to see it in its vital movement, to see it in its relation to growth. But to view it as a part of a normal growth is to secure the basis for guiding it. Guidance is not external imposition. *It is freeing the life-process for its own most adequate fulfilment.* What was said about disregard of the child's present experience because of its remoteness from mature experience; and of the sentimental idealization of the child's naïve caprices and performances, may be repeated here with slightly altered phrase. There are those who see no alternative between forcing the child from without, or leaving him entirely alone. Seeing no alternative, some choose one mode, some another. Both fall into the same fundamental error. Both fail to see that development is a definite process, having its own law which can be fulfilled only when adequate and normal conditions are provided. Really to interpret the child's present crude impulses in counting, measuring, and arranging things in rhythmic series involves mathematical scholarship—a knowledge of the mathematical formulae and relations which have, in the history of the race, grown out of just such crude beginnings. To see the whole history of development which intervenes between these two terms is simply to see what step the child needs to take just here and now; to what use he needs to put his blind impulse in order that it may get clarity and gain force.

If, once more, the "old education" tended to ignore the dynamic quality, the developing force inherent in the child's present experience, and therefore to assume that direction and control were just matters of arbitrarily putting the child in a given path and compelling him to walk there, the "new education" is in danger of taking the idea of development in altogether too formal and empty a way. The child is expected to "develop" this or that fact or truth out of his own mind. He is told to think things out, or work things out for himself, without being supplied any of the environing conditions which are requisite to start and guide thought. Nothing can be developed from nothing; nothing but the crude can be developed out of the crude—and this is what surely happens when we throw the child back upon his achieved self as a finality, and invite him to spin new truths of nature or of conduct out of that. It is certainly as futile to expect a child to evolve a universe out of his own mere mind as it is for a philosopher to attempt that task. Development does not mean just getting something out of the mind. It is a development of experience and into experience that is really wanted. And this is impossible save as just that educative medium is provided which will enable the powers and interests that have been selected as valuable to function. They must operate, and how they operate will depend almost entirely upon the stimuli which surround them and the material upon which they exercise themselves. The problem of direction is thus the problem of selecting appropriate stimuli for instincts and impulses which it is desired to employ in the gaining of new experience. What new experiences are desirable, and thus what stimuli are needed, it is impossible to tell except as there is some comprehension of the development which is aimed at; except, in a word, as the adult knowledge is drawn upon as revealing the possible career open to the child.

It may be of use to distinguish and to relate to each other the logical and the psychological aspects of experience—the former standing for subject-matter in itself, the latter for it in relation to the child. A psychological statement of experience follows its actual growth; it is historic; it notes steps actually taken, the uncertain and tortuous, as well as the efficient and successful. The logical point of view, on the other hand, assumes that the development has reached a certain stage of fulfilment. It neglects the process and considers the outcome. It summarizes and arranges, and thus separates the achieved results from the actual steps by which they were forthcoming in the first instance. We may compare the difference between the logical and the psychological to the dif/ ference between the notes which an explorer makes in a new country, blazing a trail and finding his way along as best he may, and the finished map that is constructed after the country has been thoroughly explored. The two are mutually dependent. Without the more or less accidental and devious paths traced by the explorer there would be no facts which could be utilized in the making of the complete and related chart. But no one would get the benefit of the explorer's trip if it was not compared and checked up with similar wanderings undertaken by others; unless the new geographical facts learned, the streams crossed, the mountains climbed, etc., were viewed, not as mere incidents in the journey of the particular traveler, but (quite apart from the individual explorer's life) in relation to other similar facts already known. The map orders individual experiences, connecting them with one another irrespective of the local and temporal circumstances and accidents of their original discovery.

Of what use is this formulated statement of experience? Of what use is the map?

Well, we may first tell what the map is not. The map is not a substitute for a personal experience. The map does not take the place of an actual journey. The logically formulated material of a science or branch of learning, of a study, is no substitute for the having of individual experiences. The mathematical formula for a falling body does not take the place of personal contact and immediate individual experience with the falling thing. But the map, a summary, an arranged and orderly view of previous experiences, serves as a guide to future experience; it gives direction; it facilitates control; it economizes effort, preventing useless wandering, and pointing out the paths which lead most quickly and most certainly to a desired result. Through the map every new traveler may get for his own journey the benefits of the results of others' explorations without the waste of energy and loss of time involved in their wanderings—wanderings which he himself would be obliged to repeat were it not for just the assistance of the objective and generalized record of their performances. That which we call a science or study puts the net product of past experience in the form which makes it most available for the future. It represents a capitalization which may at once be turned to interest. It economizes the workings of the mind in every way. Memory is less taxed because the facts are grouped together about some common principle, instead of being connected solely with the varying incidents of their original discovery. Observation is assisted; we know what to look for and where to look. It is the difference between looking for a needle in a haystack, and searching for a given paper in a well-arranged cabinet. Reasoning is directed, because there is a certain general path or line laid out along which ideas naturally march, instead of moving from one chance association to another.

There is, then, nothing final about a logical rendering of experience. Its value is not contained in itself; its significance is that of standpoint, outlook, method. It intervenes between the more casual, tentative, and roundabout experiences of the past, and more controlled and orderly experiences of the future. It gives past experience in that net form which renders it most available and most significant, most fecund for future experience. The abstractions, generalizations, and classifications which it introduces all have prospective meaning.

The formulated result is then not to be opposed to the process of growth. The logical is not set over against the psychological. The surveyed and arranged result occupies a critical position in the process of growth. It marks a turning-point. It shows how we may get the benefit of past effort in controlling future endeavor. In the largest sense the logical standpoint is itself psychological; it has its meaning as a point in the development of experience, and its justification is in its functioning in the future growth which it insures.

Hence the need of reinstating into experience the subject-matter of the studies, or branches of learning. It must be restored to the experience from which it has been abstracted. It needs to be *psychologized;* turned over, translated into the immediate and individual experiencing within which it has its origin and significance.

Every study or subject thus has two aspects: one for the scientist as a scientist; the other for the teacher as a teacher.

These two aspects are in no sense opposed or conflicting. But neither are they immediately identical. For the scientist, the subject-matter represents simply a given body of truth to be employed in locating new problems, instituting new researches, and carrying them through to a verified outcome. To him the subject-matter of the science is self-contained. He refers various portions of it to each other; he connects new facts with it. He is not, as a scientist, called upon to travel outside its particular bounds; if he does, it is only to get more facts of the same general sort. The problem of the teacher is a different one. As a teacher he is not concerned with adding new facts to the science he teaches; in propounding new hypotheses or in verifying them. He is concerned with the subject-matter of the science as *representing a given stage and phase of the development of experience*. His problem is that of inducing a vital and personal experiencing. Hence, what concerns him, as teacher, is the ways in which that subject may become a part of experience; what there is in the child's present that is usable with reference to it; how such elements are to be used; how his own knowledge of the subject-matter may assist in interpreting the child's needs and doings, and determine the medium in which the child should be placed in order that his growth may be properly directed. He is concerned, not with the subject-matter as such, but with the subject-matter as a related factor in a total and growing experience. Thus to see it is to psychologize it.

It is the failure to keep in mind the double aspect of subject-matter which causes the curriculum and child to be set over against each other as described in our early pages. The subject-matter, just as it is for the scientist, has no direct relationship to the child's present experience. It stands outside of it. The danger here is not a merely theoretical one. We are practically threatened on all sides. Textbook and teacher vie with each other in presenting to the child the subject-matter as it stands to the specialist. Such modification and revision as it undergoes are a mere elimination of certain scientific difficulties, and the general reduction to a lower intellectual level. The material is not translated into life-terms, but is directly offered as a substitute for, or an external annex to, the child's present life.

[Three typical evils result:] In the first place, the lack of any organic connection with what the child has already seen and felt and loved makes the material purely formal and symbolic. There is a sense in which it is impossible to value too highly the formal and the symbolic. The genuine form, the real symbol, serve as methods in the holding and discovery of truth. They are tools by which the individual pushes out most surely and widely into unexplored areas. They are means by which he brings to bear whatever of reality he has succeeded in gaining in past searchings. But this happens only when the symbol really symbolizes—when it stands for and sums up in shorthand actual experiences which the individual has already gone through. A symbol which is induced from without, which has not been led up to in preliminary activities, is, as we say, a *bare* or *mere* symbol; it is dead and barren. Now, any fact, whether of arithmetic, or geography, or grammar, which is not led up to and into out of something which has previously occupied a significant position in the child's life for its own sake, is forced into this position. It is not a reality, but just the sign of a reality which *might* be experienced if certain conditions were fulfilled. But the abrupt presentation of the fact as something known by others, and requiring only to be studied and learned by the child, rules out such conditions of fulfilment. It condemns the fact to be a hieroglyph: it would mean something if one only had the key. The clue being lacking, it remains an idle curiosity, to fret and obstruct the mind, a dead weight to burden it.

The second evil in this external presentation is lack of motivation. There are not only no facts or truths which have been previously felt as such with which to appropriate and assimilate the new, but there is no craving, no need, no demand. When the subject-matter has been psychologized, that is, viewed as an outgrowth of present tendencies and activities, it is easy to locate in the present some obstacle, intellectual, practical, or ethical, which can be handled more adequately if the truth in question be mastered. This need supplies motive for the learning. An end which is the child's own carries him on to possess the means of its accomplishment. But when material is directly supplied in the form of a lesson to be learned as a lesson, the connecting links of need and aim are conspicuous for their absence. What we mean by the mechanical and dead in instruction is a result of this lack of motivation. The organic and vital mean interaction—they mean play of mental demand and material supply.

The third evil is that even the most scientific matter, arranged in most logical fashion, loses this quality, when presented in external, ready-made fashion, by the time it gets to the child. It has to undergo some modification in order to shut out some phases too hard to grasp, and to reduce some of the attendant difficulties. What happens? Those things which are most significant to the scientific man, and most valuable in the logic of actual inquiry and classification, drop out. The really thought-provoking character is obscured, and the organizing function disappears. Or, as we commonly say, the child's reasoning powers, the faculty of abstraction and generalization, are not adequately developed. So the subject-matter is evacuated of its logical value, and, though it is what it is only from the logical standpoint, is presented as stuff only for "memory." This is the contradiction: the child gets the advantage neither of the adult logical formulation, nor of his own native competencies of apprehension and response. Hence the logic of the child is hampered and mortified, and we are almost fortunate if he does not get actual non-science, flat and commonplace residua of what was gaining scientific vitality a generation or two ago—degenerate reminiscence of what someone else once formulated on the basis of the experience that some further person had, once upon a time, experienced.

The train of evils does not cease. It is all too common for opposed erroneous theories to play straight into each other's hands. Psychological considerations may be slurred or shoved one side; they cannot be crowded out. Put out of the door, they come back through the window. Somehow and somewhere motive must be appealed to, connection must be established between the mind and its material. There is no question of getting along without this bond of connection; the only question is whether it be such as grows out of the material itself in relation to the mind, or be imported and hitched on from some outside source. If the subject-matter of the lessons be such as to have an appropriate place within the expanding consciousness of the child, if it grows into application in further achievements and receptivities, then no device or trick of method has to be resorted to in order to enlist "interest." The psychologized *is* of interest—that is, it is placed in the whole of conscious life so that it shares the worth of that life. But the externally presented material, conceived and generated in standpoints and attitudes remote from the child, and developed in motives alien to him, has no such place of its own. Hence the recourse to adventitious leverage to push it in, to factitious drill to drive it in, to artificial bribe to lure it in.

Three aspects of this recourse to outside ways for giving the subject-matter some psychological meaning may be worth mentioning. Familiarity breeds contempt, but it also breeds something like affection. We get used to the chains we wear, and we miss them when removed. 'Tis an old story that through custom we finally embrace what at first wore a hideous mien. Unpleasant, because meaningless, activities may get agreeable if long enough persisted in. *It is possible for the mind to develop interest in a routine or mechanical procedure if conditions are continually supplied which demand that mode of operation and preclude any other sort.* I frequently hear dulling devices and empty exercises defended and extolled because "the children take such an 'interest' in them." Yes, that is the worst of it; the mind, shut out from worthy employ and missing the taste of adequate performance, comes down to the level of that which is left to it to know and do, and perforce takes an interest in a cabined and cramped experience. To find satisfaction in its own exercise is the normal law of mind, and if large and meaningful business for the mind be denied, it tries to content itself with the formal movements that remain to it—and too often succeeds, save in those cases of more intense activity which cannot accommodate themselves, and that make up the unruly and *déclassé* of our school product. An interest in the formal apprehension of symbols and in their memorized reproduction becomes in many pupils a substitute for the original and vital interest in reality; and all because, the subject-matter of the course of study being out of relation to the concrete mind of the individual, some substitute bond to hold it in some kind of working relation to the mind must be discovered and elaborated.

The second substitute for living motivation in the subject-matter is that of contrast-effects; the material of the lesson is rendered interesting, if not in itself, at least in contrast with some alternative experience. To learn the lesson is more interesting than to take a scolding, be held up to general ridicule, stay after school, receive degradingly low marks, or fail to be promoted. And very much of what goes by the name of "discipline," and prides itself upon opposing the doctrines of a soft pedagogy and upon upholding the banner of effort and duty, is nothing more or less than just this appeal to "interest" in its obverse aspect—to fear, to dislike of various kinds of physical, social, and personal pain. The subject-matter does not appeal; it cannot appeal; it lacks origin and bearing in a growing experience. So the appeal is to the thousand and one outside and irrelevant agencies which may serve to throw, by sheer rebuff and rebound, the mind back upon the material from which it is constantly wandering.

Human nature being what it is, however, it tends to seek its motivation in the agreeable rather than in the disagreeable, in direct pleasure rather than in alternative pain. And so has come up the modern theory and practice of the "interesting," in the false sense of that term. The material is still left; so far as its own characteristics are concerned, just material externally selected and formulated. It is still just so much geography and arithmetic and grammar study; not so much potentiality of child-experience with regard to language, earth, and numbered and measured reality. Hence the difficulty of bringing the mind to bear upon it; hence its repulsiveness; the tendency for attention to wander; for other acts and images to crowd in and expel the lesson. The legitimate way out is to transform the material; to psychologize it—that is, once more, to take it and to develop it within the range and scope of the child's life. But it is easier and simpler to leave it as it is, and then by trick of method to *arouse* interest, to *make* it *interesting;* to cover it with sugar-coating; to conceal its barrenness by intermediate and unrelated material; and finally, as it were, to get the child to swallow and digest the unpalatable morsel while he is enjoying tasting something quite different. But alas for the analogy! Mental assimilation is a matter of consciousness; and if the attention has not been playing upon the actual material, that has not been apprehended, nor worked into faculty.

How, then, stands the case of Child *vs.* Curriculum? What shall the verdict be? The radical fallacy in the original pleadings with which we set out is the supposition that we have no choice save either to leave the child to his own unguided spontaneity or to inspire direction upon him from without. Action is response; it is adaptation, adjustment. There is no such thing as sheer self-activity possible—because all activity takes place in a medium, in a situation, and with reference to its conditions. But, again, no such thing as imposition of truth from without, as insertion of truth from without, is possible. All depends upon the activity which the mind itself undergoes in responding to what is presented from without. Now, the value of the formulated wealth of knowledge that makes up the course of study is that it may enable the educator *to determine the environment of the child*, and thus by indirection to direct. Its primary value, its primary indication, is for the teacher, not for the child. It says to the teacher: Such and such are the capacities, the fulfilments, in truth and beauty and behavior, open to these children. Now see to it that day by day the conditions are such that *their own activities* move inevitably in this direction, toward such culmination of themselves. Let the child's nature fulfil its own destiny, revealed to you in whatever of science and art and industry the world now holds as its own.

The case is of Child. It is his present powers which are to assert themselves; his present capacities which are to be exercised; his present attitudes which are to be realized. But save as the teacher knows, knows wisely and thoroughly, the race-expression which is embodied in that thing we call the Curriculum, the teacher knows neither what the present power, capacity, or attitude is, nor yet how it is to be asserted, exercised, and realized.

THE NATURE
OF SUBJECT MATTER *

1. Subject Matter of Educator and of Learner. So far as
the nature of subject matter in principle is concerned, there is
nothing to add to what has been said. It consists of the facts
observed, recalled, read, and talked about, and the ideas
suggested, in course of a development of a situation having
a purpose. This statement needs to be rendered more specific by connecting it with the materials of school instruction, the studies which make up the curriculum. What is the
significance of our definition in application to reading, writing, mathematics, history, nature study, drawing, singing, physics, chemistry, modern and foreign languages, and so on?

Let us recur to two of the points made earlier in our discussion. The educator's part in the enterprise of education is
to furnish the environment which stimulates responses and
directs the learner's course. In last analysis, *all* that the educator can do is modify stimuli so that response will as surely
as is possible result in the formation of desirable intellectual
and emotional dispositions. Obviously studies or the subject
matter of the curriculum have intimately to do with this business of supplying an environment. The other point is the necessity of a social environment to give meaning to habits
formed. In what we have termed informal education, subject

---

* From *Democracy and Education*, 1916.

matter is carried directly in the matrix of social intercourse. It is what the persons with whom an individual associates do and say. This fact gives a clew to the understanding of the subject matter of formal or deliberate instruction. A connecting link is found in the stories, traditions, songs, and liturgies which accompany the doings and rites of a primitive social group. They represent the stock of meanings which have been precipitated out of previous experience, which are so prized by the group as to be identified with their conception of their own collective life. Not being obviously a part of the skill exhibited in the daily occupations of eating, hunting, making war and peace, constructing rugs, pottery, and baskets, etc., they are consciously impressed upon the young; often, as in the initiation ceremonies, with intense emotional fervor. Even more pains are consciously taken to perpetuate the myths, legends, and sacred verbal formulae of the group than to transmit the directly useful customs of the group just because they cannot be picked up, as the latter can be in the ordinary processes of association.

As the social group grows more complex, involving a greater number of acquired skills which are dependent, either in fact or in the belief of the group, upon standard ideas deposited from past experience, the content of social life gets more definitely formulated for purposes of instruction. As we have previously noted, probably the chief motive for consciously dwelling upon the group life, extracting the meanings which are regarded as most important and systematizing them in a coherent arrangement, is just the need of instructing the young so as to perpetuate group life. Once started on this road of selection, formulation, and organization, no definite limit exists. The invention of writing and of printing gives the operation an immense impetus. Finally, the bonds which connect the subject matter of school study with the habits and ideals of the social group are disguised and covered up. The ties are so loosened that it often appears as if there were none; as if subject matter existed simply as knowledge on its own independent behoof, and as if study were the mere act of mastering it for its own sake, irrespective of any social values. Since it is highly important for practical reasons to counter-

act this tendency the chief purposes of our theoretical discussion are to make clear the connection which is so readily
lost from sight, and to show in some detail the social content
and function of the chief constituents of the course of study.

The points need to be considered from the standpoint of
instructor and of student. To the former, the significance of a
knowledge of subject matter, going far beyond the present
knowledge of pupils, is to supply definite standards and to reveal to him the possibilities of the crude activities of the immature. (1) The material of school studies translates into concrete and detailed terms the meanings of current social life
which it is desirable to transmit. It puts clearly before the instructor the essential ingredients of the culture to be per-
petuated, in such an organized form as to protect him from
the haphazard efforts he would be likely to indulge in if the
meanings had not been standardized. (2) A knowledge of the
ideas which have been achieved in the past as the outcome of
activity places the educator in a position to perceive the
meaning of the seeming impulsive and aimless reactions of
the young, and to provide the stimuli needed to direct them
so that they will amount to something. The more the educator
knows of music the more he can perceive the possibilities of
the inchoate musical impulses of a child. Organized subject
matter represents the ripe fruitage of experiences like theirs,
experiences involving the same world, and powers and needs
similar to theirs. It does not represent perfection or infallible
wisdom; but it is the best at command to further new experiences which may, in some respects at least, surpass the achievements embodied in existing knowledge and works of art.

From the standpoint of the educator, in other words, the
various studies represent working resources, available capital.
Their remoteness from the experience of the young is not,
however, seeming; it is real. The subject matter of the learner
is not, therefore, it cannot be, identical with the formulated,
the crystallized, and systematized subject matter of the adult;
the material as found in books and in works of art, etc. The
latter represents the *possibilities* of the former; not its existing state. It enters directly into the activities of the expert
and the educator, not into that of the beginner, the learner.

Failure to bear in mind the difference in subject matter from the respective standpoints of teacher and student is responsible for most of the mistakes made in the use of texts and other expressions of preëxistent knowledge.

The need for a knowledge of the constitution and functions, in the concrete, of human nature is great just because the teacher's attitude to subject matter is so different from that of the pupil. The teacher presents in actuality what the pupil represents only in *posse*. That is, the teacher already knows the things which the student is only learning. Hence the problem of the two is radically unlike. When engaged in the direct act of teaching, the instructor needs to have subject matter at his fingers' ends; his attention should be upon the attitude and response of the pupil. To understand the latter in its interplay with subject matter is his task, while the pupil's mind, naturally, should be not on itself but on the topic in hand. Or to state the same point in a somewhat different manner: the teacher should be occupied not with subject matter in itself but in its interaction with the pupils' present needs and capacities. Hence simple scholarship is not enough. In fact, there are certain features of scholarship or mastered subject matter—taken by itself—which get in the way of effective teaching *unless* the instructor's habitual attitude is one of concern with its interplay in the pupil's own experience. In the first place, his knowledge extends indefinitely beyond the range of the pupil's acquaintance. It involves principles which are beyond the immature pupil's understanding and interest. In and of itself, it may no more represent the living world of the pupil's experience than the astronomer's knowledge of Mars represents a baby's acquaintance with the room in which he stays. In the second place, the method of organization of the material of achieved scholarship differs from that of the beginner. It is not true that the experience of the young is unorganized—that it consists of isolated scraps. But it is organized in connection with direct practical centers of interest. The child's home is, for example, the organizing center of his geographical knowledge. His own movements about the locality, his journeys abroad, the tales of his friends, give the ties which hold his items of information together. But the geography of the geographer, of the one who has already developed the implications of these smaller experiences, is organized on the basis of the relationship which the various facts bear to one another—not the relations which they bear to his house, bodily movements, and friends. To the one who is learned, subject matter is extensive, accurately defined, and logically interrelated. To the one who is learning, it is fluid, partial, and connected through his personal occupations.[1] The problem of teaching is to keep the experience of the student moving in the direction of what the expert already knows. Hence the need that the teacher know both subject matter and the characteristic needs and capacities of the student.

2. *The Development of Subject Matter in the Learner.* It is possible, without doing violence to the facts, to mark off three fairly typical stages in the growth of subject matter in the experience of the learner. In its first estate, knowledge exists as the content of intelligent ability—power to do. This kind of subject matter, or known material, is expressed in familiarity or acquaintance with things. Then this material gradually is surcharged and deepened through communicated knowledge or information. Finally, it is enlarged and worked over into rationally or logically organized material—that of the one who, relatively speaking, is expert in the subject.

I. The knowledge which comes first to persons, and that remains most deeply ingrained, is knowledge of *how to do;* how to walk, talk, read, write, skate, ride a bicycle, manage a machine, calculate, drive a horse, sell goods, manage people, and so on indefinitely. The popular tendency to regard instinctive acts which are adapted to an end as a sort of miraculous knowledge, while unjustifiable, is evidence of the strong tendency to identify intelligent control of the means of action with knowledge. When education, under the influence of a scholastic conception of knowledge which ignores everything but scientifically formulated facts and truths, fails

---

[1] Since the learned man should also still be a learner, it will be understood that these contrasts are relative, not absolute. But in the earlier stages of learning at least they are practically all-important.

to recognize that primary or initial subject matter always exists as matter of an active doing, involving the use of the body and the handling of material, the subject matter of instruction is isolated from the needs and purposes of the learner, and so becomes just a something to be memorized and reproduced upon demand. Recognition of the natural course of development, on the contrary, always sets out with situations which involve learning by doing. Arts and occupations form the initial stage of the curriculum, corresponding as they do to knowing how to go about the accomplishment of ends.

Popular terms denoting knowledge have always retained the connection with ability in action lost by academic philosophies. Ken and can are allied words. Attention means caring for a thing, in the sense of both affection and of looking out for its welfare. Mind means carrying out instructions in action—as a child minds his mother—and taking care of something—as a nurse minds the baby. To be thoughtful, considerate, means to heed the claims of others. Apprehension means dread of undesirable consequences, as well as intellectual grasp. To have good sense or judgment is to know the conduct a situation calls for; discernment is not making distinctions for the sake of making them, an exercise reprobated as hair splitting, but is insight into an affair with reference to acting. Wisdom has never lost its association with the proper direction of life. Only in education, never in the life of farmer, sailor, merchant, physician, or laboratory experimenter, does knowledge mean primarily a store of information aloof from doing.

Having to do with things in an intelligent way issues in acquaintance or familiarity. The things we are best acquainted with are the things we put to frequent use—such things as chairs, tables, pen, paper, clothes, food, knives and forks on the commonplace level, differentiating into more special objects according to a person's occupations in life. Knowledge of things in that intimate and emotional sense suggested by the word acquaintance is a precipitate from our employing them with a purpose. We have acted with or upon the thing so frequently that we can anticipate how it will act and react

—such is the meaning of familiar acquaintance. We are ready for a familiar thing; it does not catch us napping, or play unexpected tricks with us. This attitude carries with it a sense of congeniality or friendliness, of ease and illumination; while the things with which we are not accustomed to deal are strange, foreign, cold, remote, "abstract."

II. But it is likely that elaborate statements regarding this primary stage of knowledge will darken understanding. It includes practically all of our knowledge which is not the result of deliberate technical study. Modes of purposeful doing include dealings with persons as well as things. Impulses of communication and habits of intercourse have to be adapted to maintaining successful connections with others; a large fund of social knowledge accrues. As a part of this intercommunication one learns much from others. They tell of their experiences and of the experiences which, in turn, have been told them. In so far as one is interested or concerned in these communications, their matter becomes a part of one's own experience. Active connections with others are such an intimate and vital part of our own concerns that it is impossible to draw sharp lines, such as would enable us to say, "Here my experience ends; there yours begins." In so far as we are partners in common undertakings, the things which others communicate to us as the consequences of their particular share in the enterprise blend at once into the experience resulting from our own special doings. The ear is as much an organ of experience as the eye or hand; the eye is available for reading reports of what happens beyond its horizon. Things remote in space and time affect the issue of our actions quite as much as things which we can smell and handle. They really concern us, and, consequently, any account of them which assists us in dealing with things at hand falls within personal experience.

Information is the name usually given to this kind of subject matter. The place of communication in personal doing supplies us with a criterion for estimating the value of informational material in school. Does it grow naturally out of some question with which the student is concerned? Does it fit into his more direct acquaintance so as to increase its efficacy and deepen its meaning? If it meets these two requirements, it is educative. The amount heard or read is of no importance—the more the better, *provided* the student has a need for it and can apply it in some situation of his own.

But it is not so easy to fulfill these requirements in actual practice as it is to lay them down in theory. The extension in modern times of the area of intercommunication; the invention of appliances for securing acquaintance with remote parts of the heavens and bygone events of history; the cheapening of devices, like printing, for recording and distributing information—genuine and alleged—have created an immense bulk of communicated subject matter. It is much easier to swamp a pupil with this than to work it into his direct experiences. All too frequently it forms another strange world which just overlies the world of personal acquaintance. The sole problem of the student is to learn, for school purposes, for purposes of recitations and promotions, the constituent parts of this strange world. Probably the most conspicuous connotation of the word knowledge for most persons to-day is just the body of facts and truths ascertained by others; the material found in the rows and rows of atlases, cyclopedias, histories, biographies, books of travel, scientific treatises, on the shelves of libraries.

The imposing stupendous bulk of this material has unconsciously influenced men's notions of the nature of knowledge itself. The statements, the propositions, in which knowledge, the issue of active concern with problems, is deposited, are taken to be themselves knowledge. The record of knowledge, independent of its place as an outcome of inquiry and a resource is further inquiry, is taken to *be* knowledge. The mind of man is taken captive by the spoils of its prior victories; the spoils, not the weapons and the acts of waging the battle against the unknown, are used to fix the meaning of knowledge, of fact, and truth.

If this identification of knowledge with propositions stating information has fastened itself upon logicians and philosophers, it is not surprising that the same ideal has almost dominated instruction. The "course of study" consists largely of information distributed into various branches of study, each study being subdivided into lessons presenting in serial cutoff portions of the total store. In the seventeenth century, the store was still small enough so that men set up the ideal of a complete encyclopedic mastery of it. It is now so bulky that the impossibility of any one man's coming into possession of it all is obvious. But the educational ideal has not been much affected. Acquisition of a modicum of information in each branch of learning, or at least in a selected group, remains the principle by which the curriculum, from elementary school through college, is formed; the easier portions being assigned to the earlier years, the more difficult to the later.

The complaints of educators that learning does not enter into character and affect conduct; the protests against memoriter work, against cramming, against gradgrind preoccupation with "facts," against devotion to wire-drawn distinctions and ill-understood rules and principles, all follow from this state of affairs. Knowledge which is mainly second-hand, other men's knowledge, tends to become merely verbal. It is no objection to information that it is clothed in words; communication necessarily takes place through words. But in the degree in which what is communicated cannot be organized into the existing experience of the learner, it becomes *mere* words: that is, pure sense-stimuli, lacking in meaning. Then it operates to call out mechanical reactions, ability to use the vocal organs to repeat statements, or the hand to write or to do "sums."

To be informed is to be posted; it is to have at command the subject matter needed for an effective dealing with a problem, and for giving added significance to the search for solution and to the solution itself. Informational knowledge is the material which can be fallen back upon as given, settled, established, assured in a doubtful situation. It is a kind of bridge for mind in its passage from doubt to discovery. It has the office of an intellectual middleman. It condenses and records in available form the net results of the prior experiences of mankind, as an agency of enhancing the meaning of new experiences. When one is told that Brutus assassinated Caesar, or that the length of the year is three hundred sixty-five and one fourth days, or that the ratio of the diameter of the circle to its circumference is 3.1415 . . . one receives what is indeed knowledge for others, but for him it is a stimulus to knowing. His acquisition of *knowledge* depends upon his response to what is communicated.

3. Science or Rationalized Knowledge. Science is a name for knowledge in its most characteristic form. It represents in its degree, the perfected outcome of learning,—its consummation. What is known, in a given case, is what is sure, certain, settled, disposed of; that which we think *with* rather than that which we think about. In its honorable sense, knowledge is distinguished from opinion, guesswork, speculation, and mere tradition. In knowledge, things are *ascertained;* they are *so* and not dubiously otherwise. But experience makes us aware that there is difference between intellectual certainty of *subject matter* and *our* certainty. We are made, so to speak, for belief; credulity is natural. The undisciplined mind is averse to suspense and intellectual hesitation; it is prone to assertion. It likes things undisturbed, settled, and treats them as such without due warrant. Familiarity, common repute, and congeniality to desire are readily made measuring rods of truth. Ignorance gives way to opinionated and current error, —a greater foe to learning than ignorance itself. A Socrates is thus led to declare that consciousness of ignorance is the beginning of effective love of wisdom, and a Descrates to say that science is born of doubting.

We have already dwelt upon the fact that subject matter, or data, and ideas have to have their worth tested experimentally: that in themselves they are tentative and provisional. Our predilection for premature acceptance and assertion, our aversion to suspended judgment, are signs that we tend naturally to cut short the process of testing. We are satisfied with superficial and immediate short-visioned applications. If these work out with moderate satisfactoriness, we are content to suppose that our assumptions have been confirmed. Even in the case of failure, we are inclined to put the blame not on the inadequacy and incorrectness of our data and thoughts, but upon our hard luck and the hostility of circumstance. We charge the evil consequence not to the error of our schemes and our incomplete inquiry into conditions (thereby getting material for revising the former and stimulus for extending the latter) but to untoward fate. We even plume ourselves upon our firmness in clinging to our conceptions in spite of the way in which they work out.

Science represents the safeguard of the race against these natural propensities and the evils which flow from them. It consists of the special appliances and methods which the race has slowly worked out in order to conduct reflection under conditions whereby its procedures and results are tested. It is artificial (an acquired art), not spontaneous; learned, not native. To this fact is due the unique, the invaluable place of science in education, and also the dangers which threaten its right use. Without initiation into the scientific spirit one is not in possession of the best tools which humanity has so far devised for effectively directed reflection. One in that case not merely conducts inquiry and learning without the use of the best instruments, but fails to understand the full meaning of knowledge. For he does not become acquainted with the traits that mark off opinion and assent from authorized conviction. On the other hand, the fact that science marks the perfecting of knowing in highly specialized conditions of technique renders its results, taken by themselves, remote from ordinary experience—a quality of aloofness that is popularly designated by the term abstract. When this isolation appears in instruction, scientific information is even more exposed to the dangers attendant upon presenting ready-made subject matter than are other forms of information.

Science has been defined in terms of method of inquiry and testing. At first sight, this definition may seem opposed to the current conception that science is organized or systematized knowledge. The opposition, however, is only seeming, and disappears when the ordinary definition is completed. Not organization but the *kind* of organization effected by adequate methods of tested discovery marks off science. The knowledge of a farmer is systematized in the degree in which he is competent. It is organized on the basis of relation of means to ends—practically organized. Its organization *as* knowledge (that is, in the eulogistic sense of adequately tested and confirmed) is incidental to its organization with reference to securing crops, livestock, etc. But scientific subject matter is organized with specific reference to the successful conduct of the enterprise of discovery, to knowing as a specialized undertaking.

Reference to the kind of assurance attending science will shed light upon this statement. It is rational assurance,— logical warranty. The ideal of scientific organization is, therefore, that every conception and statement shall be of such a kind as to follow from others and to lead to others. Conceptions and propositions mutually imply and support one another. This double relation of "leading to and confirming" is what is meant by the terms logical and rational. The everyday conception of water is more available for ordinary uses of drinking, washing, irrigation, etc., then the chemist's notion of it. The latter's description of it as H_2O is superior from the standpoint of place and use in inquiry. It states the nature of water in a way which connects it with knowledge of other things, indicating to one who understands it how the knowledge is arrived at and its bearings upon other portions of knowledge of the structure of things. Strictly speaking, it does not indicate the objective relations of water any more than does a statement that water is transparent, fluid, without taste or odor, satisfying to thirst, etc. It is just as true that water has these relations as that it is constituted by two molecules of hydrogen in combination with one of oxygen. But for the *particular purpose* of conducting discovery with a view to ascertainment of fact, the latter relations are fundamental. The more one emphasizes organization as a mark of science, then, the more he is committed to a recognition of the primacy of method in the definition of science. For method defines the kind of organization in virtue of which science is science.

4. Subject Matter as Social. Our next chapters will take up various school activities and studies and discuss them as successive stages in that evolution of knowledge which we have just been discussing. It remains to say a few words upon subject matter as social, since our prior remarks have been mainly concerned with its intellectual aspect. A difference in breadth and depth exists even in vital knowledge; even in the data and ideas which are relevant to real problems and which are motivated by purposes. For there is a difference in the social scope of purposes and the social importance of problems. With the wide range of possible material to select from, it is important that education (especially in all its phases short of the most specialized) should use a criterion of social worth.

All information and systematized scientific subject matter have been worked out under the conditions of social life and have been transmitted by social means. But this does not prove that all is of equal value for the purposes of forming the disposition and supplying the equipment of members of present society. The scheme of a curriculum must take account of the adaptation of studies to the needs of the existing community life; it must select with the intention of improving the life we live in common so that the future shall be better than the past. Moreover, the curriculum must be planned with reference to placing essentials first, and refinements second. The things which are socially most fundamental, that is, which have to do with the experiences in which the widest groups share, are the essentials. The things which represent the needs of specialized groups and technical pursuits are secondary. There is truth in the saying that education must first be human and only after that professional. But those who utter the saying frequently have in mind in the term human only a highly specialized class: the class of learned men who preserve the classic traditions of the past. They forget that material is humanized in the degree in which it connects with the common interests of men as men.

Democratic society is peculiarly dependent for its maintenance upon the use in forming a course of study of criteria which are broadly human. Democracy cannot flourish where the chief influences in selecting subject matter of instruction are utilitarian ends narrowly conceived for the masses, and, for the higher education of the few, the traditions of a specialized cultivated class. The notion that the "essentials" of elementary education are the three R's mechanically treated, is based upon ignorance of the essentials needed for realization of democratic ideals. Unconsciously it assumes that these ideals are unrealizable, it assumes that in the future, as in the past, getting a livelihood, "making a living," must signify for most men and women doing things which are not significant, freely chosen, and ennobling to those who do them; doing things which serve ends unrecognized by those engaged in them, carried on under the direction of others for the sake of pecuniary reward. For preparation of large numbers for a life of this sort, and only for this purpose, are mechanical efficiency in reading, writing, spelling and figuring, together with attainment of a certain amount of muscular dexterity, "essentials." Such conditions also infect the education called liberal, with illiberality. They imply a somewhat parasitic cultivation bought at the expense of not having the enlightenment and discipline which come from concern with the deepest problems of common humanity. A curriculum which acknowledges the social responsibilities of education must present situations where problems are relevant to the problems of living together, and where observation and information are calculated to develop social insight and interest.

Summary. The subject matter of education consists primarily of the meanings which supply content to existing social life. The continuity of social life means that many of these meanings are contributed to present activity by past collective experience. As social life grows more complex, these factors increase in number and import. There is need of special selection, formulation, and organization in order that they may be adequately transmitted to the new generation. But this very process tends to set up subject matter as something of value just by itself, apart from its function in promoting the realization of the meanings implied in the present experience of the immature. Especially is the educator exposed to the temptation to conceive his task in terms of the pupil's ability to appropriate and reproduce the subject matter in set statements, irrespective of its organization into his activities as a developing social member. The positive principle is maintained when the young begin with active occupations having a social origin and use, and proceed to a scientific insight in the materials and laws involved, through assimilating into their more direct experience the ideas and facts communicated by others who have had a larger experience.

PROGRESSIVE ORGANIZATION
OF SUBJECT-MATTER *

Allusion has been made in passing a number of times to objective conditions involved in experience and to their function
in promoting or failing to promote the enriched growth of
further experience. By implication, these objective conditions,
whether those of observation, of memory, of information procured from others, or of imagination, have been identified
with the subject-matter of study and learning; or, speaking
more generally, with the stuff of the course of study. Nothing, however, has been said explicitly so far about subject-
matter as such. That topic will now be discussed. One consideration stands out clearly when education is conceived in
terms of experience. Anything which can be called a study,
whether arithmetic, history, geography, or one of the natural
sciences, must be derived from materials which at the outset fall
within the scope of ordinary life-experience. In this respect
the newer education contrasts sharply with procedures which
start with facts and truths that are outside the range of the
experience of those taught, and which, therefore, have the
problem of discovering ways and means of bringing them
within experience. Undoubtedly one chief cause for the great

---

* From *Experience and Education*, 1938.

success of newer methods in early elementary education has been its observance of the contrary principle.

But finding the material for learning within experience is only the first step. The next step is the progressive development of what is already experienced into a fuller and richer and also more organized form, a form that gradually approximates that in which subject-matter is presented to the skilled, mature person. That this change is possible without departing from the organic connection of education with experience is shown by the fact that this change takes place outside of the school and apart from formal education. The infant, for example, begins with an environment of objects that is very restricted in space and time. That environment steadily expands by the momentum inherent in experience itself without aid from scholastic instruction. As the infant learns to reach, creep, walk, and talk, the intrinsic subject-matter of its experience widens and deepens. It comes into connection with new objects and events which call out new powers, while the exercise of these powers refines and enlarges the content of its experience. Life-space and life-durations are expanded. The environment, the world of experience, constantly grows larger and, so to speak, thicker. The educator who receives the child at the end of this period has to find ways for doing consciously and deliberately what "nature" accomplishes in the earlier years.

It is hardly necessary to insist upon the first of the two conditions which have been specified. It is a cardinal precept of the newer school of education that the beginning of instruction shall be made with the experience learners already have; that this experience and the capacities that have been developed during its course provide the starting point for all further learning. I am not so sure that the other condition, that of orderly development toward expansion and organization of subject-matter through growth of experience, receives as much attention. Yet the principle of continuity of educative experience requires that equal thought and attention be given to solution of this aspect of the educational problem. Undoubtedly this phase of the problem is more difficult than the other. Those who deal with the pre-school child, with the kindergarten

linking up outside & inside activities in school

child, and with the boy and girl of the early primary years do not have much difficulty in determining the range of past experience or in finding activities that connect in vital ways with it. With older children both factors of the problem offer increased difficulties to the educator. It is harder to find out the background of the experience of individuals and harder to find out just how the subject-matters already contained in that experience shall be directed so as to lead out to larger and better organized fields.

It is a mistake to suppose that the principle of the leading on of experience to something different is adequately satisfied simply by giving pupils some new experiences any more than it is by seeing to it that they have greater skill and ease in dealing with things with which they are already familiar. It is also essential that the new objects and events be related intellectually to those of earlier experiences, and this means that there be some advance made in conscious articulation of facts and ideas. It thus becomes the office of the educator to select those things within the range of existing experience that have the promise and potentiality of presenting new problems which by stimulating new ways of observation and judgment will expand the area of further experience. He must constantly regard what is already won not as a fixed possession but as an agency and instrumentality for opening new fields which make new demands upon existing powers of observation and of intelligent use of memory. Connectedness in growth must be his constant watchword.

The educator more than the member of any other profession is concerned to have a long look ahead. The physician may feel his job done when he has restored a patient to health. He has undoubtedly the obligation of advising him how to live so as to avoid similar troubles in the future. But, after all, the conduct of his life is his own affair, not the physician's; and what is more important for the present point is that as far as the physician does occupy himself with instruction and advice as to the future of his patient he takes upon himself the function of an educator. The lawyer is occupied with winning a suit for his client or getting the latter out of some complication into which he has got himself. If it goes beyond the case presented to him he too becomes an educator. The educator by the very nature of his work is obliged to see his present work in terms of what it accomplishes, or fails to accomplish, for a future whose objects are linked with those of the present.

Here, again, the problem for the progressive educator is more difficult than for the teacher in the traditional school. The latter had indeed to look ahead. But unless his personality and enthusiasm took him beyond the limits that hedged in the traditional school, he could content himself with thinking of the next examination period or the promotion to the next class. He could envisage the future in terms of factors that lay within the requirements of the school system as that conventionally existed. There is incumbent upon the teacher who links education and actual experience together a more serious and a harder business. He must be aware of the potentialities for leading students into new fields which belong to experiences already had, and must use this knowledge as his criterion for selection and arrangement of the conditions that influence their present experience.

Because the studies of the traditional school consisted of subject-matter that was selected and arranged on the basis of the judgment of adults as to what would be useful for the young sometime in the future, the material to be learned was settled upon outside the present life-experience of the learner. In consequence, it had to do with the past; it was such as had proved useful to men in past ages. By reaction to an opposite extreme, as unfortunate as it was probably natural under the circumstances, the sound idea that education should derive its materials from present experience and should enable the learner to cope with the problems of the present and future has often been converted into the idea that progressive schools can to a very large extent ignore the past. If the present could be cut off from the past, this conclusion would be sound. But the achievements of the past provide the only means at command for understanding the present. Just as the individual has to draw in memory upon his own past to understand the conditions in which he individually finds himself, so the issues and problems of present *social* life are in such intimate and direct connection with the past that students cannot be prepared to understand either these problems or the best way of dealing with them without delving into their roots in the past. In other words, the sound principle that the objectives of learning are in the future and its immediate materials are in present experience can be carried into effect only in the degree that present experience is stretched, as it were, backward. It can expand into the future only as it is also enlarged to take in the past.

If time permitted, discussion of the political and economic issues which the present generation will be compelled to face in the future would render this general statement definite and concrete. The nature of the issues cannot be understood save as we know how they came about. The institutions and customs that exist in the present and that give rise to present social ills and dislocations did not arise overnight. They have a long history behind them. Attempt to deal with them simply on the basis of what is obvious in the present is bound to result in adoption of superficial measures which in the end will only render existing problems more acute and more difficult to solve. Policies framed simply upon the ground of knowledge of the present cut off from the past is the counterpart of heedless carelessness in individual conduct. The way out of scholastic systems that made the past an end in itself is to make acquaintance with the past a *means* of understanding the present. Until this problem is worked out, the present clash of educational ideas and practices will continue. On the one hand, there will be reactionaries that claim that the main, if not the sole, business of education is transmission of the cultural heritage. On the other hand, there will be those who hold that we should ignore the past and deal only with the present and future.

That up to the present time the weakest point in progressive schools is in the matter of selection and organization of intellectual subject-matter is, I think, inevitable under the circumstances. It is as inevitable as it is right and proper that they should break loose from the cut and dried material which formed the staple of the old education. In addition, the field of experience is very wide and it varies in its contents from place to place and from time to time. A single course of studies for all progressive schools is out of the question; it would mean abandoning the fundamental principle of connection with life-experiences. Moreover, progressive schools are new. They have had hardly more than a generation in which to develop. A certain amount of uncertainty and of laxity in choice and organization of subject-matter is, therefore, what was to be expected. It is no ground for fundamental criticism or complaint.

It is a ground for legitimate criticism, however, when the ongoing movement of progressive education fails to recognize that the problem of selection and organization of subject-matter for study and learning is fundamental. Improvisation that takes advantage of special occasions prevents teaching and learning from being stereotyped and dead. But the basic material of study cannot be picked up in a cursory manner. Occasions which are not and cannot be foreseen are bound to arise wherever there is intellectual freedom. They should be utilized. But there is a decided difference between using them in the development of a continuing line of activity and trusting to them to provide the chief material of learning.

Unless a given experience leads out into a field previously unfamiliar no problems arise, while problems are the stimulus to thinking. That the conditions found in present experience should be used as sources of problems is a characteristic which differentiates education based upon experience from traditional education. For in the latter, problems were set from outside. Nonetheless, growth depends upon the presence of difficulty to be overcome by the exercise of intelligence. Once more, it is part of the educator's responsibility to see equally to two things: First, that the problem grows out of the conditions of the experience being had in the present, and that it is within the range of the capacity of students; and, secondly, that it is such that it arouses in the learner an active quest for information and for production of new ideas. The new facts and new ideas thus obtained become the ground for further experiences in which new problems are presented. The process is a continuous spiral. The inescapable linkage of the present with the past is a principle whose application is not restricted to a study of history. Take natural science, for example. Contemporary social life is what it is in very large measure because of the results of application of physical science. The experience of every child and youth, in the country and the city, is what it is in its present actuality because of appliances which utilize electricity, heat, and chemical processes. A child does not eat a meal that does not involve in its preparation and assimilation chemical and physiological principles. He does not read by artificial light or take a ride in a motor car or on a train without coming into contact with operations and processes which science has engendered.

It is a sound educational principle that students should be introduced to scientific subject-matter and be initiated into its facts and laws through acquaintance with everyday social applications. Adherence to this method is not only the most direct avenue to understanding of science itself but as the pupils grow more mature it is also the surest road to the understanding of the economic and industrial problems of present society. For they are the products to a very large extent of the application of science in production and distribution of commodities and services, while the latter processes are the most important factor in determining the present relations of human beings and social groups to one another. It is absurd, then, to argue that processes similar to those studied in laboratories and institutes of research are not a part of the daily life-experience of the young and hence do not come within the scope of education based upon experience. That the immature cannot study scientific facts and principles in the way in which mature experts study them goes without saying. But this fact, instead of exempting the educator from responsibility for using present experiences so that learners may gradually be led, through extraction of facts and laws, to experience of a scientific order, sets one of his main problems.

For if it is true that existing experience in detail and also on a wide scale is what it is because of the application of science, first, to processes of production and distribution of goods and services, and then to the relations which human beings sustain socially to one another, it is impossible to obtain an understanding of present social forces (without which they cannot be mastered and directed) apart from an education which leads learners into knowledge of the very same facts and principles which in their final organization constitute the sciences. Nor does the importance of the principle that learners should be led to acquaintance with scientific subject-matter cease with the insight thereby given into present social issues. The methods of science also point the way to the measures and policies by means of which a better social order can be brought into existence. The applications of science which have produced in large measure the social conditions which now exist do not exhaust the possible field of their application. For so far science has been applied more or less casually and under the influence of ends, such as private advantage and power, which are a heritage from the institutions of a prescientific age.

We are told almost daily and from many sources that it is impossible for human beings to direct their common life intelligently. We are told, on one hand, that the complexity of human relations, domestic and international, and on the other hand, the fact that human beings are so largely creatures of emotion and habit, make impossible large-scale social planning and direction by intelligence. This view would be more credible if any systematic effort, beginning with early education and carried on through the continuous study and learning of the young, had ever been undertaken with a view to making the method of intelligence, exemplified in science, supreme in education. There is nothing in the inherent nature of habit that prevents intelligent method from becoming itself habitual; and there is nothing in the nature of emotion to prevent the development of intense emotional allegiance to the method.

The case of science is here employed as an illustration of progressive selection of subject-matter resident in present experience towards organization: an organization which is free, not externally imposed, because it is in accord with the growth of experience itself. The utilization of subject-matter found in the present life-experience of the learner towards science is perhaps the best illustration that can be found of the basic principle of using existing experience as the means of carrying learners on to a wider, more refined, and better or-

ganized environing world, physical and human, than is found
in the experiences from which educative growth sets out. Hog-
ben's recent work, *Mathematics for the Million*, shows how
mathematics, if it is treated as a mirror of civilization and as
a main agency in its progress, can contribute to the desired
goal as surely as can the physical sciences. The underlying
ideal in any case is that of progressive organization of knowledge. It is with reference to organization of knowledge that we
are likely to find *Either-Or* philosophies most acutely active.
In practice, if not in so many words, it is often held that
since traditional education rested upon a conception of organization of knowledge that was almost completely contemptuous of living present experience, therefore education based
upon living experience should be contemptuous of the organization of facts and ideas.

When a moment ago I called this organization an *ideal*, I
meant, on the negative side, that the educator cannot start
with knowledge already organized and proceed to ladle it out
in doses. But as an ideal the active process of organizing
facts and ideas is an ever-present educational process. No experience is educative that does not tend both to knowledge
of more facts and entertaining of more ideas and to a better,
a more orderly, arrangement of them. It is not true that organization is a principle foreign to experience. Otherwise experience would be so dispersive as to be chaotic. The experience of young children centers about persons and the home.
Disturbance of the normal order of relationships in the family
is now known by psychiatrists to be a fertile source of later
mental and emotional troubles—a fact which testifies to the
reality of this kind of organization. One of the great advances in
early school education, in the kindergarten and early grades,
is that it preserves the social and human center of the organization of experience, instead of the older violent shift of the
center of gravity. But one of the outstanding problems of education, as of music, is modulation. In the case of education,
modulation means movement from a social and human center
toward a more objective intellectual scheme of organization,
always bearing in mind, however, that intellectual organization is not an end in itself but is the means by which social rela-

tions, distinctively human ties and bonds, may be understood and more intelligently ordered.

When education is based in theory and practice upon experience, it goes without saying that the organized subject-matter of the adult and the specialist cannot provide the starting point. Nevertheless, it represents the goal toward which education should continuously move. It is hardly necessary to say that one of the most fundamental principles of the scientific organization of knowledge is the principle of cause-and-effect. The way in which this principle is grasped and formulated by the scientific specialist is certainly very different from the way in which it can be approached in the experience of the young. But neither the relation nor grasp of its meaning is foreign to the experience of even the young child. When a child two or three years of age learns not to approach a flame too closely and yet to draw near enough a stove to get its warmth he is grasping and using the causal relation. There is no intelligent activity that does not conform to the requirements of the relation, and it is intelligent in the degree in which it is not only conformed to but consciously borne in mind.

In the earlier forms of experience the causal relation does not offer itself in the abstract but in the form of the relation of means employed to ends attained; of the relation of means and consequences. Growth in judgment and understanding is essentially growth in ability to form purposes and to select and arrange means for their realization. The most elementary experiences of the young are filled with cases of the means-consequence relation. There is not a meal cooked nor a source of illumination employed that does not exemplify this relation. The trouble with education is not the absence of situations in which the causal relation is exemplified in the relation of means and consequences. Failure to utilize the situations so as to lead the learner on to grasp the relation in the given cases of experience is, however, only too common. The logician gives the names "analysis and synthesis" to the operations by which means are selected and organized in relation to a purpose.

This principle determines the ultimate foundation for the utilization of *activities* in school. Nothing can be more absurd educationally than to make a plea for a variety of active occupations in the school while decrying the need for progressive organization of information and ideas. Intelligent activity is distinguished from aimless activity by the fact that it involves selection of means—analysis—out of the variety of conditions that are present, and their arrangement—synthesis —to reach an intended aim or purpose. That the more immature the learner is, the simpler must be the ends held in view and the more rudimentary the means employed, is obvious. But the principle of organization of activity in terms of some perception of the relation of consequences to means applies even with the very young. Otherwise an activity ceases to be educative because it is blind. With increased maturity, the problem of interrelation of means becomes more urgent. In the degree in which intelligent observation is transferred from the relation of means to ends to the more complex question of the relation of means to one another, the idea of cause and effect becomes prominent and explicit. The final justification of shops, kitchens, and so on in the school is not just that they afford opportunity for activity, but that they provide opportunity for the *kind* of activity or for the acquisition of mechanical skills which leads students to attend to the relation of means and ends, and then to consideration of the way things interact with one another to produce definite effects. It is the same in principle as the ground for laboratories in scientific research.

Unless the problem of intellectual organization can be worked out on the ground of experience, reaction is sure to occur toward externally imposed methods of organization. There are signs of this reaction already in evidence. We are told that our schools, old and new, are failing in the main task. They do not develop, it is said, the capacity for critical discrimination and the ability to reason. The ability to think is smothered, we are told, by accumulation of miscellaneous ill-digested information, and by the attempt to acquire forms of skill which will be immediately useful in the business and commercial world. We are told that these evils spring from the influence of science and from the magnification of present requirements at the expense of the tested cultural heritage from the past. It is argued that science and its method must be subordinated; that we must return to the logic of ultimate first principles expressed in the logic of Aristotle and St. Thomas, in order that the young may have sure anchorage in their intellectual and moral life, and not be at the mercy of every passing breeze that blows.

If the method of science had ever been consistently and continuously applied throughout the day-by-day work of the school in all subjects, I should be more impressed by this emotional appeal than I am. I see at bottom but two alternatives between which education must choose if it is not to drift aimlessly. One of them is expressed by the attempt to induce educators to return to the intellectual methods and ideals that arose centuries before scientific method was developed. The appeal may be temporarily successful in a period when general insecurity, emotional and intellectual as well as economic, is rife. For under these conditions the desire to lean on fixed authority is active. Nevertheless, it is so out of touch with all the conditions of modern life that I believe it is folly to seek salvation in this direction. The other alternative is systematic utilization of scientific method as the pattern and ideal of intelligent exploration and exploitation of the potentialities inherent in experience.

The problem involved comes home with peculiar force to progressive schools. Failure to give constant attention to development of the intellectual content of experiences and to obtain ever-increasing organization of facts and ideas may in the end merely strengthen the tendency toward a reactionary return to intellectual and moral authoritarianism. The present is not the time nor place for a disquisition upon scientific method. But certain features of it are so closely connected with any educational scheme based upon experience that they should be noted.

In the first place, the experimental method of science attaches more importance, not less, to ideas as ideas than do other methods. There is no such thing as experiment in the scientific sense unless action is directed by some leading idea. The fact that the ideas employed are hypotheses, not final truths, is the reason why ideas are more jealously guarded and tested in science than anywhere else. The moment they are taken to be first truths in themselves there ceases to be any reason for scrupulous examination of them. As fixed truths they must be accepted and that is the end of the matter. But as hypotheses, they must be continuously tested and revised, a requirement that demands they be accurately formulated.

In the second place, ideas or hypotheses are tested by the consequences which they produce when they are acted upon. This fact means that the consequences of action must be carefully and discriminatingly observed. Activity that is not checked by observation of what follows from it may be temporarily enjoyed. But intellectually it leads nowhere. It does not provide knowledge about the situations in which action occurs nor does it lead to clarification and expansion of ideas.

In the third place, the method of intelligence manifested in the experimental method demands keeping track of ideas, activities, and observed consequences. Keeping track is a matter of reflective review and summarizing, in which there is both discrimination and record of the significant features of a developing experience. To reflect is to look back over what has been done so as to extract the net meanings which are the capital stock for intelligent dealing with further experiences. It is the heart of intellectual organization and of the disciplined mind.

I have been forced to speak in general and often abstract language. But what has been said is organically connected with the requirement that experiences in order to be educative must lead out into an expanding world of subject-matter, a subject-matter of facts or information and of ideas. This condition is satisfied only as the educator views teaching and learning as a continuous process of reconstruction of experience. This condition in turn can be satisfied only as the educator has a long look ahead, and views every present experience as a moving force in influencing what future experiences will be. I am aware that the emphasis I have placed upon scientific method may be misleading, for it may result only in calling up the special technique of laboratory research as that is conducted by specialists. But the meaning of the emphasis placed upon scientific method has little to do with specialized techniques. It means that scientific method is the only authentic means at our command for getting at the significance of our everyday experiences of the world in which we live. It means that scientific method provides a working pattern of the way in which and the conditions under which experiences are used to lead ever onward and outward. Adaptation of the method to individuals of various degrees of maturity is a problem for the educator, and the constant factors in the problem are the formation of ideas, acting upon ideas, observation of the conditions which result, and organization of facts and ideas for future use. Neither the ideas, nor the activities, nor the observations, nor the organization are the same for a person six years old as they are for one twelve or eighteen years old, to say nothing of the adult scientist. But at every level there is an expanding development of experience if experience is educative in effect. Consequently, whatever the level of experience, we have no choice but either to operate in accord with the pattern it provides or else to neglect the place of intelligence in the development and control of a living and moving experience.

THE NATURE OF METHOD *

Subject matter dissolves into everything method, + method is everything

1. The Unity of Subject Matter and Method. The trinity of school topics is subject matter, methods, and administration or government. We have been concerned with the two former in recent chapters. It remains to disentangle them from the context in which they have been referred to, and discuss explicitly their nature. We shall begin with the topic of method, since that lies closest to the considerations of the last chapter. Before taking it up, it may be well, however, to call express attention to one implication of our theory; the connection of subject matter and method with each other. The idea that mind and the world of things and persons are two separate and independent realms—a theory which philosophically is known as dualism—carries with it the conclusion that method and subject matter of instruction are separate affairs. Subject matter then becomes a ready-made systematized classification of the facts and principles of the world of nature and man. Method then has for its province a consideration of the ways in which this antecedent subject matter may be best presented to and impressed upon the mind; or, a consideration of the ways in which the mind may be externally brought to bear upon the matter so as to facilitate its acquisition and possession. In theory, at least, one might deduce from a

* From *Democracy and Education,* 1916.

science of the mind as something existing by itself a complete theory of methods of learning, with no knowledge of the subjects to which the methods are to be applied. Since many who are actually most proficient in various branches of subject matter are wholly innocent of these methods, this state of affairs gives opportunity for the retort that pedagogy, as an alleged science of methods of the mind in learning, is futile; —a mere screen for concealing the necessity a teacher is under of profound and accurate acquaintance with the subject in hand.

But since thinking is a directed movement of subject matter to a completing issue, and since mind is the deliberate and intentional phase of the process, the notion of any such split is radically false. The fact that the material of a science is organized is evidence that it has already been subjected to intelligence; it has been methodized, so to say. Zoölogy as a systematic branch of knowledge represents crude scattered facts of our ordinary acquaintance with animals after they have been subjected to careful examination, to deliberate supplementation, and to arrangement to bring out connections which assist observation, memory, and further inquiry. Instead of furnishing a starting point for learning, they mark out a consummation. Method means that arrangement *of* subject matter which makes it most effective in use. Never is method something outside of the material.

How about method from the standpoint of an individual who is dealing with subject matter? Again, it is not something external It is simply an effective treatment *of* material—efficiency meaning such treatment as utilizes the material (puts it to a purpose) with a minimum of waste of time and energy. We can distinguish a *way* of acting, and discuss it by itself; but the way *exists* only as way-of-dealing-with-material. Method is not antithetical to subject matter; it is the effective direction of subject matter to desired results. It is antithetical to random and ill-considered action,—ill-considered signifying ill-adapted.

The statement that method means directed movement of subject matter towards ends is formal. An illustration may give it content. Every artist must have a method, a technique, in doing his work. Piano playing is not hitting the keys at random. It is an orderly way of using them, and the order is not something which exists ready-made in the musician's hands or brain prior to an activity dealing with the piano. Order is found in the disposition of acts which use the piano and the hands and brain so as to achieve the result intended. It is the action of the piano directed to accomplish the purpose of the piano as a musical instrument. It is the same with "pedagogical" method. The only difference is that the piano is a mechanism constructed in advance for a single end; while the material of study is capable of indefinite uses. But even in this regard the illustration may apply if we consider the infinite variety of kinds of music which a piano may produce, and the variations in technique required in the different musical results secured. Method in any case is but an effective way of employing some material for some end.

These considerations may be generalized by going back to the conception of experience. Experience as the perception of the connection between something tried and something undergone in consequence is a process. Apart from effort to control the course which the process takes, there is no distinction of subject matter and method. There is simply an activity which includes both what an individual does and what the environment does. A piano player who had perfect mastery of his instrument would have no occasion to distinguish between his contribution and that of the piano. In well-formed, smooth-running functions of any sort,—skating, conversing, hearing music, enjoying a landscape,—there is no consciousness of separation of the method of the person and of the subject matter. In whole-hearted play and work there is the same phenomenon.

When we reflect upon an experience instead of just having it, we inevitably distinguish between our own attitude and the objects toward which we sustain the attitude. When a man is eating, he is eating *food*. He does not divide his act into eating *and* food. But if he makes a scientific investigation of the act, such a discrimination is the first thing he would effect. He would examine on the one hand the properties of the nutritive material, and on the other hand the acts of the organism in appropriating and digesting. Such reflection upon experience gives rise to a distinction of *what* we experience (the experienc*ed*) and the experiencing—the *how*. When we give names to this distinction we have subject matter and method as our terms. There is the thing seen, heard, loved, hated, imagined, and there is the act of seeing, hearing, loving, hating, imagining, etc.

This distinction is so natural and so important for certain purposes, that we are only too apt to regard it as a separation in existence and not as a distinction in thought. Then we make a division between a self and the environment or world. This separation is the root of the dualism of method and subject matter. That is, we assume that knowing, feeling, willing, etc., are things which belong to the self or mind in its isolation, and which then may be brought to bear upon an independent subject matter. We assume that the things which belong in isolation to the self or mind have their own laws of operation irrespective of the modes of active energy of the object. These laws are supposed to furnish method. It would be no less absurd to suppose that men can eat without eating something, or that the structure and movements of the jaws, throat muscles, the digestive activities of stomach, etc., are not what they are *because* of the material with which their activity is engaged. Just as the organs of the organism are a continuous part of the very world in which food materials exist, so the capacities of seeing, hearing, loving, imagining are intrinsically connected with the subject matter of the world. They are more truly ways in which the environment enters into experience and functions there than they are independent acts brought to bear upon things. Experience, in short, is not a combination of mind and world, subject and object, method and subject matter, but is a single continuous interaction of a great diversity (literally countless in number) of energies.

For the purpose of *controlling* the course or direction which the moving unity of experience takes we draw a mental distinction between the how and the what. While there is no *way* of walking or of eating or of learning over and above the actual walking, eating, and studying, there are certain elements in the act which give the key to its more effective control. Special attention to these elements makes them more obvious to perception (letting other factors recede for the time being from conspicuous recognition). Getting an idea of *how* the experience proceeds indicates to us what factors must be secured or modified in order that it may go on more successfully. This is only a somewhat elaborate way of saying that if a man watches carefully the growth of several plants, some of which do well and some of which amount to little or nothing, he may be able to detect the special conditions upon which the prosperous development of a plant depends. These conditions, stated in an orderly sequence, would constitute the method or way or manner of its growth. There is no difference between the growth of a plant and the prosperous development of an experience. It is not easy, in either case, to seize upon just the factors which make for its best movement. But study of cases of success and failure and minute and extensive comparison, helps to seize upon causes. When we have arranged these causes in order, we have a method of procedure or a technique. ⟶ *when you say s m.v T. meth.*

A consideration of some evils in education that flow from the isolation of method from subject matter will make the point more definite. (1) In the first place, there is the neglect (of which we have spoken) of concrete situations of experience. There can be no discovery of a method without cases to be studied. The method is derived from observation of what actually happens, with a view to seeing that it happen better next time. But in instruction and discipline, there is rarely sufficient opportunity for children and youth to have the direct normal experiences from which educators might derive an idea of method or order of best development. Experiences are had under conditions of such constraint that they throw little or no light upon the normal course of an experience to its fruition. "Methods" have then to be authoritatively recommended to teachers, instead of being an expression of their own intelligent observations. Under such circumstances, they have a mechanical uniformity, assumed to be alike for all minds. Where flexible personal experiences are promoted by providing an environment which calls out directed occupations in work and play, the methods ascertained will vary with individuals—for it is certain that each individual has something characteristic in his way of going at things.

(2) In the second place, the notion of methods isolated from subject matter is responsible for the false conceptions of discipline and interest already noted. When the effective way of managing material is treated as something ready-made apart from material, there are just three possible ways in which to establish a relationship lacking by assumption. One is to utilize excitement, shock of pleasure, tickling the palate. Another is to make the consequences of not attending painful; we may use the menace of harm to motivate concern with the alien subject matter. Or a direct appeal may be made to the person to put forth effort without any reason. We may rely upon immediate strain of "will." In practice, however, the latter method is effectual only when instigated by fear of unpleasant results.

(3) In the third place, the act of learning is made a direct and conscious end in itself. Under normal conditions, learning is a product and reward of occupation with subject matter. Children do not set out, consciously, to learn walking or talking. One sets out to give his impulses for communication and for fuller intercourse with others a show. He learns in consequence of his direct activities. The better methods of teaching a child, say, to read, follow the same road. They do not fix his attention upon the fact that he has to learn something and so make his attitude self-conscious and constrained. They engage his activities, and in the process of engagement he learns: the same is true of the more successful methods in dealing with number or whatever. But when the subject matter is not used in carrying forward impulses and habits to significant results, it is just something to be learned. The pupil's attitude to it is just that of having to learn it. Conditions more unfavorable to an alert and concentrated response would be hard to devise. Frontal attacks are even more wasteful in learning than in war. This does not mean, however, that students are to be seduced unaware into preoccupation with lessons. It means that they shall be occupied with them for real reasons or ends and not just as something to be learned.

This is accomplished whenever the pupil perceives the place occupied by the subject matter in the fulfilling of some experience.

(4) In the fourth place, under the influence of the conception of the separation of mind and material, method tends to be reduced to a cut and dried routine, to following mechanically prescribed steps. No one can tell in how many schoolrooms children reciting in arithmetic or grammar are compelled to go through, under the alleged sanction of method, certain preordained verbal formulae. Instead of being encouraged to attack their topics directly, experimenting with methods that seem promising and learning to discriminate by the consequences that accrue, it is assumed that there is one fixed method to be followed. It is also naïvely assumed that if the pupils make their statements and explanations in a certain form of "analysis," their mental habits will in time conform. Nothing has brought pedagogical theory into greater disrepute than the belief that it is identified with handing out to teachers recipes and models to be followed in teaching. Flexibility and initiative in dealing with problems are characteristic of any conception to which method is a way of managing material to develop a conclusion. Mechanical rigid woodenness is an inevitable corollary of any theory which separates mind from activity motivated by a purpose.

2. *Method as General and as Individual.* In brief, the method of teaching is the method of an art of action intelligently directed by ends. But the practice of a fine art is far from being a matter of extemporized inspirations. Study of the operations and results of those in the past who have greatly succeeded is essential. There is always a tradition, or schools of art, definite enough to impress beginners, and often to take them captive. Methods of artists in every branch depend upon thorough acquaintance with materials and tools; the painter must know canvas, pigments, brushes, and the technique of manipulation of all his appliances. Attainment of this knowledge requires persistent and concentrated attention to objective materials. The artist studies the progress of his own attempts to see what succeeds and what fails. The as-

sumption that there are no alternatives between following ready-made rules and trusting to native gifts, the inspiration of the moment and undirected "hard work," is contradicted by the procedures of every art.

Such matters as knowledge of the past, of current technique, of material, of the ways in which one's own best results are assured, supply the material for what may be called *general* method. There exists a cumulative body of fairly stable methods for reaching results, a body authorized by past experience and by intellectual analysis, which an individual ignores at his peril. As was pointed out in the discussion of habit-forming there is always a danger that these methods will become mechanized and rigid, mastering an agent instead of being powers at command for his own ends. But it is also true that the innovator who achieves anything enduring, whose work is more than a passing sensation, utilizes classic methods more than may appear to himself or to his critics. He devotes them to new uses, and in so far transforms them.

Education also has its general methods. And if the application of this remark is more obvious in the case of the teacher than of the pupil, it is equally real in the case of the latter. Part of his learning, a very important part, consists in *becoming* master of the methods which the experience of others has shown to be more efficient in like cases of getting knowledge. These general methods are in no way opposed to individual initiative and originality—to personal ways of doing things. On the contrary they are reinforcements of them. For there is radical difference between even the most general method and a prescribed rule. The latter is a *direct* guide to action; the former operates indirectly through the enlightenment it supplies as to ends and means. It operates, that is to say, through intelligence, and not through conformity to orders externally imposed. Ability to use even in a masterly way an established technique gives no warranty of artistic work, for the latter also depends upon an animating idea.

If knowledge of methods used by others does not directly tell us what to do, or furnish ready-made models, how does it operate? What is meant by calling a method intellectual? Take the case of a physician. No mode of behavior more im-

periously demands knowledge of established modes of diagnosis and treatment than does his. But after all, cases are
like, not identical. To be used intelligently, existing practices, however authorized they may be, have to be adapted to the
exigencies of particular cases. Accordingly, recognized procedures indicate to the physician what inquiries to set on foot
for himself, what measures to *try.* They are standpoints
from which to carry on investigations; they economize a
survey of the features of the particular case by suggesting the
things to be especially looked into. The physician's own personal attitudes, his own ways (individual methods) of dealing
with the situation in which he is concerned, are not subordinated to the general principles of procedure, but are facilitated and directed by the latter. The instance may serve to
point out the value to the teacher of a knowledge of the psychological methods and the empirical devices found useful
in the past. When they get in the way of his own common
sense, when they come between him and the situation in which
he has to act, they are worse than useless. But if he has
acquired them as intellectual aids in sizing up the needs, resources, and difficulties of the unique experiences in which he
engages, they are of constructive value. In the last resort,
just because *everything* depends upon his own methods of response, *much* depends upon how far he can utilize, in making
his own response, the knowledge which has accrued in the experience of others.

As already intimated, every word of this account is directly
applicable also to the method of the pupil, the way of learning. To suppose that students, whether in the primary school
or in the university, can be supplied with models of method to
be followed in acquiring and expounding a subject is to fall
into a self-deception that has lamentable consequences. One
must make his own reaction in any case. Indications of the
standardized or general methods used in like cases by others—
particularly by those who are already experts—are of worth
or of harm according as they make his personal reaction
more intelligent or as they induce a person to dispense with
exercise of his own judgment.

If what was said earlier about originality of thought

seemed overstrained, demanding more of education than the capacities of average human nature permit, the difficulty is that we lie under the incubus of a superstition. We have set up the notion of mind at large, of intellectual method that is the same for all. Then we regard individuals as differing in the *quantity* of mind with which they are charged. Ordinary persons are then expected to be ordinary. Only the exceptional are allowed to have originality. The measure of difference between the average student and the genius is a measure of the absence of originality in the former. But this notion of mind in general is a fiction. How one person's abilities compare in quantity with those of another is none of the teacher's business. It is irrelevant to his work. What is required is that every individual shall have opportunities to employ his own powers in activities that have meaning. Mind, individual method, originality (these are convertible terms) signify the *quality* of purposive or directed action. If we act upon this conviction, we shall secure more originality even by the conventional standard than now develops. Imposing an alleged uniform method upon everybody breeds mediocrity in all but the very exceptional. And measuring originality by deviation from the mass breeds eccentricity in them. Thus we stifle the distinctive quality of the many, and save in rare instances (like, say, that of Darwin) infect the rare geniuses with an unwholesome quality.

3. *The Traits of Individual Method.* The most general features of the method of knowing have been given in our chapter on thinking. They are the features of the reflective situation: Problem, collection and analysis *of data*, projection and elaboration of suggestions or ideas, experimental application and testing; the resulting conclusion or judgment. The specific elements of an individual's method or way of attack upon a problem are found ultimately in his native tendencies and his acquired habits and interests. The method of one will vary from that of another (and *properly* vary) as his original instinctive capacities vary, as his past experiences and his preferences vary. Those who have already studied these matters are in possession of information which will help

teachers in understanding the responses different pupils make, and help them in guiding these responses to greater efficiency. Child-study, psychology, and a knowledge of social environment supplement the personal acquaintance gained by the teacher. But methods remain the personal concern, approach, and attack of an individual, and no catalogue can ever exhaust their diversity of form and tint.

Some attitudes may be named, however, which are central in effective intellectual ways of dealing with subject matter. Among the most important are directness, open-mindedness, single-mindedness (or whole-heartedness), and responsibility.

1. It is easier to indicate what is meant by directness through negative terms than in positive ones. Self-consciousness, embarrassment, and constraint are its menacing foes. They indicate that a person is not immediately concerned with subject matter. Something has come between which deflects concern to side issues. A self-conscious person is partly thinking about his problem and partly about what others think of his performances. Diverted energy means loss of power and confusion of ideas. Taking an attitude is by no means identical with being conscious of one's attitude. The former is spontaneous, naïve, and simple. It is a sign of whole-souled relationship between a person and what he is dealing with. The latter is not of necessity abnormal. It is sometimes the easiest way of correcting a false method of approach, and of improving the effectiveness of the means one is employing—as golf players, piano players, public speakers, etc., have occasionally to give especial attention to their position and movements. But this need is occasional and temporary. When it is effectual a person thinks of himself in terms of what is to be done, as one means among others of the realization of an end—as in the case of a tennis player practicing to get the "feel" of a stroke. In abnormal cases, one thinks of himself not as part of the agencies of execution, but as a separate object—as when the player strikes an attitude thinking of the impression it will make upon spectators, or is worried because of the impression he fears his movements give rise to.

Confidence is a good name for what is intended by the

term directness. It should not be confused, however, with *self-confidence* which may be a form of self-consciousness—or of "cheek." Confidence is not a name for what one thinks or feels about his attitude; it is not reflex. It denotes the straightforwardness with which one goes at what he has to do. It denotes not *conscious* trust in the efficacy of one's power but unconscious faith in the possibilities of the situation. It signifies rising to the needs of the situation.

We have already pointed out the objections to making students emphatically aware of the fact that they are studying or learning. Just in the degree in which they are induced by the conditions to be so aware, they are *not* studying and learning. They are in a divided and complicated attitude. Whatever methods of a teacher call a pupil's attention off from what he has to do and transfer it to his own attitude towards what he is doing impair directness of concern and action. Persisted in, the pupil acquires a permanent tendency to fumble, to gaze about aimlessly, to look for some clew of action beside that which the subject matter supplies. Dependence upon extraneous suggestions and directness, a state of foggy confusion, take the place of that sureness with which children (and grown-up people who have not been sophisticated by "education") confront the situations of life.

2. Open-mindedness. Partiality is, as we have seen, an accompaniment of the existence of interest, since this means sharing, partaking, taking sides in some movement. All the more reason, therefore, for an attitude of mind which actively welcomes suggestions and relevant information from all sides. In the chapter on Aims it was shown that foreseen ends are factors in the development of a changing situation. They are the means by which the direction of action is controlled. They are subordinate to the situation, therefore, not the situation to them. They are not ends in the sense of finalities to which everything must be bent and sacrificed. They are, as foreseen, *means* of guiding the development of a situation. A target is not the future goal of shooting; it is the centering factor in a present shooting. Openness of mind means accessibility of mind to any and every consideration that will throw light upon the situation that needs to be

cleared up, and that will help determine the consequences of acting this way or that. Efficiency in accomplishing ends which have been settled upon as unalterable can coexist with a narrowly opened mind. But intellectual growth means constant expansion of horizons and consequent formation of new purposes and new responses. These are impossible without an active disposition to welcome points of view hitherto alien; an active desire to entertain considerations which modify existing purposes. Retention of capacity to grow is the reward of such intellectual hospitality. The worst thing about stubbornness of mind, about prejudices, is that they arrest development; they shut the mind off from new stimuli. Open-mindedness means retention of the childlike attitude; closed-mindedness means premature intellectual old age.

Exorbitant desire for uniformity of procedure and for prompt external results are the chief foes which the open-minded attitude meets in school. The teacher who does not permit and encourage diversity of operation in dealing with questions is imposing intellectual blinders upon pupils—restricting their vision to the one path the teacher's mind happens to approve. Probably the chief cause of devotion to rigidity of method is, however, that it seems to promise speedy, accurately measurable, correct results. The zeal for "answers" is the explanation of much of the zeal for rigid and mechanical methods. Forcing and overpressure have the same origin, and the same result upon alert and varied intellectual interest.

Open-mindedness is not the same as empty-mindedness. To hang out a sign saying "Come right in; there is no one at home" is not the equivalent of hospitality. But there is a kind of passivity, willingness to let experiences accumulate and sink in and ripen, which is an essential of development. Results (external answers or solutions) may be hurried; processes may not be forced. They take their own time to mature. Were all instructors to realize that the quality of mental process, not the production of correct answers, is the measure of educative growth something hardly less than a revolution in teaching would be worked.

3. Single-mindedness. So far as the word is concerned,

much that was said under the head of "directness" is applicable. But what the word is here intended to convey is *completeness* of interest, unity of purpose; the absence of suppressed but effectual ulterior aims for which the professed aim is but a mask. It is equivalent to mental integrity. Absorption, engrossment, full concern with subject matter for its own sake, nurture it. Divided interest and evasion destroy it.

Intellectual integrity, honesty, and sincerity are at bottom not matters of conscious purpose but of quality of active response. Their acquisition is fostered of course by conscious intent, but self-deception is very easy. Desires are urgent. When the demands and wishes of others forbid their direct expression they are easily driven into subterranean and deep channels. Entire surrender, and whole-hearted adoption of the course of action demanded by others are almost impossible. Deliberate revolt or deliberate attempts to deceive others may result. But the more frequent outcome is a confused and divided state of interest in which one is fooled as to one's own real intent. One tries to serve two masters at once. Social instincts, the strong desire to please others and get their approval, social training, the general sense of duty and of authority, apprehension of penalty, all lead to a half-hearted effort to conform, to "pay attention to the lesson," or whatever the requirement is. Amiable individuals want to do what they are expected to do. Consciously the pupil thinks he is doing this. But his own desires are not abolished. Only their evident exhibition is suppressed. Strain of attention to what is hostile to desire is irksome; in spite of one's *conscious* wish, the underlying desires determine the main course of thought, the deeper emotional responses. The mind wanders from the nominal subject and devotes itself to what is intrinsically more desirable. A systematized divided attention expressing the duplicity of the state of desire is the result.

One has only to recall his own experiences in school or at the present time when outwardly employed in actions which do not engage one's desires and purposes, to realize how prevalent is this attitude of divided attention—double-mindedness. We are so used to it that we take it for granted that a considerable amount of it is necessary. It may be; if so, it is the more important to face its bad intellectual effects. Obvious is the loss of energy of thought immediately available when one is consciously trying (or trying to seem to try) to attend to one matter, while unconsciously one's imagination is spontaneously going out to more congenial affairs. More subtle and more permanently crippling to efficiency of intellectual activity is a fostering of habitual self-deception, with the confused sense of reality which accompanies it. A double standard of reality, one for our own private and more or less concealed interests, and another for public and acknowledged concerns, hampers, in most of us, integrity and completeness of mental action. Equally serious is the fact that a split is set up between conscious thought and attention and impulsive blind affection and desire. Reflective dealings with the material of instruction is constrained and half-hearted; attention wanders. The topics to which it wanders are unavowed and hence intellectually illicit; transactions with them are furtive. The discipline that comes from regulating response by deliberate inquiry having a purpose fails; worse than that, the deepest concern and most congenial enterprises of the imagination (since they center about the things dearest to desire) are casual, concealed. They enter into action in ways which are unacknowledged. Not subject to rectification by consideration of consequences, they are demoralizing.

School conditions favorable to this division of mind between avowed, public, and socially responsible undertakings, and private, ill-regulated, and suppressed indulgences of thought are not hard to find. What is sometimes called "stern discipline," i.e., external coercive pressure, has this tendency. Motivation through rewards extraneous to the thing to be done has a like effect. Everything that makes schooling merely preparatory works in this direction. Ends being beyond the pupil's present grasp, other agencies have to be found to procure immediate attention to assigned tasks. Some responses are secured, but desires and affections not enlisted must find other outlets. Not less serious is exaggerated emphasis upon drill exercises designed to produce skill in action, independent of any engagement of thought—exercises have no purpose but the production of automatic skill. Nature abhors a mental vacuum. What do teachers imagine is happening to thought and emotion when the latter get no outlet in the things of immediate activity? Were they merely kept in temporary abeyance, or even only calloused, it would not be a matter of so much moment. But they are not abolished; they are not suspended; they are not suppressed—save with reference to the task in question. They follow their own chaotic and undisciplined course. What is native, spontaneous, and vital in mental reaction goes unused and untested, and the habits formed are such that these qualities become less and less available for public and avowed ends.

4. Responsibility. By responsibility as an element in intellectual attitude is meant the disposition to consider in advance the probable consequences of any projected step and deliberately to accept them: to accept them in action, not yielding a mere verbal assent. Ideas, as we have seen, are intrinsically standpoints and methods for bringing about a solution of a perplexing situation; forecasts calculated to influence responses. It is only too easy to think that one accepts a statement or believes a suggested truth when one has not considered its implications; when one has made but a cursory and superficial survey of what further things one is committed to by acceptance. Observation and recognition, belief and assent, then become names for lazy acquiescence in what is externally presented.

It would be much better to have fewer facts and truths in instruction—that is, fewer things supposedly accepted,—if a smaller number of situations could be intellectually worked out to the point where conviction meant something real— some identification of the self with the type of conduct demanded by facts and foresight of results. The most permanent bad results of undue complication of school subjects and congestion of school studies and lessons are not the worry, nervous strain, and superficial acquaintance that follow (serious as these are), but the failure to make clear what is involved in really knowing and believing a thing. Intellectual responsibility means severe standards in this regard. These standards can be built up only through practice in following up and acting upon the meaning of what is acquired.

Intellectual *thoroughness* is thus another name for the attitude we are considering. There is a kind of thoroughness which is almost purely physical: the kind that signifies mechanical and exhausting drill upon all the details of a subject. Intellectual thoroughness is *seeing a thing through*. It depends upon a unity of purpose to which details are subordinated, not upon presenting a multitude of disconnected details. It is manifested in the firmness with which the full meaning of the purpose is developed, not in attention, however "conscientious" it may be, to the steps of action externally imposed and directed.

Summary. Method is a statement of the way the subject matter of an experience develops most effectively and fruitfully. It is derived, accordingly, from observation of the course of experiences where there is no conscious distinction of the personal attitude and manner from material dealt with. The assumption that method is something separate is connected with the notion of the isolation of mind and self from the world of things. It makes instruction and learning formal, mechanical, constrained. While methods are individualized, certain features of the normal course of an experience to its fruition may be discriminated, because of the fund of wisdom derived from prior experiences and because of general similarities in the materials dealt with from time to time. Expressed in terms of the attitude of the individual the traits of good method are straightforwardness, flexible intellectual interest or open-minded will to learn, integrity of purpose, and acceptance of responsibility for the consequences of one's activity including thought.

THE EDUCATIONAL SITUATION:
AS CONCERNS
SECONDARY EDUCATION *

I should feel hesitant indeed to come before a body of teachers, engaged in the practical work of teaching, and appear to instruct them regarding the solution of the difficult problems which face them. My task is a more grateful one. It is mine simply to formulate and arrange the difficulties which the current state of discussion shows teachers already to have felt. Those concerned with secondary school work have realized that their energies must be peculiarly concentrated at certain points; they have found that some problems are so urgent that they must be met and wrestled with. I have tried in the accompanying syllabus to gather together these practical problems and to arrange them in such form as to show their connections with one another; and by this classification to indicate what seemed to me the roots of the difficulty.

I. Problems relating to the articulation of the secondary school in the educational system.

    1. Adjustment to the grades.
        a) Dropping out of pupils: extent and causes.
        b) Different sorts of preparation of teachers; methods of rectifying, etc.

---

* From *The Educational Situation*, 1902.

    c) Abrupt change of ideals and methods of teaching and discipline.

    d) Introduction of traditional high-school studies into the upper grades; the science course, etc.

2. *Adjustment to college.*

    a) Modes of entering college; examination, certification, etc.

    b) Varieties of entrance requirements.

    c) Different problems of public and private high schools.

    d) Coaching for specific results vs. training and method.

II. Problems relating to the adjustment of preparation for college to preparation for other pursuits in life.

1. Is it true that the same education gives the best preparation for both?

2. If so, which shall be taken as the standard for measuring the character of the other?

3. If not so, by what principles and along what lines shall the work be differentiated?

4. If not so, shall specialized or definite preparation be made for other future callings as well as for the college student?

III. The adjustment of work to the individual.

1. The nature and limits of the elective principle as applied to particular subjects, and to courses and groups of subjects.

2. Acquaintance with the history, environment, and capacity of individuals with reference to assisting in the selection of vocation.

3. Does the period of adolescence present such peculiarities as to call for marked modifications of present secondary work?

IV. Problems arising from social phases of secondary-school work.

1. The educational utilization of social organizations: debating, musical, dramatic clubs; athletics.

2. School discipline and government in their social aspects.
3. Relations to the community: the school as a social center.

V. Preceding problems as affecting the curriculum: conflict of studies and groups of studies.

1. The older problem: adjustment of the respective claims of ancient and modern languages, of language and science, of history and social science, civics, economics, etc., of English literature and composition.

2. The newer problem:
   a) The place of manual training and technological work.
   b) The place of fine art.
   c) Commercial studies.

In what I have to say this morning, I shall make no attempt to go over these points one by one. I shall rather try to set clearly and briefly before you the reasons which have led me to adopt the classification presented. This will take me into a discussion of the historic and social facts which lie back of the problems, and in the light of which alone I believe these problems can be attacked and solved. If it seems unnecessarily remote to approach school problems through a presentation of what may appear to be simply a form of social philosophy, there is yet practical encouragement in recognizing that exactly the same forces which have thrust these questions into the forefront of school practice, are also operative to solve them. For problems do not arise arbitrarily. They come from causes, and from causes which are imbedded in the very structure of the school system—yes, even beyond that, in the structure of society itself. It is for this reason that mere changes in the mechanics of the school system, whether in administration or in the externals of subject-matter, turn out mere temporary devices. Sometimes, when one has made a delicate or elaborate arrangement which seems to him exactly calculated to obviate the difficulties of the situation, one is tempted to accuse his generation as stiff-necked when the scheme does not take—when it does not spread; when, in the language of the biologist, it is not selected. The explanation, however, is not in the hard-heartedness or intellectual blindness of others, but in the fact that any adjustment which really and permanently succeeds within the school walls, must reach out and be an adjustment of forces in the social environment.

A slight amount of social philosophy and social insight reveals two principles continuously at work in all human institutions: one is toward specialization and consequent isolation, the other toward connection and interaction. In the life of the nation we see first a movement toward separation, toward marking off our own life as a people as definitely as possible to avoid its submergence, to secure for it an individuality of its own. Commercially we pursue a policy of protection; in international relations one of having to do as little as possible with other nationalities. That tendency exhausts itself and the pendulum swings in another direction. Reciprocity, the broadening of our business life through increased contacts and wider exchange, becomes the commercial watchword. Expansion, taking our place in the sisterhood of nations, making ourselves recognized as a world-power, becomes the formula for international politics. Science shows the same rhythm in its development. A period of specialization—of relative isolation—secures to each set of natural phenomena a chance to develop on its own account, without being lost in, or obscured by generalities or a mass of details. But the time comes when the limit of movement in this direction is reached, and it is necessary to devote ourselves to tracing the threads of connection which unite the different specialized branches into a coherent and consecutive whole. At present the most active sciences seem to be spelled with a hyphen; it is astro-physics, stereo-chemistry, psycho-physics, and so on.

This is not a movement of blind action and reaction. One tendency is the necessary completion of the other. A certain degree of isolation or detachment is required to secure the unhindered and mature development of any group of forces. It is necessary in order to master them in their practical workings. We have to divide to conquer. But when the proper degree of individualization is reached, we need to bring one thing to bear upon another in order to realize upon the benefits which may be derived from the period of isolation. The sole object of the separation is to serve as a means to the end of more effective interaction.

Now as to the bearings of this abstract piece of philosophy upon our school problems. The school system is a historic evolution. It has a tradition and a movement of its own. Its roots run back into the past and may be traced through the strata of the successive centuries. It has an independence, a dignity of its own comparable to that of any other institution. In this twenty-five-hundred-year-old development it has, of necessity, taken on its individuality at the expense of a certain isolation. Only through this isolation has it been disentangled from absorption in other institutions: the family, government, the church, and so on. This detachment has been a necessity in order that it might become a true division of labor and thus perform most efficiently the service required of it.

But there are disadvantages as well as advantages. Attention has come to be concentrated upon the affairs of the school system as if they concerned simply the system itself, and had only a very indirect reference to other social institutions. The school-teacher often resents reference to outside contacts and considerations as if they were indeed outside—simply interferences. There can be no doubt that in the last two centuries much more thought and energy have been devoted to shaping the school system into an effective mechanism within itself than to securing its due interaction with family life, the church, commerce, or political institutions.

But, having secured this fairly adequate and efficient machine, the question which is coming more and more to the front is: what shall we do with it? How shall we secure from it the services, the fruits, which alone justify the expense of money, time, and thought in building up the machine?

It is at this point that particular conflicts and problems begin to show themselves. The contemporary demands—the demands that are made in the attempt to secure the proper interaction of the school—are one thing; the demands that arise out of the working of the school system considered as an independent historical institution are another. Every teacher has to work at detailed problems which arise out of this conflict, whether he is aware of its existence or not, and he is harassed by friction that arises in the conflict of these two great social forces. Men divide along these lines. We find one group instinctively rather than consciously ranging themselves about the maintenance of the existing school system, and holding that reforms are to be made along the line of improvement in its present workings. Others are clamorous for more radical changes—the changes which will better adapt the school to contemporary social needs. Needless to say, each represents a necessary and essential factor in the situation, because each stands for the working of a force which cannot be eliminated.

Let me now try to show how, out of this profound social conflict and necessity of social adjustment, the particular problems arise which I have arranged under five heads in the accompanying syllabus. Our first concern is with the articulation of the high school into the entire educational system. The high school looks towards the grades on one side and toward the college on the other. What are the historic influences which have shaped this intermediate position, and placed peculiar difficulties and responsibilities upon the secondary school? Briefly put, it is that the elementary school and the college represent distinctly different forces and traditions on the historic side. The elementary school is an outgrowth of the democratic movement in its ethical aspects. Prior to the latter half of the eighteenth century the elementary school was hardly more than a wooden device for instructing little children of the lower classes in some of the utilities of their future callings—the mere rudiments of reading, writing, and number. The democratic upheaval took shape not merely in a demand for political equality, but in a more profound aspiration towards an equality of intellectual and moral opportunity and development. The significance of such an educational writer as Rousseau is not measured by any particular improvement he suggested, or by any particular extravagances he indulged himself in. His is a voice struggling to express the necessity of a thoroughgoing revolution of elementary education to make it a factor in the intellectual and moral development of all—not a mere device for teaching the use of certain practical tools to those sections of society before whose development a stone wall was placed. What Rousseau as a writer was to the emotions of the France of his day, Horace Mann as a doer was to the practical situation of the United States in his time. He stood, and stood most effectively, for letting the democratic spirit, in all of its ethical significance, into the common elementary schools, and for such a complete reorganization of these schools as would make them the most serviceable possible instruments of human development.

In spite of all the influences which are continually operative to limit the scope and range of elementary education, in spite of the influences which would bring back a reversion to the type of the limited utilitarian school of the seventeenth century, that part of the school system which stands underneath the high school represents this broad democratic movement. To a certain extent, and in many of its phases, the high school is an outgrowth of exactly the same impulse. It has the same history and stands for the same ideals; but only in part. It has also been profoundly shaped by influences having another origin. It represents also the tradition of the learned class. It maintains the tradition of higher culture as a distinct possession of a certain class of society. It embodies the aristocratic ideal. If we cast our eyes back over history, we do not find its full meaning summed up in the democratic movement of which I have just spoken. We find the culture of the ancient world coming down to us by a distinct channel. We find the wisdom and enlightenment of the past conserved and handed on by a distinct class located almost entirely in the colleges, and in the higher academies which are to all intents and purposes the outgrowth of the colleges. We find that our high school has been quite as persistently molded and directed through the agencies which have been concerned with keeping alive and passing on the treasure of learning, as through the democratic influences which have surged up from below. The existing high school, in a word, is a product of the meeting of these two forces, and upon it more than upon any other part of the school system is placed the responsibility of making an adjustment.

I do not mention the tradition of learning kept up in the universities of the Middle Ages and the higher schools of the Renaissance, and refer to it as aristocratic for the sake of disparaging it. Eternal vigilance is the price of liberty, and eternal care and nurture are the price of maintaining the precious conquest of the past—of preventing a relapse into Philistinism, that combination of superficial enlightenment and dogmatic crudity. If it were not for the work of an aristocracy in the past, there would be but little worth conferring upon the democracy of today.

There are not in reality two problems of articulation for the high school—one as regards the grades and the other as regards the college. There is at bottom but one problem— that of adjusting the demand for an adequate training of the masses of mankind to the conservation and use of that higher learning which is the primary and essential concern of a smaller number—of a minority. Of course, elementary school and college alike are affected by the same problem. Part of the work of the grades today is precisely the enrichment of its traditional meager and materialistic curriculum with something of that spirit and wealth of intelligence that are the product of the higher schools. And one of the problems of the college is precisely to make its store of learning more available to the masses, make it count for more in the everyday life.

But the high school is the connecting link, and it must bear the brunt. Unless I am a false prophet, we shall soon see the same thoughtful attention which for the past fifteen years has characterized discussion of the relation of high school and college, speedily transferring itself over to the problem of a more organic and vital relation between the high school and the grades. The solution of this problem is important in order that the democratic movement may not be abortively arrested—in order that it may have its full sweep. But it is equally important, for the sake of the college, and in the interests of higher learning. The arbitrary hiatus which exists at present reacts as unfavorably in one direction as in the other.

First, it limits the constituency of the college; it lessens the actual numbers of those who are awakened to the opportunities before them, and directed towards the college doors. Secondly, it restricts the sphere of those who sympathetically and vicariously feel the influence of the college, and are thus led to feel that what concerns the welfare of the college is of direct concern to them. The attitude of the mass of the people today towards the college is one of curiosity displaying itself from afar rather than of immediate interest. Indeed, it sometimes would seem that only athletic exhibitions form a direct line of connection between the college and the average community life. In the third place it tends to erect dams which prevent the stream of teachers flowing from the college walls from seeking or finding congenial service in the grades, and thereby tends automatically to perpetuate whatever narrowness of horizon or paucity of resource is characteristic of the elementary school. Fourth, it operates to isolate the college in its working relations to life, and thereby to hinder it from rendering its normal service to society.

I pass on now to the second main line of problems—those having to do with preparation for college on one side, and for life on the other. Ultimately this is not a different problem, but simply another outgrowth of the same question. A few years ago a happy formula was current: the proposition that the best preparation for college was also the best preparation for life. The formula was such a happy one that if formulae ever really disposed of any practical difficulty, there would be no longer any problem to discuss. But I seem to observe that this proposition is not heard so frequently as formerly; and indeed, that since it was uttered things seem to be taking their own course much as before.

The inefficiency of the formula lies in its ambiguity. It throws no light on the fundamental problem of Which is Which? Is it preparation for college which sets the standard for preparation for life, or is it preparation for life which affords the proper criterion of adequate preparation for college? Is the high-school course to be planned primarily with reference to meeting the needs of those who go to college, on the assumption that this will also serve best the needs of those who go into other callings in life? Or, shall the high school devote its energies to preparing all its members for life in more comprehensive sense, and permit the college to select its entrance requirements on the basis of work thus done?

I shall not attempt to solve this problem, and for a very good reason. I believe that there are forces inherent in the situation itself which are working out an inevitable solution. Every step in the more rational development of both high school and college, without any reference to their relationships to each other bring the two more closely together. I am optimistic enough to believe that we are much nearer a solution of this vexed question than we generally dare believe. Quite independent of any question of entrance requirements, or of high-school preparation, the college is undergoing a very marked development, and even transformation, on its own account. I refer to such developments within the college course as the introduction not only of the Ph.B. and B.S. courses side by side with the older classical courses, but also to the forward movement in the direction of a specific group of commercial and social studies; and to the tendency of all universities of broad scope to maintain technological schools. I refer also to the tendency to adapt the college work more and more to preparation for specific vocations in life. Practically all the larger colleges of the country now have a definite arrangement by which at least one year of the undergraduate course counts equally in the professional course of law, medicine, or divinity as the case may be. Now, when these two movements have reached their fruition, and the high school has worked out on its own account the broadening of its own curriculum, I believe we shall find that the high school and the college have arrived at a common point. The college course will be so broad and varied that it will be entirely feasible to take any judicious group of studies from any well organized and well managed high school, and accept them as preparation for college. It has been the narrowness of the traditional college curriculum on one side, and the inadequacy of the content of high-school work on the other, which have caused a large part of our mutual embarrassments.

I must run rapidly over the problems referred to under my third and fourth main heads—those having to do with adjustment to individual needs, and to the social uses of the school. I take it that these illustrate just the same general principle we have been already discussing. The school has a tradition not only regarding its position in the educational system as a whole, and not only as regards its proper curriculum, but also as regards the methods and ideals of discipline and administration in relation to its students.

There can be no doubt that many of these traditions are out of alignment with the general trend of events outside the school walls—that in some cases the discrepancy is so great that the high-school tradition cuts abruptly across this outside stream. One of these influences is found in the tendency equally marked in the family, church, and state, to relax the bonds of purely external authority, to give more play to individual powers, to require of the individual more personal initiative, and to exact of him a more personal accountability. There may be difference of opinion as to the degree in which the school should yield to this tendency, or should strive to counteract it, or should endeavor to utilize and direct it. There can be no difference of opinion, however, as to the necessity of a more persistent and adequate study of the individual as regards his history, environment, predominant tastes and capacities, and special needs—and please note that I say needs as well as tastes. I do not think there can be any difference of opinion as to the necessity of a more careful study of the effect of particular school studies upon the normal growth of the individual, and of the means by which they shall be made a more effective means of connection between the present powers of the individual, and his future career. Just the limits of this principle, and its bearings upon such problems as the introduction of electives, I shall not take up. We have no time for a detailed discussion of these disputed points. As I have just indicated, however, I do not see how there can be dispute as to the fact that the individual has assumed such a position as to require more positive consideration and attention as an individual, and a correspondingly different mode of treatment. I cannot leave the topic, however, without stating that here also I believe the ultimate solution will be found, not along the line of mechanical devices as to election or non-election, but rather through the more continued and serious study of the individual in both his psychological make-up and his social relations.

I have reserved the group of problems bearing upon the formation of a curriculum until the last. From the practical side, however, we probably find here the problems which confront the average teacher most urgently and persistently. This I take it is because all the other influences impinge at this point. The problem of just what time is to be given respectively to mathematics, and classics, and modern languages, and history, and English, and the sciences—physical, biological—is one the high-school teacher has always with him. To adjust the respective claims of the different studies and get a result which is at once harmonious and workable, is a task which almost defies human capacity. The problem, however, is not a separate problem. It is so pressing just because it is at this point that all the other forces meet. The adjustment of studies, and courses of study, is the ground upon which the practical solution and working adjustment of all other problems must be sought and found. It is as an effect of other deep lying and far-reaching historic and social causes that the conflict of studies is to be treated.

There is one matter constantly accompanying any practical problem which at first sight is extremely discouraging. Before we get our older problems worked out to any degree of satisfaction, new and greater problems are upon us, threatening to overwhelm us. Such is the present educational situation. It would seem as if the question of adjusting the conflicts already referred to, which have so taxed the time and energy of high-school teachers for the past generation, were quite enough. But no; before we have arrived at anything approaching consensus of opinion, the larger city schools at least find the conflict raging in a new spot—still other studies and lines of study are demanding recognition. We have the uprearing of the commercial high school; of the manual-training high school.

At first the difficulty of the problem was avoided or evaded, because distinct and separate high schools were erected to meet these purposes. The current now seems to be in the other direction. A generation ago it was practically necessary to isolate the manual-training course of study in order that it might receive due attention, and be worked out under fairly favorable influences. Fifteen years ago the same was essentially true of the commercial courses. Now, however, there are many signs of the times indicating that the situation is ripe for interaction—the problem is now the introduction of manual-training and commercial courses as integral and organic parts of a city high school. Demands are also made for the introduction of more work in the line of fine art, drawing, music, and the application of design to industry; and for the introduction of a larger number of specifically sociological studies—this independent of those studies which naturally form a part of the so-called commercial course.

At first sight, as just intimated, the introduction of these new difficulties before we are half way through our old ones, is exceedingly distressing. But more than once the longest way around has proved the shortest way home. When new problems emerge, it must mean, after all, that certain essential conditions of the old problem had been ignored, and consequently that any solution reached simply in terms of the recognized factors would have been partial and temporary. I am inclined to think that in the present case the introduction of these new problems will ultimately prove enlightening rather than confusing. They serve to generalize the older problems, and to make their factors stand out in clearer relief.

In the future it is going to be less and less a matter of worrying over the respective merits of the ancient and modern languages; or of the inherent values of scientific *vs.* humanistic study, and more a question of discovering and observing certain broader lines of cleavage, which affect equally the disposition and power of the individual, and the social callings for which education ought to prepare the individual. It will be, in my judgment, less and less a question of piecing together certain studies in a more or less mechanical way in order to make out a so-called course of study running through a certain number of years; and more and more a question of grouping studies together according to their natural mutual affinities and reinforcements for the securing of certain well-marked ends.

For this reason I welcome the introduction into the arena of discussion, of the question of providing courses in commerce and sociology, in the fine and applied arts, and in technological training. I think henceforth certain fundamental issues will stand out more clearly and have to be met upon a wider basis and dealt with on a wider scale. As I see the matter, this change will require the concentration of attention upon these two points: first, what groups of studies will most serviceably recognize the typical divisions of labor, the typical callings in society, callings which are absolutely indispensable to the spiritual as well as to the material ends of society; and, secondly, not to do detriment to the real culture of the individual, or, if this seems too negative a statement, to secure for him the full use and control of his own powers. From this point of view, I think that certain of the problems just referred to, as, for instance, the conflict of language and science, will be put in a new perspective, will be capable of approach from a different angle; and that because of this new approach many of the knotty problems which have embarrassed us in the past will disappear.

Permit me to repeat in a somewhat more explicit way the benefits which I expect to flow from the expansion of the regular high school in making room for commercial, manual, and aesthetic studies. In the first place, it will provide for the recognition and the representation of all the typical occupations that are found in society. Thus it will make the working relationship between the secondary school and life a free and all around one. It will complete the circuit—it will round out the present series of segmental arcs into a whole. Now this fact will put all the school studies in a new light. They can be looked at in the place they normally occupy in the whole circle of human activities. As long as social values and aims are only partially represented in the school, it is not possible to employ the standard of social value in a complete way. A continual angle of refraction and distortion is introduced in viewing existing studies, through the fact that they are looked at from an artificial standpoint. Even those studies which are popularly regarded as preparing distinctively for life rather than for college cannot get their full meaning, cannot be judged correctly, until the life for which they are said to be a preparation receives a fuller and more balanced representation in the school. While, on the other hand, the more scholastic studies, if I may use the expression, cannot relate themselves properly so long as the branches which give them their ultimate *raison d'être* and sphere of application in the whole of life are non-existent in the curriculum.

For a certain type of mind algebra and geometry are their own justification. They appeal to such students for the intellectual satisfaction they supply, and as preparation for the play of the intellectual in further studies. But to another type of mind these studies are relatively dead and meaningless until surrounded with a context of obvious bearings—such as furnished in manual-training studies. The latter, however, are rendered unduly utilitarian and narrow when isolated. Just as in life the technological pursuits reach out and affect society on all sides, so in the school corresponding studies need to be imbedded in a broad and deep matrix.

In the second place, as previously suggested, the explanation of the high school simplifies instead of complicates the college preparatory problem. This is because the college is going through an analogous evolution in the introduction of similar lines of work. It is expanding in technological and commercial directions. To be sure, the branch of fine and applied arts is still practically omitted; it is left to the tender mercies of over-specialized and more or less mercenary institutions—schools where these things are taught more or less as trades, and for the sake of making money. But the same influences which have already rescued medical and commercial education from similar conditions, and have brought to bear upon them the wider outlook and more expert method of the university, will in time make themselves also felt as regards the teaching of art.

Thirdly, the wider high school relieves many of the difficulties in the adequate treatment of the individual as an individual. It brings the individual into a wider sphere of contacts, and thus makes it possible to test him and his capacity more thoroughly. It makes it possible to get at and remedy his weak points by balancing more evenly the influences that play upon him. In my judgment many of the problems now dealt with under the general head of election *vs.* prescription can be got at more correctly and handled more efficiently from the standpoint of the elastic *vs.* the rigid curriculum— and elasticity can be had only where there is breadth. The need is not so much an appeal to the untried and more or less capricious choice of the individual as for a region of opportunities large enough and balanced enough to meet the individual on his every side, and provide for him that which is necessary to arouse and direct.

Finally, the objection usually urged to the broader high school is, when rightly considered, the strongest argument for its existence. I mean the objection that the introduction of manual training and commercial studies is a cowardly surrender on the part of liberal culture of the training of the man as a man, to utilitarian demands for specialized adaptation to narrow callings. There is nothing in any one study or any one calling which makes it in and of itself low or meanly practical. It is all a question of its isolation or of its setting. It is not the mere syntactical structure of etymological content of the Latin language which has made it for centuries such an unrivaled educational instrument. There are dialects of semi-barbarous tribes which in intricacy of sentential structure and delicacy of relationship, are quite equal to Latin in this respect. It is the context of the Latin language, the wealth of association and suggestion belonging to it from its position in the history of human civilization that freight it with such meaning.

Now the callings that are represented by manual training and commercial studies are absolutely indispensable to hu-

man life. They afford the most permanent and persistent occupations of the great majority of human kind. They present
man with his most perplexing problems; they stimulate him to
the most strenuous putting forth of effort. To indict a whole
nation were a grateful task compared with labeling such occupations as low or narrow—lacking in all that makes for
training and culture. The professed and professional representative of "culture" may well hesitate to cast the first
stone. It may be that it is nothing in these pursuits themselves
which gives them utilitarian and materialistic quality, but
rather the exclusive selfishness with which he has endeavored
to hold on to and monopolize the fruits of the spirit.

And so with the corresponding studies in the high school.
Isolated, they may be chargeable with the defects of which
they are accused. But they are convicted in this respect only
because they have first been condemned to isolation. As rep-
resentatives of serious and permanent interests of humanity,
they possess an intrinsic dignity which it is the business of the
educator to take account of. To ignore them, to deny them a
rightful position in the educational circle, is to maintain
within society that very cleft between so-called material and
spiritual interests which it is the business of education to
strive to overcome. These studies root themselves in science;
they have their trunk in human history, and they flower in the
worthiest and fairest forms of human service.

It is for these various reasons that I believe the introduction of the new problem of adjustment of studies will help
instead of hinder the settlement of the older controversies.
We have been trying for a long time to fix a curriculum
upon a basis of certain vague and general educational ideals:
information, utility, discipline, culture. I believe that much of
our ill success has been due to the lack of any well-defined
and controllable meaning attaching to these terms. The discussion remains necessarily in the region of mere opinion
when the measuring rods are subject to change with the standpoint and wishes of the individual. Take any body of persons,
however intelligent and however conscientious, and ask them
to value and arrange studies from the standpoint of culture,
discipline, and utility, and they will of necessity arrive at very

different results, depending upon their own temperament and more or less accidental experience—and this none the less because of their intelligence and conscientiousness.

With the rounding out of the high school to meet all the needs of life, the standard changes. It ceases to be these vague abstractions. We get, relatively speaking, a scientific problem—that is a problem with definite data and definite methods of attack. We are no longer concerned with the abstract appraisal of studies by the measuring rod of culture or discipline. Our problem is rather to study the typical necessities of social life, and the actual nature of the individual in his specific needs and capacities. Our task is on one hand to select and adjust the studies with reference to the nature of the individual thus discovered; and on the other hand to order and group them so that they shall most definitely and systematically represent the chief lines of social endeavor and social achievement.

Difficult as these problems may be in practice, they are yet inherently capable of solution. It is a definite problem, a scientific problem, to discover the typical vocations of society, and to find out what groupings of studies will be the most likely instruments to subserve these vocations. To dissipate the clouds of opinion, to restrict the influence of abstract and conceited argument; to stimulate the spirit of inquiry into actual fact, to further the control of the conduct of the school by the truths thus scientifically discovered—these are the benefits which we may anticipate with the advent of this problem of the wider high school.

THE WAY OUT OF
EDUCATIONAL CONFUSION *

I recur now to the main theme of which this particular problem supplies one instance. It is fair for an objector to ask
what is the substitute, the alternative, to organization of
courses on the basis of adherence to traditional divisions and
classifications of knowledge. The reply which goes furthest
to the left is found in reference to the so-called "project,"
"problem," or "situation" method, now adopted for trial in
many elementary schools. I shall indicate later that I do not
believe that this is the only alternative. But the method has
certain characteristics which are significant for any plan for
change that may be adopted, and accordingly I shall call attention to these features. The method mentioned is called a
method; it might be taken, therefore, to be *only* a method. In
fact, like anything that *is* a method other than in name, it
has definite implications for subject-matter. There cannot be a
problem that is not a problem of *something*, nor a project
that does not involve doing something in a way which demands inquiry into fresh fields of subject-matter. Many so-
called projects are of such a short-time span and are entered

* This was published originally as a pamphlet by the Harvard University Press, 1931.

upon for such casual reasons, that extension of acquaintance with facts and principles is at a minimum. In short, they are too trivial to be educative. But the defect is not inherent. It only indicates the need that educators should assume their educational responsibility. It is possible to find problems and projects that come within the scope and capacities of the experience of the learner and which have a sufficiently long span so that they raise new questions, introduce new and related undertakings, and create a demand for fresh knowledge. The difference between this procedure and the traditional one is not that the latter involves acquisition of new knowledge and the former does not. It is that in one a relatively fixed and isolated body of knowledge is assumed in advance; while in the other, material is drawn from any field as it is needed to carry on an intellectual enterprise.

Nor is the difference that in one procedure organization exists and in the other it does not. It is a difference in the type of organization effected. Material may be drawn from a variety of fields, number and measure from mathematics when they are needed, from historical, geographical, biological facts when they carry forward the undertaking, and so on. But the central question acts as a magnet to draw them together. Organization in one case consists in formal relations within a particular field as they present themselves to an expert who has mastered the subject. In the other case, it consists in noting the bearing and function of things acquired. The latter course has at least the advantage of being of the kind followed in study and learning outside of school walls, where data and principles do not offer themselves in isolated segments with labels already affixed.

Another feature of the problem method is that activity is exacted. I suppose that if there is one principle which is not a monopoly of any school of educational thought, it is the need of intellectual activity on the part of teacher and student, the condemnation of passive receptivity. But in practice there persist methods in which the pupil is a recording phonograph, or one who stands at the end of a pipe line receiving material conducted from a distant reservoir of learning. How is this split between theory and practice to be explained?

Does not the presentation in doses and chunks of a ready-made subject-matter inevitably conduce to passivity? The mentally active scholar will acknowledge, I think, that his mind roams far and wide. All is grist that comes to his mill, and he does not limit his supply of grain to any one fenced-off field. Yet the mind does not merely roam abroad. It returns with what is found, and there is constant exercise of judgment to detect relations, relevancies, bearings upon the central theme. The outcome is a continuously growing intellectual integration. There is absorption; but it is eager and willing, not reluctant and forced. There is digestion, assimilation, not merely the carrying of a load by memory, a load to be cast off as soon as the day comes when it is safe to throw it off. Within the limits set by capacity and experience this kind of seeking and using, of amassing and organizing, is the process of learning everywhere and at any age.

In the third place, while the student with a proper "project" is intellectually active, he is also overtly active; he applies, he constructs, he expresses himself in new ways. He puts his knowledge to the test of operation. Naturally, he does something with what he learns. Because of this feature the separation between the practical and the liberal does not even arise. It does not have to be done away with, because it is not there. In practical subjects, this doing exists in laboratories and shops. But too often it is of a merely technical sort, not a genuine carrying forward of theoretical knowledge. It aims at mere manual facility, at an immediate external product, or a driving home into memory of something already learned as a matter of mere information.

I have referred, as already indicated, to the "project" method because of these traits, which seem to me proper and indispensable aims in all study by whatever name it be called, not because this method seems to be the only alternative to that usually followed. I do not urge it as the sole way out of educational confusion, not even in the elementary school, though I think experimentation with it is desirable in college and secondary school. But it is possible to retain traditional titles and still reorganize the subject-matter under them, so as to take account of interdependencies of knowledge and connection of knowledge with use and application. As the time grows to a close let me mention one illustration, Julian Huxley's and H. G. Wells' recent volumes on Life. They cut across all conventional divisions in the field: yet not at the expense of scientific accuracy but in a way which increases both intellectual curiosity and understanding, while disclosing the world about us as a perennial source of esthetic delight.

I have referred to intellectual interest. It is only too common to hear students (in name) say in reference to some subject that they "have *had* it." The use of the past tense is only too significant. The subject is over and done with; it is very much in the past. Every intelligent observer of the subsequent career of those who come from our schools deplores the fact that they do not carry away from school into later life abiding intellectual interests in what they have studied. After all, the period from, say, fourteen to twenty-two is a comparatively short portion of a normal life time. The best that education can do during these years is to arouse intellectual interests which carry over and onwards. The worst condemnation that can be passed is that these years are an interlude, a passing interval. If a student does not take into subsequent life an enduring concern for some field of knowledge and art, lying outside his immediate profession preoccupations, schooling for him has been a failure, no matter how good a "student" he was.

The failure is again due, I believe, to segregation of subjects. A pupil can say he has "had" a subject, because the subject has been treated as if it were complete in itself, beginning and terminating within limits fixed in advance. A reorganization of subject-matter which takes account of outleadings into the wide world of nature and man, of knowledge and of social interests and uses, cannot fail save in the most callous and intellectually obdurate to awaken some permanent interest and curiosity. Theoretical subjects will become more practical, because more related to the scope of life; practical subjects will become more charged with theory and intelligent insight. Both will be vitally and not just formally unified.

I see no other way out of our educational confusion. The obvious objection is that this way takes too abrupt a turn. But what alternative is there save a further cluttering up of the curriculum and a steeper dividing wall between the cultural and liberal? The change is in many respects revolutionary. Yet the intelligence needed to bring it about is not lacking, but rather a long-time patience and a will to coöperation and coördination. I can see schools of education leading in the movement. They will hardly do much to reduce the existing confusion if they merely move in the direction of refining existing practices, striving to bring them under the protective shield of "scientific method." That course is more likely to increase confusion. But they can undertake consecutive study of the interrelation of subjects with one another and with social bearing and application; they can contribute to a reorganization that will give direction to an aimless and divided situation.

For confusion is due ultimately to aimlessness, as much of the conflict is due to the attempt to follow tradition and yet introduce radically new material and interests into it—the attempt to superimpose the new on the old. The simile of new wines in old bottles is trite. Yet no other is so apt. We use leathern bottles in an age of steel and glass. The bottles leak and sag. The new wine spills and sours. No prohibitory holds against the attempt to make a new wine of culture and to provide new containers. Only new aims can inspire educational effort for clarity and unity. They alone can reduce confusion; if they do not terminate conflict they will at least render it intelligent and profitable.

MY PEDAGOGIC CREED *

ARTICLE I—*What Education Is*

I Believe that

—all education proceeds by the participation of the individual in the social consciousness of the race. This process begins unconsciously almost at birth, and is continually shaping the individual's powers, saturating his consciousness, forming his habits, training his ideas, and arousing his feelings and emotions. Through this unconscious education the individual gradually comes to share in the intellectual and moral resources which humanity has succeeded in getting together. He becomes an inheritor of the funded capital of civilization. The most formal and technical education in the world cannot safely depart from this general process. It can only organize it or differentiate it in some particular direction.

—the only true education comes through the stimulation of the child's powers by the demands of the social situations in which he finds himself. Through these demands he is stimulated to act as a member of a unity, to emerge from his original narrowness of action and feeling, and to conceive of himself from the standpoint of the welfare of the group to which he belongs. Through the responses which others make to his own activities he comes to know what

---

* This was published originally as a pamphlet by E. L. Kellogg and Co., 1897.

these mean in social terms. The value which they have is reflected back into them. For instance, through the response which is made to the child's instinctive babblings the child comes to know what those babblings mean; they are transformed into articulate language, and thus the child is introduced into the consolidated wealth of ideas and emotions which are now summed up in language.

—this educational process has two sides—one psychological and one sociological—and that neither can be subordinated to the other, or neglected, without evil results following. Of these two sides, the psychological is the basis. The child's own instincts and powers furnish the material and give the starting-point for all education. Save as the efforts of the educator connect with some activity which the child is carrying on of his own initiative independent of the educator, education becomes reduced to a pressure from without. It may, indeed, give certain external results, but cannot truly be called educative. Without insight into the psychological structure and activities of the individual, the educative process will, therefore, be haphazard and arbitrary. If it chances to coincide with the child's activity it will get a leverage; if it does not, it will result in friction, or disintegration, or arrest of the child nature.

—knowledge of social conditions, of the present state of civilization, is necessary in order properly to interpret the child's powers. The child has his own instincts and tendencies, but we do not know what these mean until we can translate them into their social equivalents. We must be able to carry them back into a social past and see them as the inheritance of previous race activities. We must also be able to project them into the future to see what their outcome and end will be. In the illustration just used, it is the ability to see in the child's babblings the promise and potency of a future social intercourse and conversation which enables one to deal in the proper way with that instinct.

—the psychological and social sides are organically related, and that education cannot be regarded as a compromise between the two, or a superimposition of one upon the other. We are told that the psychological definition of education is barren and formal—that it gives us only the idea of a development of all the mental powers without giving us any idea of the use to which these powers are put. On the other hand, it is urged that the social definition of education, as getting adjusted to civilization, makes of it a forced and external process, and results in subordinating the freedom of the individual to a preconceived social and political status.

—each of these objections is true when urged against one side isolated from the other. In order to know what a power really is we must know what its end, use, or function is, and this we cannot know save as we conceive of the individual as active in social relationships. But, on the other hand, the only possible adjustment which we can give to the child under existing conditions is that which arises through putting him in complete possession of all his powers. With the advent of democracy and modern industrial conditions, it is impossible to foretell definitely just what civilization will be twenty years from now. Hence it is impossible to prepare the child for any precise set of conditions. To prepare him for the future life means to give him command of himself; it means so to train him that he will have the full and ready use of all his capacities; that his eye and ear and hand may be tools ready to command, that his judgment may be capable of grasping the conditions under which it has to work, and the executive forces be trained to act economically and efficiently. It is impossible to reach this sort of adjustment save as constant regard is had to the individual's own powers, tastes, and interests—that is, as education is continually converted into psychological terms.

In sum, I believe that the individual who is to be educated is a social individual, and that society is an organic union of individuals. If we eliminate the social factor from the child we are left only with an abstraction; if we eliminate the individual factor from society, we are left only with an inert and lifeless mass. Education, therefore, must begin with a psychological insight into the child's capacities, interests, and habits. It must be controlled at every point by reference to these same considerations. These powers, interests, and habits must be continually interpreted—we must know what they mean. They must be translated into terms of their social equivalents—into terms of what they are capable of in the way of social service.

ARTICLE II—*What the School Is*

I Believe that

—the school is primarily a social institution. Education being a social process, the school is simply that form of community life in which all those agencies are concentrated that will be most effective in bringing the child to share in the inherited resources of the race, and to use his own powers for social ends.

—education, therefore, is a process of living and not a preparation for future living.

—the school must represent present life—life as real and vital to the child as that which he carries on in the home, in the neighborhood, or on the playground.

—that education which does not occur through forms of life, forms that are worth living for their own sake, is always a poor substitute for the genuine reality, and tends to cramp and to deaden.

—the school, as an institution, should simplify existing social life; should reduce it, as it were, to an embryonic form. Existing life is so complex that the child cannot be brought into contact with it without either confusion or distraction; he is either overwhelmed by the multiplicity of activities which are going on, so that he loses his own power of orderly reaction, or he is so stimulated by these various activities that his powers are prematurely called into play and he becomes either unduly specialized or else disintegrated.

—as such simplified social life, the school life should grow gradually out of the home life; that it should take up and continue the activities with which the child is already familiar in the home.

—it should exhibit these activities to the child, and reproduce them in such ways that the child will gradually learn the meaning of them, and be capable of playing his own part in relation to them.

—this is a psychological necessity, because it is the only way of securing continuity in the child's growth, the only way of giving a background of past experience to the new ideas given in school.

—it is also a social necessity because the home is the form of social life in which the child has been nurtured and in connection with which he has had his moral training. It is the business of the school to deepen and extend his sense of the values bound up in his home life.

—much of present education fails because it neglects this fundamental principle of the school as a form of community life. It conceives the school as a place where certain information is to be given, where certain lessons are to be learned, or where certain habits are to be formed. The value of these is conceived as lying largely in the remote future; the child must do these things for the sake of something else he is to do; they are mere preparations. As a result they do not become a part of the life experience of the child and so are not truly educative.

—the moral education centers upon this conception of the school as a mode of social life, that the best and deepest moral training is precisely that which one gets through having to enter into proper relations with others in a unity of work and thought. The present educational systems, so far as they destroy or neglect this unity, render it difficult or impossible to get any genuine, regular moral training.

—the child should be stimulated and controlled in his work through the life of the community.

—under existing conditions far too much of the stimulus and control proceeds from the teacher, because of neglect of the idea of the school as a form of social life.

—the teacher's place and work in the school is to be interpreted from this same basis. The teacher is not in the school to impose certain ideas or to form certain habits in the child, but is there as a member of the community to select the influences which shall affect the child and to assist him in properly responding to these influences.

—the discipline of the school should proceed from the life of the school as a whole and not directly from the teacher.

—the teacher's business is simply to determine, on the basis of larger experience and riper wisdom, how the discipline of life shall come to the child.

—all questions of the grading of the child and his promotion should be determined by reference to the same standard. Examinations are of use only so far as they test the child's fitness for social life and reveal the place in which he can be of the most service and where he can receive the most help.

ARTICLE III—*The Subject-Matter of Education*

I Believe that

—the social life of the child is the basis of concentration, or correlation, in all his training or growth. The social life gives the unconscious unity and the background of all his efforts and of all his attainments.

—the subject-matter of the school curriculum should mark a gradual differentiation out of the primitive unconscious unity of social life.

—we violate the child's nature and render difficult the best ethical results by introducing the child too abruptly to a number of special studies, of reading, writing, geography, etc., out of relation to this social life.

—the true center of correlation on the school subjects is not science, nor literature, nor history, nor geography, but the child's own social activities.

—education cannot be unified in the study of science, or so-called nature study, because apart from human activity, nature itself is not a unity; nature in itself is a number of diverse objects in space and time, and to attempt to make it the center of work by itself is to introduce a principle of radiation rather than one of concentration.

—literature is the reflex expression and interpretation of social experience; that hence it must follow upon and not precede such experience. It, therefore, cannot be made the basis, although it may be made the summary of unification.

—once more that history is of educative value in so far as it presents phases of social life and growth. It must be controlled by reference to social life. When taken simply as history it is thrown into the distant past and becomes dead and inert. Taken as the record of man's social life and progress it becomes full of meaning. I believe, however, that it cannot be so taken excepting as the child is also introduced directly into social life.

—the primary basis of education is in the child's powers at work along the same general constructive lines as those which have brought civilization into being.

—the only way to make the child conscious of his social heritage is to enable him to perform those fundamental types of activity which make civilization what it is.

—in the so-called expressive or constructive activities as the center of correlation.

—this gives the standard for the place of cooking, sewing, manual training, etc., in the school.

—they are not special studies which are to be introduced over and above a lot of others in the way of relaxation or relief, or as additional accomplishments. I believe rather that they represent, as types, fundamental forms of social activity; and that it is possible and desirable that the child's introduction into the more formal subjects of the curriculum be through the medium of these activities.

—the study of science is educational in so far as it brings out the materials and processes which make social life what it is.

—one of the greatest difficulties in the present teaching of science is that the material is presented in purely objective form, or is treated as a new peculiar kind of experience which the child can add to that which he has already had. In reality, science is of value because it gives the ability to interpret and control the experience already had. It should be introduced, not as so much new subject-matter, but as showing the factors already involved in previous experience and as furnishing tools by which that experience can be more easily and effectively regulated.

—at present we lose much of the value of literature and language studies because of our elimination of the social element. Language is almost always treated in the books of pedagogy simply as the expression of thought. It is true that language is a logical instrument, but it is fundamentally and primarily a social instrument. Language is the device for communication; it is the tool through which one individual comes to share the ideas and feelings of others. When treated simply as a way of getting individual information, or as a means of showing off what one has learned, it loses its social motive and end.

—there is, therefore, no succession of studies in the ideal school curriculum. If education is life, all life has, from the outset, a scientific aspect, an aspect of art and culture, and an aspect of communication. It cannot, therefore, be true that the proper studies for one grade are mere reading and writing, and that at a later grade, reading, or literature, or science, may be introduced. The progress is not in the succession of studies, but in the development of new attitudes towards, and new interests in, experience.

—education must be conceived as a continuing reconstruction of experience; that the process and the goal of education are one and the same thing.

—to set up any end outside of education, as furnishing its goal and standard, is to deprive the educational process of much of its meaning, and tends to make us rely upon false and external stimuli in dealing with the child.

ARTICLE IV—*The Nature of Method*

I Believe that.

—the question of method is ultimately reducible to the question of the order of development of the child's powers and interests. The law for presenting and treating material is the law implicit within the child's own nature. Because this is so I believe the following statements are of supreme importance as determining the spirit in which education is carried on:

—the active side precedes the passive in the development of the child-nature; that expression comes before conscious impression; that the muscular development precedes the sensory; that movements come before conscious sensations; I believe that consciousness is essentially motor or impulsive; that conscious states tend to project themselves in action.

—the neglect of this principle is the cause of a large part of the waste of time and strength in school work. The child is thrown into a passive, receptive, or absorbing attitude. The conditions are such that he is not permitted to follow the law of his nature; the result is friction and waste.

—ideas (intellectual and rational processes) also result from action and devolve for the sake of the better control of action. What we term reason is primarily the law of orderly or effective action. To attempt to develop the reasoning powers, the powers of judgment, without reference to the selection and arrangement of means in action, is the fundamental fallacy in our present methods of dealing with this matter. As a result we present the child with arbitrary symbols. Symbols are a necessity in mental development, but they have their place as tools for economizing effort; presented by themselves they are a mass of meaningless and arbitrary ideas imposed from without.

—the image is the great instrument of instruction. What a child gets out of any subject presented to him is simply the images which he himself forms with regard to it.

—if nine-tenths of the energy at present directed towards making the child learn certain things were spent in seeing to it that the child was forming proper images, the work of instruction would be indefinitely facilitated.

—much of the time and attention now given to the preparation and presentation of lessons might be more wisely and profitably expended in training the child's power of imagery and in seeing to it that he was continually forming definite, vivid, and growing images of the various subjects with which he comes in contact in his experience.

—interests are the signs and symptoms of growing power. I believe that they represent dawning capacities. Accordingly the constant and careful observation of interests is of the utmost importance for the educator.

—these interests are to be observed as showing the state of development which the child has reached.

—they prophesy the stage upon which he is about to enter.

—only through the continual and sympathetic observation of childhood's interests can the adult enter into the child's life and see what it is ready for, and upon what material it could work most readily and fruitfully.

—these interests are neither to be humored nor repressed. To repress interest is to substitute the adult for the child, and so to weaken intellectual curiosity and alertness, to suppress initiative, and to deaden interest. To humor the interests is to substitute the transient for the permanent. The interest is always the sign of some power below; the important thing is to discover this power. To humor the interest is to fail to penetrate below the surface, and its sure result is to substitute caprice and whim for genuine interest.

—the emotions are the reflex of actions.

—to endeavor to stimulate or arouse the emotions apart from their corresponding activities is to introduce an unhealthy and morbid state of mind.

—if we can only secure right habits of action and thought, with reference to the good, the true, and the beautiful, the emotions will for the most part take care of themselves.

—next to deadness and dullness, formalism and routine, our education is threatened with no greater evil than sentimentalism.

—this sentimentalism is the necessary result of the attempt to divorce feeling from action.

ARTICLE V—*The School and Social Progress*

I Believe that

—education is the fundamental method of social progress and reform.

—all reforms which rest simply upon the enactment of law, or the threatening of certain penalties, or upon changes in mechanical or outward arrangements, are transitory and futile.

—education is a regulation of the process of coming to share in the social consciousness; and that the adjustment of individual activity on the basis of this social consicousness is the only sure method of social reconstruction.

—this conception has due regard for both the individualistic and socialistic ideals. It is duly individual because it recognizes the formation of a certain character as the only genuine basis of right living. It is socialistic because it recognizes that this right character is not to be formed by merely individual precept, example, or exhortation, but rather by the influence of a certain form of institutional or community life upon the individual, and that the social organism through the school, as its organ, may determine ethical results.

—in the ideal school we have the reconciliation of the individualistic and the institutional ideals.

—the community's duty to education is, therefore, its paramount moral duty. By law and punishment, by social agitation and discussion, society can regulate and form itself in a more or less haphazard and chance way. But through education society can formulate its own purposes, can organize its own means and resources, and thus shape itself with definiteness and economy in the direction in which it wishes to move.

—when society once recognizes the possibilities in this direction, and the obligations which these possibilities impose, it is impossible to conceive of the resources of time, attention, and money which will be put at the disposal of the educator.

—it is the business of every one interested in education to insist upon the school as the primary and most effective interest of social progress and reform in order that society may be awakened to realize what the school stands for, and aroused to the necessity of endowing the educator with sufficient equipment properly to perform his task.

—education thus conceived marks the most perfect and intimate union of science and art conceivable in human experience.

—the art of thus giving shape to human powers and adapting them to social service is the supreme art; one calling into its service the best of artists; that no insight, sympathy, tact, executive power, is too great for such service.

—with the growth of psychological service, giving added insight into individual structure and laws of growth; and with growth of social science, adding to our knowledge of the right organization of individuals, all scientific resources can be utilized for the purposes of education.

—when science and art thus join hands the most commanding motive for human action will be reached, the most genuine springs of human conduct aroused, and the best service that human nature is capable of guaranteed.

—the teacher is engaged, not simply in the training of individuals, but in the formation of the proper social life.

—every teacher should realize the dignity of his calling; that he is a social servant set apart for the maintenance of proper social order and the securing of the right social growth.

—in this way the teacher always is the prophet of the true God and the usherer in of the true kingdom of God.